The Animation Bible

A Guide to Everything from Flipbooks to Flash

The Animation Bible

A Guide to Everything— from Flipbooks to Flash

Maureen Furniss

Laurence King Publishing

Published in 2008 by
Laurence King Publishing Ltd
361-373 City Road
London EC1V 1LR

tel: +44 20 7841 6900
fax: +44 20 7841 6910
email: enquiries@laurenceking.co.uk
www.laurenceking.co.uk

A catalogue record of this book is available
from the British Library.

ISBN 13: 978-1 85669-550-3

Designed by Struktur Design

Cover designed by Struktur Design
Permission to use image of Felix provided
courtesy of Don Oriolo and FTCP, Inc.
© 2008 and ™ Felix the Cat Productions, Inc.

Printed and bound in China

Frontispiece: Image from Donna Cameron's
Newsw. © 2006 by Donna Cameron. All
rights reserved © Papercamfilms.™

To Kerry and Kelly

Contents

Animation as a discipline has a long history and a greatly varied nature, with applications in such diverse fields as medicine, entertainment, fine art, forensics, and education. As media have been developed, animated imagery has infiltrated new realms, from print (in flipbooks, for example), film, and video to various digital contexts, including the World Wide Web. Animation appears to us now in many forms: as virtual reality, as two-dimensional images in the familiar "cartoon" format, as three-dimensional objects created using both digital and stop-motion techniques, and as seamlessly integrated effects that appear within the context of ostensibly live-action motion pictures, among other manifestations.

Now animation is being created for wider audiences, increasingly appealing to adults as well as younger viewers. Audiences have grown partly due to expanded exhibition opportunities, which include international festivals, cable television networks devoted to animation, and of course the Web, which provides easy access to work made across the globe. As audiences have become larger, and especially as more money has been earned, educational programs, studios, and whole industries have grown in size across the world, sometimes being supported by government initiatives to encourage animation production. The trend of international co-production also has increased, allowing studios from different countries to join together to create animation projects. Even bigger shifts have been caused by a steady influx of technologies that contribute to production in the field.

Today, animation students prepare themselves for careers in a world where computers are ubiquitous, providing the infrastructure of day-to-day life. As a result, educational programs sometimes feel they must offer students two whole areas of coursework: a full spectrum of traditional animation art practices, *plus* media, technology, and methods introduced in more recent years, including animation approaches using a range of software. But how can that be done? A four-year BFA or three-year MFA program is adequately long for one of these two approaches. An animation student who is asked to cover twice the material probably leaves a degree program understanding it half as well as he or she should.

As an alternative, academic programs can focus primarily on one or the other: mastering traditional skills or learning the newest technologies. Technical training may result in immediate job placement, but it provides students with a narrow set of workplace skills and relatively little flexibility when industry positions or technologies change. In contrast, fundamental art skills travel with an individual to a range of work settings as the world of animation experiences its inevitable shifts; technical training is useful for specific positions in the short term, while broader foundations in art provide long-term knowledge applicable in many contexts. Programs in higher education that emphasize the foundations of animation art recognize that any given technology provides just one of many possible ways to realize a project. Though the industry may stipulate the widespread use of computers, artists turn back to their hands, pencils, brushes, and various art materials to stay directly connected to their work, using them along with digital media to enhance production.

Content

It is important to nurture an experimental approach to animation, so that new talents in the field continue to develop its potential as art, entertainment, and communication. Unfortunately, the majority of writing on animation production methods has been devoted primarily to mainstream commercial work and conventional animation methods. The experimenters and individualists working outside the studio system are too often overlooked, or when they are mentioned, theorists and historians generally do not provide detailed accounts of their production methods so others can learn from them. This book takes a close look at productions from a wide range of practitioners, including students and hobbyists along with well-known "stars" and pioneers in the field. It includes in-depth case studies and practical applications of animation techniques, some of which have been contributed by experts in a particular area: Leslie Bishko on developing characters, Devon Damonte on images in direct filmmaking, and Richard Reeves on direct sound. Anyone reading this book will find detailed information on not only drawn character animation methods, but also a wide range of other techniques.

The first four chapters provide overviews of essential information related to the production of animation in general. Chapter One covers the issues of concept, medium, and style to demonstrate how choices at these levels affect the outcome of the animated production. Chapter Two deals with the

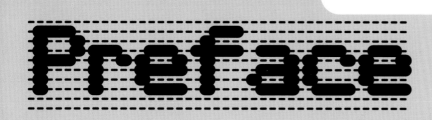

Preface

importance of structure and presentation, and attention is given to such issues as sound design and color theory. Chapter Three details the steps of pre-production, while Chapter Four covers production and post-production; consideration is given to the contexts of drawn and painted animation, GIF and Flash production, stop-motion, and wire-framed digital animation.

The remaining chapters explore particular approaches to animation. Chapter Five examines the history and diversity of motion devices. It begins with a discussion of automata, motion studies, and magic lanterns, and then covers thaumatropes, kaleidoscopes, phenakistoscopes, zoetropes, praxinoscopes, and flipbooks.

The next two chapters explore the diverse range of practices that fall under the category of "direct filmmaking"— that is, working directly on a piece of film. Chapter Six begins with an overview of related art practices, such as batik and miniatures, and then discusses a number of animators who work directly on film. Chapter Seven looks at perceptual issues related to direct film and also covers direct sound, the productions of collaborative groups, and other topics.

Various 2D approaches are described in the following two chapters, which are devoted to the general topics of drawing and painting. Chapter Eight covers ways of working with cels, as well as mixed and dry media, while Chapter Nine looks at water- and oil-based media. The next chapters are on stop-motion. Chapter Ten discusses the use of sand, cutouts, folded paper, found objects, brickfilms, and clay. Chapter Eleven focuses on animation within real world contexts, including puppet films of various types, pixilation, and installations.

While all the chapters include some information on digital media, the last two in the book focus on this topic in detail. Chapter Twelve describes the development of computer animation and includes practical information about digital technology. Chapter Thirteen demonstrates the range of ways in which digital media can aid the animation process, as well as their limitations.

Acknowledgments

My name appears as author of this book, but in fact I never could have written it on my own. For much of the content, I have to thank the artists who appear within it. They spent a significant amount of time being interviewed, correcting text, and adding details to my descriptions. I especially want to thank Leslie Bishko, Devon Damonte, and Richard Reeves, who contributed practical exercises. I'd also like to thank Lillian Schwartz and Cecile Starr, who provided inspiration to me as I wrote this book, not only because of their pioneering roles in the field of experimental animation, but also for the books they co-authored: Lillian's *Computer Artist's Handbook: Concepts, Techniques, and Applications*, written with her son Laurens R. Schwartz, and Cecile's *Experimental Animation*, written with Robert Russett. Thanks also to Cecile for her dedication to promoting experimental animators and, from a personal perspective, for helping me at various points in my career.

Also at the top of my list of people to thank is David Ehrlich, who suggested my name when my publisher was looking for someone to write a book on animation production. David has been a mentor and friend to me literally from the moment I entered this field—when I wanted to write my thesis on independent animation but knew no one and had no idea where to start. It has been a great experience to work with Laurence King Publishing, including Lee Ripley, John Jervis, and Donald Dinwiddie. The individuals at Laurence King Publishing have high ideals for the design and content of their work, and the support I've been given has been terrific. Thanks also to Eric Himmel at Harry N. Abrams for his enthusiasm for my work.

It goes without saying that a book on animation must be well illustrated. The National Film Board of Canada was exceptional in providing an array of pictures, and allowing its artists to send me extensive numbers of images. However, the vast majority of other illustrations used in this book were donated by artists working independently or in relatively small-scale studios. Some went out of their way to dig up documents that had been in storage for years. Some had old films reprinted so that digital images could be made, or re-created production materials so that illustrations would be more complete. Many spent time digitizing or photographing items so that they could be sent to me for publication. Collectors and archivists also contributed significantly to the illustrations. Thanks to all of them, this book contains a wide range of visual materials that I hope will make it very useful as a guide to innovative production techniques. However, having said this, I would add that I could not get all the images I had hoped for. Language barriers, the complexity of finding rights owners, and a lack of available materials were among the factors preventing me from illustrating some of the topics discussed in the book. Fortunately, the Internet has increased our ability to see hard-to-find items, and I hope you will take advantage of this resource when images are not available here.

Along the way, I've worked with a few great graduate assistants, who moved on from college and became colleagues: Greg Singer, Pierce Scantlin, Stormy Gunter, and Jeremy Schwartz. Each contributed to this book in some way. Also thanks to other student contributors who shared their knowledge and talents to make this a better book, including Musa Brooker, Dae In Chung, Ke Jiang, Andrew Zimbelman, Max Winston, Erin Ross, Brent Johnson, Dina Noto, and Hlynur Magnússon, as well as Jesse Gregg, Allyson Haller, and Adam Fox, who provided wonderful illustrations. Among the other researchers, faculty, and colleagues who helped me are Andy Voda, Michael Frierson, Jean Théberge, Linda Simensky, Chris Robinson and the Ottawa International Animation Festival staff, Giannalberto Bendazzi, Pat Beckman, Steven Brown, Stephen Chiodo, Tom Klein, Brian Wells, Thorsten Fleisch, Craig Smith, Clare Kitson, and Jeremy Butler. I especially want to thank Nancy Beiman, who provided extensive, extremely helpful feedback on my work—I cannot thank her enough.

Some of my research was supported financially through a Presidential Fellowship I received from the Savannah College of Art and Design. I taught at SCAD before I moved back to California in 2005 to begin teaching at California Institute of the Arts. I would like to thank my dean, Steve Anker; my department chairs, especially Myron Emery and Frank Terry; my colleagues at Cal Arts; and the office staff in the School of Film and Video for making my transition there so easy. It's wonderful to be at a place where people like and respect each other; what a joy it is to love my job. This environment has helped me stay focused on my work, and has given me perspective on the important things in my life and career. Among my other supporters are friends and family, including Susan Fox, Vicki and John Callahan, Kris Ibarra, and Kay Kaye.

Finally, my two daughters, Kerry Anar and Kelly Bibikhanum, whose entire lives in America have been accompanied by this book. Perpetually grumpy from the fatigue of late nights of typing, I have been given countless backrubs and been told that I'm the best cook in the world, even when we were reduced to eating not-so-tasty leftovers and food that didn't turn out very well. Pragmatist that I am, I like to say "I'm not the greatest mother in the world, but I'm not the worst"—so while I've typed my way through a good part of their childhood, I hope if nothing else this book has shown my daughters that complex goals are obtainable, that you can and should love your work, and that you should strive to do something that in some way makes the world a better place. I believe all things happen for a reason, though we don't always understand why at the time—and I believe that these two smart, talented, kind, and beautiful girls from Kazakhstan came to me for an important reason, and that they will achieve something great in their lives. In fact, they already have, by giving their love to me despite the challenges we've faced. To Kerry and Kelly, I dedicate this book and what I hope are the many expressions of beauty that it inspires.

Maureen Furniss, Ph.D.

Concept, Medium, and Style

Despite the diversity of approaches to animation, every animator confronts the same challenges when he or she begins a new project: namely, getting a good idea and finding a way to make that idea come to life. This chapter provides an overview of creative aspects of animation production in its many forms, including two-dimensional (2D) animation primarily created with dry and wet media (such as pencils and paints), stop-motion (including puppets and clay), and computer-generated imagery (2D and 3D).

Concept

Behind every great animated work there is a great concept—but how does the concept come about? There is a mystique around art and artists that suggests "great art" comes from a streak of inspiration deep within the mind's creative center. However, it takes more than a stroke of genius to make successful animation. The idea itself is just the first step toward achieving this goal: research, considerations of audience, value assessments, and critical review all contribute to the development of a concept for an animated work.

Getting a Good Idea

Sometimes an artist is fortunate and a great project idea comes to mind quite easily. Other times, he or she has to search for a concept, perhaps suffering from the inevitable creative block that everyone experiences once in a while. Here are some recommendations for keeping good ideas coming:

- Keep a journal: Creativity is dependent upon being able to open up emotionally and intellectually, so it is important to practice these skills on an ongoing basis.
- Read books and newspapers: These resources expand an artist's understanding of history and contemporary society, which helps in the development of interesting narratives.
- Study many different subjects: A broad knowledge base brings about a wide range of concepts.
- Find out what people like: Ask your grandparents what they enjoy in a film, or visit a preschool center and see what makes the children happy.
- Ask two or three people to join you: A group think session will stimulate new ideas and you can throw away any concepts that don't work after everyone has left.
- Randomly open a reference book: Reading an entry in a dictionary or encyclopedia can inspire a good concept.
- Write down your goals: Seeing a clear statement on paper helps to develop a creative strategy. Consider the issues

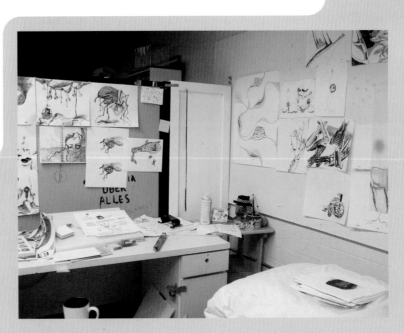

Inspirational sketches fill the work-space of animator Nandita Kumar.

related to the type of work you are envisioning, whether it's a short-subject film for a festival, a film for your professional reel, a feature-length concept, or perhaps promotional work to sell products or services for a client. Think in terms of primary and secondary objectives—for example: "How can I sell a product, but also create an environmentally friendly image?"

– Create a deadline: The project has to start at some point—no matter what state it's in.

– Doodle randomly: This can warm you up and overcome a freeze in creativity. Animators should always carry a sketchbook for impromptu drawings that will provide inspiration and help in the development of ideas.

– Don't be afraid to make mistakes: Self-censorship creates huge barriers in the creative process.

– And don't be afraid to admit you've made a mistake: Use your critical eye to determine what works for the current project and what needs to be stored elsewhere for future development.

– Finally, don't overlook the obvious: Eat well, exercise, use media and equipment (like chemicals and computers) safely, and get enough sleep.[1]

Once you have identified some concepts you would like to pursue, your ideas should move through a thoughtful process of research and development.

Research

Research takes many forms and is an ongoing process. Its purpose is to enable an artist to grow in his or her range of expression, to increase an understanding of the world, and provide models and inspiration. Research doesn't just come from books: It also involves physical and emotional experience on a broad level. Such experience allows an animator to take on many roles. He or she should know how it feels to be a well-trained warrior taking part in a battle or a burro plodding through dusty streets. He or she should be capable of making an abstract form look excited and energized—or a character look bold and powerful—by sensing how these figures feel.

When taking on a specific project, it is important to compile a notebook of visual references, including figures, props, environments, and other images that in some manner depict or inspire the images in the animation. These references can be taken from newspapers, magazines, the Internet, or any other source of visual material—and, of course, they can be drawn. An artist's sketchbooks are valuable sources of inspiration; they should contain quick sketches (completed in ten- and thirty-second, and one-minute poses) as well as more detailed drawings. Visual references also include motion picture works that relate to

Images by Stephen Silver from his *Sketchbook*.

Stephen X. Arthur's notebook of visual references for his film *Transfigured*.

the production. These films can be viewed repeatedly to keep the artist in the proper frame of mind, and are invaluable for giving assistants and others involved with the production a sense of what is being achieved. Other sources of inspiration—music, paintings, books, sculptures, toys—should be placed within the work-space, to guide the project from beginning to end. An animator can, of course, also do more formal research, gathering facts about the topic by reading books, interviewing individuals, and making direct observations.

Audiences

If a work is to be universal, it has to touch on themes that are familiar to people all over the world. More often, animated productions are culturally specific, reflecting the national and local contexts, as well as historical realities, in which the animation is produced—and very likely the age, economic status, life experience, and gender of the artist(s) involved.

In the process of creating an animated work, it is useful to consider such factors as viewers' age ranges, values, motivations, and experience. Envisioning probable audiences helps animators when they submit work for competitions in festivals, as well as in professional contexts when it is important to understand the goals of a client or perhaps the needs of development departments seeking programming for

television. Technological factors are an issue, too. When creating animation for online exhibition, the animator must think about the audience's ability to view the work, given variations in computers, software, and speed of delivery. Artists also should consider that the animation will be viewed internationally, so culturally specific references are likely to be missed. Stereotypes considered humorous on a local level might not play so well across the world. Animation that relies heavily on dialogue in a given language also limits potential worldwide viewers. And large numbers of people are hearing- and vision-impaired; animation design issues affect their ability to access a work as well. All these factors fall under a consideration of audience.

If an artist hopes to make an animated work for a specific audience it is, of course, important to understand the perspectives of these viewers and not rely on personal

The video reference library used to research Virgil Widrich's *Fast Film*.

Suggestions for Research

— Observe and draw human and animal figures, still and in motion, and study the skeletal and muscle structures that underlie them; an animator should carry a sketchbook at all times and draw in it constantly.

— Learn the basics of physics to better understand the possibilities of motion and visual effects.

— Become familiar with technology, including at least basic study of computer languages and programming.

— View works of art (including animated productions), both representational and abstract.

— Read about animation aesthetics, history, and theory.

— Understand the history of art and its relationship to culture; learn about the experiences of other artists through lectures or personal interviews.

— Become familiar with a wide range of storytelling traditions.

— Take improvisational acting and dancing courses to enhance your ability to feel and move.

— Study music and figures in motion to develop timing and rhythm.

— Investigate the ways in which audiences learn and make sense of information in different stages of life (especially through childhood development).

— Study world cultures, sociology, psychology, and history to better understand human experience.

opinions about what that group might like. Generalizations about peoples' interests, motivations, and desires too often fall into the category of stereotypes. In order to fully understand an intended audience, it is ideal to spend time with people in that group, observing the way they function, the activities they enjoy, the skill levels they possess, and other related factors. It may be helpful to call an informal focus group composed of these individuals to get feedback as part of the research process. It is also advisable to consult experts who have studied the group in depth: educators who understand particular age-specific skills, social workers assisting particular communities, psychologists, healthcare professionals, and others who can contribute to the content and approach of a work.

There is an increasing concern with representation issues and certain types of content, especially those involving violence, sexual acts, religious practices, extreme political beliefs, and even some portrayals of race and gender. Feelings surrounding these topics are intense and, as a result, there are strong tendencies toward censorship on the one hand and arguments for creative license on the other. Even while espousing "academic freedom," colleges often have policies that regulate students' depictions of these topics, in images or text, on their websites. Certainly, commercial institutions

weigh the connotations of all affiliated media very carefully; even website host services might refuse clients who post what they see as undesirable material. In today's global society, attempts to censor are complicated by access; what is deemed acceptable in a relatively liberal user's household might not play so well in a very conservative one, and vice versa.

Clearly, there is no one right way to express any given topic. However, creative decisions can have significant repercussions on festival judges, employers, general viewers, and others in a position to support an animator's work. Artists should consider the impact of hot topics and weigh the implications of what they intend to do, especially in light of desired audiences. Still, some animators choose to work without considering the implications of their productions—seeing the issues as limiting personal freedoms, or being irrelevant to the creative process. In any case, provocative work very often has captured the public's attention. As animator Nancy Bieman points out, "Some of the most successful animation is the most controversial. What about 'South Park' or 'The Simpsons'? Controversy can be very popular!"[2] It can also inspire important work: The eastern European animators Yuri Norstein and Jan Svankmajer created great films by defying the censors in their countries.

Life drawing is the foundation on which animated movement is built. Examples include; left to right, (top) female figure study, thirty-second poses, (bottom) one-minute poses, quick sketches of figures in motion, and a squash-and-stretch study. Drawings by J. Adam Fox.

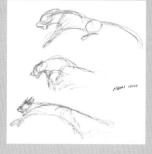

Value

Animation, as a medium of communication, can entertain, inform, or persuade. However, it also can represent intangible concepts, such as spirituality or the experience of death. As an art form, it functions on an aesthetic level, perhaps for the purpose of being delightful, beautiful, and profound—as in the work of Frédéric Back, who has devoted his career to making films related to environmental issues, a cause he also champions in his day-to-day life.

However an artist defines the function of his or her work, it is important to consider its value. What will it ultimately achieve? Is it a practice exercise in preparation for future animated works? In that case it would be of research—and possibly professional—value. An animated piece also might have the practical value of helping the artist secure employment, as part of a demo reel. If so, it should clearly demonstrate the skills he or she wants future employers to see. In some cases, the value of a work is measurable—for example, if the animation is sold, you can count how many copies of it were purchased and how much money it made. This type of value is monetary. Business clients who hire artists are interested in the value of their work to sell products, promote a particular image, or achieve other aims.

Artists also can see the value of a work as something far less tangible, and in fact highly personal: They are driven to animate by the pleasure it brings during production, through the process of self-growth and discovery on technical, spiritual, and intellectual levels. When this spirit—the love of the work—imbues a project, it almost invariably is evident in the outcome of the piece. Some people think of animation in technical terms—that they can learn a particular skill and be qualified to work in the field. Exceptional artists have a much deeper connection to what they create. It is difficult work, often isolating and physically demanding, but the animator feels compelled to persist at it. Truly exceptional works are not only highly personal; they also connect with viewers in a way that proficient, even "entertaining" animation does not.

Feedback

A good concept goes through a process of critical evaluation before it is developed very far. In a studio or classroom, this review generally takes place through various stages of required approval and discussion with supervisors and peers. With experience, artists gain objectivity in determining what is worthwhile and what needs to be removed, and find it is almost always useful to get feedback. This process can be painful, as the animator might be dealing with personal

Frédéric Back has devoted his life's work to environmental issues. This image is from *La fleuve aux grandes eaux.*

perspectives and even be plagued by self-doubt. It is important to remember that the critical opinions of others are not always right—but they aren't always wrong. Mature artists weigh feedback and give serious consideration to all opinions, even if they ultimately do not act on them. Sometimes it helps to remember that items removed from a work do not have to be thrown out; often they can be saved for future development. In any case, it is best to get feedback early in the production process, before a work is nearly or fully completed. If comments come too late, nothing can be done to correct any problems—or if changes are made, they probably will cost a great deal in lost time and money.

When seeking the opinions of others it is best to find relatively neutral reviewers. Close friends or relatives probably do not want to risk hurting the artist's feelings, so may be overly positive in their assessments. A blind review—when people comment on works without knowing who created them—provides more objective comments. However, not everyone is trained to be a critic. The perspectives of experienced individuals—teachers, mentors, development professionals, and so on—often are more useful than the responses of "average" viewers, who might not know how to articulate their reactions in a meaningful way. Animators can cultivate self-editing skills by taking part in critical discussions of other artworks (informal salons are great in this respect). It is relatively easy to spot the flaws in other people's art, but eventually the critic should be able to apply the lessons learned to his or her own work.

Some websites give viewers the opportunity to provide feedback on animated productions that appear there. Often the criticism is very direct, including stinging commentary about works deemed unsuccessful by a given viewer. Reading through the comments at a movie site such as Atomfilms (www.atomfilms.com) is a good way to experience animation through the eyes of "average" viewers.

Medium

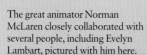

Some artists begin with a concept and look for a medium that can express it. Others specialize in specific media and are pulled toward concepts that lend themselves to these media. Each medium defines possibilities within the visual field of an animated work. As a result, it is important to carefully consider not only the production media used to create animated imagery, but also the recording and distribution media used to capture and screen the work.

The great animator Norman McLaren closely collaborated with several people, including Evelyn Lambart, pictured with him here.

Michael Dudok de Wit selected water-based media to create the fluid images of *Le moine et le poisson.*

Dominant Animation Media

For many years, the most common media used to create animation were acrylic paints and acetate-adhering inks that were used on clear sheets called "cels." The practice originated in the 1910s.[3] At first, cels were nitrate-based, which made them highly flammable; it wasn't until the 1950s that safety stock became the norm for both film stock and animation cels. The Disney studio is largely responsible for the dominance of cel animation worldwide. Because it was so successful, other companies sought to duplicate its style, using cels that were inked and painted. The American film industry was set up to accommodate cel animation, which proved to be the most economical way to make animated films, and people working in this way floated from studio to studio with relative ease. This flexibility helped solidify the power of the American animation industry as a whole.

In recent years, cel animation has been challenged by other media. When the stop-motion film *The Nightmare Before Christmas*, directed by Henry Selick, was released in 1993 (also by Disney), its great success made the American film industry take note. The same year, stop-motion animation got a further boost from the immense popularity of director Nick Park's "Wallace and Gromit" short film, *The Wrong Trousers* (1993), produced by Aardman Animations in England.

However, it took the computer and digital technology to truly dismantled the reign of cel animation. While students today are still trained in many of the 2D production techniques previously employed with cels, in most cases the images they create are rendered digitally rather than with ink and paint. In some contexts, stop-motion animation has been displaced by digital technology, as computers are now used widely to create effects found in feature films, games, training programs, and other contexts. But digital equipment also has contributed to some growth in stop-motion, as it has made the production process more efficient (for example, mistakes during shooting can be fixed using editing software).

Digital media have changed the face of animation production, in part because they have made it potentially cheaper and more accessible. But no matter how significant they are, digital media represent only some of many different production approaches employed by innovative animators.

3D computer-generated images by Ke Jiang.

Frank Mouris (ca. 1972) shooting artwork under a rostrum camera designed and built by Jerry Strawbridge.

Production Media

Many 2D animators choose to work in dry media such as pencils and charcoal, or wet media such as watercolors or oil paints. Increasingly, these analog media are combined with digital tools, which may be used for image capture, image manipulation, compositing (combining images), or editing in the final stages of production. Of course, not every animator gravitates toward digital media. For example, sometimes artists opt to create animation using a bare minimum of technology, drawing and painting directly on a piece of film.

Each medium lends itself to a different way of working. Drawing on paper is conducive to an assembly-line approach, where many people work on different aspects of a production simultaneously. In contrast, painting on glass is a technique that must be done "under the camera" by one artist working alone, or at least with a minimum of help. This is a "modified base" stop-motion technique; instead of many images being produced, the same base object is altered over and over. The base is filmed after every alteration to achieve the appearance of animated movement.

Figures fashioned of clay, latex, wood, and other materials are among the choices for animators who prefer to work in actual three-dimensional environments rather than virtual ones.

Stop-motion objects are lit and photographed in much the same way as live-action images. These figures obey the laws of gravity, have actual texture, and cast real shadows; they naturally create perspective as they move through planes of space. Clay can be manipulated and reshaped to animate it. Wood cannot because it is rigid; however, figures made of either substance can be animated through the "replacement method," creating alternate body parts that are used in sequence to develop animated movement.

The selected media should be considered not only for the way they affect the art, but also for how they affect the artist. It is important to learn the risks involved with materials and equipment.[4] There are well-publicized guidelines to preventing physical problems when using computers, and it is advisable to read labels carefully and to wear gloves, use a mask, and ventilate rooms when using hazardous substances (or, better yet, just choose other media).

Distribution and Exhibition Media

Artists make choices about media in terms of not only production, but also exhibition and distribution. These decisions should not be afterthoughts, since they often affect

Clive Walley painting on glass.

Some artists choose to draw and paint directly on film stock.

The process of working directly on film lends itself to collaboration. Pictured here are the Crackpot Crafters, organized by Devon Damonte.

the parameters of what can be achieved with the animation. Installation animation set up in a gallery or other space can incorporate a wide range of media: film, video, or even slide projectors that reveal each frame in an animated sequence. In this context artists have many choices, but animators are often more limited in what they can design. The image size of a film projected in a theater is large compared to that of animation shown on television—and huge compared to the screen on a mobile device, where a fair amount of animation is playing these days. Clearly, Disney-style full animation is useless in a cell phone or Personal Digital Assistant (PDA) setting, or even on most computer monitors, where processing speed, limited colors, and resolution issues cancel out details of shading, line quality, and subtle movement. On the other hand, animation made for television or even the Web can look overly simple on a theater screen. Very saturated (bright) red, blue, cyan, and yellow can be "illegal" in some contexts; for example, they do not reproduce correctly in the North American National Television Standards Committee (NTSC) format. Still, it is possible to find such bright colors in some animated productions (generally in small doses).

Various media have different screen dimensions, or aspect ratios. The standard ratio for 16mm film projection—the Academy format—is similar to that of standard television screens, which means they are generally compatible. In contrast, CinemaScope or other widescreen images will not fit easily on standard television screens—that is, unless

additional steps are taken to adjust the image. One option is letterboxing, where a black bar is placed at the top and bottom of the screen to allow the full wide picture to show on the otherwise narrow screen. If letterboxing is not used, the widescreen film would have to be altered in another way—by cutting off the outer part of the frame or by "pan and scan" technology that incorporates cuts and what appears to be camera movement in a production to include various parts of the image. This process often results in awkward framing choices never anticipated by the creators of the work. Today, animators creating images for mobile technology face great design challenges because the aspect ratios of phones and other hand-held communication devices vary widely.

The amount of art needed for a work differs according to how it will be shown. For film, it is necessary to create 24 frames of images per second, whereas in some contexts (such as North America) video runs at 30 frames per second, or fps (25 fps in most other parts of the world). Some animators work at film speed (because it requires less work and remains the industry standard) and rely on technology to make the transition to video, adjusting the image and sound so they run properly. Animation created for the Web is a different matter altogether—frame rates vary (for example, Flash animations can run at 12 fps).

Distribution media also limit the longevity of a work. Animators working with particular software applications should be concerned about the compatibility of the

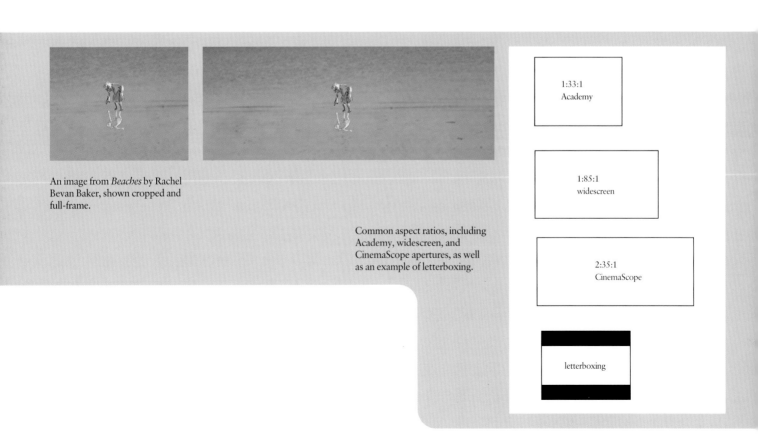

An image from *Beaches* by Rachel Bevan Baker, shown cropped and full-frame.

Common aspect ratios, including Academy, widescreen, and CinemaScope apertures, as well as an example of letterboxing.

1:33:1
Academy

1:85:1
widescreen

2:35:1
CinemaScope

letterboxing

completed work with future software releases, including operating systems and possibly Web browsers, such as Safari or Internet Explorer. Hardware standards also change as technology is developed and planned obsolescence results in new products. In any case, distribution media have an inherently limited lifetime. The life expectancy of videotapes (under ideal storage conditions) is about ten years, and DVD formats also deteriorate, though they have not been around long enough to say exactly how many years they will last. More information on preservation issues can be found at the website of the Association of Moving Image Archivists.[5]

Style

An animator's style is apparent in the way his or her chosen media are used to convey images and ideas. Styles develop from a variety of influences, including conventions within the field of animation and developments within the fine and popular arts.

Image design and movement are two components of style in animation. Other considerations include structure, genre and conventions, presentation of images, sound design, and color, all of which are covered in Chapter Two.

Image Design

Animation is largely defined within the categories of 2D and 3D. By definition, two-dimensional art has only height and width: The illusion of depth, when desired, must be created. Drawn and painted animation, including cel animation, fits into this category. Three-dimensional art has height and width, but it also has actual depth—for example, the sets for stop-motion animation made with wooden, clay, or other types of figures take up real space in all three dimensions. Animation that is primarily computer-generated simulates 2D and 3D environments, though its imagery is virtual, existing only as digital data. Such animation is described by its appearance: If it looks like it was drawn or painted in a "flat" manner, a work typically is called 2D, and if it looks like it incorporates a real-world environment or deep space, light, and shadow, for example, it is described as 3D.

The aesthetics of a given image are affected by choices in form, texture, and line.

Form The shapes of forms can be described as organic or geometric. Organic shapes typically are those found in nature and tend to be curved, soft, and irregular. They usually impart a comforting feel. Geometric forms are the named shapes often associated with mathematical figures: the triangle, the

Depth is drawn into this two-dimensional direct-film image from *Red Ball Express* by Steve Segal.

Depth exists naturally in this three-dimensional stop-motion set from *The Magic Portal* by Lindsay Fleay.

square, the sphere, and so forth. These forms are more orderly and regular, and so tend to create a feeling of structure and strength. Because geometric figures tend to be symmetrical, or the same on both sides, they feel balanced. In contrast, the irregular construction of organic forms generally results in asymmetrical figures, or forms that are not as balanced in structure.

Texture Texture refers to the way a surface looks: smooth, rough, velvety, hairy, crystallized, porous, metallic, and so on. Textures create visual interest and subtly provide information to viewers. The three-dimensional objects used in stop-motion animation are inherently textured, 2D animation and computer-generated images can be textured in the process of creating them. One of the biggest aesthetic challenges of digital animation has been the development of widely varied surfaces, particularly in terms of organic materials. Flat, hard, and reflective materials (metal, plastic, and smooth wood) dominate early computer animation. In recent years, hair, skin, and other irregular, organic surfaces appear with increasing frequency. Artists often scan textures from surfaces covered with paints, charcoals, or other media and apply them to digitally produced images in order to achieve varied looks.

Line Line quality is the domain of 2D animation, where artists have many choices. Hard-edged lines are rigid and firm. Gestural lines are free-flowing and spirited, and can energize a work. Lines also can be soft or smudged, dashed, uneven in pressure, brushed on using wet media, or applied in different ways. Unfortunately, in industrial animation, lines often serve a purely utilitarian function. Computer-generated art and photocopying processes generally standardize them, and the greatest flexibility comes in the decision to use a certain color or perhaps no lines at all around colored forms.

Typography represents a subcategory within the realm of line quality. Animated text presents its own considerations—largely concerned with legibility. While type, like other shapes

Venues for Animation

Animation is ubiquitous in society today. Here are just a few places where animation can be found:

— television series
— television advertising
— theatrical features
— independent short works found online or in festivals
— Web series
— interfaces for cell phones and PDAs
— gaming
— interdisciplinary performance pieces
— gallery installations
— research and training applications in scientific fields such as medicine and forensics
— software used for military training programs

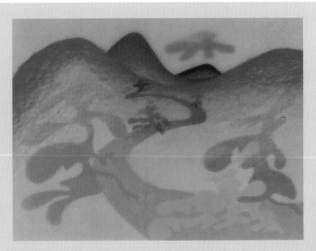

Curved, soft organic forms are found in *Dance of Nature*, co-directed by David Ehrlich and Karin Johansen Sletton.

Hard-edged geometric forms in Stephanie Maxwell's *Please Don't Stop*.

onscreen, creates generalized meaning through the way it appears, it also relays specific information, in terms of what it says. Ornate fonts, or all capital letters, make content much harder to access because the eye tends to slide over the words, rather than take in their meaning.

Interesting examples of animation that utilize typography include *The Man with the Beautiful Eyes* (2000) by Jonathan Hodgson. This film incorporates words into a story based on a Charles Bukowski poem about a group of children who are fascinated by a mysterious man in their neighborhood. Also of interest is *The Child* (1999) by the French animation studio H5, created entirely out of type set into geometric forms, suggesting the streets and buildings of a city. In this three-minute computer-generated short, which was a music video for the Alex Gopher song of the same name, a woman is rushed to hospital to give birth to a child. She and her husband, the taxi driver, some policemen who chase the cab, and everything else in the film are defined by the meaning and form of the onscreen words that describe them.

Character Design Many expectations about character design in animation come from conventions developed at the Disney studio. Its impact has been huge; it is impossible to name any single live-action studio that had the same kind of influence on its industry. In his *Hollywood Cartoons: American Animation in its Golden Age*, Michael Barrier details the evolution of the studio style from the norms of silent animation to a specialized aesthetic reflective of not only Walt Disney's own sensibilities, but also of the influence of particular animators (such as Norman Ferguson and Freddie Moore) and a multitude of inspirational sources. A number of others also have explored the studio's aesthetics, including the influence of European storytelling traditions and art.

Despite Disney's dominance, its reign certainly has not been absolute. Stylistically, one of the earliest challenges came from Chuck Jones at Warner Bros. in *The Dover Boys* (1942). During the post-World War II era, United Productions of America (UPA) and, later, Zagreb Film became known for their stylized imagery, quite unlike that of Disney, as well as the use of limited animation techniques and stories propelled by narration. UPA's best-known works include a series of films created around the characters of Gerald McBoing Boing and Mr. Magoo. Also well-known are UPA titles aimed at adult viewers, like *Rooty Toot Toot* (1952), directed by John Hubley, which visualizes "The Ballad of Frankie and Johnny," a classic American song about a jealous woman who shoots her cheating boyfriend. Although UPA was center stage for

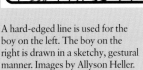

Ornate fonts can create meaning through style, but also can be difficult to read.

A hard-edged line is used for the boy on the left. The boy on the right is drawn in a sketchy, gestural manner. Images by Allyson Heller.

only about a decade, its impact has been very long lasting. Today the UPA style continues to exert influence on a range of television series in the United States, particularly on The Cartoon Network.

The cartoonists of the Zagreb School began creating animation in 1950. Their first steps were in the then-dominant Disney style, but during the mid-1950s they began to think about new possibilities, an impulse that was furthered by exposure to the work of UPA and other inspirational sources. Animators such as Dusan Vukotić, Vlado Kristl, Vatroslav Mimica, Zlatkco Grgic, Borivoj "Bordo" Dovnikovic, Zlatko Bourek, and others are stylistically diverse and yet all reflect a distinctive sensibility that arose in opposition to the fairy-tale characters and cute animals of the Disney style. Instead, they favored (though not exclusively) human characters who interact in settings of stylized reality. Internationally acclaimed, Zagreb animation tends to be geared toward adult viewers more than children, or at least to include "mature" content. In 1962, Vukotić became the first director from outside the United States to win an Oscar for animation—it was awarded to *Surrogat* (Ersatz, 1961), a humorous film that explores a world filled with inflatable substitutes.

Whereas imagery associated with the Disney studio tended to be relatively "photorealistic," the characters designed by UPA and Zagreb artists generally have been more "iconic" in nature. These tendencies form two of the three "vertices" Scott McCloud identifies in describing the "pictorial vocabulary of the visual arts"—the third one being "abstraction."[6] In his book, *Understanding Comics*, McCloud places these tendencies within a triangle, demonstrating that every image can be placed somewhere within an intersection of them: the "picture plane" (culminating in abstraction), "reality" (epitomized by a photographic representation of an entity), and "language" (represented by icons, including words). Images in comics—and most animation—tend to gravitate between iconic and photorealistic tendencies, just as the UPA, Zagreb, and Disney images do.

McCloud explains that the term "icon" means "any image used to represent a person, place, thing, or idea," and recognizes two types: pictorial (the stick figure of a woman on a washroom door) and nonpictorial (the word "women" that accompanies it). Both pictorial and nonpictorial icons can stand for the same thing: The two examples here both represent a person of female gender. To take another example, Homer Simpson and his entire yellow-skinned family are iconic representations of people; they are recognizably human, but nonetheless are unlike any people we've ever seen. In McCloud's view, icons create the greatest opportunities for viewers to identify with a character because, with their lack of specificity, they easily accommodate a viewer's self-perception.

Images from *Gerald McBoing Boing*, directed by Robert "Bobe" Cannon, reflect the influential UPA style. Courtesy iota Foundation.

In contrast, abstract images lend themselves to a more generalized experience (sometimes suggestive of dream states) and representational images create a more specific and therefore limited-perception of what the entity represents. Simply put, an iconic smiley face is more universal than a photo-like image of a blonde, blue-eyed girl in her teens.

Today the use of photorealism is growing, especially in the realms of special effects for live-action feature films and gaming, aided by the growth in digital technology. However, various methods of creating highly realistic images have existed throughout animation history. Rotoscoping, an animation process patented in 1917 by Max Fleischer, provides one example. It involves tracing over live-action images to harness the vitality of a live performer and transform it into an animated figure. Rotoshop, which is a computer program developed by Bob Sabiston, provides a recent variation on this technique. Instead of live-action filmed footage that is traced onto paper and reshot with a camera, the Rotoshop process involves digitized imagery that can be altered using a graphics tablet. Images of this sort were used in the films *Waking Life* (2001) and *A Scanner Darkly* (2006), both directed by Richard Linklater.

Digital technology has greatly aided our ability to create highly realistic human and animal characters. At first, this objective was hampered by limitations in software; a film like *Tin Toy*, directed by John Lasseter and released by Pixar in 1988, includes a baby that is relatively monstrous because it has pocked skin, artificial-looking movements, and an inability to react to the forces of gravity (when it falls down, it seems to hover above the ground). However, advances in creating fur, skin, and more complex organic forms during the 1990s resulted in relatively realistic human and animal figures—for example, in *Toy Story 2* (1999), *Monsters Inc.* (2001), and *Final Fantasy: The Spirits Within* (2001). Within the field of gaming, photorealism has been especially pervasive, sometimes resulting in controversy. For example, "first person shooter" games typically employ realistic images in a context where the player assumes the role of a shooter, literally looking through the character's eyes. Critics have argued that this scenario allows for close identification between the player and the killer, which could lead to relatively violent impulses in real life as well.

The third vertex McCloud identifies, the abstract image, also has a long history and continues to be widely used today. When abstraction was appearing in western art movements during the early twentieth century, the cinema also was emerging as an art form (the first public screening took place in Paris in 1895 and cinema came of age over the next twenty years). It is not surprising, then, that fine artists embraced the

2

Stylistically, character design can be relatively iconic, photorealistic, or abstract.

Production from the Zagreb School has been characterized by iconic figures, limited animation, and mature themes. Included here are images by Borivoj "Bordo" Dovnikovic, pictured right.

new technology of film as a way to expand the vocabulary of the visual arts, exploring abstract images not only on canvas but also on screen. From those early years to the present, abstract animation has been produced in a variety of styles, ranging from minimalist uses of color and form, such as the color-field animation of Jules Engel's *Landscape* (1971), to playful explorations of the process of painting, as in Clive Walley's "Divertimenti" series (1991–94).

Backgrounds Image design is not limited to moving figures and props; it also includes backgrounds, which have an important function in not only framing the action but also providing the emotional context in which it takes place. Igor Kovalyov is known for his richly textured backgrounds, which set the scene for introspective stories about human relationships. His award-winning film *Milch* (2005) runs fifteen minutes in length and contains little in the way of dialogue, letting the visuals carry the story.

Through the late 1910s, backgrounds of 2D animation tended to be simple (perhaps just a horizon line) because every image in a frame had to be entirely redrawn on paper. Cels eventually allowed for more complexity, since backgrounds could be painted once and then overlaid with a clear sheet containing the moving figures. Individuals began to specialize in background design and were recognized as artists in their own right—one of the best known is Maurice Noble, who worked with director Chuck Jones, among others. When computer animation emerged during the 1980s, backgrounds again became simplified, as in the use of a spotlight effect (eliminating details with darkness) in John Lasseter's *Luxo Jr.* (1986). At that time, it was difficult to create even the central object of a computer-generated film, so it made sense to simplify extraneous background details. As a conventional lighting method, the spotlight saved time and money without being obvious.

During the 1920s and 1930s, multiplane camera setups were developed to facilitate manipulation of foreground, mid-range, and background spaces to a greater extent than standard camerawork allowed. Probably the best known comes from the Disney studio (used, for example, in the 1937 feature *Snow White*), but during the mid-1920s Lotte Reiniger used a multiplane setup to create her cutout paper animation film *The Adventures of Prince Achmed* (1926), which employed sliced wax and other media to create visual effects in the background. Variations on these multiplane cameras are still in use, especially in the work of animators employing such techniques as oil on glass and sand animation. The use of multiple levels of glass solves the problem of preserving

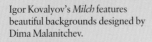
Igor Kovalyov's *Milch* features beautiful backgrounds designed by Dima Malanitchev.

background images made of soft materials (like wet oil paints) as characters move across them. Today, artists can also use many layers with relative ease by employing software designed for this purpose; for example, Photoshop images can be broken into virtual layers, so that one level can be manipulated while another is untouched.

No matter which technique is used, backgrounds should be designed to facilitate the interaction of central figures while maintaining the overall aesthetics of the work. A central question is consistency: whether to use the same media to create backgrounds and the moving figures. Different media can help to separate figures from an environment, but using the same media is useful for creating a more unified diegesis, or film world, in which the action can take place. In either case, sometimes simpler is better. Complex backdrops may distract from the action and make central figures hard to see, especially if many colors are used. It takes careful planning to ensure that colors used on backgrounds complement the ones used on characters that pass in front of them.

Environments for stop-motion are much like the sets designed for live-action cinema in terms of having "real-life" depth, scale, texture, and lighting. The scope of background detail varies significantly depending on aesthetics, budget, time, and available technology, not to mention the skills of the artists. For example, backgrounds for narrative-based, high-budget stop-motion works often contain intricate lighting setups that can take days to accomplish. Low-budget student animation usually relies on simpler setups with occasional use of lighting effects. Stop-motion animation shot outdoors (for example, pixilation involving live actors) can rely on natural light, which sounds convenient but can cause a lot of problems; the sun moves, causing shadows to shift, and lighting intensity changes as clouds move and the day comes to an end.

Choices in perspective also play an important role in creating backgrounds. In some instances, a lack of perspective is desirable; flattened environments can create a sense of claustrophobia or help to accentuate the images within them. Flat space also can enhance humor, while depth tends to add drama. Paul Driessen from the Netherlands plays with shifting perspectives in his *On Land, at Sea, and in the Air* (1980), which uses three panels that mainly show action horizontally; one panel briefly shifts to an overhead view and the separation between the panels partially dissolves at the end. German animator Raimund Krumme is well-known for using varied perspectives in his work; for example, in *Crossroads* (1991) a simple meeting of two roads provides a place for exploring spatial dimensions as characters walk and climb through and

Disney's multiplane camera increased the dimensionality of backgrounds in films such as *Snow White*. © Disney Enterprises Inc.

Maya Yonesho utilized a multiplane setup to animate flipbooks for her film *Üks Uks*.

around the area created by lines representing the intersection. Environments can be designed to incorporate depth of field and perspective to heighten a sense of realism. The illusion of depth is enhanced by laying out scenes to include horizon lines that are angular (receding into the distance), opening up the background. Atmospheric effects (bluish overtones and softer focus) can be incorporated into the design of drawn and painted backgrounds to add to the perception of depth.

Movement

The movement of figures is of course a central concern for animators. In some respects, the process boils down to basic formulas—for example, working out how many individual images are needed to create a second of action. In the case of motion picture film, where there are 24 fps, every second of a figure's movement could be broken into 24 increments, referred to as animating "on ones." If an artist wants to reuse images—to save time and money and/or create stylized movement—the action could be broken into 12 images per second, 8 images, 6 images, and so on, requiring each setup to be shot two times (animating on twos), three times (animating on threes), four times (animating on fours), and so on. Animating on ones produces smoother animation than animating on twos or higher numbers, as the breakdown of a

figure's movement is subtler when there are 24 increments per second rather than 12 or fewer. This formula is different for various media. Phase Alternating Line (PAL) and Séquentiel couleur à mémoire (SECAM) video run at 25 fps, while the NTSC standard is 30 fps. Images created with Flash to run off the Web are variable in speed, but often are paced at 12 fps.

The movement of any figure—human, animal, or an abstract shape—tells a great deal about its personality and mood. Animators who study acting or dance gain insight into the way humans interpret poses and actions to create meaning. We can perceive such emotions as elation, despair, or apprehension, for example, just by looking at the way a form holds itself and the movements it makes. One well-known exercise given to aspiring animators involves an animated sack of flour: A skillful artist can make even this anonymous object express a full range of feelings.

Animating a human character can be more of a challenge, especially if the aim is to achieve a high degree of realism. To do so, some animators have relied on rotoscoping and motion-capture. Max Fleischer's rotoscope process was used to create elements in his studio's "Out of the Inkwell" and "Betty Boop" films between the late 1910s and mid-1930s, and notably in its 1939 feature, *Gulliver's Travels*. However, rotoscoping has been used perhaps most famously in Ralph

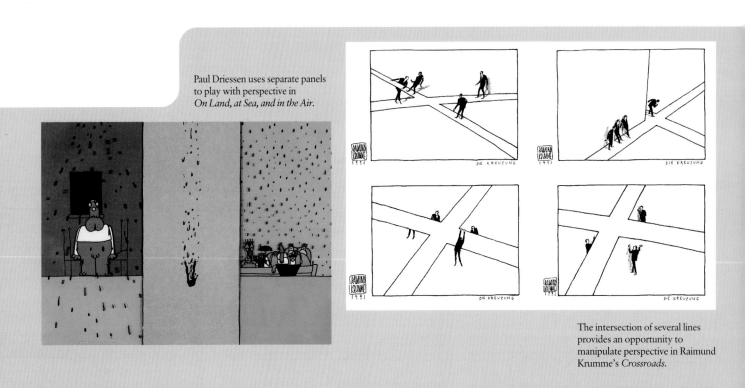

Paul Driessen uses separate panels to play with perspective in *On Land, at Sea, and in the Air.*

The intersection of several lines provides an opportunity to manipulate perspective in Raimund Krumme's *Crossroads.*

Bakshi's feature-length films, including *Wizards* (1977), *The Lord of the Rings* (1978), and *American Pop* (1982). Other artists who have employed rotoscoping to interpret live-action footage in interesting ways include the Australian animator Denis Tupicoff. In *His Mother's Voice* (1996), he used the process to depict the content of a radio interview involving the mother of a young man who was shot and killed in a high-profile case. Tupicoff selected two professional actors to play the mother and her interviewer, and filmed them performing to the playback of this audio. Other roles were acted by nonprofessionals—high school students and friends. The interview is heard twice, accompanied by different imagery in each case. The first focuses mainly on the crime scene. It was created using cel animation, mainly in black and white with solid patches of intense color woven into the designs. The murdered boy was drawn with a wax pencil to give him a soft quality. The second reenactment takes viewers around the home of the woman being interviewed. It is created in soft charcoal on paper and features tight framing on the woman's eyes, as well as a poignant shot of a whimpering dog. Though essentially the same soundtrack is used, the results are drastically different, partly because of the change in visuals and partly because of the shifts in media used to depict them. The film asks viewers to consider how their emotions are manipulated by what they see on the screen and, even more specifically, to question the way that "documentary" coverage has its own point of view.

In recent years, motion capture has succeeded in bringing very realistic movement to animation. It uses live performers who are rigged in suits containing data points that transmit information back to computers via a series of cameras set up in the performance area. This data forms the basis of animated characters, either in real time or after extensive manipulation of the input. Motion-capture animation is widely found in the contexts of gaming and effects for live-action features.

Creating "Character" "Character animation" is the term used to describe conventions of character-driven work released by most commercial studios producing features and television series. Originally, style in this sort of animation was highly influenced by the Disney studio. During the 1930s, it shifted from the "rubber hose" style—so called because characters moved in a rubbery fashion, without regard to anatomy—to a more naturalistic approach, developed from the study of live models and filmed reference footage. This change took place partly in art courses that Disney arranged for the large number of artists it hired in the mid-1930s, as it geared up for feature-film production. In these courses,

2

Ralph Bakshi is well-known for his use of rotoscoped images, such as these characters from *The Lord of the Rings*.

In *His Mother's Voice*, Denis Tupicoff renders rotoscoped images in two different styles.

many of which were led by Don Graham, artists viewed and analyzed movement in films, observed and drew human and animal models, and discussed the ways in which body movements, such as a manner of walking, could suggest how a character feels. Motion was so important that Disney artists began to draw figures without mouths to test the action of characters during dialogue scenes—the body had to be in sync with the words being spoken before moving lips were added.

The aesthetic of "squash and stretch," as the body shifts shape for dramatic and comedic effect, became one component in the studio's development of "personality animation"—which includes the movement, as well as the design and voice, given to a character to define it as a distinctive type. However, personality animation is not limited to cel animation or even 2D imagery. The Aardman film *Creature Comforts* (1990), directed by Nick Park, provides an example of the technique using modeling clay. Each of the animals featured is given a distinctive personality, so it becomes an individual, rather than an anonymous zoo creature.

Disney's best-known productions provide examples of "full animation." In contrast, the term "limited animation" can be used to describe the work of the influential UPA studio and, for the most part, made-for-television series and Web animation. The two approaches can be compared in terms of frequency of images, use of dialogue, and camera movement. Full animation tends to be animated on ones, while limited animation can be animated on threes or higher. To minimize the movement needed, limited animation relies on "holds" (a full stop in the action) and "cycles" (reusing a series of animated movements, as in a walk cycle) to a larger extent than full animation. It also tends to "explain" actions rather than "show" them, using dialogue (including voice-over narration) to provide plot details. Extensive camera movement across still art minimizes the number of individual drawings limited animation requires, thus reducing the cost and amount of time necessary to create it.

Limited animation is pervasive within Japanese "anime," in part because of the relatively rapid production schedules and low budgets afforded to most of the industry's output. But its techniques also reflect the origins of much of anime in comic books, which, of course, are not in motion. A good example of a comic-book aesthetic is found in *Hadashi no Gen* (*Barefoot Gen*, 1983), directed by Mori Masaki, the story of a boy who survives the bombing of Hiroshima in World War II. The designs and highly stylized expressions of its characters closely mirror the look of the autobiographical manga by Keiji Nakazawa on which the film is based.

The characters in Disney's *The Skeleton Dance* are the same in design and movement, revealing that the studio had not yet shifted to its use of personality animation. These images illustrate the "rubber hose" style of animation. © Disney Enterprises, Inc.

Though limited animation is an economical process, it can certainly be used stylistically. Jules Engel, who worked at both Disney and UPA, disliked the term, because it could imply that it was less effective than full animation. According to Engel, "There is no such thing as limited animation, only limited talent."[7] If the art is strong enough, he contended, it does not require constant movement to make it visually compelling. Motion should be employed in ways that are consistent with the aesthetics of the work as a whole. Through movement, animators should be able to endow forms with levels of energy appropriate to their "qualities of being"—not just to reflect the simple conditions of happiness or sadness, for example, but a more complex array of emotional states that make a character or any other image come alive.

Understanding the relationship between motion and a quality of being, and having the ability to depict that in animation, generally takes a combination of sensitivity and training. Animator Leslie Bishko has long advocated a dance-related approach, developed from Laban Movement Analysis (LMA), to assist visual artists with creating motions for their forms. She explains that Laban-based analysis assists the animator in the process of ascribing movements to characters by articulating "formal components of movement, associating them with specific mental aspects of human existence."[8]

Other methods are also useful in developing character movements. For example, Lorin Salm is a mime who regularly holds a "character movement for animators" workshop. He explains, "Careful analysis of the human body and its possibilities in natural and stylized movement is invaluable. Theatrical mime offers animators a greater understanding of the potential of a character's physical expression."[9] Whereas traditional acting classes stress the need to understand a character from the inside, mime concentrates on the outward physical expression of a state of being; in its caricature-like nature, it is readily adaptable to the needs of animators. Studying the film work of such diverse "physical comedians" as Charlie Chaplin, Buster Keaton, Stan Laurel, Oliver Hardy, and Jacques Tati also helps with understanding the use of the body in comedy.

Metamorphosis Movement can, of course, be used to transport a form from one place to another, but it also can be used to alter the physical state of that entity. Such shape-shifting, or metamorphosis, is at the heart of animation. Some media are particularly suitable for this. For example, oil-based clay can be reshaped easily, as can sand and oil paint, which stays wet for a relatively long time. Quite often, animated forms are changed over a series of images—this is the way cel

The Three Little Pigs is credited as the first Disney film to incorporate personality animation: characters who are differentiated in various ways, including design and movement. Its characters move using "squash and stretch" and are in other ways typical of the full-animation style. © Disney Enterprises, Inc.

animation works, as does most dry media (like colored pencils) and computer-generated animation. Stop-motion that involves fabric, latex, plastic, or wood figures usually achieves shape-changing through the replacement method, when expressions and alterations in form are made by removing and replacing the changing portion of the figure (such as a speaking mouth, a winking eye, or a limb that bends). To create synchronized speech for the character U.D. Chunk, Chris Sickels of Red Nose Studio created a series of heads with mouths in various positions. Chunk appears in a short film called *Innards: The Metaphysical Highway* (2004), directed by Stephen Chiodo. He is a piece of undigested food that refuses to be absorbed into the corrupt system of an unhealthy body.

Timing Animation in all its forms is concerned with timing, or the manner and speed of an object's movements, which typically is closely tied to the sound elements within the production. Sometimes animation is tightly synchronized to a music score that provides the pace for the action (an approach that in narrative contexts sometimes is described as "mickey mousing" because Disney did it in many films—for example, *The Skeleton Dance*, 1929). However, in features, television series, and games, the dialogue track generally supplies the framework for timing. It is common for animators to incorporate "anticipation" into their characters' movements by adding a physical reaction a split second before a verbal one. Anticipation also occurs before other actions, to provide emphasis and make a movement more convincing, possibly adding humor or drama. In classic Hollywood cartoons, the bodies of characters often "wind up" for a moment before they take off in a burst of speed.

Creative timing incorporates variations in the speed of an action, which adds visual interest. A movement can begin slow and suddenly take off, as in a "wind up"—or it can be just the opposite, with the last steps the slowest. Sometimes a humorous effect can be achieved by altering the normal tempo of the speed, using slow motion (a slower-than-normal set of movements) or fast motion (where everything moves overly fast). Time-lapse animation is a form of variable speed cinematography, where a live object is captured frame by frame over a long period of time, so its action is greatly accelerated during playback; a typical example is a seed growing into a plant in perhaps five seconds, which might be seen in an educational film.

Timing is also tied to the laws of physics. For example, animators "ease in" and "ease out" the motion of a figure, gradually accelerating the speed as it starts to move and decelerating as it stops. The effects of gravity are particularly significant in the production of stop-motion animation. While drawn and painted figures can be depicted hovering in the air

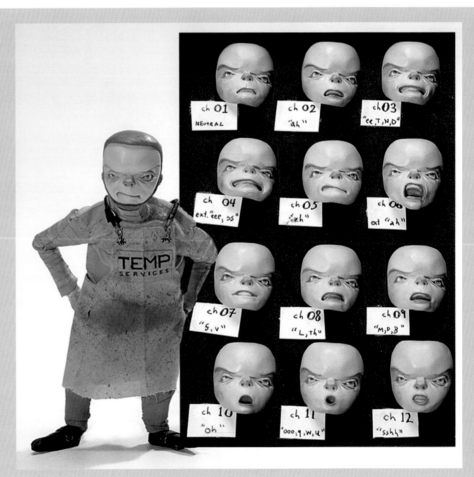

Replacement heads used for lip-sync animation of a character from *Innards: The Metaphysical Highway*, directed by Stephen Chiodo. Sculpture by Chris Sickels of Red Nose Studio.

or in other ways defying real-world physics, a stop-motion clay figure is bound by its physical nature. Without the use of supports, it cannot be paused in the air in order to animate it gradually flying up or down. Even walking and running are challenging. The one-legged slide of Art Clokey's famous clay figure, Gumby, is not only charming; it is also practical because it keeps him anchored to the floor of the set. Stop-motion animators generally have to use creative angles, strategically placed wires, and possibly computer technology to achieve such gravity-defying effects. Sometimes, flying and other difficult movements are achieved by placing a side view of the character on a sheet of glass and animating it from above, using a "rostrum" camera, held vertically over the artwork on a column. Aardman Animations used this technique in *The Wrong Trousers* to depict an evil penguin as it was catapulted through the air. Background elements were moved quickly behind the character, so it appears to be traveling at a rapid speed, adding humor to the scene.

Variations in speed are attractive to the eye, relieving the monotony of a constant pace. Variations in the directions in which an object moves on the screen also can be visually attractive, particularly when it comes to dynamic motion across various planes of action. Movements left and right can be described as occurring on the "x axis," while movements up and down are on the "y axis." Movements in depth are on the "z axis," and are the most dynamic of all. Like an optical illusion, they can pull the eye into the frame or pop out and surprise the viewer. Z-axis movements are the most difficult to create in 2D because they rely not only on an ability to draw in perspective, but also on a strong sense of timing. Stop-motion characters, on the other hand, move most easily on the z axis (backward and forward) as well as the x axis (left and right); for them it is the y axis (up and down) that presents problems.

The Walk Cycle One of the most basic and yet challenging types of movement for character animators is the walk cycle. To draw one, the artist must have a detailed understanding of the dynamics of movement. This is where the study of dance, theatrical mime, or other aspects of performance really comes in handy. The walk cycle is developed around two extremes, or key positions, of outstretched legs that are connected by a series of in-between drawings—simple to describe, but much harder to do, especially when character-related nuances are added to the gait. As animator and author Tony White explains, the body is "a complex piece of machinery and does not lend itself easily to simple procedures. The head, arms, body, and legs all seem to move independently so that it appears impossible to 'get into' the action."[10] The central motion of the walk cycle is located in the legs and lower body,

"Creating animated movement is a triadic process of experience, observation, and description. The animator's uniqueness comes through selection or perceptual biases from experience and observation in the natural world."

Leslie Bishko

with the weight of the figure typically staying in balance with the position of the legs. In the "passing position," the halfway-point movement between the two extremes, the body is lifted slightly higher due to the straightening of one leg under the body. White's full walk cycle takes a series of seventeen drawings to complete, but this number can vary.

Lip Sync Another challenge faced by character animators is "lip sync"—moving a character's mouth as though it were speaking particular words. There are various approaches to lip sync, some relatively complex and others fairly simple. White says it is important to emphasize vowel sounds. He writes, "As a general rule, the mouth open [vowel] sounds tend to dominate the action. If the open positions hit their sounds accurately, then the lip sync is usually successful … Certain consonants, however, are equally important when tackling lip sync. In particular, b, f, m, and l should, ideally, be held for a least two frames."[11] In any case, it is not necessary to animate the mouth for every letter of a word.

Dialogue can be described in terms of "phonemes," or units of sound, that can be broken down into nine basic mouth shapes (though more can be used). Simply uttering these sounds reveals that, indeed, the mouth shape is approximately the same when it says the letters in any one of the groups. However,

a mouth moves differently when a character experiences different emotions. For example, an angry mouth will not look like a happy one. Also characters talk in different ways due to their mouth shapes (a horse mouth is not like a human one). A potential problem is that animation originally synced for mouth movements in one language will not be in sync if the production is dubbed into another one. Even people who speak the same language have different accents that can affect the way their mouths move.

There are ways to minimize the problems of lip syncing. Computer programs that automate some of the process are an example, though predictably they tend to produce movements that look mechanical. Stop-motion animation using the replacement method can rely on a series of preformed mouth shapes to speed production. In Japan, unlike in the United States, it is common to record voices when the animation has been completed, and there is little concern with lip sync (Japanese animation typically employs only three distinct mouth movements).[12] As anime historian Patrick Drazen points out, there are probable historical precedents for this practice. He notes, "In the unmoving mouths of Bunraku puppets, and in Noh theater, in which the protagonists usually wear masks, Japan has a history of giving the audience mouths that move without speaking or speech from a mouth

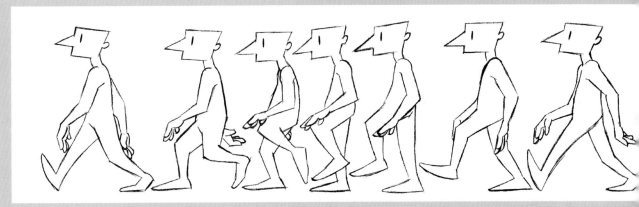

A walk cycle is one of the most basic skills of character animation, and yet one of the most challenging movements to create. The walk cycle is structured around the "extremes" of outstretched legs, which are "in-betweened" with several mid-stride poses, as seen in this series of images by Musa Brooker.

that doesn't move."[13] As this example suggests, lip sync, like other aesthetic choices, is understood differently in various contexts. In any case, beginning animators should be cautious when attempting it. Many viewers will see limitations in lip sync as reflecting low production values or poor animation skills—or both.

Image design and the approach to movement are but two aspects of style in an animated work. The following chapter details additional stylistic considerations—factors related to how a story is told.

Mouth Shapes: The Basic Groups

1:    A, I
2:    O
3:    E (as in sweet)
4:    U
5:    C, K, G, J, R, S, TH, Y, Z
6:    D, L, N, T
7:    W, Q
8:    M, B, P
9:    F, V[14]

2

The ways in which lips are synchronized to dialogue vary according to the language, mouth shapes, and conventions of production. Depicted here are nine basic mouth movements associated with English-language dialogue.

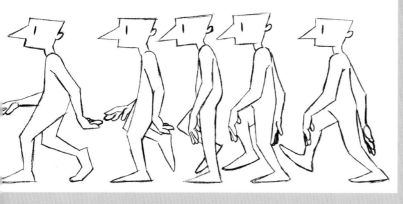

Storytelling Strategies

Animated concepts generally involve storytelling. A story about a product or service is conveyed in advertisements in order to make it appealing. Instructional works might tell a story about a procedure, or focus on an important concept, in order to inform or caution an audience. Architectural animations reveal the "story" of a building, including its various features and overall appeal. Animated features tell stories that often are humorous in nature for entertainment purposes, but they—like animated series on television—typically also have a merchandising function; their characters become products that consumers can purchase. In a less tangible way, even abstract works—or any so-called "non-narrative" animation—can tell a kind of story; it might be the process through which a work is created, revealed onscreen through time, or it might be an exploration of form that develops in some structured manner. Even "chaos" or lack of a formal structure in a work can tell a story—about the existence of chance or the absence of order in our lives. Some abstract animations function as meditational aids that help viewers explore experience within themselves—not exactly storytelling, but these works still fall within a general cause-and-effect framework. Of course, animators are not obligated to think of their work in terms of story, but doing so can be a helpful way to conceptualize a production.

Stories help make sense of what might otherwise be perceived as random bits of data. They can be entertaining, fun, and inspirational, and can leave viewers with the satisfaction of having expanded their knowledge or experience base. They also can be used to persuade people in various ways: to follow rules, to rebel, to consume products, and to consider new ideas. The power of the message rests in part on the difference between "telling a story" and true "storytelling." A progression of events or facts about a situation forms only the backbone of any narrative. What makes a story or exploration captivating is the artist's unique approach to imparting the information. Skillful animators are those who read widely, watch motion pictures of all types, and experience life in various contexts. They understand cultural communication and how to appeal to a wide audience. In addition, to be great storytellers, animators must understand how to utilize various components of the motion picture form, including structure, presentation of images, sound, and color.

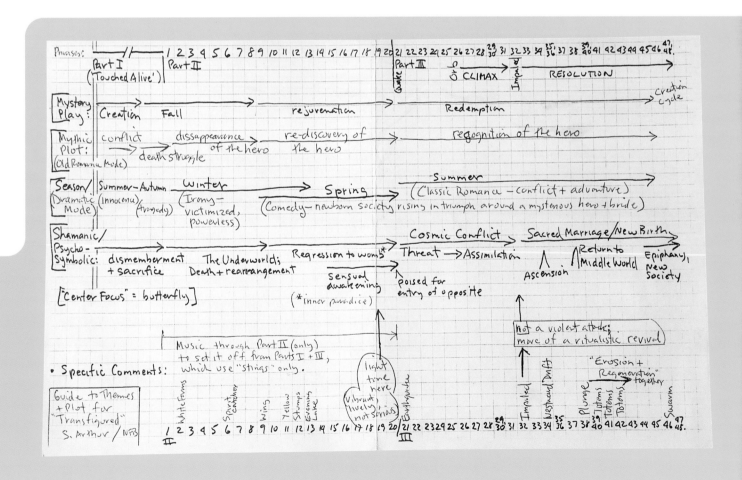

Structure

At the basic level of storytelling, determining how to impart the content of a work, the animator has many options. For example, a story may be visualized within a particular "genre," or classification of storytelling, as an extension of some existing group of works that share formal or thematic similarities. It also can be considered in terms of narrative design, or the manner in which story elements are ordered temporally. This section focuses on these and other issues concerning the structure of an animated work.

Conventional Forms

"Genre" defines a recognizable category in literature, motion pictures, and other types of communication, which is based upon repeated patterns, or conventions, in character, story, setting, and other aspects of a work. There is no set number of genres, and they are always evolving. Some common genre classifications include the musical, the western, and horror. However, these genres often overlap—for example, the distinction between horror and science fiction is at times hazy, and a film like *The Triplets of Belleville* (directed by Sylvain Chomet, 2003) blends qualities of a mystery and a musical with comedy. Producers find genres are desirable because they

can be used as indicators of success; if science-fiction anime is popular in a given market, there is a strong chance that another film incorporating the same conventions will make money.

Historically, animation has not been widely classified in terms of genre. One reason is the dominance of Disney for so long—for many, the term "animation" was synonymous with its feature films. Studio style became a stand-in for genre: For example, the "Warner Bros. style" was much more dependent than Disney on physical humor, and the UPA and the Zagreb School styles were associated with a modern-art approach and limited animation. However, there are true genres within animation. "The Flintstones," "The Simpsons," and "Family Guy" all qualify as animated family sitcoms. And a variety of genres are associated with Japanese animation: for example, "mecha," which involves large warrior robots, generally controlled by humans. Mecha series include "The Super Dimension Fortress Macross" and "Giant Robo."

Animation can follow formulas in other ways as well—for example, by using similar characters in different contexts. During the silent era, American animators cashed in on a wave of popular felines, which included Krazy Kat, Felix the Cat, and Julius from Disney's "Alice Comedies." In the Robert Zemeckis film *Who Framed Roger Rabbit* (1988), the sexy singer Jessica Rabbit was a super-sized version of the

Disney, like other animation studios, often has relied on conventional characters. Julius, from the studio's 1920's "Alice Comedies," was based on a series of popular cat characters, including Felix the Cat. Many years later, Jessica Rabbit, from *Who Framed Roger Rabbit*, was developed as a parody of a sexy female "type" found throughout much of American animation. Julius © Disney Enterprises, Inc. Jessica Rabbit © Touchstone Pictures & Amblin Entertainment, Inc. All Rights Reserved.

Stephen X. Arthur developed a kind of story structure (opposite) for his abstract film *Transfigured* (above), which is built around the paintings of Jack Shadbolt.

stage performer animated by Preston Blair in a series of Tex Avery shorts that include *Red Hot Riding Hood* (1943) and *Swing Shift Cinderella* (1945); Jessica functions as both an homage, or tribute, to the Blair character and a commentary on changing morality, especially in contrast with the sexuality of the once "scandalous" Betty Boop, who makes a cameo appearance in the film. The reuse of characters is central to machinima, the practice of creating cinema using the game engines of various real-time interactive software packages (such as "Quake," "Unreal Tournament 2003," and "The Sims 2"), as opposed to 3D animation software such as 3ds Max. In addition to characters, other resources within the games can be accessed, such as backgrounds, levels, and skins, and creators also use tools like camera angles and editors. The popular machinima series "Red vs. Blue," by Rooster Tooth Productions, is a parody of "Halo," the game used to create it.

Using repeated patterns can be practical, and can even promote creativity. There are good reasons why so much animation has incorporated stories from the Brothers Grimm and other traditional sources: People are familiar with the basic structure of the work, which means there is less need to develop characters and their motivations. Viewers basically know what to expect. As a result, the animation director can dwell on the action being depicted and the design of the work. Part of the reason why Tex Avery's *Red Hot Riding Hood* is so funny is that it is based on a well-known fairy tale, in this case involving an innocent little girl and a hungry wolf—in Avery's version, they grow up to be a sexy singer and a lust-filled

animal who salivates for a different reason. The humor works precisely because viewers are familiar with the original version. Avery subverts their expectations and, in so doing, creates a great parody of the traditional tale. Of course, he was a great storyteller, and so succeeded in his rendition. The use of conventions also comes with risks—mainly by creating results that are too similar to the previous work, rather than being original in their own terms.

Narrative Design

The structure of an animated production's narrative design can be described in various ways, including:

– Linear: the most common type of structure for features, television programs, and short films. Generally begins with an introduction to the character(s), progresses to introducing a conflict or dramatic/comedic situation, and ultimately ends with resolution and possibly some type of character "arc" (that is, change).

– Multilinear: A number of stories are told simultaneously, by dividing the frame into various parts or cross-cutting between scenes; relatively rare in animation, this technique is seen in some of Paul Driessen's work—for example, in *The End of the World in Four Seasons* (1998), where up to 9 frames of action occur onscreen at one time.

– Interactive (sometimes called nonlinear): used for creating stories where the user influences the events in some manner. The story usually changes every time it is told.

The production team of Rooster Tooth Productions (right) created the machinima series "Red vs. Blue" (above) as a parody of the game "Halo," using the software's game engine.

- Gag: common in animated series on television. Although its underlying structure generally is linear, the content consists of a series of humorous events, often based on physical comedy, occurring in rapid succession with little concern for a fleshed-out story.
- Episodic: The story is broken into parts, or episodes, though typically the same characters continue to appear. Some or all story elements may progress from episode to episode; this structure is typical of television series and some Web animation.
- Compilation: a variation on episodic structure. A group of artists creates animated works (generally quite short) based on a given topic, which are linked together in one film. David Ehrlich has headed efforts of this sort, including *Academy Leader Variations* (1987), which involved artists from the United States, Switzerland, Poland, and China.
- Cyclical: The "story" returns to the point of origin, rather than moving toward a resolution and change in the character(s). To provide just one example, the animation seen on a zoetrope wheel repeats in an endless loop, beginning over and over again, and so is cyclical in nature. George Griffin's film *Viewmaster* (1976), which was inspired by early motion studies, features an unending cycle of action as characters move around the border of a circle.
- Thematic: an in-depth exploration of a topic that is not concerned with forward or even cyclical movement. Meditational films provide an excellent example since they explore stasis. Some motion graphics (animated television station logos, for instance) can be considered thematic insofar as they primarily express a single image.
- Effect: The primary purpose of the animation is to enhance another visual. Examples include rollover effects on websites, animated overlays on a map, or special effects in live-action films. Effects might not actually tell a story, but certainly they are structured in that they have dynamic movement with a beginning and ending.

This list provides examples of the wide range of ways in which animation can be structured, in terms of how content, or narrative, is imparted.

Running Time

Another component of structure, running time (or length), quite often is dictated by budgets, in terms of both money and time. Length also can be limited by the function of the animation. Station identifications (interstitials) and television commercials typically run between a few seconds and half a minute. The structure of a television series depends on the context in which it is exhibited. Commercials may affect not only the running time of an episode (for example, a typical "half hour" show in the United States runs for only twenty-two minutes to accommodate advertisements), but also the dramatic structure: Key moments in the narrative typically occur just before an advertising break, to keep viewers from

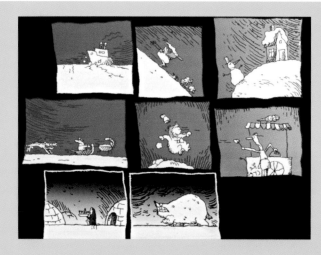

Paul Driessen's *The End of the World in Four Seasons* depicts action in several frames simultaneously.

George Griffin's *Viewmaster* employs a cyclical structure involving a series of walk cycles.

From early in film history, animation has been used to create effects in live-action films, as seen in this series of frames from the 1902 film *Fun in a Bakery Shop*, directed by Edwin S. Porter for the Edison studio.

changing channels. Theatrical features might follow a classic three-act structure, and typically run for about ninety minutes—theater owners would be unhappy with a three-hour film because fewer customers would be seated each day.

The attention span of a viewer is another consideration in structuring a work. For example, knowing how selection committees operate can improve the chances of an animated production being accepted for a festival. Members of these committees typically watch many hours of submitted work for days on end, knowing that the majority will not be accepted for screening at the event. To help speed up the selection process, they often have the option to turn off a work before it ends. It is safe to say that most committees will watch an entry from start to finish if it runs under three minutes, but longer animations that are in any way questioned will probably be rejected after a minute or so. Productions that start slowly might get turned off before a grand finale takes place.

For other reasons, too, short works are desirable. At a festival, it can be tedious to watch a series of longer films, even for the most devoted cineast. Short animations that make a big impact help break up the pace of screening several longer works in a row, so programmers tend to like them.

Other Structural Concerns

Aside from narrative design and running time, other aspects of structure include:

– The number and type of characters or objects depicted, and their relationship to each other: For example, is the work a character study, about a conflict or attraction involving two entities, or an ensemble performance featuring a number of central characters? What is the back story that motivates the actions of each major character? In animation concerned with forms rather than with characters, which principles are guiding development of its elements to give it consistency?

– The depth at which story details are given: Is the product or character depicted known to viewers or new to them? Is the animation retelling a traditional story, so viewers know what is likely to happen? If a work is abstract, to what extent is the audience given access to it through familiar music or visual devices? To what extent is it intended to be easy—or challenging—to watch?

– Placement of key actions: What type of pacing is desired? Does the animation begin strongly, to attract viewers? How does the rise and fall of action occur throughout the body of the work? Is there a clear resolution at the end, or should elements be left unresolved, either for intellectual reasons or to make viewers want to "tune in next time"?

– The balance between visuals and sound: To what extent is information made clear through dialogue or other types of sound rather than visuals? Which elements of the soundtrack will be emphasized: dialogue, sound effects, or music?

– Thematic elements: What underlying structures and essential truths inform the work? What are the repeated elements, or motifs? If the animation is part of a series, to what extent are thematic elements dictated by past productions?

– Desired emotional and physical responses: Should viewers laugh, be enlightened, be moved to action, or learn something new? How should their bodies react? What kind of thoughts should be in their minds?

A common flaw, particularly when an animator is inexperienced, is a tendency to pack too much into a production, sacrificing depth for superficial story development and perhaps the showcasing of technical abilities. Long before production begins, story details should be designed carefully, and reworked after discussion with peers or advisors, or at the very least thoughtful reflection by the artist.

An establishing shot or "master shot" (left) provides environmental details that establish the general action in a particular space. Detail shots (right) bring the viewer into the action, revealing small but important facets of the plot, such as the emotional states of characters. These establishing and detail shots are from *Steinflug* directed by Susanne Horizon-Fränzel.

Presenting Images

The conventions of language are learned by groups of people, allowing them to understand the images they see, as well as the sounds they hear. The extent to which we experience different types of art—our "visual literacy"—affects our appreciation of various forms of expression. Sometimes people see something unfamiliar and are instantly attracted to it. More often, they gravitate toward things that relate to their past experience and shared cultural norms. For example, people who have very little familiarity with abstract art often dislike it, or at least find it difficult to appreciate, in part because it seems meaningless to them; the abstract imagery does not constitute a language they understand.

No two individuals have exactly the same perception of any experience, because factors such as cultural identity impact interpretation. People who identify with subcultures within dominant societies can ascribe culturally specific meanings to what they see, regardless of the intentions of the creator. In his book *Tinker Belles and Evil Queens: The Walt Disney Company from the Inside Out* (2000), Sean Griffin has written about how gay viewers can read Disney imagery and find shared cultural meaning within the company's productions and theme parks.[1] Historical shifts also affect perceptions.

Like any language, the conventions of visual art evolve through time, so what was largely undesirable for one generation may seem perfectly natural to another. For example, both television and, more recently, the Internet have had a profound effect on the way we communicate, not just in terms of writing, but also in respect of visual culture. Though limited animation has been practiced widely since the earliest years of animation, it typically suffered from being described as a "second-rate" production practice. However, generations of television and Web animation viewers have done much to validate limited techniques, so in series such as "The Simpsons" and "South Park" this style is not only acceptable but valued as an aesthetic choice. Today, limited animation is ubiquitous, and hardly the subject of negative criticism.

Other aspects of motion picture language, such as the norms of editing and cinematography, also have evolved over many years. They are now so pervasive that most people probably do not think of them as being a constructed set of rules, reflecting a particular aesthetic sensibility, but rather see them as the "natural" way to create quality productions. All animators should understand these normalized production practices, though they are under no obligation to conform to them—choices in editing and cinematography should always be thoughtfully integrated into the overall design of a work.

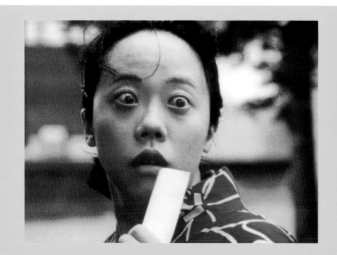

Editing

Throughout most of their history, motion pictures have been strongly identified with a form of editing described as "continuity style." This cinematic language is embedded not only in live-action films throughout much of the world, but also in animation. On the whole, the conventions of continuity editing are intended to abbreviate the action to essential details while providing viewers with a sense of understanding and pleasure in their mastery of the visuals. This is accomplished through the use of such techniques as:

– Establishing shots: wide views of a location whenever a scene changes to a different place.
– Detail shots: close shots of important information, perhaps a critical object or a facial reaction, to add emphasis and emotional impact.
– Consistent screen direction when cutting between shots: For example, if the hero's car was driving to the left in shot A, it must be driving in the same direction after a cut to shot B.
– Shot/reverse shot: sequences where two individuals are shown in separate frames while talking to each other, after a wide shot showing both people in close proximity establishes their presence in the same physical space.

There are various ways of structuring transitions between these and other shots. The most common is the "cut," which is simply butting one set of frames up against another. At the point of the cut, the final frame of shot A is followed by the first frame of shot B. Fades are also used for transitions. A "fade in" begins with a black frame, indicating that the camera's shutter (which allows it to "see" the image) is closed. Gradually, the shutter is opened until the image is at full exposure; this can occur over 24 frames for a one-second fade in (for film), or at any other speed. A fade in is a gentle way to start a production or introduce a new scene. It is also possible to "fade out," when the shutter is gradually closed, causing an image to eventually turn to black. A "dissolve" occurs when a fade out is placed over a fade in, so that one image leaves while another emerges. There is no black since the gradual darkness of the fade out is compensated by the emerging light of the fade in that rests on top of it. If the dissolve is slow, there may be a few moments when images are "superimposed" on one another, so that both can be seen at the same time. Done quickly, a dissolve acts like a cut but is softer to the eye. Another transitional device is the "wipe," when frames of a first scene are gradually replaced by those of a second scene from left to right, top to bottom, or in some other side-by-side manner. Wipes are obtrusive and should be used sparingly, if at all, unless they are stylistically motivated.

A significant change in image size allows a smooth transition when these images are edited together. The continuity style also requires consistency in screen direction, as seen in these images from Lindsay Fleay's *The Magic Portal*.

Under the rules of continuity style, changes from shot to shot within a scene require a significant shift in the size of the image and/or its angle, so that viewers can clearly register the difference between shot A and shot B. For example, if shot A of a given character is tightly framed on its head, it is jarring to viewers if shot B is of the same character at the same angle in a tight framing of its chest and head—the image sizes of A and B are too similar. However, the character could be shown from the same angle if shot B were increased to show its full body within its environment, since that represents a significant change in size. In most cases, though, it is desirable to change both angle and image size when a cut occurs.

If these rules of continuity are not observed, it is likely that a "jump cut" will result. In other words, when an object appears in one position, and has moved only slightly onscreen after a cut, it will seem to jump—and again the transition will be jarring to viewers. There is nothing inherently wrong with this technique, or any editing choice, but it is not consistent with continuity style and viewers usually read it as an error unless it is used for stylistic reasons. However, jump cutting is an accepted convention of a documentary style of cinema, usually combined with what looks like hand-held filming, which appears shaky because in theory the camera is not on a stabilizing tripod. Of course, in animation these effects must be drawn in or created by purposefully moving the artwork under the camera. The jump cut gives a disjointed feeling to a story—or, in the case of a documentary, it suggests the conventions of realism because it looks spontaneous.

Typically, it takes about three seconds for viewers to comfortably comprehend an image that appears onscreen, though it is possible to sense imagery that is presented much more rapidly. By editing several images together quickly, the animator creates a "montage" that can be exhilarating, adding speed to the action. However, the result can be visually exhausting if carried on too long. Today's viewers are far more accepting of rapid editing than older generations were. Many people believe the aesthetics of the MTV cable network (which appeared in the early 1980s) are largely responsible for this shift. An alternative to quick editing is the "long take," a continuous shot that lasts more than ten seconds. It usually involves wide shots that allow action to play out without cutting. Productions shot mostly with long takes can feel quite slow in pacing—which may, of course, be the desired effect. Flash Web animation is generally designed with relatively long takes (or at least an absence of rapid cutting) to avoid scene changes that slow download times.

Shot/reverse shot sequences are commonly used to depict characters having a conversation.

Cinematography

One way to avoid cutting is to move the camera within a shot. There are a number of possibilities in the context of live-action cinema, including:

- Zoom in/out: The camera remains still but its lens is adjusted to create the effect of getting closer to or farther from the subject.
- Dolly: The camera moves toward or away from the subject.
- Tilt: The camera tips to look toward the ground or the sky.
- Crane: A pedestal is used to elevate or lower the camera over the action.
- Pan: The camera is rotated left or right from its fixed position on a tripod.
- Canted, or "Dutch angle": The camera stays on a tripod but tips to the left or right so that the subject is at an angle.

In animation, camera movement may be simulated through drawings—the view seems to shift through space because things are drawn to look that way. A rostrum camera is limited in what it can do; it can be moved down or up its column to capture a relatively smaller or larger field size of the artwork, and sometimes artwork can be moved side to side underneath it. Animators also can rely on software to achieve certain "camera" effects after filming has occurred.

Stop-motion camerawork can be orchestrated in much the same way as in a live-action context, except that exposures are made frame by frame and the scale is usually pretty small. As a result, some types of camera movement are difficult. Breakaway sets (which open up to allow a camera to enter the space more easily) and large- or small-scale figures (which give the impression that the subject is closer to or farther from the camera) can allow for more versatility in stop-motion cinematography. A programmable motion-control camera unit may be used to capture complex movement through a set.

Images develop meaning by the way they are captured within the borders of the picture area. A high-angle shot (looking down on a subject) conventionally suggests weakness, while a low-angle shot (looking up at a subject) gives the impression of strength. Canted shots, which put the world at an angle, can be used to suggest disorientation. Staging can achieve similar effects: Centered images tend to be perceived as strong, whereas subjects situated at the edge of a frame appear weakened or off balance. Images that are staged to be symmetrical in form and move in uniformity emit power and authority, while asymmetrical organization and chaotic movement create energy and a sense of unpredictability.

The angle used to depict a character affects our interpretation of him or her. From left to right, a high angle suggests weakness, a low angle creates strength, and a canted angle reveals uncertainty.

Images can be framed in various sizes: extreme close-up (an eye), close-up (a head), medium shot (chest and head), full shot (whole body), wide shot or long shot (whole body and a fair amount of environment), and extreme long shot (environment with little suggestion of a body in the distance). Each size carries a different level of emotional attachment, depending on the subject's "proximity" to viewers. Generally, the closer an image appears to be, the greater its emotional impact. Proximity also affects objects within the frame. For example, two characters staged in close proximity are more emotionally charged (with fear, hate, or love) than ones separated by various objects (which might add to the drama of getting them together) or set far from each other. The Web has added another dimension to framing. Rollovers, pop-up

Dimensions

In animation, there is yet another consideration related to the size of images: the dimensions of the artwork being filmed. The development of 2D drawn and painted images is typically planned using a "field guide," (see page 76) which indicates standard increments typically ranging between 1 field and 12 field (2 is the smallest in practical use and 10 is about average) that synchronize with measurements on animation camera stands. Not all artists work with field sizes; they mean nothing to stop-motion animators working on a set, or to animators working directly on film.

Size takes on additional significance for animators using digital media. For example, often they are concerned with file sizes, or the amount of memory used to save a work. Many factors potentially affect the size of a digital file, including the number of colors used, the complexity of animated movement, and the resolution (or amount of fine detail) of saved images.

Hlynur Magnússon adjusts a motion-control camera used to record complex movements through stop-motion sets.

From left to right; an extreme close-up (ECU), close-up (CU), medium shot (MS), full shot (FS), and long shot (LS).

windows, and page frames complicate discussions involving standard concepts of framing. Using such devices it is possible to depict multiple perspectives, details, parallel actions, or any number of story-deepening elements.

Sound

Animated works of the highest quality are carefully crafted in terms of sound as well as visuals, which are designed in a complementary relationship. This point is echoed by Sven E. Carlsson, publisher of the website Filmsound.org, who writes, "Humans are pattern-seeking creatures. … The gifted animator, along with the music director/composer and the editor, understands the psychology of musical design and seeks to trigger parallel responses through conscious manipulation of various visual patterns: repetition and rhythm; the movement of characters and background; the predictability of a story; and the pacing and editing of finished work."[2]

Working with Sound
It is ideal to consult a sound designer relatively early in the production process, as he or she can make suggestions and provide samples that might influence the final look of the film. To work with sound professionals effectively, it is useful to be knowledgeable about the nature of sound, and terminology related to it. At a basic level, sound is created as vibrations pass through matter (such as air) in wave formations and reach the ears, where they are sensed by nerves and then perceived by the brain as sounds. Many factors affect the ability to hear sounds, as well as the type of experience those sounds evoke.

For the most part, sound today is recorded digitally. This offers advantages over analog processes (such as the use of reel-to-reel tape), which can pick up unwanted machine hiss and other noises, and are susceptible to generational loss (copies are never as good as the original). In contrast, digital re-recordings can be exactly the same as the original recording, copy after copy.

Components of the Soundtrack
Each component of the soundtrack—dialogue, score, sound effects, and well-placed silence—contributes to the overall impression of an animated production.

Dialogue A central question in sound design is whether dialogue will be included. If voice actors are used, their selection should be one of the first steps in pre-production planning; typically, voices are recorded well before animation takes place. This can be done in essentially two ways: as an ensemble, or individually with each actor reading dialogue at

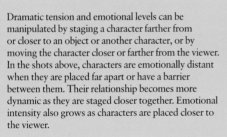

Dramatic tension and emotional levels can be manipulated by staging a character farther from or closer to an object or another character, or by moving the character closer or farther from the viewer. In the shots above, characters are emotionally distant when they are placed far apart or have a barrier between them. Their relationship becomes more dynamic as they are staged closer together. Emotional intensity also grows as characters are placed closer to the viewer.

a different time. An advantage of ensemble recording is the group dynamic, which generally energizes the delivery. Disadvantages relate to editing. When voices overlap it is difficult to make corrections, and when one performer makes a mistake everyone has to do a retake (and their collective time can add to production costs).

Voice recordings are compiled into a "scratch track" that contains the dialogue in order from start to finish. When the scratch track is synchronized with images from the storyboard, the result is an animatic that suggests the overall pace of the work; it is useful for showing to production crews, faculty, funding agencies, or others wanting an early preview. Editing software indicates how many frames of action accompany the dialogue, revealing the required timing of individual movements within the production—thus the scratch track is also useful for detailed planning.

Pre-recording voices is not universal; in Japan, animation generally takes place first and dialogue is later dubbed onto the work. Internationally, many animated films contain no dialogue at all. Such films avoid the problems of lip syncing and having to be dubbed or subtitled for international screenings and the hearing-impaired. Christoph and Wolfgang Lauenstein's award-winning film *Balance* (1989) uses only a few sound effects to suggest vast emptiness. The film tells the story of several characters standing on a platform

suspended in space. They find themselves competing for ownership of a new possession, a music box that brings a small bit of liveliness—through sound—to their drab existence. The French-based international co-production *The Triplets of Belleville*, was immensely successful in part because it contains very little dialogue. The lyrics of its songs emphasize the widely understood French word *rendez-vous*, but audiences don't have to know what is being sung. Viewers across the world relied on visuals, music, and sound effects, rather than dialogue, to interpret the story. The classic holiday film *The Snowman* (1982), directed by Dianne Jackson for the British television network Channel 4, provides a related example; relying on music and sound effects, the twenty-six-minute work re-creates Raymond Briggs's popular children's story about a boy who dreams that his snowman comes to life.

Score Some films lack dialogue because they are not overtly narrative in form; in this case, the score usually plays a relatively significant role. An excellent example is Sara Petty's *Furies* (1977), a short film that explores the energy of two cats dashing through a house, fighting, and playing, accompanied only by a dramatic score as they shift from iconic to abstract forms and back again. Other examples can be found within the tradition of visual music—much of the work of Oskar

Understanding Sound

The following are some of the terms used to discuss sound.[3]

— Frequency: the number of oscillations a sound wave makes per second, measured in Hertz (Hz); 1 Hz equals one oscillatory cycle per second. Humans typically hear sounds in the frequency range between 20 Hz and 20,000 Hz (or 20 kHz), and are most sensitive to those in the 250 Hz to 5,000 Hz range.

— Pitch: determined by the frequency of the sound waves; it can be described as low (bass), mid-range, or high (treble). Low pitch tends to connote power and warmth, whereas high pitch suggests energy and sound "presence," or the feeling of being close to its point of origin.

— Harmonics: Also known as "overtones," they are secondary frequencies that result from the frequency of vibrations emitted from a given object.

— Amplitude: the intensity of the sound. Perception of amplitude, or volume, can be affected by other sounds, as well as frequency—for example, mid-range sounds at about 3,500 Hz will be perceived as louder than higher

or lower frequency sounds at the same amplitude. The volume of sound can be measured in decibels (dB), which are dependent on the distance of the sound's source from the person hearing it. A sustained sound pressure level (SPL) of 85 dB or greater can be harmful to human hearing.

— Ambience: the ambiguous "noise" or acoustics of an empty room that gives a sense of space and realism to the environment; it is used in place of the complete absence of sound, which generally is perceived as an accidental "drop out" on the soundtrack.

— Rhythm: recurring patterns of sounds that range from dominant to subordinate.

— Envelope of sound, composed of three components: Attack (the speed at which sound builds to a peak—a gunshot has a fast attack, whereas paper being ripped has a slow one); sustain (the length of time for which the peak sound remains before the source sound stops); and decay (the time it takes for a sound to fall into silence after its source has stopped making the noise).

Fischinger and Norman McLaren, the legendary National Film Board of Canada animator, falls into this category. Primarily, visual music works are concerned with creating a visual equivalent to music using design, motion, cinematography, editing, and other components of motion picture production. Sometimes productions are concerned with interpreting specific musical works that accompany the visuals, and other times the visuals are shown in silence, as they are supposed to generate their own sense of "music." Within this tradition, some animators have drawn or photographed images in the optical sound portion of film to see what the images "sound" like. The results of these synthetic sound experiments can range from various types of noise to "music" with an electronic sound quality. Norman McLaren was a master of the use of drawn and photographed sound; some of it can be heard in his film *Neighbours* (1952).

A music score generally is used to create an appropriate emotional context for a work. It also can affect the perceived pacing of visual information and create a bridge between images. Instrumental pieces are likely to affect the viewer on a somewhat subliminal level. Music containing vocals can have a much different effect, because the words of a song tell their own story; thus they compete with the visuals for primacy—or take the primary role, in the case of a music video, for example. When animators decide to use existing music, rather than have something composed for their work, it is important that rights are cleared before the animation begins—it is shortsighted to animate to music that cannot be used legally, since the finished work cannot be shown at festivals or distributed. Using copyrighted popular music for a scratch track to help with pacing (assuming the intention is to replace it later with original music) is a common practice, and can be useful for composers as it gives them an idea of the tempo of the music they are to create.

Sound Effects Sound elements can be "diegetic," emanating from inside the world of the film (dialogue, a character's footsteps as he walks across the floor, music from his guitar), or "nondiegetic," from outside it (voice-over narration, a music score). Diegetic sounds can be onscreen, coming from sources that can be seen, or they can be offscreen, opening up the frame of the film to the world beyond its borders (the chirping of unseen birds, the honking of horns outside a window). Sound effects, which typically are added to the soundtrack after animation has been completed, are especially useful for developing spatial and temporal aspects of the visuals.

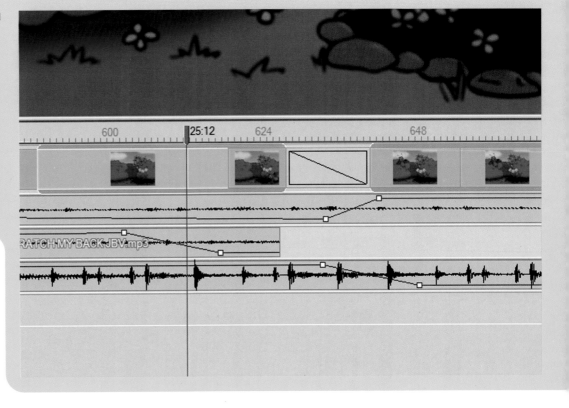

This screenshot shows how sound and images can be synchronized visually. Toon Boom Storyboard offers an advanced timeline to control timing and automatically generate an animatic with soundtracks and transitions between shots.

Quite often, animated action happens more quickly than it does in real life; it is speeded up for humorous or dramatic effect. As a result, pre-recorded "library" sound effects sometimes used in live-action soundtracks are not always useful when it comes to animation, though creative results can be achieved by manipulating and layering them.

Original sound effects can be created using a wide range of objects. This process is known as "foley," named after Jack Foley, a pioneer in recording live sound effects in synchronization with motion pictures. Some possibilities in foley sound include:
- Fire: crumpled cellophane
- Rain: salt sprinkled on paper
- Footsteps in mud: hands in soggy newspaper
- Footsteps in snow: grinding cornstarch
- Birds in flight: flapping a pair of leather gloves together
- Champagne bubbles: effervescent medicine dissolved in water[4]

Throughout much of animation history, zany sounds like jet engines, vibrating metal, and cowbells have been used to highlight the antics of cartoon characters. Some great examples can be found in the work of Treg Brown at Warner Bros., and in films directed by Chuck Jones and Bob Clampett during the golden age of Hollywood animation.

The Sound Mix The separate sound elements of a film are ultimately combined in a re-recording mix, when various components are made relatively louder or quieter. In life, numerous streams of sound often occur simultaneously, but people tend to be selective listeners and perhaps tune in to only one or two at a time. In terms of motion picture sound design, viewers have become so accustomed to conventional practices that if sound were designed to be like it is in reality, most of them would find it unappealing. The sound designer must be able to determine how to balance elements at different points in the story, in order to manipulate the perception of the viewer/listener.

Though dialogue is generally at the top of the hierarchy—or loudest—there may be moments when sound effects or the score dominate a scene. Sounds are often amplified in an attempt to get the viewer's attention, but the opposite approach can be just as—or more—effective. For example, if dialogue cannot be heard because it is under other sounds or played at a very low volume, this may add to suspense or create curiosity about what has been said. In general, silence directs viewers' attention to the visuals and heightens the impact of the sounds that come before and after it.

Too Much Sound

A constant barrage of sound is problematic for some people—in particular, the hearing and visually impaired. Captions used by the hearing impaired often describe only dialogue, and leave out the music and assortment of sound effects central to so much animation. Spoken words from video descriptions for low-vision viewers have to be squeezed between sounds in the animation; when there are few silent moments in a work, decisions must be made about what parts of the sound to talk over.[5]

Color

Color is usually perceived before imagery; as a result, it tends to make the initial impression in a composition.[6] Animators who spend a great deal of time focusing on character design and movement do themselves a disservice by using it arbitrarily, without considering how various colors impart meaning and create effects—individually or in combination with others. In today's world of varied and ever-changing technology, artists also must consider how different colors come across in various contexts, such as computer monitors, projected film, and television.

Dimensions of Color

Color can be discussed in terms of its four dimensions: hue, temperature, value, and intensity.

Hue A "hue" is the name of a color; it is pure if it contains no white, black, gray, or complementary color. Primary hues are those that cannot be created by mixing other colors: They are red, blue, and yellow using a pigment wheel (for paint, for example)—or magenta, cyan, and yellow using a process wheel (the standard for photography and color printing). When primary hue pigments (as in paints) are mixed together in equal amounts, the result is black. Mixed in unequal amounts, they result in broken hues—earth colors, often described as ochers. Because broken hues contain elements of all the primaries, they tend to go well with all colors.[7]

A first step in designing color might be the selection of hues for a color palette—one that complements the storytelling, adds meaning to the work, is compatible with the selected technology, and is readable by the target audience. A "monochromatic" color scheme includes variations of a single hue created by adding white or black; it may be useful for developing a serious tone, or a sense of unity—or for creating a neutral backdrop for other more colorful elements in a given scene. An "analogous" color scheme uses colors that are next to each other on a color wheel (up to one-quarter of the wheel) to create a sense of harmony and balance. A "complementary" color scheme uses hues that are opposite each other on the wheel, and creates a more energized effect. Another option is no color at all: designing in black and white. As any photographer knows, this tends to accentuate form within a composition. As a result, black-and-white images can be read easily by a wide range of viewers. Keep in mind that a

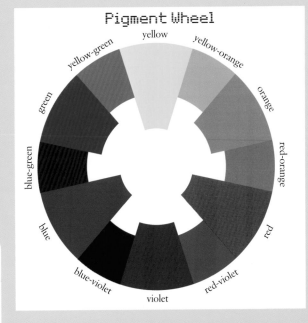

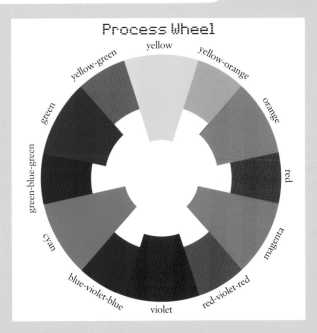

A pigment wheel (above) is built around the primaries red, blue, and yellow, whereas a process wheel (right) is developed around magenta, cyan, and yellow.

portion of the population has partial or color-deficient sight; when designing for the biggest audience, it is wise to consider color combinations that everyone can view with ease. Generally, the most universally readable colors tend to be dark hues of blue, violet, purple, and red placed against light hues of blue-green, green, yellow, and orange.[8]

Temperature Colors are often described as having "temperature"; they can be warm (red, yellow, and orange) or cool (green, violet, and blue), imparting physical sensations of warmth or coolness. Black, too, can be characterized as warm or cool. Commercially mixed, it is cool, which generally is best for depicting man-made objects. Black made from a combination of primaries is warm (likewise, grays produced by mixing it with white are warm). Warm black works well for natural objects, including cloth. However, every color's temperature is relative; a pure hue can be either warm or cool depending on what surrounds it. If a warm hue is placed next to a warmer one, it looks relatively cool. If that same warm hue is placed next to a cool one, it looks warmer.[9] When selecting colors for an animated work, it is useful to consider how a "warm" or "cool" environment can support the work's thematic values.

Value The effects of various hues come in part through their "luminosity," or glowing quality, which results from the amount of light they reflect. Luminosity is an important factor when mixing paint. It takes very little black to darken a luminous hue such as yellow, but a larger quantity of white to lighten it. In contrast, it takes a large amount of black to affect a dark hue, such as violet, but just a little white to lighten it. Adding white to a hue to create a tint, or black to create a shade, affects the "value" of that hue. White is the lightest value, while black is the darkest, and grays make up the middle range. The values of pure hues range from lightest to darkest in the following order: yellow, yellow-orange, orange, yellow-green-yellow, red-orange, yellow-green, green-yellow-green, red, green, red-violet, green-blue-green, blue-green, blue-green-blue, blue, violet, and blue-violet. Obviously, there is a correspondence between value and luminosity. Colors with the lightest value have the greatest luminosity and vice versa.

Intensity A hue's saturation or chroma can be described as its intensity. It defines the degree of a color's purity; that is, how bright (as opposed to light) or dull (as opposed to dark) it is. All pure hues are at their full chroma, though the strength of that intensity varies; pure hues with light values have the

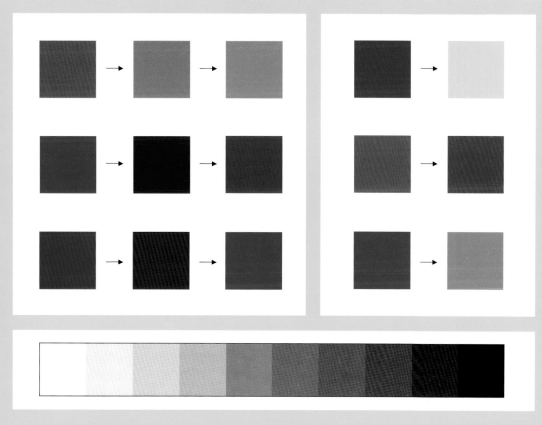

"Analogous" color schemes include colors that appear next to each other on up to one-quarter of a color wheel. Some examples are shown (far left). "Complementary" colors (left) are across from each other on a color wheel.

White, gray, and black create a range of values.

strongest chromas. White, black, and shades of gray have no saturation at all, and thus are described as achromatic. Unfortunately, the subtleties of intensity and luminosity and other qualities of color may be lost through the duplication of images and distribution of final works, depending on the type of media that is being used. Still, it is important for the well-rounded artist to understand the varied qualities of color as one of many important considerations in the art of animation.

The Aesthetics of Color

Recognizing the dimensions of color—hue, temperature, value, and intensity—is merely the start for an animator wishing to use color in sophisticated ways. Increased awareness comes not only through study, but also experience and sensitivity. People across the world have theorized about the aesthetics and power of color, influencing the production of art throughout history and in specific cultural contexts. However, there is no one meaning associated with a given color or with various combinations of colors. Like other aspects of art, the way people see color is affected by individual as well as social experience, and by perceptual differences.

In her book *Colour*, Edith Anderson Feisner analyzes the aesthetics of color. She writes that primary hues (red, blue, yellow) are most stable, tend to attract the eye, are most easily recognized, and offer the greatest contrast. All other hues are seen in relation to them, so for balance they often are used in small amounts toward the top of a composition (unless the desired effect is to pull the eye to the bottom, in which case they can be placed lower down). Secondary hues (orange, green, violet), she writes, are less stable than primaries, but are compatible with other colors and function well in large masses and at the bottom of a composition. The tertiary colors (red-orange, red-violet, blue-green, blue-violet, yellow-green, and yellow-orange) are the least stable and have the least amount of contrast; they, too, work well in large amounts and placed in lower positions.[10] Guidelines like these provide a starting point for experimentation.

At commercial animation studios, color key departments have been responsible for testing all color combinations to be sure they are suitable for a given production. If a character's color is like that of a background element, it will blend into its environment. Because animated compositions are dynamic, rather than static, the selection of color schemes is all the more complicated. It is necessary to consider how an object moves across its background and interacts with other characters and props, not just how it looks within a single composition. Poor decisions in color design are not just

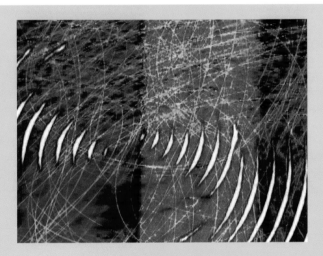

The use of primary colors in *All That Remains* by Stephanie Maxwell creates a bold impression.

Secondary colors, which dominate this frame from Maxwell's *All That Remains* are relatively subtle in their effect.

unattractive—they can also make the animation much less effective. Some of the worst color offenses are on the Web, where we can see colors of text and animated graphics that seem to vibrate on top of their backgrounds, or colors that irritate the eyes (bright yellows and reds) constituting large portions of a screen. If images are hard to look at, Web users will not stay around for long.

It is important to consider how color operates within specific exhibition contexts because it manifests itself in various ways depending on the media in question. Differences occur in part because of the varied nature of color. For example, the process of mixing paint is "subtractive," because as more pigments are mixed together, less and less light is reflected and the color gets darker. However, the process of mixing light, which occurs in the transmission of television images or stage lighting, for example, is "additive," since the mixture becomes lighter as more colors are added.

Media choices also affect the range of colors that can be used. While the color palette for painting might seem limitless, the colors suited to the Web have been relatively few: In the past designers generally worked with a palette of 216 "Web colors"—using only the ones that were available in both Windows and Macintosh applications. However as the technology has changed, the number of widely usable colors has increased considerably. Color on television presents its own challenges and not only because most sets have poor resolution capabilities. Background artist Jenny Baker estimates that about 50 percent of image quality in television work, including color, is lost during the production process, including scanning, printing, painting in a subcontractor studio, post-production, and then broadcasting.[11] As a result, in television series it is impossible to suggest the kinds of fine color detail that might be achieved in animated features, or projected animated films of any kind. Another potential problem is the use of "illegal" colors; very saturated red, blue, cyan, and yellow do not read properly on NTSC television monitors.

The analogous color scheme of blues and greens seen here in Bärbel Neubauer's *Play of Particles* creates a cool feeling.

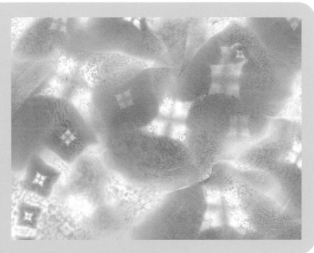

Red, orange, and yellow appear as warm hues in Neubauer's *Play of Particles*.

Applications I
Hearing Sound

Humans are selective listeners. Although there are a multitude of sounds in our environments, we tend to focus on only one or two at a time. Though motion picture soundtracks generally are constructed to give an impression of real space, they rarely are true to reality. This exercise develops a greater understanding of the complexity of sound in everyday life. It also provides an opportunity to start exploring the ways in which sounds work together to create an environment and mood.

Objectives:

To increase the awareness of our actual sound environments and how we hear sounds selectively, and to create a recording of sound that represents a given theme.

You will need:

– Access to three environments
– Portable sound recording equipment
– Writing utensil
– Sketchbook

1

Select two or three environments where you will hear a variety of different sounds.

2

In each of these environments, close your eyes or at least avoid looking around. Instead, try to listen only to what is going on around you.

3

Remain in the environment for two or three minutes, making a mental note of not only the sounds you hear, but the relative loudness of each one.

4

In your sketchbook, write down as many sounds as you can, placing them within categories of "soft," "medium," and "loud," depending on how you perceive the sound.

5

Choose five or six sources and walk close to them, so you can record twenty seconds or more of each sound. Write down the sources of the sounds, so that you can keep a record of your work.

6

Play back each of your recordings, and as you do, create a visualization of that sound in your sketchbook. It might be a repeated pattern, an abstract composition, or possibly a representational form.

7

If possible, ask other people to draw visualizations of your sounds, and compare their drawings with your own.

8

Think of a way to arrange some of what you've heard into a sound collage that represents a theme of your choosing. Walk back to various sources and record sounds one by one to create an interesting composition. You might like to consider concepts such as repetition and contrast. Don't get too worried about the overall integrity of the piece; no post-production editing is needed.

Dynamics of Color

Step 2

Step 1

Color is perceived before form, and has a significant impact on our understanding of any visuals. It is important to think about not only the colors of individual parts of a composition, but also the way they interact with each other as they are placed side by side and as objects move around.

Objective:

To develop color palettes and analyze their suggested meanings.

You will need:

- Sixteen to twenty sheets of approximately 8¹/₂ x 11-inch (21.5 x 27.5-centimeter) paper in eight to ten colors; two sheets each (be sure to include white and black)
- Writing paper
- Glue stick
- Scissors
- Writing utensil

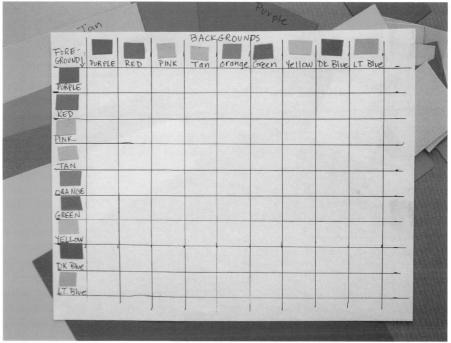

Step 3

1

Divide the paper into two piles, each containing one sheet of each color. Set one pile aside for use as backgrounds. Mark the back of each background sheet with the name of its color (dark red, light red, forest green, lime green, white, black, etc.).

2

Take the sheets in the other pile and cut three squares measuring approximately 2 x 2 inches (5 x 5 centimeters) out of each one.

3

Make a chart that will be used to record your impressions of various color combinations. Write the names of the background colors across the top of a sheet of writing paper. List the colors of the cutout squares down the side of the same sheet of paper. Paste a small piece of the color next to each name, as a visual reference.

Dynamics of Color

4

Take one of the background sheets and place one square of another color in the middle of it.

5

Record your impression of this combination on the chart where the background color and square color meet.

6

Using the same background, place each of the other color squares in the middle of it, one at a time, and record your impression on the chart.

7

Repeat the process on the other backgrounds, one at a time, and record your impressions.

8

You can also try combinations of one background with two or more squares, recording your impressions on a separate chart.

Step 5

9

Select five background and square(s) color combinations and glue each one together. On the back of each, write your impression of the effect of the color combination, and possible scenarios where it would work effectively. If you select a combination that you feel is ineffective, explain why you think it doesn't work well. It is useful if some of your combinations contain a few of the same colors, to show how they change in different contexts.

Color Rhythms

Many animators have explored relationships between sound, image, color, and motion. Musical concepts are ideal for establishing patterns of movement that can be used in animated visuals, providing a structure that is pleasing on various levels.

Objective:
To develop visual rhythms using color.

You will need:
- Sheets of paper in a wide range of solid colors
- Glue stick
- Large poster board or foam-core board
- Writing utensil

Step 3 (above and left)

1

Look at each sheet of paper and consider what sort of tone or "sound" its color suggests.

2

Cut each of the sheets into 1-inch (2.5-centimeter) squares, and put them into separate piles.

3

Use the various colors to create patterns that suggest fast and slow pulse; high and low pitch; loud and soft volume; a composition with a beginning, middle, and end, or other structure; repetitions and intervals; and/or other musical concepts of your choosing.

4

The colors can be continuous in one long "composition" or they can be placed in individual, unrelated "phrases" of various lengths.

5

Glue the sequences of color music that you feel satisfied with onto your board. On the back, write a description of the "sound" of each sequence.

Developing Personality

Contributed by Leslie Bishko,
Emily Carr Institute of Art+Design+Media

Leslie Bishko is an experimental animator, Certified Laban Movement Analyst, and Associate Professor of Animation at Emily Carr Institute of Art+Design+Media. She integrates the rich movement theories of Laban Movement Analysis (LMA) with her art and teaching. Her research investigates movement styles in animation, and the use of animated imagery for LMA studies.

Her works include:
Gasping for Air (1993)
Website: www.eciad.ca/~lbishko

Developing the personality of animated characters is an important part of animation production and should not be left to story development alone. You must know who your characters are before you can animate them. This exercise will help you develop a character's life story, worldview, and attitude and relate them to how the character responds to circumstances, and ultimately how it moves. It employs the Laban Movement Analysis theory of "Effort," which is the outward manifestation of inner intent through various qualities of movement. Effort provides a way to observe how intent mobilizes the Flow of Weight in Space and Time. It is a useful tool for evaluating and refining what a character is communicating.

Objective:
This exercise aids in the development of complex characters who reflect their personalities through action. The goal is to design a character that is authentically expressive of the effect their life's experiences have on their view of themselves within the world around them.

The first step is to develop a back history for the character. Then its movements are created in response to a given scenario, according to your gut feelings. Results are observed to see what movement qualities were chosen for the character's personality. Finally, movements are refined, using Effort to accentuate the key communication points of the character's actions.

You will need:
– Paper
– Writing utensil

3

Back History

Age
Family, friends
Goals/ambition
Sex life
Weaknesses
Environment
Gender
Religion
Morals
Intelligence
Obstacles
Self view
Era
Profession
Physical health
Education
Values
Flaws
Culture
Income
Hygiene
Need/purpose
Sense of humor
Talent
Ethnicity
Dreams
Diet
Idiosyncrasies
Fears
Addictions
Childhood

1

Develop the character's back history by writing a few notes for each item on the list to the left. The goal is to be imaginative and create a character that has a rich background of life experiences, yet is consistent and believable.

2

Write a few paragraphs that summarize the character; form the most significant parts of his history into a descriptive narrative. Be colorful! This is where you bring the character to life.

3

What is this character's motto? The motto's scope should include his view of himself as well as his view of the world around him.

4

Now you're ready to explore the personality a little more deeply. Based on what you've developed so far, how does the character evaluate situations, make decisions, and take action in the world? Using the chart below, rate him along each of the spectra. How strongly does your character exhibit one characteristic or the other? If he has the ability to swing in either direction, indicate the extent.

Attention / Thinking / Where

Explores all possibilities, takes in multiple points of view. Flexible.

Focuses on one thing at a time, gets right to the point. Narrow point of view.

Intention / Sensing / What

Handles situations with gentle consideration.

Takes a firm stance and applies pressure to get things done.

Commitment / Intuition / When

Takes time, lingers over decisions.

Ready to take action now.

Progression / Feeling / How

Doesn't hold back, open, goes freely with circumstances.

Hesitates, resists, fights against the situation.

Developing Personality

How do these factors influence the way the character expresses himself through movement? Let's place him in one of several scenarios. Based on his preferences in the previous exercise, write a one-paragraph narrative that tells the story of what happens when:

– Driving alone on an empty highway, the car runs out of gas …
– A friend gives your character a very tacky birthday gift…
– The character receives news about the death of a close relative . . .
– The character wins the lottery …

The final stage is to plan the animation of your chosen scenario using thumbnail sketches. Start by roughing out the actions; imagine the scenario you described and go with your intuition about how the scene should unfold. Work quickly and spontaneously until all actions have been sketched on paper.

Now evaluate what message comes from the animation you've planned. At this point you may wish to do a line test of your thumbnail sketches so that you can observe how the character communicates in time. To conduct the evaluation, see how decision-making styles described can be associated with Effort qualities of movement, using the following chart.

Attention/Thinking /Where	Explores all possibilities, takes in multiple points of view. Flexible.	Focuses on one thing at a time, gets right to the point. Narrow point of view.
Space Effort	Indirect: moves with full, three-dimensional gestures that indicate the surrounding space; joints are loose and bendable.	Direct: moves toward a single point in space; focused, zeroing in, pinpointed.
Intention/Sensing/What	Handles situations with gentle consideration.	Takes a firm stance and applies pressure to get things done.
Weight Effort	Light: handles objects with a light touch; moves with lightness and delicacy.	Strong: uses strong, forceful movement; powerful, vigorous, and impactful.
Commitment/Intuition /When	Takes time, lingers over decisions.	Ready to take action now.
Time Effort	Sustained: leisurely, no rush, taking all the time in the world; gradual changes or variations of speed.	Sudden: urgency, hasty, hurried, anxious, quick, or sudden changes of speed.
Progression/Feeling/How	Doesn't hold back, open, freely going with circumstances.	Hesitates, resists, fights against the situation.
Flow Effort	Free: relaxed, easy, abandoned, ready to go.	Bound: controlled, precise, restrained, ready to stop.

8

Observe your thumbnail sketches—does the animation you planned reflect some of these movement qualities? Do you find that the personality choices you made are reflected in the character's movement qualities?

Here's an example to help you see how this works. Let's say your character is an exploring, urgent hesitator who considers things delicately, and has run out of gas. He sits in the car thinking about all the possibilities for dealing with this situation—his eyes seem to be looking at many thoughts inside his head as he sits quietly for a few moments. With sudden tension, he reaches for the door handle but rests his hand there lightly as he changes his mind about what to do. He looks around inside the car with tense anxiety, trying to decide on a plan of action. Then with a sudden moment of focus, he decides, sitting upright and punching his fist down on the dashboard. With one quick, agile movement, he opens the car door and lands on his feet with a firm thud of conviction. He scans the horizon for signs of other traffic on the road and, gradually, headlights appear. As the car zooms by, the character becomes unsure once again—perhaps it's not safe to flag down a stranger? His waving gesture has little force behind it, as if his hand disappears into thin air, retreating in toward his torso with hesitancy and restraint.

The character's personality reflects Indirect Space, Light Weight, Sudden Time, and Bound Flow as movement preferences. Throughout the sequence of his postures and gestures, these different movement qualities ebb and flow, combining in different ways. While he is generally unsure of what to do, there are two accented moments when he combines Sudden Time with Strong Weight (punching the dashboard, landing with a thud), which shows momentary confidence toward taking action.

Tips and Cautions:

— Keep the ideas flowing and don't analyze or judge them! This is a preliminary exercise, and it is best to analyze and modify your character's actions only after you have committed initial ideas to paper.

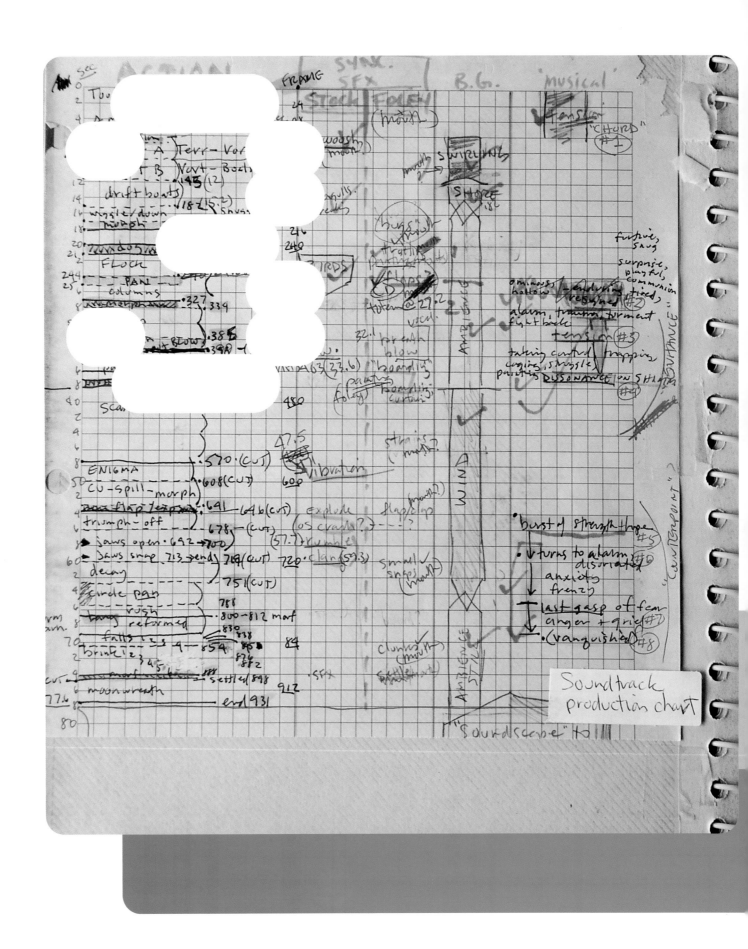

Soundtrack production chart

3

Pre-production

Animation exists in a wide range of forms and is displayed within a variety of contexts, so the actual methods of its production processes vary a great deal. Even similar types of animation—for example, contemporary made-for-television series—are not produced in the same ways from country to country, as industrial factors, television exhibition contexts, censorship, budgets, and levels of technology differ. And it goes without saying that the production process of animation created at a major production studio turning out feature films is much different from that of an individual working at home with a crew of one (the artist, with occasional help from family and friends).

Pre-production is the first step in producing an animated work, the vital planning stage where the producer and director consult each other to lay the groundwork for the production. It encompasses all the activities necessary before finished art is produced and image recording begins. The actual animation of images is labor-intensive, and the cost of materials and artist labor can be high. No one wants to spend unnecessary time creating images that cannot be used. Careful pre-production planning is the key to efficient production.

Personnel

The producer and director are the two key individuals in a production. The producer deals with the business concerns of the work, including funding the project, arranging the facilities, and scheduling the workflow, and keeps people motivated and on schedule. The director leads the creative side; the primary storyteller, he or she supervises the work of the other artists and makes creative decisions that enable efficient and meaningful production.

There are many other possible positions on a production crew, depending on the overall size of the studio, the budget, the medium in use, and other factors affecting the work. Student and independent animated productions are often solo efforts, in which the artist takes on all aspects of the work. This provides great experience, as it gives individuals the opportunity to learn all aspects of the process.

Developing the Concept

Producers and directors are not always the originators of a project. They may be hired to oversee production of a concept created by someone else. Sometimes an investor has bought an option to develop and produce a news story or book as a motion picture, or a concept may originate with a client who wants an advertisement or instructional short. The works of independent animators arise from a virtually limitless array of inspirations—visual music artists might be inspired by the mathematical nature of musical compositions, and painters might want to explore the "process" of their work through time. In college courses, the concept often arises from a specific assignment.

Every scenario is somewhat different, but in each case it is important to go through a period of concept development. In *Producing Animation*, Catherine Winder and Zahra Dowlatabadi describe the development phase as "the time when the creative foundation for a project is set up through visual and written materials."[1] A series of questions should be

Andrew Zimbelman employed a computer to work in the style of 2D silhouette animation.

answered, in order to better define the work that needs to be done and the path it takes to its completion—in other words, to create a production plan. They include:

- What is the central goal or storyline?
- What are the main characters or images that will be included?
- Are any special permissions needed, perhaps for the use of copyrighted properties?
- What specific content items, if any, are required by a client or other outside party?
- What are the restrictions on content, if any?
- Which media will be used within the work?
- Which techniques will be used to realize the project?
- Are there other works (animated or otherwise) that could provide inspiration for the current one, or perhaps compete with it? If so, how are they similar or different?
- What is the visual style of the work?
- What is the aspect ratio and probable screen size of the completed work?
- What type of sound design will be used?
- How will the titles look and what information will they, or must they, contain?
- Who is the audience?
- How will the work be made accessible for special-needs audiences?
- What is the desired outcome of the project?
- Who will "greenlight" the project, or allow production to begin?
- Who will evaluate the project before it is completed?

- What is the timeline, including the work's due date?
- What technical resources are available?
- What financial resources are available?
- Who will be on the crew?
- What skills do crew members bring with them?
- What skills will crew members need to learn?
- Are outside (subcontractor) services needed and, if so, what are the costs?
- What are the potential problems in realizing the project?
- How will the work be exhibited, and what are the requirements and limitations of the format(s), including color requirements?
- How will the work be distributed?
- What are the main selling points of the work? Is there anything that makes it unique?
- If applicable, what are the merchandising possibilities of the project?
- How will the production process of the work be documented, both in terms of paperwork and photographic or motion picture images that can be used in creating a "making of" documentary or assembling a production-related website?
- How will artwork, digital files, and other components of the work be archived when they are no longer in production?
- After the project is complete, could it be extended into other forms? What is the long-term potential of the concept?

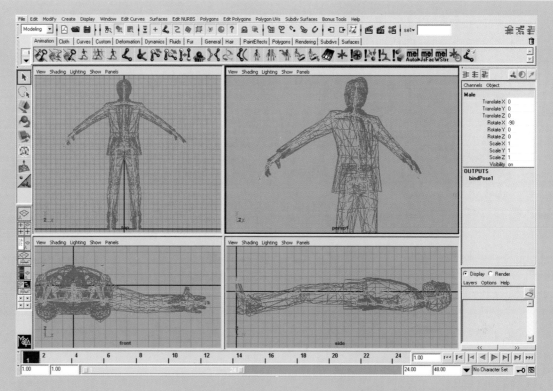

Ke Jiang's development of a computer-generated figure.

Answers to these questions can be used as a basis for critical self-evaluation, as well as a means of preparing to move ahead. If any aspect of the production seems unrealistic, pre-production is the time to make corrections.

The vast majority of animation productions, particularly in commercial contexts, begin with a script, storyboard, layout materials, and written plans; the approval of financial backers, clients, professors, or others involved generally requires their presentation. They are part of the project's visual development materials, which also include line drawings, conceptual paintings, and other indications of how characters, props, and locations will look. A brief sample of animation is also helpful. With these written and visual aids, it should be possible to demonstrate the direction a work will take, even if the evaluator reviewing them has little experience with animated media.

Pitching the Project

Many animated projects start with a "pitch," or short descriptive statement (up to a couple of minutes in length), and a longer written treatment that describes the entire project; both incorporate salesmanship to make the work sound desirable.

The pitch varies depending on the proposed format. For television, it should include a distinct concept and a defined target audience, while for features it should indicate a clear beginning, middle, and end of the story.[2] A short experimental film may be pitched by describing the technical exploration involved, the way in which it extends the artist's previous work, or possibly issues of concern to the organization receiving the pitch.

Usually, the individual presenting a pitch should prepare three or four of his or her best concepts, and be able to expand on them verbally. Although alternate pitches might not be appropriate if an artist is intent on creating one particular film, it is helpful to be open to a variety of approaches. If the opportunity arises, a pitch can be detailed through presenting a treatment; it describes the essence of the project, its characters and visual highlights, the story or concept from start to finish, perhaps a few bits of dialogue, and anything else that is vital. Treatments range from a page or two for short animations to twenty or so for a feature. Like the pitch, a treatment should be lively and interesting.[3]

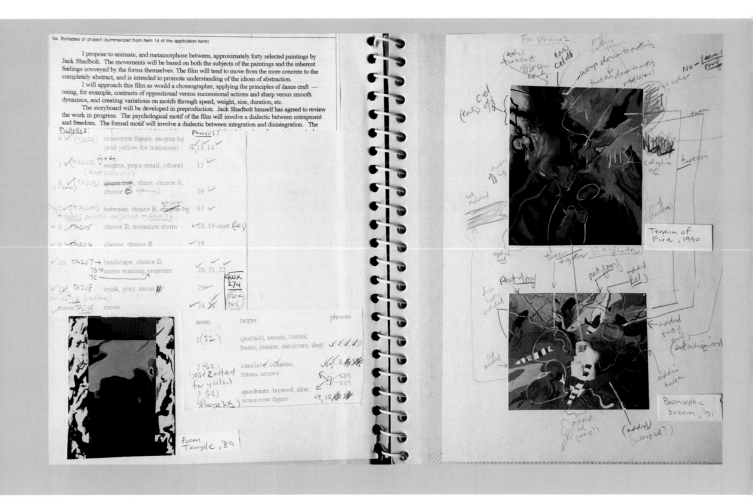

Scripts

Scripts are the backbone of television production. Short films might have no script at all. Features may develop around rough outlines that are transformed into scripts after being rewritten numerous times as ideas synthesize and the project evolves. In an industrial context, a script may pass through several hands, and the end result can look nothing like the original. Student animators generally have control over a script from start to finish—which may or may not be a good idea, depending on their ability to analyze the work critically and make corrections before progressing to later stages of production.

There is no single approach that works for everyone: The creative process is as individual as the writer. However, it is important to remember that while a good script begins with a good idea, it is the remaining 99 percent of the work that makes it a success—and this work is often repetitive, detail-oriented, demanding, and even painful (when it comes to throwing out material that has taken a long time to develop and might be dear to the writer's heart). Scriptwriters benefit from researching similar productions to see how they are structured. Careful analysis can reveal a great deal about why a particular production works well, and this can help writers in structuring their own work.

Typically, a script includes dialogue and indications of sound effects, if any, and written descriptions of visual elements such as character action and environmental details. But the script not only imparts the content of the finished work; it also serves as a technical guide. Therefore, it is imperative that scriptwriters be able to consider their work from various perspectives: those of the designers, animators, actors, and anyone else who will seek guidance from the script. Perhaps the most common admonition found in writing guides is that scripts should be visual in their orientation. Likewise, they should be written in the present tense, using active speech (not passive), to keep the actions they describe alive in the mind of the reader. It is important that paragraphs are brief, and that their content paints a vivid, fully dimensional picture of the actions and environments in the work.

In *How to Write for Animation*, Jeffrey Scott explains that a first step in developing a television script's framework is to compile a series of "story beats," one-line descriptions of the most significant action in each scene; he suggests that fifteen to twenty beats be used in a half-hour script.[4] Actions also can be described visually. The Fleischer studio developed a "story mood chart" that indicated the highs and lows of suspense and other sensations in its feature *Mr. Bug Goes to Town* (1941).[5] The same kind of model could be useful for conceptualizing abstract animation and other non-narrative work.

Typically, each page of a script accounts for about a minute of screen time. A game script can be hundreds of pages long, translating into several hours of dialogue and action. Advertisements typically run thirty seconds or less. A typical independently produced short for film festivals is unlikely to

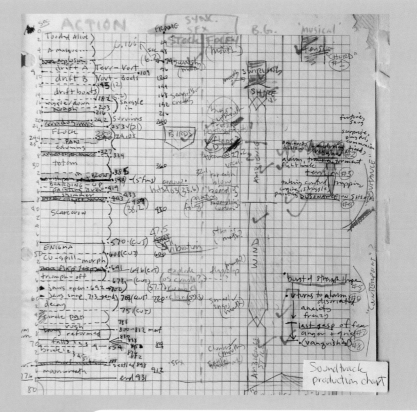

This production notebook (opposite) for Stephen X. Arthur's film *Transfigured* includes a copy of his project pitch, images from the film and various production notes. Sequences from the film, are listed and annotated on a chart (right) that allows him to conceptualize the abstract film's structure in writing.

run more than twenty minutes; eight to ten is probably average, though shorter works are quite common. During Hollywood's "golden age" of theatrical animation, a cartoon typically ran seven minutes. Today, in the United States the placement of television commercials means that episodes of half- hour prime-time series are closer to twenty-two minutes in length. In contrast, *The Wrong Trousers* (1993), directed by Nick Park, runs thirty minutes. It was shown on the BBC in the United Kingdom, and there were no commercials to reduce its running time. Animated feature films are more flexible, though most last about ninety minutes, or sometimes less (especially when they are "direct to video" productions).

Sound Design

There is no best way to create sound design. However, the best results are achieved by considering the soundtrack—dialogue, sound effects, and score—early in the pre-production process. Sometimes animators create their own sound, perhaps interweaving the process of creating visuals and audio so that the end result is a tightly interrelated whole (as in visual music). More often, sounds and images are developed separately, though as closely related creative

pursuits. To maximize the impact of sound, directors might call on two types of sound specialist: a composer, who creates music to accompany the work, and a sound designer, who creates, manipulates, and organizes nonmusical sonic elements.[6]

When a sound designer is consulted early in pre-production, his or her suggestions can add to the visual development of the work. This individual probably will want to look at scripts and storyboards, which are useful for determining the type and number of sounds required. As production progresses, the sound designer may also engage in a "spotting session," watching the animated footage and making a list of necessary sonic elements. The designer determines which of these sounds will come from pre-recorded libraries and which will be original, recorded for the production as "raw" sounds from field recordings or through foley (see page 51).

Voice recording typically takes place during the pre-production process. Generally, it is the director's job to prepare performers to deliver their lines, meeting with them several times prior to the recording day, so they can ask questions about how to pronounce words and how to deliver lines.[7] Animator Nancy Beiman advises, "At Disney we brought model sheets and storyboards for the actors to consult when recording

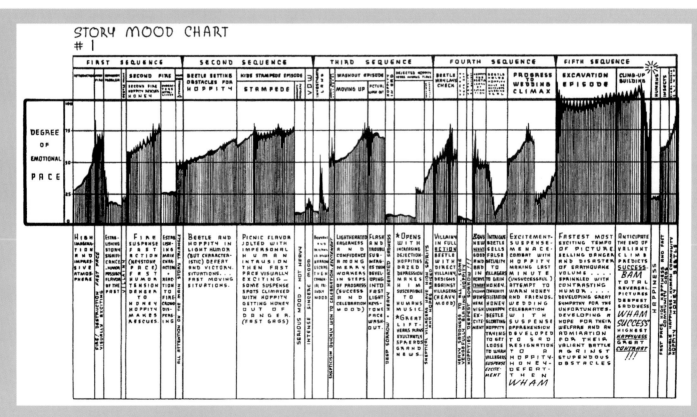

The Fleischers used a "story mood chart" to describe the narrative structure of their film *Mr. Bug Goes to Town* in text and graphically.

the script. This was particularly helpful when dealing with fantasy characters. They are a lot more helpful to the actor than anything written. How do you explain that they are playing the part of a talking dresser unless you show them the dresser?"[8]

The director must know the characters very well before rehearsals begin, so he or she can give performers authoritative guidance. Actors can be given written "biographies" of their characters, indicating not only "who" but also "how" they are—their emotional and physical states of being. It may be useful to include a list of key descriptors, such as "egotistical," "heartbroken," "emotionally remote," or "not easily provoked." But character development does not end there. A good actor is able to bring added dimension to a character, revealing qualities that may surprise even the scriptwriter or director, and often voice inflections can later be used during animation production to enhance the character's actions. When animation has been created using only a preliminary dialogue track, final readings are recorded using a process known as Automated Dialogue Replacement (ADR).

Every director has his or her own way of working with performers, and every performer works best under different conditions—though experienced directors and actors are able to modify their styles to accommodate the situation at hand. After providing actors with a copy of the script and personal details about the characters, some directors find it useful to allow performers to explore their roles with relatively little guidance. Initial rehearsals offer an opportunity for the cast to run through performances, but they should be carefully managed. It is important not to over-rehearse or overdirect performers, which can destroy their ability to deliver dialogue spontaneously—or they might even lose self-confidence or their ability to re-create the characters in their own minds.

On the day of recording, the actors should be given a schedule showing the order in which dialogue will be recorded, so they can anticipate when their parts will be read, and should be allowed to rehearse as necessary prior to the final recording. In the recording facility, script pages should be laid out flat on a table and not moved, to avoid rustling noises. Each recording is slated, being assigned a "take number" that is written down along with comments that will be useful in evaluating the reading. It is best to record entire scenes, if not an entire production, in one day to avoid changes in sound quality that can occur when a studio is used at different times. And it is important for the director to listen to all the recordings before actors are dismissed, to be sure that the required performance has been achieved.

Eventually, information about dialogue (and/or music) probably will be transferred to an exposure sheet , or "dope

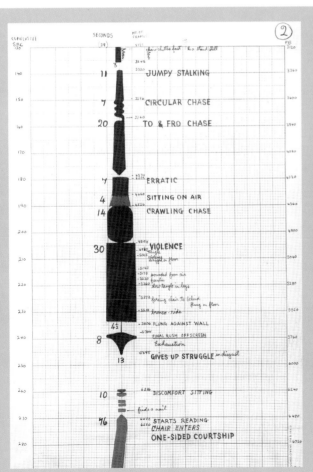

Norman McLaren used graphic forms to suggest the development of action in *A Chairy Tale*.

"The contrast between slow against fast, pause against action is at the heart of animation timing. When drawing the phases of animation— the in-betweens—you would only use perfectly even spacing if you were animating a machine. Nothing alive moves in evenly spaced increments of your 24-frame seconds."[9]

Gene Deitch

sheet," that tells the camera operator or others involved in production how all the elements of the film are to be combined. This sheet can also contain information related to backgrounds, effects, camera movement, and anything else pertaining to the combination of images and sounds.

Timing

In works that include speaking parts, dialogue typically controls the pacing of the action. Sometimes animated visuals are tied to music, so the score becomes the central element in determining timing. Where sound is not recorded until after animation occurs, timing is determined through other means, such as acting out scripted actions and measuring their length with a stopwatch. With abstract work, one can apply mathematical formulae to the development of visuals. In any case, most experienced animators develop some kind of timing guidelines.

When pre-recorded sound controls timing, it is necessary to "read" the soundtrack to determine how many frames of visuals are required to accompany it. This used to be done manually using a "bar sheet" printed on paper, but today digital technology offers some automation of the process—editing software generally includes a "timeline" that shows each frame associated with a given sound element. Digital readings are transferred to digital or paper exposure sheets, to be used as a reference for the animation process.

Though a variety of factors potentially affects the timing of action, it is important that timing be considered as a significant factor in itself; in other words, the animator should be aware of timing as a vital component of storytelling that must be assessed on its own merits. Animator Gene Deitch discusses it in terms of "contrast" between particular animated movements, but this perspective can be extended to the timing of a work as a whole. It is vital to consider the rise and fall of action throughout an animated production.

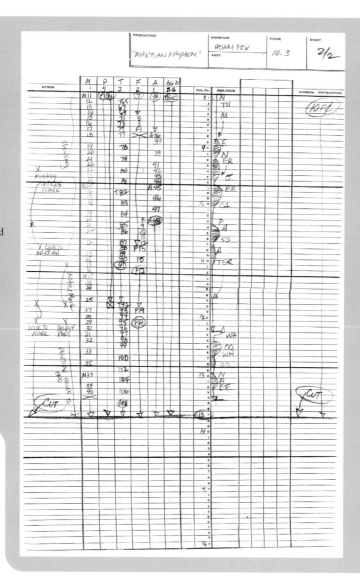

An exposure sheet can be used to track the timing of a film at the level of each frame, including layers, sound, and other associated elements.

Storyboard

The storyboard generally combines text elements from the script with sketches of the visuals that accompany them. However, a storyboard might be created before the script, to help the writer visualize imagery or movement. In any case, a script usually is not finalized until the storyboard is complete. Works that dispense with a script altogether are primarily planned using storyboarded images.

The storyboard includes details about visuals, character action, dialogue, and camera movements, plus any special components that must be included in the final art. It is the place where shots are initially set up, so it is important to think creatively when it is being developed. Once the dialogue has been recorded, its running time can be added as well—a process called "slugging the storyboard."

In the early stages of designing a project, a board should not be overworked. Ideally, it goes through several revisions, beginning with "thumbnails" that are relatively quick and loose; later boards can also be comparatively loosely

rendered, but they should be increasingly comprehensive and eventually include a new image for every change of action, camera angle, or mood.[10] Presentation boards done later in a project can be detailed and cleaned up, but for small-scale productions it is important that an artist's energy is saved for creating the images actually used in the animation. In many cases, a relatively rough storyboard is all that is needed. At other times, the board evolves into a detailed blueprint for the production. *The Nightmare Before Christmas* (1993), directed by Henry Selick, relied on about fifty boards, each containing sixty-six drawings, so for the seventy-five-minute production, there was one image for an average of every 1.5 seconds of the finished film.[11]

Inexperienced artists sometimes overlook the importance of a strong title sequence and closing credits, which make the first—and last—impressions. They should look as professional as the work itself, and it is a good idea to include them on the storyboard, to indicate how they will frame the production. The rest of the board should, of course, also be visually engaging. A publication called "Storyboarding the

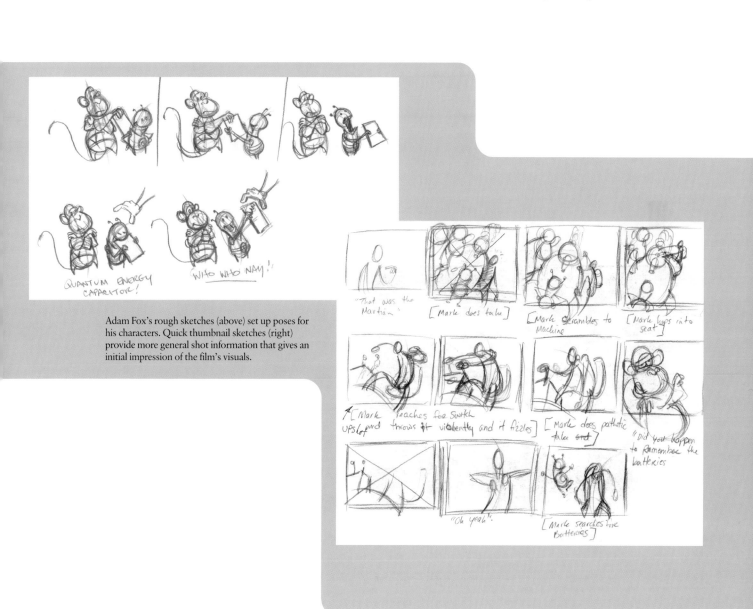

Adam Fox's rough sketches (above) set up poses for his characters. Quick thumbnail sketches (right) provide more general shot information that gives an initial impression of the film's visuals.

Simpsons Way" provides useful suggestions for enhancing presentation. One is to select interesting angles. It describes a straight-on view of Homer as "Boring! Flat! Uninspired!" and says a slightly angled perspective is better. It suggests showing at least three planes in a room, and trying to avoid floor lines that are exactly parallel to the bottom of the frame.[12] Placing characters at different heights suggests who holds the power in a shot (the highest in the frame being dominant), and lowering the horizon line can add drama to a composition. Composing shots is an art form in its own right, and there are numerous ways to create a pleasing balance in the visuals pictured onscreen: leaving sufficient "nose room" during close framings of a face, balancing screen elements in one-third portions of the total space, framing background action with foreground elements, and so forth.

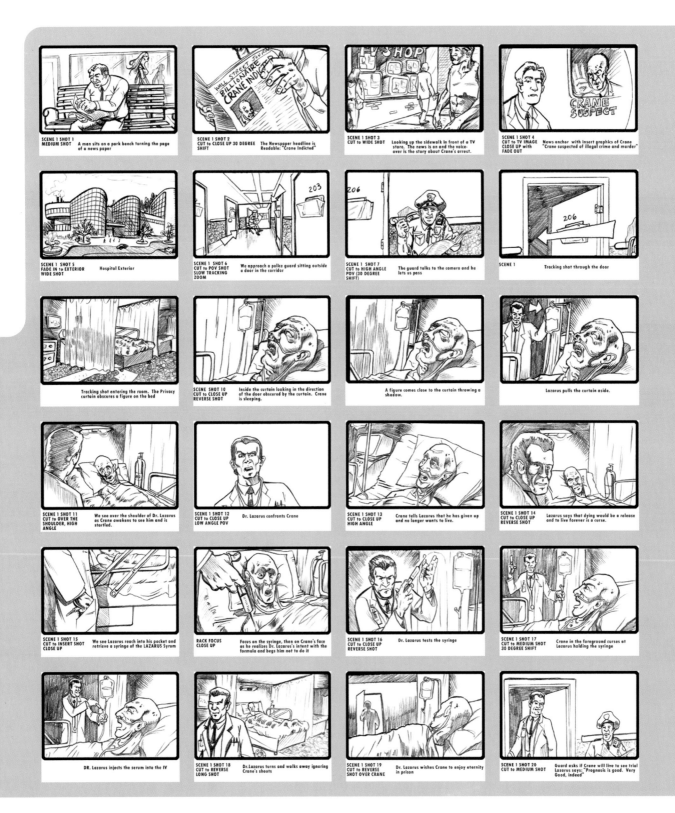

Animatic

The storyboard is used in conjunction with the soundtrack to create another important component of pre-production: the animatic or story reel (also known as a "leica reel"). Individual images from the storyboard are recorded to coincide with timing of the dialogue or other structuring sound elements, such as the score. As a result, an animatic provides a sense of how the finished work will look and sound, even though the images may be still and the sound can be rough. The story reel reflects the eventual running time of the film fairly accurately. If it runs over the desired length or the action seems too slow, it can be shortened before production begins. If viewers find it hard to follow the action, dialogue and visual information can be changed.

As the production progresses, the animatic can be updated. As each section of animated footage is completed, it is cut into the animatic, until eventually all the still storyboard images are replaced by moving imagery.

Layout

The layout process resolves the logistics of creating and depicting the animated world. Ideally, a layout artist has strong skills in perspective drawing, as well as knowledge of cinematography (including camera angles, composition, lighting, and staging) and the entire animation process. He or she follows the storyboard and designs for locations closely, but must be able to think in terms of levels of action (or "layers") and effects, and how they fit into the surroundings.[13] Layout artists are responsible for setting up scenes cinematically, typically using establishing shots followed by close shots of characters in their settings. It is important that they understand staging and the power of proximity in creating drama between characters or between characters and objects; at the same time, they must avoid compositions that are so tightly framed that characters cannot move around. In their work, layout artists compose images for 2D animation in terms of various field sizes and determine how moving parts can be designated to appear on different layers of the composition.

Adam Fox's storyboard (left) uses a variety of shot sizes, including establishing shots, close-ups, and cut-aways to guide the viewer through his story. The use of perspective as well as high and low angles create visual interest and enhances meaning.

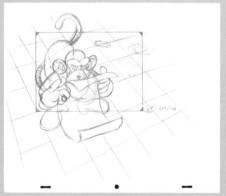

Within his layouts, Adam Fox has indicated framing that enhances the composition of his layouts.

Field Guides

In 2D drawn and painted animation, layout artists use a "field guide"—a clear plastic sheet marked with black rectangles that indicate "fields"—to establish how images will form. Typically they are formatted in the standard Academy aspect ratio (see page 20), for 16mm film and standard television screens, in either 12- or 16-field maximum dimensions (a different field guide is required for widescreen animation). The field guide indicates how large a space is being used to frame the animation: 2 field (about 2 x 1 ½ inches [5 x 4 centimeters]) is very small, while 10 field (about 10 x 7 ¼ inches [25 x 18 centimeters]) is a commonly used average size. A field guide can also contain the "TV cutoff area," which indicates how images and lettering will be seen on a standard television screen. By working within this area, layout artists help to ensure that significant imagery stays in view.

It is useful to cut out a series of frames corresponding to each field size, using heavy black paper. These frames can be placed around drawings to help visualize how images will look when they are onscreen, and to simulate camera movement or editing; for example, a layout can be composed within the 10-field frame, and then an object within that environment can be envisioned within a 4-field frame, suggesting the effect of a zoom-in or perhaps a cut to a close-up shot.

Layers of Artwork

The animation process is made more efficient by the use of layers that enable an object to move without disturbing other elements in a scene; for example, moving eyes could be placed on the top level, while the motionless face behind them appears on the next level below. When artists worked with acetate cels, they were limited to using about five levels at any given time due to the density of the material, which affected the appearance of images at the lower layers (less light made it through each successive level). With computer technology, there are no longer such restrictions; digital layers are virtual, not actual, and an image at the bottom of the "stack" can appear to have the same quality as an image on the top. Theoretically, an infinite number of levels may be used. However, a layout artist must use discretion in designating layers, and not create too many levels of visual material just because it's possible. Additional layers can create additional complications.

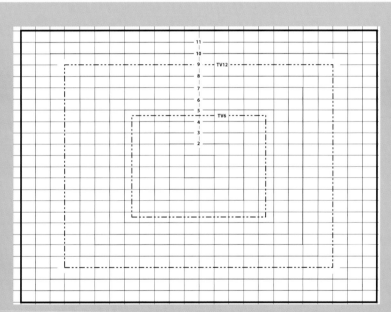

A field guide is used to indicate various framing choices within a given layout or production art.

Stop-Motion Layouts

Predictably, layouts used for stop-motion differ from those for 2D animation. Not only do they indicate how characters move through space but they also must accommodate options for lighting and the placement, and possibly movement, of a camera. There is often a need for architectural-type blueprints for sets, which may include trap doors in the floor (to allow animators to get nearer to figures) and breakaway walls. In addition, stop-motion sets generally incorporate tie-downs of some sort, which anchor the figures to the bottom of the set, and which need to be incorporated into its overall design so that they are not visible. The floor plans of sets are also useful for charting characters' actions.

Scheduling and Budgeting

While clients, studio executives, professors, and other supervisors are interested in the concept, story, and visuals of a work, they tend to be equally interested in the bottom line: what it will take to get the production done, on time and within the budget. As a result, a significant part of the pre-production process focuses on scheduling and budgeting.

Scheduling involves careful structuring of the "production pipeline" and estimating the time it takes to complete its various steps. Once a work is in production, a "lead sheet" should be used to track its progress. The lead sheet lists all the scenes in a film and the steps toward completing it, which vary depending on the type of project that is undertaken and the media being used. In the case of a 2D work, the lead sheet for a relatively simple animation without dialogue might include columns for storyboards, timing/exposure sheets, layouts, backgrounds, model sheets (showing character designs), key frames, animation, cleanup, color, and sound. Winger and Dowlatabadi provide a detailed breakdown for an episode of a 2D television series that includes, among other steps, model design, storyboard rough, recording of dialogue, creation of animatic, storyboard cleanup, soundtrack reading

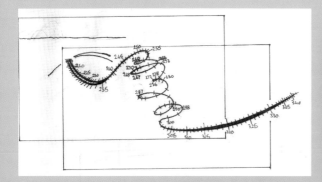

Clive Walley used a graphical representation (above) to indicate the movement of a paint-on-glass line through time (right).

(to determine speed of action), sheet timing, background keys, color styling, checking, shipping, subcontractor production, retakes, mixing audio, and final mix of picture and sound.[14] It is imperative to figure in extra "contingency" time—for computer crashes, software glitches, personal emergencies, and other likely production problems—to ensure that the work is completed when it is due.

Accurate budgeting depends on the development of a well thought-out production plan and a realistic schedule. The items listed in a budget may include facilities and maintenance, personnel, equipment, materials, lab work, marketing and promotion, and insurance. As with scheduling, it is important to build a contingency into the budget, to ensure there is an emergency fund to finish the project, if necessary.

It is important to keep accurate records of all expenditures. Even students, whose budgets might include only a few hundred dollars for the purchase of art materials, can be asked to account for their spending, especially if their personal funds are supplemented with outside support. Financial sources (including grant-givers and school accounting departments) want to see a record of how money was spent, with receipts documenting it. Expense records are also useful when the

time comes to plan funding for a future production, as they provide a good starting point for the next budget.

The producer of a project should investigate funding through grants from sources of different types: college, community, corporate, and government, for example. Searching for money is challenging and can become a full-time endeavor. The application process is often time-consuming and may require up to a year or more of pre-planning. Careful attention to application procedures and presentation details such as spelling and grammar are imperative to make a good impression.

Unless an institution's funds are intended for newcomers, first-time artists may have a difficult time winning a grant; without a track record, they can find it hard to convince the grant-giver they will use the money wisely and come through with the proposed project. Associating a well-known name with the project is sometimes the answer—for example, a "star" voice talent, or perhaps an executive producer who might contribute little to the production process but will lend credibility to the project. Creating perhaps a minute or two of the planned animation, and sending it with an application, can also help. Even though it is hard to get a grant the first time, applying is still a valuable experience. It is likely that the

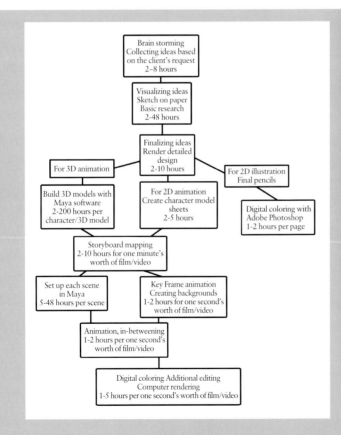

This flow chart illustrates the relative differences in animator Ke Jiang's production of 2D and 3D animation, as well as illustrations.

Comparative Schedules and Budgets

In 2001, Winger and Dowlatabadi provided sample budgets and schedules for features and direct-to-video and television projects. They estimated that a feature using three-dimensional computer-generated imagery averaged two to three and a half years in production, with a budget of between $25 million and $100 million. In contrast, a direct-to-video animation had a production schedule of one to two years, with an accordingly lower budget: $5 million to $25 million. An episode of an animation series for cable television, they estimated, was in production for between three and twelve months per episode, at a budget of between $250,000 and $850,000.[15]

Karen Raugust's figures in *The Animation Business Handbook*, published in 2004, were similar, though she added some lower-end prices, as well as the cost of producing an interactive console game at $500,000 to $20 million, and an Internet short at $1,000 to $45,000.[16]

organization will look upon a second application, in a later funding cycle, more favorably, especially if the artist has been productive. And look at it this way: once all the basic materials (narrative statement, budget, resume, and so on) are compiled for the first application, it becomes easier to send them out to other grant-giving organizations.

Producers should think of creative ways to secure support. For example, a women's organization might finance animation about prenatal care, or a sailing association could be attracted to a work about boat safety for children. A local hardware store might donate wood or hardware for building sets. It is also possible to recoup costs through distribution: An animated work that can be used in social services settings, or as an educational aid in the classroom, is likely to be of interest to a specialized distributor. Ideally, such special-interest groups are contacted early in the pre-production process, so they have the chance to be involved with planning and approving elements of the production. They also like to be there at the end: Funding sources generally want to be acknowledged in film titles and possibly written programs distributed at the screening of the film.

Marketing and Promotion

Marketing departments in studios spend a great deal of time creating trailers and "making of" videos, photographing production scenes, contacting media, writing press releases, and making deals to merchandise products, all to ensure that their animation will be promoted to as many people as possible. A lot of independent artists don't realize that it's not only the "big guys" who should budget for marketing—it is equally important for the small-scale animator.

The first step is to identify design elements in the animation that give a quick impression of its form and content; they should be relatively simple, but make an impact. The design concept should also include the names of the creative principals (such as the director and producer), a one- to three-line summary of the work, and contact information. The same concept should be used on all promotional materials, such as the DVD cover and a postcard to promote screenings. It should also appear on a professional-looking website dedicated to the animation, which is an ideal place for a "making of" documentary or, at the very least, a series of still images detailing how the work was created.

Image from *The Secret Adventures of Tom Thumb* by the Bolex Brothers.

Title card from Virgil Widrich's "making of" documentary for his *Fast Film*.

The pre-production stage is the time to begin making marketing plans—researching venues for screenings, writing press releases, and developing a list of local media contacts. With enough lead time, even small-scale screening events can be promoted free through listings in newspapers' event columns or radio programs that air local happenings. Inexpensive but memorable gifts can be given to audience members when a work is shown. At a San Francisco screening of the Bolex Brothers' *The Secret Adventures of Tom Thumb* (1993), people received small plastic flies as they left the theater (the insects play a prominent role in the film). The creation of marketing materials can be delegated to a trusted graphic artist or Web designer, or perhaps a budding advertising creative looking to enhance his or her portfolio, leaving the animation artist to work on the production. Otherwise, promotional work should be undertaken by the producer.

Rights and Ownership

The producer is responsible for contacting the copyright owners of music or other materials that will be incorporated into the animation, to seek permission to use the property. The process can take a long time, so securing rights should be one of the first things to be done. Works that are of a certain age or produced under certain conditions can be in the "public domain"—they can be used for free because their copyright has expired. In some circumstances it may be legal to use parts of copyrighted material without licensing it, but that does not guarantee that an artist will not be brought to court. Sometimes students and nonprofessionals may be allowed to use a copyright-protected work for reduced fees, possibly with restrictions. It is important to read all contracts carefully and seek the advice of experienced professionals, especially when considering restrictions placed upon licensed material. Perhaps the best advice is to avoid using copyrighted materials altogether.

Insects play a prominent role in *The Secret Adventures of Tom Thumb* by the Bolex Brothers.

Copyright Facts

Ninety-six countries worldwide abide by an umbrella treaty, the Berne Convention, which recognizes the rights of copyright owners, but each country has its own procedures for copyrighting. In the United States, copyright registration is obtained from the Library of Congress (www.loc.gov). Animated productions fall into the category "original works of expression," which includes, among others, literary works, sound recordings, architectural works, and motion pictures of all kinds. All productions, whether they are formally registered or not, are owned by the individual who creates them. By affixing a copyright symbol (©), the word "copyright," or the abbreviation "Copr.," along with the date and the name of the individual who owns the copyright, a formal declaration of ownership is made. It is vital that this information appears on any materials "published" through distribution of any kind. Letting a neighbor watch a work in progress does not constitute publication, but sending tapes to prospective employers does. Copyright registration should not be confused with a "patent," which covers a process, or a "trademark," which protects a word, name, or symbol.

Typically, copyrighting a work requires filling out a form, paying a processing fee, and depositing one or more copies of the work. This registration protects the copyright holder if his or her material is stolen, though of course it will not prevent theft, or reuse by others.

Theoretically, copyright is granted automatically, at the moment words are written or visual art is created, but in practice it is not always that simple. Institutions sometimes claim partial or complete ownership of work produced within their facilities: For example, many universities claim rights to their students' productions. If an artist is animating a work as regular paid employment, it is likely to be considered "work for hire," which means the company probably owns it all (from original artwork to completed film). Some studios even claim the copyright of an employee's production when it has been created after work in his or her own home. It is important to fully understand issues related to ownership, which usually are specified in contracts signed upon entering a school or beginning work at a studio. But even independent artists might face complicated issues of copyright. If an animated work involves multiple creators and a production team, all participants must understand from the beginning where ownership rests. Animation creators are naïve if they overlook the importance of securing rights to ownership of their own work and all tangible expressions associated with it.

In recent years, the concept of "creative commons" has begun to supplement the older form of ownership. The nonprofit Creative Commons organization has developed "a flexible range of protections and freedoms for authors, artists, and educators … [building] upon the 'all rights reserved' concept of traditional copyright to offer a voluntary 'some rights reserved' approach."[17] People who are willing to let their material be used relatively freely by others can provide a creative commons license, so users do not have to formally seek permission every time they want to reproduce it. This is especially useful in such contexts as education, where a teacher can distribute print materials to his or her students, and in the art world, to facilitate creation of derivative works. Creative commons licenses do not negate the rights of copyright holders, but rather extend selected rights to users. More information can be found at the organization's website, creativecommons.org.

The Studio

The producer, working with the director, is responsible for deciding on the facilities needed for a production. Budget is obviously a factor, but the choice is also determined by working methods. For example, a great deal of television production is handled by subcontractors. Initial creative work might be done in the studio, while the animation, coloring, and recording could be sent to a company in another country. In contrast,

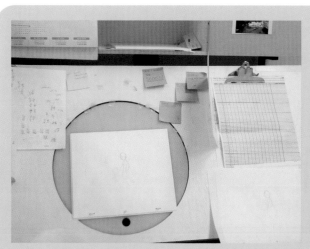

A 2D animation space including an angled drawing surface, exposure sheets, a drawing disk, peg bars, and punched animation paper used for a pencil test.

Gil Alkabetz at work in his home studio.

an independent Web animator creating an animated short for his or her personal website is likely to control all aspects of production, and might work with a computer setup and an Internet connection, but very little else.

Elements that are essential for a small animation studio are listed below:

- Field guides (or TV cutoff guides) and field guide frames in various field sizes; use standard Academy format or widescreen, depending on the finished product's aspect ratio.
- Exposure (dope) sheets.
- Media for rendering final production art (including software, if applicable).
- Most animation requires technology to assist with creating, manipulating, and recording images, including production stills, though what is needed varies significantly: possibly a rostrum camera (independent animators could rent time on one), a digital still SLR (single lens reflex) camera and tripod, a webcam, and/or a computer setup.
- Lenses, if necessary; for stop-motion work, the camera lens must be able to focus at short distances, typically with a macro setting or adaptive "dioptre" lens that allows close-ups to be shot.
- Wall boards, both cork and dry erase.
- Mirrors, so artists can look at themselves while performing actions.
- Stopwatch for timing action.

- An animation drawing disc; required for most animation projects, this is a circular frosted glass plate that rotates within a cutout space in a desktop and is lit underneath to allow artists to see through layered paper.
- Peg registration system; typically embedded into the drawing disc, it keeps artwork lined up during the drawing process and under the camera; paper is punched with perforations that match "pegbars," or strips of punched paper are stuck to the bottom of artwork ("pegging"); a peghole punch is relatively expensive but can be a good investment, and will probably be necessary if nonstandard paper is used.
- A lot of paper in various sizes, as needed.
- Pencils and other drawing media.
- Scissors and cutting blades.
- Digital imaging program/"frame grabber" system for capture and playback during "pencil testing" of line drawings before rendered art is filmed, playback of frames of recorded stop-motion animation to check flow and placement of figures, toggling between recorded and "live" images to aid in development of movement, editing and changing timing, and even the final output of images.
- Facilities for viewing reference videos/DVDs, and work in progress, depending on how it is recorded.
- Sound recording equipment, depending on how audio is developed (dialogue recording will probably be done outside the animation studio).

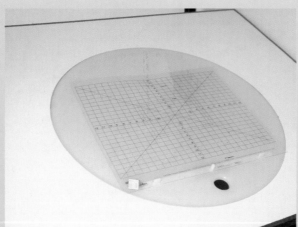
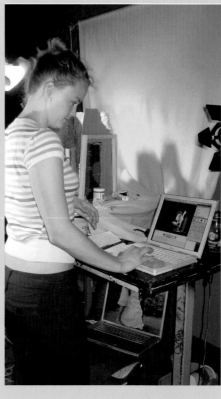

Assorted brushes (above); a drawing disk and peg bars (above right); facilities for viewing work of various types (right), set up in Jules Engel's office.

Stop-motion animator Erin Ross (above) using a video capture unit.

- Lighting equipment if the animation is filmed with a camera; this will vary depending on the shooting setup and lighting effects, but might include an underlight and at least two toplights, all of which can be dimmed; "barn doors" to put on the outside of lights to focus them; and colored gels that can be placed in front of lights to alter their quality.
- Digital editing program.
- Compressed air and soft brushes for cleanup during general production or while shooting; a small, gentle vacuum cleaner could also be useful.
- Safety equipment, including gloves and face masks, and clearly labeled containers of cleaning materials—especially paint solvents and other potentially dangerous materials; a list of hazardous materials should be readily available to anyone working with or near them.

Artists working with three-dimensional figures need additional materials, some of which are also useful to 2D artists when they create maquettes, or three-dimensional models of characters and objects. For example:

- Materials for creating armatures, the supports inside figures; armatures are commonly made of wire or metal parts.
- Materials for creating the bodies of figures: aluminum foil, modeling clay, latex, fabric, and other materials.

- Buckets, bowls, and mixing utensils.
- Sculpting tools for shaping, creating textures, and otherwise designing figures.
- Gauges (manual or digital) for measuring the movement of figures.
- Tweezers.
- Paints and other coloring media.
- Possibly a sewing machine to make fabric items; also patterns for the same.
- Building tools and materials, including wire, wirecutters, nuts, screws, bolts, wingnuts, screwdrivers, wrenches, clamps, pliers, drills, and saws.
- Clear fishing line for suspending figures.
- Adhesives, including a glue gun, glue sticks, permanent epoxy, FunTak (or other temporary adhesive), Velcro, and tapes including duct, masking, clear, and double-sided.
- Staple gun and staples.
- Box cutter and blade knives.
- Materials and props for creating sets.
- Foam-core boards, Styrofoam, balsa wood, and thin Plexiglas for general building purposes.
- Large, dedicated space for the set—including camera placement—that can be lit without incidental light from other sources.[18]

The work area of stop-motion animator Max Winston contains the wide range of items used in his work.

Hlynur Magnússon on the set of his stop-motion film.

Style Guides

A style guide is central to art direction. Its content varies, depending on the medium used as well as the type of animation being created. Typically, it includes designs for characters, props, locations, and backgrounds, as well as keys for the colors used throughout the film.[19]

An important component of a style guide is documentation of how characters look. For two-dimensional work, model sheets are created showing emotionless characters in a "rotation": forward, side, three-quarter, and back views. These help keep characters the same—"on model"—as various artists draw them during the production process. The sheets can also include examples of characters in motion, experiencing different emotions, in scale to other characters, and going through a walk cycle.[20] During the development of a 2D animation style guide, it is helpful to create maquettes, or sculptures, of major characters and props in the work. Maquettes allow artists to fully visualize objects, especially as they rotate in space. They can also be used with various lighting setups as aids to depicting shadows effectively.

For stop-motion production, scale-size drawings of all characters are also needed. The set must be built around the figures, so they should be kept under a foot in height (though they must be large enough to be animated). For planning purposes, it is advisable to also create three-dimensional scale models of the figures. These prototypes serve two general functions, beyond defining how the figures look: They are used to perfect the internal framework of the figures, and they help designers visualize the size of costumes and props. In some cases, sets, props, and figures (including armatures, exterior bodies, and costumes) are created in various scales to accommodate all the requirements of the script.

There are many factors to consider in terms of art direction. One of the most important is how an animation will be exhibited. Film is known for its relatively high resolution (the fineness of the grain of captured images) and relatively large projection size. Television, on the other hand, has historically had poor resolution and has been fairly small in scale. As a result, designing for it has required restrained use of color and figures that aren't highly complex. The simplified boys of "South Park" are ideal for it because they "read" (or are understood by the viewer) very clearly on the screen. In recent years television has changed, and larger screens and high definition are more readily available.

Variations in model sheets are illustrated here (above and right) with images from Igor Kovalyov's *Milch*.

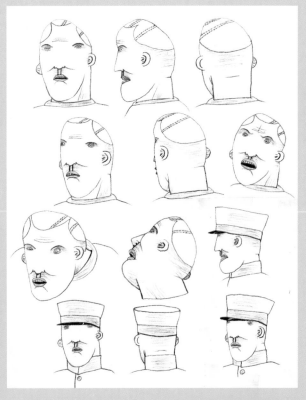

Jesse Gregg's model sheets (right) show his character Puck in rotation and experiencing various emotions.

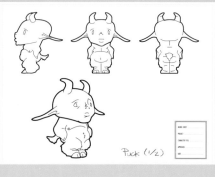

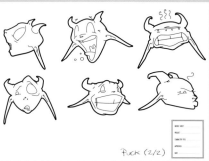

Now there is a new technology associated with relatively simple animation: mobile communication devices. On a small-scale monitor, including a cell phone or PDA screen, simple shapes and colors work best. Most animation for the Web is also relatively low-end in terms of detail. Small file sizes (that is, restricted amounts of visual data) are required to reduce the time it takes to transmit information. Despite fast cable and DSL (Digital subscriber lines) that can be used in conjunction with computers to process data very quickly, many users across the world access the Internet via phone lines and use older computers powered by slower processors.

To reach the most people, one must design with the greatest limitations in mind—which is not necessarily a bad thing. By working around self-imposed restrictions, an artist has to come up with creative solutions. Among them should be considerations of "universal design"; issues of accessibility should figure into selections of color, sound, and so on. Works that are designed with the limitations of certain viewers in mind (particularly those with vision- or hearing-related impairments) can be creative and also appeal to a wide audience.

The Test Run

The best way to see how aspects of style are working is to create short pieces of test animation. This provides an opportunity to experiment with all the design elements of a production, trying them in conjunction with the chosen media. Do colors work together? Can a particular figure be animated effectively? Are tie-downs on a stop-motion set strong enough and yet easy to use? Is the lighting creating the appropriate atmosphere? Are huge file sizes overloading the software? All these questions and more can be answered by simply testing parts of the process before the artist makes a commitment to move ahead with full-scale production. Test animation falls under the general category of research—and it is time well spent!

2D animator Philippe Vaucher created this three-dimensional model (right), or maquette, to guide the production of charcoal drawings used in his film *Chasse Papillion*.

This image shows Iain Gardner's color key for the red knight character in *The Squire's Tale*.

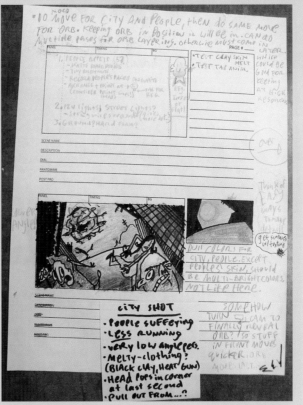

Notes by Max Winston used to create tests for stop-motion productions.

Production and Post-production

Once pre-production has been completed, it is time to put plans to the test and see a vision become a reality. During the production process, artwork is created and recorded, and then the project moves into post-production, where it is readied for exhibition.

Production

Because there are so many contextual factors affecting the production of an animated work, there can be great variation in the processes through which they are realized. It is important to accommodate the unique qualities of specific projects as they are considered individually within the generic production process.

Drawn Animation

The term "2D" describes a drawing or any artwork that has height and width, but no depth; it is flat, but can be made to look three-dimensional by applying the rules of perspective. Two-dimensional animation encompasses a wide range of techniques, including drawing on paper, ink and watercolor on paper, oil on glass, and cel animation. Animation devices

such as flipbooks and zoetropes (see pages 126–127) also feature 2D imagery. This section focuses primarily on animation that is drawn on paper or painted on cels, but some of its content can be applied to other 2D methods.

For many years, the commercial animation industry mainly employed cel animation, a 2D technique that involved applying inks and paints onto acetate sheets ("cels"). First, a line drawing was made on paper. Then, a clear cel was placed on top of it, so the line drawing could be traced with ink onto the acetate. After the ink dried, the cel was flipped over and painted with an acetate-adhering acrylic paint. When the completed cel was viewed from the front, the color appeared under the glossy surface, surrounded by the black ink outline.

Cel animation was patented in the United States in 1915 by Earl Hurd. Largely because of the influence of the Disney studio, but reinforced by virtually the whole American animation industry, it became the norm for the production of short films and animated features worldwide. Part of the reason 2D animation—and cel animation in particular—was embraced so wholeheartedly in an industrial context is that it lent itself to a "factory line" system of production. It could be created by large groups of employees, each of whom did a relatively focused part of the work. During the 1930s and

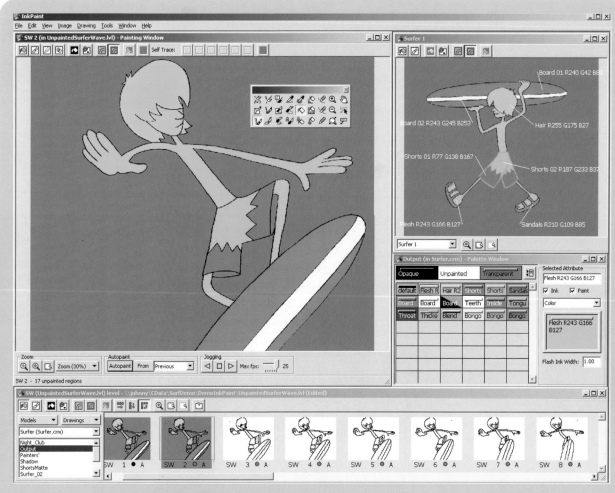

For many years, the clear cels used to create the majority of 2D animation were inked and painted by hand. Now 2D animation generally is colored using digital ink and paint software such as Animo (above).

1940s, the golden age of animation, most of these people, such as the legions of women in "ink and paint" departments, were part of an anonymous group of workers. The famous producers and directors who created feature and short films (and, later, animated works for television) made up only a very small proportion of the people involved in the industry.

Today, the situation is similar. Although many young people entering animation programs describe their career goal as "animator," the term is sometimes ambiguous—their actual work is likely to be much different. Certainly, an independent artist working alone on a project is doing the work of an animator (and probably everything else). However, in an industrial studio, relatively few people are animators, compared with those who do all the other animation-related jobs.

Nonetheless, a large-scale industrial project might involve a series of animators who are differently specialized. For example, a "lead animator" oversees the movement of a specific character or supervises the artists who handle its scenes. If characters are caught in rough seas during a storm, an "effects animator" is responsible for depicting the water battering their boat.

An animator typically creates the "key frames" (or "extremes") in a scene, which represent significant points within a series of animated movements (such as the beginning and end of an action). After these poses have been created, the next step in a hand-drawn picture is to fill in the missing images and finalize drawings, to make the character or object move as desired. Depending on the scale of the production, this work could be passed to an "assistant animator" who fills in a few frames, and then to an "in-betweener" who creates the remaining ones, and finally to "cleanup," where an individual removes stray lines and ensures the art is ready to move ahead in production. Today, animators sometimes rely on digital technology to "tween" images between scanned key-frame poses, doing away with the role of the in-betweener.

Approaches to Animation The process described above is known as "pose to pose" animation, which is common in an industrial setting. One of the advantages of this method is that it allows the breakdown of labor. Because the work can be "assembly lined," the most skillful artists (who are paid the highest salaries) are able to focus only on its most complex aspects, which requires a relatively advanced level of expertise. In theory, the people who draw any of the in-between poses do not have to be as skilled; the scope of their contributions is limited by the animator's drawings, which appear every few

Character Animation

The following are some of the most important elements in animating figures and objects:

— Walk cycles: the series of movements a character goes through in one complete stride of walking. One of the most fundamental and yet most difficult aspects of animation, a walk cycle can reveal a great deal about a character's personality.

— Squash and stretch: exaggerated movement that creates the impression of an elastic body on a character or object, generally associated with physical humor and gags. Squash and stretch informs viewers about the flexibility or solidity of the object. This approach can be contrasted with the "rubber hose" style seen early in animation history, when arms, legs, and bodies stretched and bent without regard to consistent volume or a sense of actual physical form.

— Slow in and slow out: Movements do not occur at a consistent speed. They begin with gradual acceleration, typically reach their peak speed at the mid-point, and decelerate at the end.

— Anticipation: the preface to an action, generally involving movement in the opposite direction to the action (a head looking slightly to the left before it snaps to the right).

— Follow through: the terminal part of an action, in which the character or object continues to move slightly beyond the required movement.

— Overlapping action: movement in a secondary area, generally as the result of the movement in a primary one (often seen in clothing that drapes behind a moving figure). It adds complexity to the animation.

— Line of action: animating movements so that an entire figure looks unified. The move must continue through the character in a convincing way.

— Secondary action: adding a supplemental movement to support the impact of the primary one. For example, if a character's eyes bulge out of his eye sockets, his fingers might extend to reinforce the impression of shock.

— Exaggeration: taking whatever is necessary and adding a bit more, in terms of design, movement, sound, and/or story; typical of humorous animation in a "cartoon" style.

frames. This method also ensures that the character's actions, volume, and timing remain relatively consistent, and also that the production comes in at the required length.

A second approach, "straight ahead" animation, offers different advantages and is the only way to work with some media. Using this method, the animator begins at the first frame and creates images consecutively until the required animated movement—one scene or an entire film—is complete. Painting on glass requires a straight-ahead approach because it is among the "modified base" techniques, meaning that only one object is manipulated to create the animation, and each movement is made and recorded in succession. However, drawn animation also can be created straight ahead. Advocates of this method appreciate its ability to incorporate spontaneity into the process of animating, but because it is not easy to guarantee a running time this way, it tends to be less desirable in a commercial context.

Creating Images Usually, 2D figures are first drawn on bond paper. A "nonphoto blue" pencil is often used to create an image composed of loosely sketched under-drawings, which is later refined by tracing selected lines with a black graphite pencil, pen, or other media; when the image is photocopied, only the black lines reproduce. Some artists prefer to use a regular pencil rather than a nonphoto blue one

for rough sketches; final drawings are created by laying a new sheet of paper on top and making "clean" images on it (if a mistake is made, the original sketches aren't damaged). Sometimes, software makes it possible to paint "roughs" easily and eliminate cleanup.

Creating sequential images generally requires an underlit drawing disc or light table (a glass surface with a light source underneath) containing registration pegs. After the first drawing is completed, a piece of paper is laid on top of it. The next image in the sequence is drawn and a piece of paper is placed on top of this second drawing. If the artist is animating straight ahead, more and more drawings are created until the stack becomes so thick that the underlighting cannot show through. At that point, the lowest (first drawn) images are removed to thin the stack, and the drawing process resumes. Pose to pose animators tend to work differently. They will usually have only two or three key frames on the pegs at any one time and will roll them to view progressive movement. To keep drawings organized, they should be numbered as they are created, according to their scene and frame numbers.[1]

In his *Encyclopedia of Animation Techniques*, Richard Taylor recommends starting by animating a sequence in the middle of a production, particularly if the artist is working on a project alone. He explains, "Working single-handed is slow work; it may take a year or more to complete a film, in which

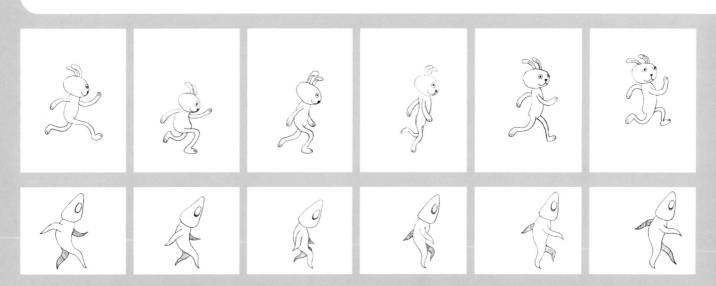

In these two series of movements, animator Dae In Chung creates distinctly different personalities.

time your idea of a character may develop without your being aware of it. … If you start work on the film somewhere in the middle of the story rather than in sequence from the beginning, variations in the character can be merged in more easily. Also, because the early scenes in the film will be more mature in drawing, the opening will be stronger."[2]

The Pencil Test   As scenes are completed, they can be flipped by hand to check for smooth movement, and then made into a "pencil test" (also known as a "line test") using a video or digital recording system. If the pencil-tested line drawings look right, they are ready to be made into the final art that will be used to create the animation, using whatever media have been selected.

Digital Ink and Paint   Today, it is relatively common to scan line drawings into a computer and use software to achieve the digital equivalent of inking and painting, potentially saving a great deal of time. However, these systems are not foolproof. Unlike a human painter, a computer is not good at making judgments. If the lines that define a form on a character (such as the edges of his shirt) aren't closed well enough, the color placed in it might leak out to surrounding areas. Consequently, it is important that scanned images are created with solid lines that can be identified easily by the computer.

GIFs and Flash

While people are often encouraged to "think big" in terms of goal setting, the motto for animators creating online animation should be the opposite: "think small." Though we find ourselves hoping to transmit more and more elaborate material online, we must face reality. Web users in many parts of the world still receive data over slow phone lines, and files must remain relatively compact if they are to be widely disseminated internationally.[3] At this point, the animation best suited for use on Web and mobile communication technology typically employs small images that can be reused, limited amounts of movement, relatively simple lines, and restrained color schemes, all to keep file sizes as compact as possible and pictures clear in their sometimes tiny dimensions. The challenge of getting concepts across within these constraints is a significant aspect of the art of Web and mobile device animation.

This sort of animation can be created in a variety of ways and for a range of contexts: decoration (including screensavers), functional objects related to interactivity, animated series, three-dimensional models for e-commerce, games, and more. The production of each is dependent on understanding various software packages—technology that is evolving constantly.

Animator Bill Plympton uses a standard no. 2 pencil and bond paper to create his images.

This series of drawings by Adam Fox (below) demonstrates the principle of "squash and stretch" animation.

GIF Animations GIF stands for "graphic interchange format," a term used to identify certain types of graphic files. Though GIF animations are losing their place to other innovations, animators should still know what they are. GIF images are typically composed of groups of solid colors. GIF animations tend to serve as relatively small functional or decorative visuals on a website and can be made using virtually any drawing software, or from scanned images saved in the GIF format. Sequential movement is created by importing the images into a GIF animation program, such as GifBuilder for Macintosh or Gif Construction Set for Windows. The program lines the separate GIF images up into a kind of flipbook, so they appear in succession as animated movement. The animations are easily recognizable by browsers, but tend to be relatively data-heavy and are not suited to long or complex works.

GIF animations can be composed of two or more images, and so might last only a fraction of a second or a few seconds. Consequently, the pre-production process is not nearly as extensive as that of most other animation. Still, there are a number of important considerations when developing GIFs, including:

– The most important question: Is the image worth using? Overly animated sites can be less attractive than completely static ones, and constant movement causes problems for universal access.

– Within the animation, can an image be reused or is a new one required?
– What is the smallest number of frames that can be used to create the desired movement?
– How long should each image stay onscreen?
– Can the image be smaller in visual terms and still function effectively, without causing difficulty for vision-impaired viewers?

"Optimizing" the images in various ways—reducing their file sizes and thus their load times—is important. Webpage users are unlikely to wait more than ten seconds (if that long) for a page to download. During production it is a good idea to upload the GIF to the server and test it using a variety of Web browsers in different versions, to check for compatibility as well as actual running speed, which may differ from the running speed within the program.[4]

A major factor that affects download time is bandwidth, essentially the amount of data that can move through an Internet user's communication system at any one time. It is a good idea to consider how long it takes for information to travel through modems of various speeds used with dialup phone connections, in comparison with DSL or cable modems; charts containing this information are widely available. Fast-running GIF animations will have relatively few frames, low bit

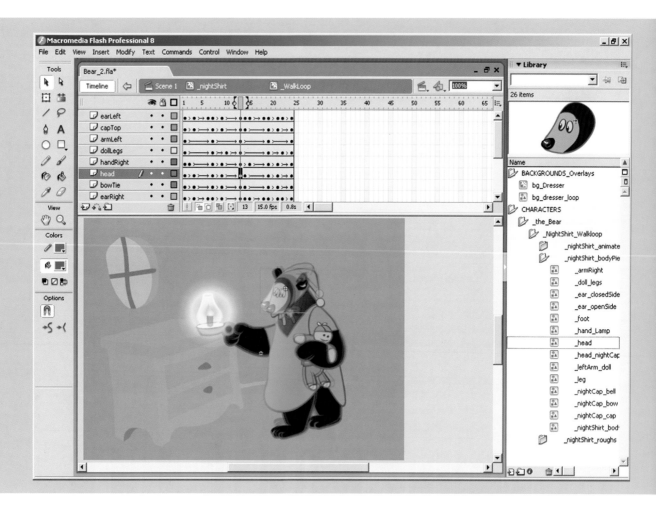

depth (which determines the range of colors), flat color (rather than detailed photographic images), and highly optimized frames that work with previously used backgrounds. Needless to say, such efficiency requires a good deal of pre-planning.

Flash Animation GIF animations can be viewed by anyone using a Web browser such as Internet Explorer or Safari. In contrast, Flash animation requires a special "plug-in" that must be acquired by downloading (free) or in another fashion—new computers commonly come with a Flash plug-in already installed. Adobe Flash Player is a software program that is marketed as being easy enough for anyone to use, and also sophisticated enough to be the industry standard for creating high-end animation for online use. It can be seen in many contexts, including complex effects on websites and animated series online. From its inception, it was designed as a Web application, which partly explains why it is so well suited to that context.[5] Since about 2003, there have been significant advances in adapting Flash for use on mobile technology, which presents challenges because of the many differences among phones and PDAs.

The Flash program employs a range of terms that bridge various contexts of art production. A Flash production is called a "movie," and is composed of various "scenes." Performance takes place on a stage—where artwork is drawn or imported, and other features such as sound and text are added. Also familiar is the term "toolbox," which is widely used in digital contexts to describe a place containing buttons that control drawing tools, brushes, paint buckets, inks, selection arrows, and so forth. Like much other software, Flash provides several floating panels that can be kept active or removed, depending on the user's preference; these help in the viewing, organizing, and changing of elements in a movie.

The library is where reusable images are stored—Flash's small file sizes are partly due to its capacity to reuse images effectively. Items kept in the library are "symbols," and each time they are placed on the stage represents an "instance" of their use. Each instance of a symbol can be modified on the stage without changing the original image in the library—or the library symbol can be modified and the change will affect each instance of it in the work.

Historically, an exposure sheet has been used to chart the structure of an animated production. Flash uses the term "timeline" to describe its system for organizing and controlling a movie's content over time. The timeline is composed of a series of lines containing numbers that represent each frame. The animator moves the playhead over the numbered lines to select the desired frame. Rows below the frame numbers provide a visual reference to where different aspects of the work occur.

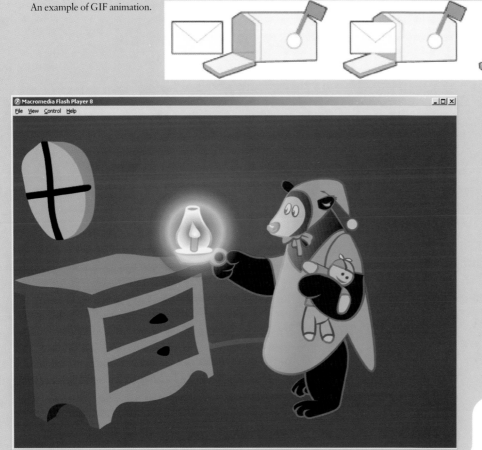

An example of GIF animation.

The screenshot (opposite) shows components of the Flash software interface used by Adam Fox to create this image (left).

Flash allows either frame-by-frame animation, where each image is created by hand, or motion and shape "tweening," which involves selecting a key frame where the action begins and a final frame where it ends, and letting the computer create the in-between movements. Just as in traditional animation with cels, a work can be created on layers that organize its content. If a background appears on one layer, it does not interfere with a moving character on another when moving the figure across the screen.

One of Flash's key features is that its images can be saved as vector graphics; in other words, images created from lines and curves, rather than bitmapped with dots (pixels)—though bitmapped images can be imported into the program. Vector graphics can be rescaled (in particular, enlarged) without the distortion that occurs when pixels are blown up.

There are some potential downsides to Flash, one of the most significant being speed. In order to smoothly translate mathematical formulae into visuals, Flash requires a relatively large amount of processing capacity. Computers sold in recent years tend to have sufficient processors built in, but typically startup time is still required before the animation begins. Viewers can lose interest or close a window if the wait seems too long (ten seconds being the probable limit). To hold the viewer's interest, Flash animators are encouraged to create a

"pre-loader," a small image that comes on before the start of the animation. Common pre-loaders include a countdown timer, a simple animated figure, or even a flashing "loading" sign.

Flash file sizes can be minimized by simplifying images, optimizing elements to condense information, using fewer key frames, and reducing the number of images moving at the same time. It also helps to reduce the frame rate, which is variable. In contrast to the fixed 24 fps of sound film and 25 or 30 fps for video, the generally recommended rate for Flash is 12 fps. However, lowering the frame rate affects the overall quality of movement in the finished work—one of the Flash animator's biggest challenges is to combine creativity and efficiency.

Stop-motion

Stop-motion encompasses an endless variety of materials and approaches. The term describes any animation process in which an object is filmed, moved incrementally, filmed again, and so on, to create the perception of fluid motion. Two-dimensional approaches that employ a modified base, such as oil on glass and manipulated cutouts fall into this category, though most stop-motion work involves three-dimensional materials—objects that have volume as well as height and width. Wooden and latex figures are often used, along with beads, rocks, candy, yarn, office supplies, rubber chickens,

In his pre-production drawing (left) Adam Fox indicates how the bear's body parts will be divided into layers. The final Flash image combines these layers seamlessly to form the character (above).

plants, people, and so on. Some of the most popular stop-motion materials are oil-based clays; they are used to create work often referred to as "claymation," a term trademarked by the Will Vinton studio, though it has fallen into general usage. Objects made of clay can retain an ability to change shape, or they can be hardened through drying and baking. Sometimes soft, malleable clay is used in conjunction with silicone, hardened clay products, or other materials, so that part of a figure is flexible enough to be reshaped and part of it is more permanently formed. The following overview focuses mainly on clay-related techniques, though much of the information also relates to other media.

Tie-down Systems   Before production begins, it is important to decide on tie-down systems for all objects on the set. Everything—including the tabletop, camera, and lights—must be anchored tightly. From the perspective of Aardman Animations, "There is one simple golden rule in the model-animation studio. Nothing should move unless you want it to. When most people start experimenting with animation … the most common fault is that either the set, the shadows from the lights, the camera, or the environment itself moves almost as much as the animated puppet."[6]

While it is certainly true that figures must be immobile during shooting, they also must be easily freed, so that they can be moved around without too much trouble. To that end, it is important to work with tie-downs that facilitate the production process, taking into account the media used, set (especially floor) construction, the distance the animator must reach, camera angles, and other related concerns. Possible tie-down options include wire that is pulled through the figure's foot and anchored below the set, bolts fastened below the set, pins pushed through the foot into the floor of the set, sticky substances that create a temporary bond, and magnets placed under the set to hold down the metal in the figure's foot. Each option has its drawbacks: Wire takes a long time to twist and untwist; screws are visible if a foot is raised; pins and sticky substances are not reliable; and magnets are relatively easy to move, but must be strong enough to keep figures in place as their balance shifts.

Armatures   An armature is the skeletal system that supports a stop-motion figure. They, too, come in a wide variety, as a result not only of preference, but also considerations of cost, manufacturing time, and durability. Some stop-motion figures do not need an armature; even oil-based clay sometimes has enough body that it can stand up on its own. An example can

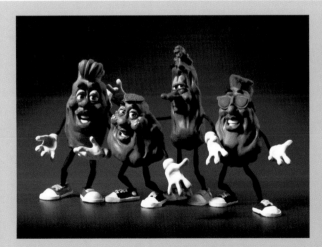

The California Raisins, animated by the Will Vinton studio, were a big hit and helped popularize the term "claymation."

Hlynur Magnússon has used bolts and wing nuts as tie downs for this stop-motion figure.

be found in *Gumbasia* (1953), where Art Clokey has used a variety of small geometric forms that basically slide or roll along the ground, without the need for support. However, if characters have any height, or if they engage in complex movement, a supportive armature is necessary. It helps keep a figure upright, even under warm lights that tend to soften clay, and allows for the construction of joints that can be moved back and forth. Twisted wire, which can be bent in various directions to support the torso, head, legs, and arms of a figure, is one type of armature; when Clokey moved into production of his "Gumby" series, he used it to build his characters. Often, a twisted wire armature is reinforced with resin, a hardening clay product, or other substance at the hips and upper body. It is fairly easy to construct.

A second type is a machined armature, which is custom-made from steel with finely tuned ball-and-socket joints, and tends to be used in well-financed productions, such as theatrical features. It must be produced by someone who has specialized knowledge and tools. Chiodo Bros. Productions, a Los Angeles-area studio, is large enough to create metal armatures in-house. An example is a *Tyrannosaurus rex* figure from Sid & Marty Krofft's "New Land of the Lost" series, which aired on American television during the mid-1990s; the Chiodos

(brothers Charles, Stephen, and Edward) were co-producers of the show and supervised the effects work.

There are significant differences between these supports. One is related to manufacturing time. A twisted wire armature can be made in a matter of hours, if not minutes, by virtually anyone. Most independent animators would have to order a machined armature from an individual who works on his or her own schedule, and quick delivery would be unlikely. Cost is also an important factor: The best wire available from a local hardware store is nowhere near as expensive as a professionally built steel frame. On the other hand, whereas one figure created with a machined armature is likely to be sufficient, the animator will have to buy a lot of wire and clay (or other media) and spend time creating backup figures. Wires break easily after being bent several times: Clokey prepared about twenty Gumbys every time he shot an episode.

Whatever type of armature is selected, a prototype should be tested before production of additional figures takes place. As part of the test, the armature should be tied down to the base of the set and moved through the actions required by the script—creating a good opportunity for a test run of camera angles as well.

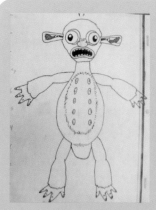 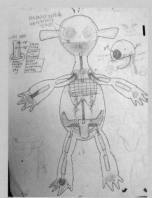

In these sketches, stop-motion animator Max Winston first sketches his character (above left) and then re-draws the figure, designing an armature that will support it (above right).

Twisted wire armatures provide an economical way to create a stop-motion puppet. The twisted wire form (above) is reinforced with a hardened substance (right).

Types of Clay A number of clay materials can be used to cover armatures. Oil-based modeling clays (commonly known as plastiline, and also by the product name of Plasticine) don't harden, which makes them useful for animation. The downside is that it can easily be misshaped by accident during the production process, though any fingerprints that appear can be smoothed out with mineral oil. There is also a range of polymer clays that can be dried or baked into fixed figures that cannot be reshaped—though they can break, and crumbling can be a problem, especially when parts are thin. Among the most popular are Fimo and Sculpey Premo. These clays are relatively stiff and must be conditioned by kneading before they can be shaped into figures.

There are many options open to the creative sculptor. Colors can be blended together, and baked pieces can be painted or varnished. Some stop-motion figures combine hard and soft materials: For example, eyeballs and even lips can be created with hard materials (beads, resin, baked clay, etc.) and inserted into a clay-modeled figure. However, when selecting materials and creating a figure, it is important to keep weight and size in mind. For example, heavy arms and legs are relatively difficult to animate, and a large head will throw a lightweight body off balance.

Clay objects can be created using molds, which are useful for mass production, or shaped by hand, possibly using carving and texturing tools, such as dental equipment, pointed sticks, paintbrushes with the bristles removed, and so on. Whatever method is used, production should take place in a clean area, as clay picks up anything it comes in contact with, including other clay. Hands must be kept clean when a variety of colors is used because pigment transfers easily if residue remains on fingers; applying petroleum jelly to the skin before starting work will help to prevent it sticking.

Typically, polymer clays are applied over an armature that has been wrapped with crinkled tinfoil. When it is ready, the clay figure is baked in an oven according to the manufacturer's instructions. For example, Fimo typically bakes in a 265° F (130°C) oven for about thirty minutes. Although the clays are labeled nontoxic, at temperatures over 350° F (175 °C), or if they burn, they can give off hydrogen gas and produce an irritating smell. In any case, the room where baking occurs should be well ventilated.

Latex and Rubber In recent years, commercial stop-motion studios increasingly have used foam latex or silicone rubber puppets. Examples can be found in the work of Chiodo Bros. Productions, which has fabricated and manipulated

Professional stop-motion productions generally employ machined armatures that include ball-and-socket joints. They are expensive, but very durable. This dinosaur was designed and sculpted by Stephen Chiodo at Chiodo Bros. Productions, Inc. The armature was constructed by Peter Marinello.

Sculpey products are among the oil-based clays used by stop-motion animators.

stop-motion and marionette figures for the features *Pee Wee's Big Adventure* (directed by Tim Burton, 1985), *Team America: World Police* (directed by Trey Parker, 2004), and their own *Killer Klowns from Outer Space* (directed by Stephen Chiodo, 1988), among other works. For most of its productions, Chiodo Bros. brings in a team of specialists to create maquettes, armatures, remote-control units, latex figures, costumes, and sets, and to animate stop-motion action or puppets before the camera.

A casting process is used to create latex and silicone rubber figures. First comes the development—or modeling—of a figure that is typically rendered in clay. This model is then prepared so that plaster or some other material can be poured around it to make a mold. After the plaster is dry, the mold is taken apart and treated, and then reassembled for the casting process. The latex or rubber is poured or injected into the mold, and cooled or dried. It can be difficult to time this process, since the prepared material tends to set relatively quickly; several tries might be necessary before the technique is mastered. The final stage, once the mold has been removed, is to treat the surface of the cast work—for example, by buffing and painting. Rubber figures are relatively expensive in contrast to clay. However, because they are typically more durable, fewer are needed for any given production. Like other production materials, foam latex and silicone rubber should be used with caution, and health-related warnings on labels should be heeded.

Sets and Lighting The human figures in most Aardman films are about 8 to 10 inches (20 to 25 centimeters) tall.[7] Although it might be easier to animate larger objects, bigger figures need bigger environments, which not only cost more but also can be relatively difficult to work in. Stop-motion is typically created at a relatively small scale to allow the animator to adjust figures comfortably. If a set is overly wide, reaching across the space can cause back strain. A trap door is sometimes fitted in the middle of the floor so that figures can be reached conveniently. Ideally, walls can be easily removed, which is good for both the animator and the camera operator, who is able to shoot from more angles. The set should be suspended high enough to prevent back stress from constant bending, and allow the animator to get below it to adjust characters' tie-downs.

Some of the most impressive stop-motion films employ minimal sets. The background of Kihachiro Kawamoto's *Kataku* (*House of Flames*, 1979) is simply designed, suggesting the context of a theatrical set. In his series of award-winning clay animations—including *Uncle* (1996), *Cousin* (1998),

Three production images from Virgil Widrich's *Fast Film*, including both horizontal and vertical shooting methods.

Three replacement heads above the basic clay prototypes, created by Erin Ross.

The three components of a cast figure: the plaster mold, the clay original around which it is built, and the resulting object cast in rubber. Models by Brent Johnson.

Brother (1999), and *Harvie Krumpet* (2003)—Adam Elliot often used relatively simple backdrops illuminated by a spotlight that casts a strong shadow behind the characters or shapes the space in some manner.

Though Elliot frequently uses stylized lighting, many stop-motion productions rely on standard "three-point lighting," so named because it involves three lights. A "key light" is the strongest light source; it is typically set in front of the subject, off to one side. A "fill light" illuminates the other side of the figure, filling light in where there would otherwise be a dark shadow; it also is placed in front of the subject, but on the side opposite to the key light. A "backlight" is used to separate the subject from its background; a relatively weak light source, it is placed behind the figure being lit. A set that is brightly and evenly lit is generally described as "high key," while sets filled with pools of light and shadows are "low key."

Movement When a stop-motion figure is animated, it seems to come to life. However, there is a significant difference between the recorded movements of a three-dimensional object that is animated and an actual living being moving naturally. Live figures move continuously as a camera captures them in real time, creating "motion blur" on each frame, whereas animated figures are captured in a series of still poses,

which are not blurred at all. The difference may be subtle, but it is perceptible. To create more realism in stop-motion movement, animators can use a process called "go motion," in which objects are moved slightly in front of an open camera shutter. The procedure was first used in the feature *Dragonslayer* (1980). A slightly different technique has been used at Aardman for the Wallace and Gromit films:

> In the train chase in *The Wrong Trousers* and the lorry chase in *A Close Shave*, we blurred the background by using long exposures (one or two seconds) and by physically moving the camera during the exposure. To take the train example, the train on its track was attached to the camera, which was mounted on a dolly. For each frame, we pushed the dolly about 3 to 4 inches (8 to 10 centimeters) and this carried the train along with it. At the same time we pressed the button to expose the film. The characters on the train come out sharply defined because they are moving with the camera but in the course of the two-second exposure the camera moves fractionally past the wallpaper in the background, and this comes out blurred.[8]

Blur effects also can be created through the use of software.

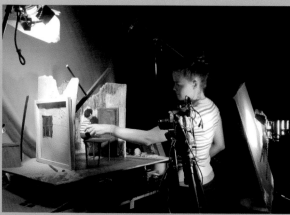

An image from Adam Elliot's *Brother* (left).

Erin Ross (above) adjusting figures on a set employing various lighting methods.

Stop-motion complicates movement in various other ways as well. For one thing, objects cannot leap upward the way living beings can. One solution is to suspend the figure by wires, clear fishing line, or rods while it is filmed frame by frame. In *The Wrong Trousers* (1993), Aardman overcame this problem when it depicted the evil penguin flying through the air, about to be captured within a bottle: a side view of the character was shot against glass while the background, which consists of white clouds on a field of blue, was moved behind it. Lord reveals, "… the penguin is largely still, though from time to time we altered the position of his feet and the sack across his shoulder. The illusion of falling comes mainly from the sky itself, which we moved from side to side during a series of long exposures."[9] Running figures are also a problem, as Peter Lord explains: "Because the movement is fast, the gaps between frames are large. This means that although the effect is energetic, it is seldom smooth."[10]

Wireframed Digital Images

Due to the growth in three-dimensional digital animation processes in recent years, a number of software packages are available to create 3D work. An overview of wireframed digital animation is difficult partly because of the vastness of the field, but also because of the relative complexity of the tools themselves. This section provides a brief description of general processes used to produce 3D animation, leaving the technical details for more advanced study.

The production of 3D computer-generated animation has quite a bit in common with live-action methods. As Winder and Dowlatabadi explain, "sets must be built, lit, and painted, much in the way that sets are constructed for live-action films. CGI also resembles live-action filmmaking in terms of spatial conceptualization, lighting, cinematography, scene hook-ups and blocking of actor's movements."[11] The authors summarize the many phases of design and development a 3D figure goes through on its path to completion. The specific steps they identify flow in the following order: design, modeling, rigging, surfaces (texture and color), staging/workbook, animation, lighting, effects, rendering, compositing, touchup, and final film/video output.[12]

A blurring effect is used to create the sensation of high speed movement in *The Wrong Trousers*.

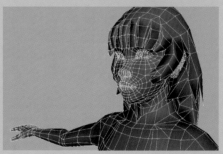

A series of images (above and opposite) created by Ke Jiang illustrates steps in the process of creating a 3D CGI character.

Modeling Computer-generated figures generally have both an exterior surface and an internal structure, similar to the sculpted and armatured objects used in stop-motion animation; these component parts are envisioned and refined during a design phase, just as in other types of animation production. In the 3D realm, the process of creating the basic form of a figure is known as "modeling." This involves developing a "primitive object," or basic shape, which can be transformed in terms of its size, form, and position within the frame, and also rotated in space.

Whereas the most basic forms in 2D animation are the dot and the line, in 3D digital animation the equivalents are the "vertex" (a point in space) and the "vector" (the line connecting two points in space). When a number of vertices are connected by segments, it is possible to create polygons such as squares and rectangles, which are linked together to form the basis for a computer-generated figure. Often, the resulting wireframe can be saved and regenerated into other characters, which saves both time and labor.

Rigging and Texturing Rigging and texturing are processes that add complexity to a wireframe model. A model is "rigged"—that is, controls are added to its form—to give it the ability to move in certain ways. An important part of the animation process is "parenting" objects: Essentially, a group of separate shapes are linked together so that when one moves, it is possible to move all of them simultaneously. "Texturing" is the development of surface coverings that appear on characters, objects within a scene, or backgrounds. Textures are generally supplied within software programs, but artists often decide to import textures of their own; they create and scan interesting materials that can lend originality and authenticity that might be lacking with prefabricated selections. "Alpha channels" control the opacity of an object, or the extent to which items can be seen through it.

Staging, Animation, and Lighting The processes of staging, animation, and lighting further refine characters and their environments. "Staging" can be compared to layout in traditional production terms. This process is concerned with the spatial relationship of characters to other characters, objects, and the environment, and ensures that the actions envisaged

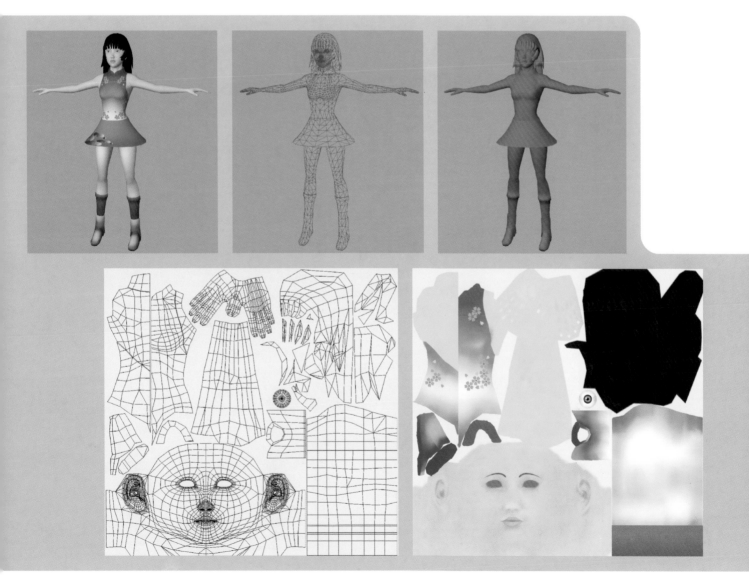

in scenes are possible. Only after workable staging is achieved can the "path" for animation be created. The animation process involves creating key frames, which can be compared to the "extremes" of drawn animation, and calculating the number of frames needed to realize a given action along its path. During a later stage, the computer will determine the in-between positions that will complete the movement. During "lighting," sources of light are positioned and manipulated to create shadows and dimensionality as objects move through space and shift in relationship to the viewer's point of view.

Effects Effects animation encompasses visual design elements that range from subtle to extreme. At industrial studios, the tools used to achieve them are often developed in-house as "proprietary" software, meaning that it can only be used within the company that created it; they allow the studio to produce unique effects, and gain an edge on competing firms. Eventually, most innovations find their way into general use, and effects once difficult to achieve, such as morphing one shape into another and the "particle animation" of dust or rain, are built into commercial software packages. Some of the biggest challenges in computer animation have been the depiction of fur, hair, fire, and realistic human figures with complex muscle structures and skin that is of the right opacity to be convincing. Today's software aids in the depiction of even these hard-to-create images.

Rendering and Compositing Near the end of the production process, figures are rendered and composited. Rendering takes the information generated in earlier stages and combines it to create the moving figure within its environment. Compositing involves combining elements so that they appear as one seamless production; an example is the incorporation of animated visual effects into a live-action film.

Post-production

Post-production processes include everything necessary to get the animated imagery ready for exhibition. It includes editing and preparing for distribution in various formats, as well as archiving elements of the work.

Editing

Because each frame of animation is labor-intensive in production, and therefore costly, it is ideal to animate each scene only once. Consequently, the animation editor typically has fewer choices than a live-action one for assembling the final film. Usually, continuous editing takes place during production; as images are completed, they are input into a digital animatic and built up as a leica reel. That way, any necessary retakes can be done while production is in progress.

Charles daCosta created an appealing, colorful title image and informal lettering to complement his film's content: an interview with an elderly woman who reminisces about childhood memories.

In the days before computer technology, editing effects such as dissolves and superimpositions might be achieved with an "optical printer." This equipment essentially combines a projector with a camera: The exposed film is loaded into the projection side and projected frame by frame onto unexposed stock in the camera side of the optical printer. Mattes can be used to mask images and enable printing of more than one image or several partial images onto the final print. Live-action and animation combinations could be achieved this way. Today it is common to create such effects with a computer. A range of digital editing and graphics programs provide professional results for even modestly budgeted films.

The editing process involves the addition of titles to the project. Titles should be designed to integrate with the work as a whole, and not look like an afterthought; ideally, they should be in production along with the film itself. Typically, the title sequence includes the name of the film, the names of the crew members and voice talent, a copyright symbol and the year of the film's release, and the name of any copyright holder. Sometimes the content is dictated in part by outside parties. For example, unions regulate how its members are listed; and a school may mandate acknowledgment that students used its facilities. Funding agencies typically require mention of their names. It is also common practice to thank institutions and individuals who have helped out, but the list of names should be considered carefully. Title sequences should be kept as short as possible, while giving adequate credit to those involved. The main point is that they should be well designed and professional.

Sound and Subtitles The edited picture is mixed with sound elements such as pre-recorded dialogue, foley sound effects, and voices recorded in ADR to accompany the visuals. If the work is to be seen in more than one country, the dialogue is dubbed—recorded in the relevant languages—or subtitles are added. Preferences for dubbing and subtitling vary in different regions in the world.

Many countries also require captioning for the hearing-impaired; video description for the vision-impaired is mandated to a lesser extent. Both processes take place during post-production. Most producers contract the work out, but in-house captioning and video description help to retain creative control over the finished product.

Distribution

To accommodate various exhibition contexts, the finished work might be distributed in a number of formats. In 2006 the Academy of Motion Picture Arts and Sciences in the

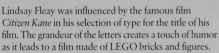

Lindsay Fleay was influenced by the famous film *Citizen Kane* in his selection of type for the title of his film. The grandeur of the letters creates a touch of humor as it leads to a film made of LEGO bricks and figures.

United States revised its guidelines for short films to allow submission of DVDs, reflecting what is likely to be the prevailing attitude. DVDs are popular—and practical. They are relatively inexpensive to produce, and they are lightweight, so are economical to mail. They are also easy to make, using software that is widely available. However, like all aspects of the production, the DVD itself should be well designed. Overly complex interfaces can discourage viewers from playing the material, so DVD menus should be simple and accessible. It is useful to include supplemental materials that relate directly to the main production—for example, production stills or a "making of" documentary.

Despite the prevalence of DVD and video technology, some film festivals still require competition works to be screened on film. Most animators prefer to edit digitally but ultimately want to print to film because of its fine resolution. Some filmmakers shoot on 16mm and "print up" to 35mm—the imagery of the smaller-gauged film is blown up so that it can be projected on the larger format.

Filmmakers who have worked on a widescreen format, 70mm for example, are faced with the problem of shrinking the imagery to fit onto film or video of a different aspect ratio (see page 20). There are two general solutions. One is "pan and scan," a kind of optical printing process in which the wide film is panned over to get the most significant imagery into the smaller frame. The operator sometimes opts to cut between parts of a frame, rather than pan over it. In either case, transitions are introduced where none existed in the original. Sometimes the transfer is not pan and scan, but includes imagery from only the middle of the frame, cutting off the edges of the widescreen original; anything on the outer left or right doesn't appear in the new version.

A second resizing option is "letterboxing," which places black lines at the top and bottom of a standard television screen in order to display the widescreen original in its entirety. Although some people complain about the smaller overall picture, the lines are handy for subtitles and captions, which can be placed on the black region, away from the image field.

Global Standards When a work is transferred to video or DVD, global standards are a concern. In the case of videos, they affect not only the recording but also the playback, as monitors are standardized to recognize the line rate of their own formats. It is possible to purchase a "multistandard deck" that will allow playback of various tapes, but it is important that it adjusts the output to the standard of the monitor being used.[13] DVDs can be recorded for use in any combination of six different regions across the world, including an "all region" option that allows the work to be played worldwide. The regions have been devised in part to confront "bootlegging," illegal copying and selling of motion pictures.

The actual distribution of the work can be handled in various ways. Work produced at a large studio might be distributed by an internal arm of the organization, or it might be handled by an outside company. Independent animators sometimes choose to self-publish and sell the work themselves, possibly using a personal website and online payment service like PayPal.

Video Formats

The world is divided into three video formats: PAL (Phase Alternating Line, developed in 1961); SECAM (Séquential couleur à mémoire, developed in 1957); and NTSC (National Television System Committee, developed in 1948).

— NTSC dominates in North America and parts of Latin America, for example.

— SECAM can be found in France, Russia, eastern Europe, and parts of Africa, among other locations.

— PAL is used in the United Kingdom, Scandinavia, much of continental Europe, parts of Africa, Australia, China, and other countries.

DVD Regions

— Region 1: Bermuda, the United States, U.S. territories, and Canada.

— Region 2: The Middle East, Western Europe, Central Europe, Egypt, French overseas territories, Greenland, Japan, Lesotho, South Africa, and Swaziland.

— Region 3: Southeast Asia, Hong Kong, Macau, South Korea, and Taiwan.

— Region 4: Australasia, Central America, the Caribbean, Mexico, Oceania, and South America.

— Region 5: The rest of Africa, the former Soviet Union, the Indian subcontinent, Mongolia, and North Korea.

— Region 6: China.

Packaging Design A DVD or video should be neatly packaged for distribution, and the promotional art created during pre-production should be used consistently to establish a visual identity for the work. Computers can print color labels and inserts; think twice before handing out a DVD or video in a generic paper cover with a handwritten title. Consider the many hours that went into planning and executing the work—the cover makes the first impression.

Each DVD and video should include vital identifying information on the label, box, and printed insert containing text:
– The title.
– The format (NTSC or PAL, for example, for a video— or the DVD region).
– The running time.
– The year of production.
– The director (at the very least, plus possibly other significant cast and crew).
– A two- to three-sentence plot summary or description of the work's objectives.
– The production's website address.
– Contact information, such as an email address, company address, and phone number.
– A copyright notice.

At the very least, the title, director's name, and copyright notice should appear on a label on the DVD or videocassette, in case it is separated from its case.

Archiving Elements

Archiving the materials used during a production should be done as soon as their function within the project is complete. The potential value of such artifacts can be immense. Digital information can provide the basis for upcoming projects. Two-dimensional artwork might be sold in the future or used as portfolio pieces for teaching and job interviews. Archived materials are also useful in making a documentary about the work, which can be distributed as a DVD supplement or posted on a website.

Papers All paper-based artistic materials should be kept in archival-standard preservation cases, such as acid-free storage boxes, in a cool, low-humidity environment. It also helps if acid-free paper is used during the creation of the work. That way, elements used in making a film will be in as good a condition as possible when they are needed in the future, possibly for exhibition, sale, or even reuse in a future production.

There are several distributors of archival-quality storage materials, including Gaylord; its website, www.gaylord.com, includes a number of practical articles about preservation of various materials, including documents, prints, drawings, pamphlets, magazines, newspapers, postcards, textiles, and photographs.

It is important to create a design concept that can be used to promote the work on posters, DVD covers, postcards, websites, and through other means.

Digital Files Keep in mind that digital formats change rapidly and there is no guarantee that in twenty (or even five) years files made today will be easy to view. As technology changes, old machinery is thrown out and replaced by something new. A good example is Super 8mm film, which was overtaken by home video formats. Ironically, many people transferred their home movies to video and threw out the originals, only to find that the video deteriorated some ten years later (while the Super 8mm would have held out fairly well in terms of picture quality—though color fading might have been a problem). The best solution might be to have a high-quality digital video transfer made. Options and updates can be found at the website of the Association of Moving Image Archivists, www.amianet.org.

Even with good intentions, it may be difficult to properly archive production artifacts. Unfortunately, many of the materials used in stop-motion production do not last long. Latex is among the worst in terms of longevity; it crumbles after a relatively short time. Students who move from place to place often hasten the demise of their artworks, throwing out production materials rather than storing them for the long term. In the case of studio-produced works, artists may have no choice in the matter. Typically, an employer owns all production materials and can do with them as it sees fit.

Final Details

The animated production may be finished, but there is still work to do. Marketing and promotion will ensure that your work gets the attention it deserves.

The Debut

By the time the premiere draws near, a good publicist will have written releases and collated press kits containing a still from the film, a plot summary, production information, a list of the principal crew members and voice talents, and—most crucially—contact information. Be sure to include a physical address, phone and fax numbers, an email address, and a website. Press kits should be sent to the local press two weeks in advance, along with an invitation to attend the screening.

There are many ways to stage a debut screening. Theatrical features are promoted in dramatic ways, with a great deal of money committed to publicity. Small-scale debuts might be as simple as a screening in a college classroom or at someone's home, followed by a wine-and-cheese party or even a potluck. Oftentimes, colleges organize an end-of-year event that brings together parents, press, potential employers, faculty, and of course the production crews. An independently owned movie theater may be willing to show a locally produced film before its feature presentation.

First Look is an annual screening held by the animation program at the University of Southern California to debut its students' films.

The main reason to hold a debut screening and party is to celebrate the completion of many months, if not years, of hard work with the people who made it possible: financial sources, cast and crew, family, friends, faculty, local businesses, or other people and institutions that were involved. This is the time to enjoy your success and thank others for their help. It is wise to distribute copies of the animation to those involved with it, and very important to write "thank you" letters (email is not enough), which can go a long way in securing help for future productions. Local libraries and film archives should be given copies of the production, along with a press kit.

Festivals

Early in the production process, the producer or publicist should list the festivals likely to show interest in the work. Animation World Network (www.awn.com) publishes a calendar of upcoming events, with links to websites. The year in which a work was released is typically the basis for its acceptance at a festival, so it is important to watch deadlines. Generally, there are categories based on various criteria, possibly including length (for example, under or over ten minutes) or production context (for example, sponsored animation, student-produced work, television series, etc.). Subtitles in the language of the country in which the festival is held are sometimes required, though English may be allowed as a default.

While submitting to festivals can be time-consuming and somewhat expensive, there are advantages to being accepted. One is that festival screenings give an artist credibility—a stamp of approval that even nonanimators (like financial sources) will understand. A second benefit is that festival screenings are seen by many people, usually including distributors who could offer to represent the animator's work, and potential employers on the lookout for new talent.

With a multitude of festivals occurring worldwide, there are opportunities to screen virtually every kind of film.

Applications II
Timing Action

In order to understand the principles of successful timing, it is useful to study various models of existing work. All animation, whether narrative or non-narrative, can be assessed in terms of the rise and fall of action. This exercise increases recognition of the timing of elements within animated productions, using both written descriptions and abstract representations of the action.

Objective:
Increasing sensitivity to the pacing of visual elements within animated productions.

You will need:
- A timer
- Several large sheets of paper
- A writing utensil
- Access to a short animated production that can be paused during play and watched repeatedly
- Means of viewing the animation (computer, television, videocassette recorder, etc.)

1

Select an animated production of a particular type: abstract work set to music, dramatic narrative short subject, or short gag-oriented cartoon.

2

Play the work through from start to finish. Watch the animation as you would normally.

3

Watch the animation again, but this time attempt to document its action in an abstract way. As the action occurs, graph it on a piece of paper using lines to create peaks, plateaus, and valleys, depending on your perception of what you see. There is no right or wrong way to create this document, though it is helpful to maintain a consistent forward motion in your graph. The main point is to demonstrate the number of instances where action rises and falls, and the general point where these changes occur within the production as a whole.

4

The third viewing will be a bit more precise. On one sheet of paper, write numbers corresponding to the running time of the film, using increments of thirty seconds. If the film runs three minutes and ten seconds, for example, the paper would list :30, 1:00, 1:30, 2:00, 2:30, 3:00, and 3:30.

5

Watch the animation for the third time, using the timer to note the pacing of the action during each thirty-second increment. It might take more than one viewing to assess and record the rhythm being established. Write descriptive phrases of your choosing to describe the action within the thirty-second period that has elapsed.

6

If the animation is gag-oriented, watch the piece once more, using the timer to measure the time that elapses between gags or instances of physical humor. You can do this by estimating: Count the number of gags within each thirty-second period and then find the average by dividing thirty by the number of gags (for example, thirty seconds divided by five gags equals an average of one gag every six seconds). Do the gags start and stop at various points, or do they occur continuously, delivered at a constant rate? Make a note as to whether gags are verbal, physical, or both. If both, how does the timing of verbal gags compare with that of physical gags?

7

If the animation is dramatic or abstract, watch the piece again, counting the time that elapses between the beginning and what you judge to be pivotal moments in the storytelling or action. Is there a steady rise in action or is the storytelling and/or choreography of images characterized by rising and falling throughout the duration of the work?

Tips and Cautions:
- Take care that your perception of the action is not overly influenced by sound components—especially score. Dialogue contributes to the delivery of verbal gags and so must be considered in a gag-oriented work. Otherwise, it could be useful to view the production with and without the sound on, to get a better perception of how the visuals are working—and an understanding of how much sound influences our perceptions.

Developing Frames

Our perception of images in motion pictures is greatly impacted by choices in framing. Wide shots provide environmental information, while close ones heighten our emotional response to the figure being depicted. Field guide frames can be used to consider different ways of framing images within a single piece of production art.

Objective:

To create a series of field guide frames and use them to make choices in framing compositions.

You will need:

- Academy format field guide
- Sheets of white photocopy paper, larger than the field guide
- Access to a photocopier
- Scissors
- Blade knife
- Cutting board or other appropriate surface
- Metal ruler
- Several large sheets of black card stock paper
- Two or three large images containing backgrounds and multiple figures or objects
- Black permanent marker, thin point
- Light-colored writing utensil

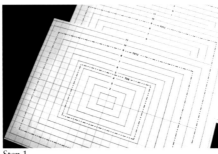

Step 1

Step 2

Step 3, a and b

1

Make eleven photocopies of the field guide on the white paper.

2

Using the metal ruler and blade, on the first copy, cut out the rectangle representing 2 field; on the second copy, cut out the rectangle representing 3 field; on the fourth copy, cut out the rectangle representing 4 field; and so on, through 11 field. Avoid cutting through the outer edge of the frame as you remove the inner rectangle. You should be left with a series of frames containing different sizes of windows.

3

Trace each frame onto the black paper using a light-colored writing utensil. Using the metal ruler and blade, cut out the rectangular centers—again, do not cut through the outer edge of the frame. Label each frame with its appropriate field size (2 field, 3 field, etc.), depending on the size of its cutout rectangle.

Developing Frames

Step 4

Step 5a

Step 5b

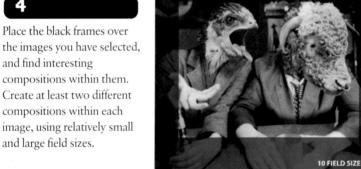

Step 5c

Step 5d

Step 6

4

Place the black frames over the images you have selected, and find interesting compositions within them. Create at least two different compositions within each image, using relatively small and large field sizes.

5

When you have determined which framings you like, use the black marker and draw around the images you've selected, just inside each frame.

6

You can use a photocopier to enlarge the "framed" areas so that all the images are one size (for example, if you created a 4-field and an 8-field image, you might enlarge them so they are both 11-field). This will give you a sense of how these portions of the art would look after being captured at the field size you have chosen.

Tips and Cautions:

— Use caution with the cutting blade. It is best to use a sharp blade and to avoid the use of strong downward pressure. If you are having difficulty getting through the thickness of the material, score the paper several times by lightly retracing the cutting line, and do not attempt to cut it with a single pass of the knife.

Twisted Wire and Clay Figure

Many animators like using twisted wire armatures because they are inexpensive and comparatively easy to create. And although they tend to break and aren't suitable for lengthy, complex animation, they work well for many purposes—including getting acquainted with stop-motion production.

To create a human figure, use various gauges of wire for the body, limbs, and extremities, and twist them for added support. A sturdy material is used to anchor the nonmoving parts around the upper torso and pelvic region, and to provide rigidity in the arms and legs. There are various ways to attach the hands, feet, and head and give flexibility to jointed areas, such as elbows and knees—and a number of options for anchoring the figure to the ground. This exercise is a basic approach that can be modified depending on time, money, skills, and needs.

Objective:
To create a simple twisted wire figure covered with clay.

You will need:
- Bond paper
- Access to a photocopier
- Light- and medium/heavy-gauge armature wire
- Two pairs of pliers, or one pair of pliers and a drill with a chuck that can be used to clamp the wire
- Plumber's steel putty
- Gloves and other protective gear (as needed)
- Nondrying oil-based modeling clay
- Small Styrofoam ball to form the basis for the head

Step 1

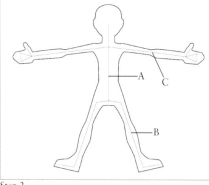

Step 2

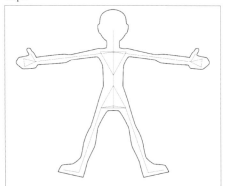

Steps 3 and 4

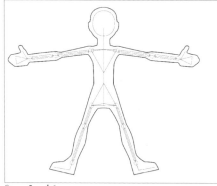

Steps 5 and 6

1

Draw the outline for a simple human character. It should be relatively short and stocky, rather than tall and thin or top-heavy. Do not worry about drawing details like hair and facial features or even muscle tone.

2

Within this outline, create three lines that represent the armature. Line A connects the arms and legs, and so acts as the spine. Line B begins at one of the feet, arches upward to the bottom of line A, and then arches downward to the other leg and the foot. Line C extends from hand to hand, passing through the top of line A.

3

Over the shoulder area, draw the top line of a triangle that points downward. The upper edge should run along the shoulders and the downward angle should intersect the spine in the upper body area. This triangular area represents the collarbone and the rib-cage region, a nonmoving part of the figure that gives strength to its upper body.

4

Draw another triangular shape in the lower part of the torso, connecting it to the leg line. This represents the pelvic region, a nonmoving part of the figure that will be reinforced to give strength to its lower body.

5

Draw circles on the armature lines for the head and at each place where joints should occur to allow movement: the shoulders, elbows, wrists, hips, knees, and ankles.

6

On the arms and legs, draw small rectangular shapes on the spaces not occupied by the circled joints. These represent the bones of the upper and lower arms and legs, which do not bend. They will be reinforced to give strength to your figure.

Twisted Wire and Clay Figure

Step 9

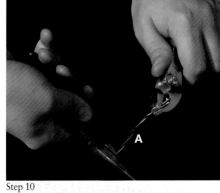

Step 10

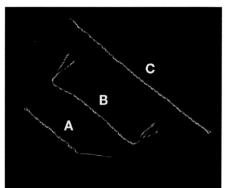

Step 11

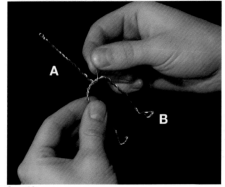

Step 12

Step 13a

Step 13b

7

Measure lines A, B, and C, and make a note of their size.

8

Cut a piece of medium or heavy wire so that it is 2½ times longer than line A. Repeat the process, using the measurements for lines B and C.

9

Fold each of the three lengths of wire in half.

10

Grip the fold of wire A with pliers, a drill chuck, or other clamp. Place a second pair of pliers on the other end of the wire, about 1 inch (2.5 centimeters) away from the end. Twist the wire until the two pieces are tightly wrapped around each other. Be sure to leave a small open loop at the fold of the wire (the arms will be threaded through this). The 1 inch (2.5 centimeters) of untwisted wire at the end will wrap around the legs.

11

Twist the folded wire B along its entire length; folding the ends up slightly for feet will help identify it as the legs. Twist folded wire C.

12

Curve wire B to form legs. Using your drawn image as a guide, wrap the loose ends of wire A around wire B in the lower torso region, with each end going down a different leg. Cut a length of thin wire and wrap it around this junction to reinforce it. Be sure to also go down each leg and up the spine a short distance.

13

At the top of wire A, in the loop that remains open, insert wire C. Twist wire A to tighten the intersection of the two pieces. Cut another length of thin wire and twist it around this intersection, reinforcing the spine and upper arms of the figure. The ends of the thin wire should extend upward above the spine, providing prongs to hold a Styrofoam head.

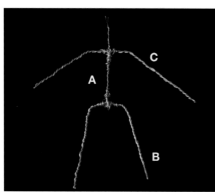

Step 14

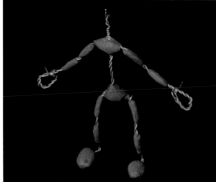

Step 15

14

You now have a wire figure that is ready to be reinforced in the upper and lower torso regions, as well as in the bone areas of the upper and lower arms and legs. Use a hardening putty product—but be sure to read the directions on the package carefully, noting all warnings. Some putties are highly toxic and you should apply them in a well-ventilated area, possibly wearing gloves and other protective gear, or select another product.

15

Take the putty and wrap it around the wires as indicated by the triangles and rectangles in your drawn guide; the putty must encircle the wires completely. Be sure there is plenty of room between the putty arm and leg "bones" for the figure's joints, as indicated by circles on your guide. And make sure the putty is dispersed in a balanced way, to avoid creating a figure that is top-heavy and loses its balance easily. Harden the putty, following directions on the product.

16

When the putty has hardened, place the Styrofoam head on the prong extending above wire A in the neck region. Shape modeling clay into thin strips and wrap it around the armature and head, building up the figure gradually, in layers. Continue until the figure's body is formed.

Tips and Cautions:

— When twisting the wire, it can be easier if two people hold it—one on each end. It is also possible to clamp one end by placing it under the leg of a chair, then sitting on the chair and twisting the other end with pliers or a drill.

— Be sure that the circular "joint" areas are large enough to allow the wires to bend easily and in more than one location. A wire that is constantly bent in one place will break quickly.

— Make sure the head you choose is not too large. Top-heavy figures fall over easily.

— Feet must be large enough to balance the body. Tie-down features are generally incorporated into them—for example, a piece of metal that can be used in conjunction with magnets, wires extending downward that can be tied to a set, or bolts that will accommodate nuts placed under metal grids on the floor of a set.

— Crumpled aluminum foil can be wrapped around the armature before modeling clay is applied, so that less clay has to be used; the result is a lighter and less expensive figure.

— Extra touches can be added using clay tools and accessories such as beads, which can be inserted as eyes.

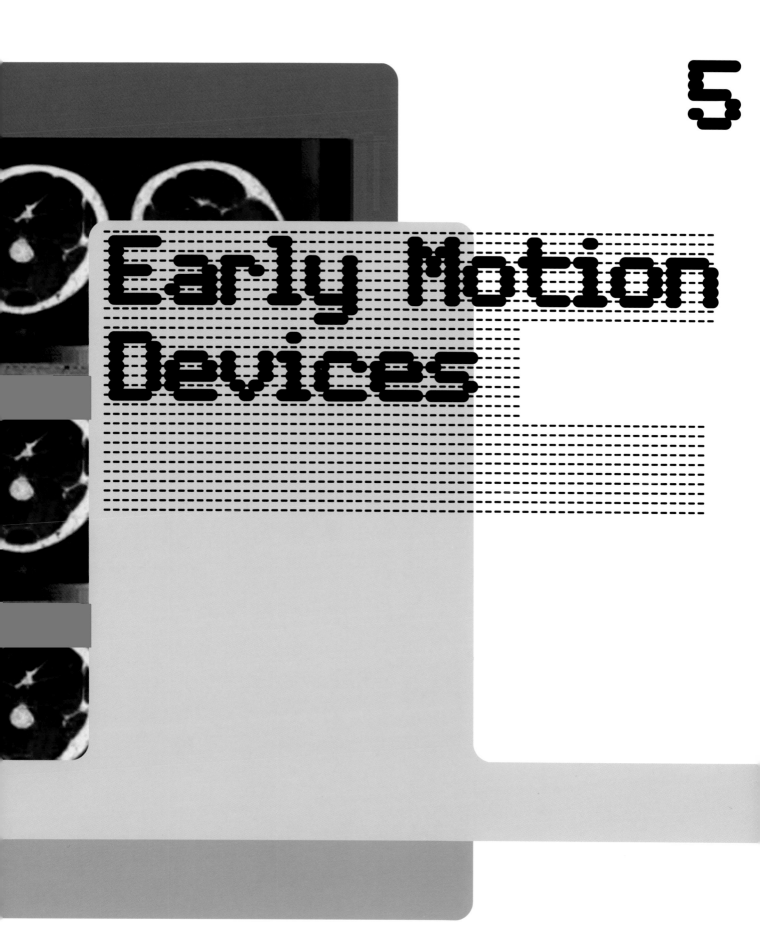

Early Motion Devices

The first animated films were projected more than a century ago, only a few years after the Lumière brothers' first public screening of live-action films, which took place in Paris in 1895. Since then, animation has developed alongside an ever-changing base of technology. However, even artists who intend to work with digital media can find inspiration in revisiting the techniques their predecessors used long before the computer made its way into everyday life.

Automata

Automata are three-dimensional inanimate objects—depicting humans, animals, and other figures—that are capable of automated movement. Some of the the earliest documentation of these devices dates from the third century BCE in writings and diagrams by Hero of Alexandria, which detail complex machines that made figures turn and move by means of hydraulic and pneumatic power. They include a figure of Hercules shooting an arrow at a hissing dragon lying under a tree, and singing birds that were operated by water pressure.[1] Throughout the world, automata have been created for many purposes, including education, entertainment, and art. They have ranged from expensive, complex curiosities created from fine materials to mass-produced, relatively simple toys made of tin, balsa wood, and heavy paper. They have often been powered by clockwork mechanisms, though

they have also been driven by air, water, mercury, and electricity, or manually. Following are examples of this diverse art practice, which is driven by impulses similar to that of animation: the desire to bring figures to life.

Theatrum Mundi

First seen in Germany in the late seventeenth century, *theatrum mundi* spread to England, France, Russia, and elsewhere during the next hundred years. They contained multiple figures and typically illustrated a historical scene; reenactments of battles and depictions of major cities were popular subjects. Some *theatrum mundi* were very complex. In *Judgement universel* (*Universal Judgment*), created by Ardax du Mont Liban in Reims, France, in 1775, 3,500 bas-relief figures moved along the stage in predetermined order, accompanied by a live commentary.[2]

Variations on *theatrum mundi* included crib scenes, which reenacted the birth of Christ. The first documented example in a church dates from 1716, in Vienna,[3] and by the mid-eighteenth century, church-based performances were supplemented by traveling ones staged by individual businesspeople from various trades, known as "mechanicians."

Human Figures

From early in the history of automata, their makers have attempted to re-create humans and their actions. For example, in the thirteenth century the English monk Roger Bacon

The "autoperipatetikos," or "self-walking" doll, patented by Enoch Rice Morrison in 1862.

reportedly made a talking head out of bronze. Around 1641, Athanasius Kircher, a German Jesuit known for inventing a wide range of early "magical machines," created a dancing female figure that performed on a stage surrounded by mirrors. A magnet manipulated the dancer's movements, and the mirrors multiplied its image, creating the impression that it was surrounded by many others. In 1838, Cornelis Jacobus van Oeckelen of the Netherlands created a life-size robot, "Android Clarinetist," that performed four classical pieces on a thirty-two-note clarinet. It appeared in the major cities of the Netherlands, as well as in Boston and New York.[4]

Children's Toys

Automated toys for children existed as early as the eighteenth century, and eventually went into large-scale production in Germany. By the mid-1800s, one of two methods of activation was typically employed: a squeezebox or a simple boxed mechanism run by a crank. In England, John Hempel produced commercially available automata that had plaster heads and wooden body frameworks held together by leather hinges and wire springs.[5] Walking and speaking dolls and tin toys made for a mass market were among the specialties that appeared within the United States. George W. Brown was the most significant of the American producers of inexpensive automata for children; he is well-known for manufacturing self-propelled trains and other toys, including walking dolls. However, the most famous walking doll was patented by

American Enoch Rice Morrison in 1862. His "autoperipatetikos" (Greek for "self-walking") employed a key-wound clockwork mechanism that operated each foot separately, allowing the doll to move on rollers concealed under metal boots. Its head was made from various materials, including wax and china, and it was the first mass-produced doll to move forward with individual steps.

Talking dolls became available during the late nineteenth century with the invention of sound-recording devices. In early 1890, the first mass-produced talking doll was manufactured in the United States by Thomas Edison, who made a fortune marketing the phonograph and other new technologies (including motion pictures). However, he was not so successful with toys. His Talking Doll, which recited a nursery rhyme, spoke by means of a sound device—a grooved wax-covered disc read by a needle—concealed within its metal body; it was the first time pre-recorded "records" had been available to the public. Edison's doll had jointed wooden limbs and a German bisque head, and was operated manually. The sound discs began to wear out after just forty or fifty uses, which proved to be problematic. The dolls were on sale for only about three weeks, after years of development. As a result, they represent one of Edison's biggest failures.

During the late nineteenth century, the French were the world's foremost creators of automata, including a moving doll known as a "bébé," which had articulated limbs and a face containing moving eyes that could shut for "sleep." Bru, a

Pre-recorded disks read by a needle (above) provided the voice for the Talking Doll, manufactured by Thomas Edison in 1890 (right). Collection of René Rondeau.

leading manufacturer of the toy, furthered this realism by patenting a nursing doll with a bottle, Bébé Teteur, in 1879; a feeding baby, Bébé Gourmand, in 1881; and a doll that threw kisses, Bébé Baiser, in 1895. In 1892, the firm created a doll that could talk, sleep, and even "breathe": a key-wound music box played a tune as its eyes closed in sleep and a small device in its chest simulated breathing. The Jumeau company's Bébé Phonographe came on the market in 1893.[6] At the Paris Exhibition of 1900, an entire room was devoted to this talking "phonograph doll." Using a wax cylinder, a young customer could record his or her voice, which became the voice track for the toy.

Display Automata

Many automata have been regarded as fine art, seen at first in the parlors of wealthy patrons, and later in museums and galleries. Paris is considered to have been the center of the finest production of this sort during the late nineteenth century, in what is described as the "golden age" of automata. French display automata typically included human figures with German bisque heads which were run by Swiss clock mechanisms and enclosed in glass.[7] However, French automaton makers also created a number of noteworthy animal figures. During the mid-eighteenth century, Jacques de Vaucanson made a mechanical duck that stood on a cabinet and was driven by more than a thousand moving parts, which allowed it to move about, eat food, digest it, and then excrete it "in a natural way."[8]

Some of the figures produced in Switzerland during the late eighteenth and early nineteenth centuries are among the most complex ever made. Those of Pierre Jaquet-Droz, one of the leading clock and automaton makers of this period, are particularly remarkable. His three greatest works, the Draughtsman, the Writer, and the Lady Musician, are said to "represent the peak of automata manufacture and mark the beginning of the modern development of the art; other figures are always judged against them."[9] The Lady Musician is the most complex of the three, with remarkable breathing and head movements. She served as a model for many future designers.[10]

Karakuri

Japan's interest in making automata—*karakuri*—began in the seventeenth century, probably because western examples were brought into the country at this time. The eighteenth century saw the popularity of the *chahakobi ningyo*, a doll that could serve tea. After receiving a cup from the host, it walked to the guest and waited; when the empty cup was returned, the automata went back to the host. Details about these figures can be found in Hosokawa Hanzo Yorinao's *Karakuri zui* (*Illustrated Miscellany of Automata*, 1798).[11] Hosokawa, Tanaka Hisashige, and Benikichi Ono were among the most famous of Japan's *karakuri* makers. They worked during the late eighteenth and early nineteenth centuries, and were considered to be scientists and visionaries in the field of technology (notably, Tanaka founded what is today known as the Toshiba Corporation).

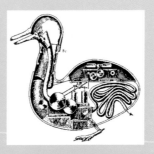 

During the mid-eighteenth century, Jacques de Vaucanson created a mechanical duck that sat on a cabinet and was able to demonstrate the digestive process.

Modern Automata

Usually much less "luxurious" than the parlor pieces of years past, modern automata, which began to appear during the 1970s, tend to be satirical and self-aware. There is less emphasis on life-like realism than on the mechanisms themselves, which are commonly open to view. Some of today's leading automata makers, including Tim Hunkin, Sokari Douglas Camp, Tim Lewis, Paul Spooner, Ron Fuller, and Andy Hazell, were among those who particpated in a group exhibition, Devious Devices, organized by filmmaker Terry Gilliam in 1998. Gilliam set themes based on eighteen objects he selected as representing the twentieth century, such as a movie camera, a test-tube baby, a car, a psychiatrist's couch, and a vinyl record.

Automata play a significant role in the theatrical performances of mime Stephen Mottram. In his hour-long critically acclaimed "The Seed Carriers," small wooden beings are captured, bred, and harvested when they are found to contain valuable seeds. The little figures writhe and wiggle in his hands and inside the small bags in which they are placed; more than forty animated objects and automata are employed. Mottram feels the figures appeal to viewers at a psychological level because they address internalized questions about the mysteries of life, birth, and death. He says, "Birth and death are events where the line between what is alive and what is not is very obscure. I have a feeling that the global fascination of puppet theater is similarly bound up with the way puppets refer to life and death at the same time. Puppets are dead things.

They are also very alive—in the right hands."[12] In his work, Mottram explores the essence of movement—an effort that is aided by the lack of dialogue, which keeps viewers' attention on the figures onstage. He draws inspiration for his work from many sources, including the animation of the Brothers Quay and the pixilation films of Norman McLaren.

Motion Studies

During the mid-nineteenth century, the development of photography opened the door for motion studies—the use of sequential photographic images to analyze human and animal locomotion. The most famous research came from two practitioners who approached their work from different angles: the showman Eadweard Muybridge and the scientist Etienne-Jules Marey. Their recordings, and those of other motion studies pioneers, can generally be classified as "series photography," in which different photographic plates are used to record individual increments of movement, and "chronophotography," where all the images of a given movement are captured on a single plate.

Eadweard Muybridge

Eadweard Muybridge (originally Edward Muggeridge) was born in 1830, in Kingston upon Thames, England.[13] He moved to the United States in 1851, and in 1867, in California, he

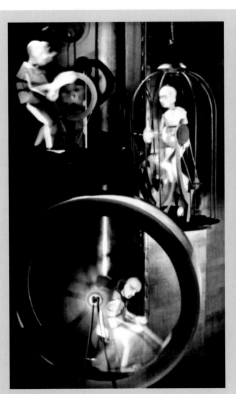

Mime Stephen Mottram performs with automata figures in "The Seed Carriers."

became a professional photographer.[14] Leland Stanford, a former governor of California and president of the Central Pacific Railroad, had bet that a trotting horse would at times have all four feet off the ground, and asked Muybridge to prove this; he did so with a series of photographs taken in 1873.[15] In 1877, Stanford sponsored additional experiments; Muybridge used a series of cameras each with a special shutter designed to release when a horse ran by and tripped a thread attached to it. The exposure speed was approximately 1/500 second, with 1/25 second elapsed time between shots.[16] The result was a series of still images demonstrating the concept of incremental movement that underlies animation.

In 1883, Muybridge received a grant of $40,000 from the University of Pennsylvania for additional work,[17] and the following years were productive: In 1884 and 1885, he took more than one hundred thousand photographs of men, women, children, animals, and birds. Muybridge himself was photographed, along with professional models, students, teachers, and others.[18] Estimates suggest that five hundred to six hundred negatives were exposed on productive days. Almost twenty thousand of these images were reproduced in Muybridge's *Animal Locomotion: An Electro-photographic Investigation of Consecutive Phases of Animal Movements*

(1887). Though it has been described as "the most comprehensive analysis of movement ever undertaken," some images are not as documentary as they seem, since there are duplicate images as well as "sequences" apparently edited together from different sets of movements.[19] Nonetheless, Muybridge's studies remain a valuable reference for animators.

Etienne-Jules Marey

Born in Beaune, France, Etienne-Jules Marey attended medical school and later proved to be an outstanding scientist. In 1859, he produced an influential thesis on the circulation of blood, and he invented the sphygmograph, which records the pulse. He also devised or adapted other instruments, including the thermograph, to track heat changes in the body, and the pneumograph, to study respiration.

In 1869 and 1870, long before motion-capture equipment recorded the movements of objects in space, Marey created harnesses for birds to register the frequency of wing movements, their relative duration, movements signaled by the wing tip, and the trajectory of the wing in flight.[20] This research eventually contributed to the development of airplane technology. In 1872, he created experimental shoes to record data related to the step and pressure of a runner's feet.[21] The same year, he made leather anklets for a horse, to register its gaits.[22]

The information Marey gathered with his devices was recorded as graphs, most of which were fairly abstract; for example, wing tracings appeared as a series of lines on the

A motion study by Etienne-Jules Marey (left) provided the inspiration for Devon Damonte's film *Rolling Man* (above).

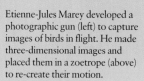

Etienne-Jules Marey developed a photographic gun (left) to capture images of birds in flight. He made three-dimensional images and placed them in a zoetrope (above) to re-create their motion.

horizontal and vertical (x and y) axes of a standard graph. Using data from the horse anklets, he created bar charts that allowed him to graphically note "the length of time each hoof had been on the ground as well as the position of each limb in each pace and the moment of transition from one pace to another."[23] The problem was that the graphing instruments could not capture movements in terms of external form.[24] Marey was inspired by Muybridge's photographs of running horses, and by February of 1882 he had developed a "photographic gun,"[25] operated by a clockwork mechanism located behind the barrel and containing a photographic lens. A shutter in the form of a disc let light through from the lens twelve times a second, for 1/720 second each time.[26] Marey used the gun, which captured twelve images on a circular dry plate, to photograph birds and bats in flight.[27]

In August of 1882, Marey received a grant of land and money from the French government to continue with his experiments in the publicly funded Station Physiologique in Bois de Boulogne.[28] There he designed his first Chronophotographe camera, which exposed images on a single fixed plate. It had a rotating disc shutter, 4¼ feet (1.3 meters) in diameter, pierced with narrow slits that exposed images ten times a second, at a shutter speed of about 1/1000 second. The camera was built inside a unit that moved on rails.[29] In 1891, Marey's assistant George Demeny developed a device called a Phonoscope. It employed a disc containing photographs of a face to demonstrate lip movements to deaf individuals, in order to teach them to speak.[30] Unfortunately,

it did not work too well, because it was difficult to see the photographed speaker's tongue.[31] However, Marey continued to develop his technology, increasing the frames per second rate for exposing negatives, and eventually altering his camera so that it could employ a strip of photographic material containing multiple frames, it was available in France by late 1888.[32]

Marey's and Muybridge's studies of studies of movement were not only useful in scientific terms; they have also inspired many artists. Marcel Duchamp's famous *Nude Descending a Staircase No. 2* (1912) reflects the influence of motion studies in its depiction of multiple poses within the single canvas.[33] Devon Damonte (see page 167) is among the animators who have incorporated Marey's studies into a film—his one-and-a-half-minute *Rolling Man* (1999), which is offered as "cinematic proof that what goes around does indeed come around."[34] George Griffin (see page 128) describes his *Viewmaster* (1976) as a "cartoon homage to Eadweard Muybridge"; it features a range of characters engaged in a perpetual walk cycle.[35] Marty Hardin, too, has incorporated motion studies into his work. In *Corpus*, he uses both looped motion studies of a man engaged in various actions, and images produced by modern visualization techniques that allow the human form to be dissected in ways Marey could only have imagined.

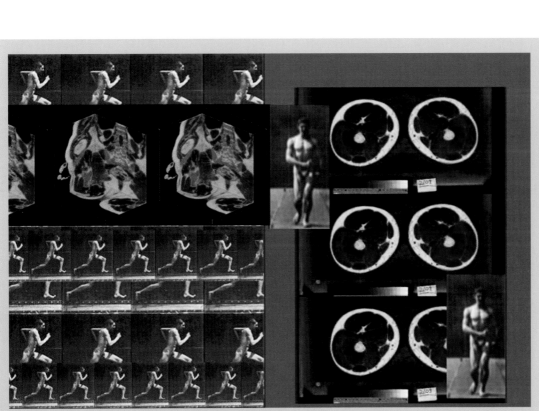

In *Corpus*, Marty Hardin has combined nineteenth-century motion studies with images created using modern visualization techniques.

Magic Lanterns, Slides, and Animated Effects

Magic lanterns are early slide projectors which employed handpainted and photographic glass plates that sometimes included stereoscopic dimensional views. They are important to the development of animation insofar as they are one of the first widely used projecting devices, and they allowed animated movement to occur. Also, magic lantern performances provided narrative conventions for the emerging field of motion picture films, including animation.

Magic Lanterns

Most sources suggest that the magic lantern was invented by Christiaan Huygens, a Dutch astronomer and inventor of the pendulum clock, in 1660.[36] Athanasius Kircher described a similar device in a 1671 version of his *Ars magna lucis et umbrae* (*The Great Science of Light and Dark*);[37] and less than a hundred years later, by the mid-eighteenth century, magic lantern shows were a well-known form of popular entertainment, particularly in France. One of the most famous magic lantern showmen was Etienne Gaspar Robert ("Robertson"), a Belgian who performed frequently in Paris from 1799. Using a portable lantern, a Phantascope, his "phantasmagoria" shows included spectacular effects, such as smoke, thunder, and lightning, as

well as unearthly content, with ghosts and phantoms playing major roles. Typically, the lanterns—as many as eight were sometimes in use simultaneously—were operated behind the screens on which they projected. Several assistants walked around with small lanterns strapped on their bodies, creating a host of eerie creatures. As the nineteenth century progressed, shows became more sophisticated, in part because performers became less itinerant, tending to play in a single established location. And illumination had improved—from the candle or small oil lamp used in the early years to the very bright light of a limelight burner, which was invented in 1826. By the mid-1850s, the use of photographic slides supplemented the older painted ones, and afforded lanterns a new scientific basis.[38]

Magic lanterns became relatively sophisticated, with a wide range of parts to enhance the performances. At the end of the nineteenth century, equipment might have featured objective lenses used for focusing; a focus knob, which moves the objective lenses; a filter slot, which holds a colored glass filter; a flap to soften the light; condenser lenses to keep the light trained on the slide; a chimney for oil-burning illuminants, smoke, and heat; a concave mirror at the back to reflect the light of the burner; a door with an inspection window and tinted glass for adjustments to the burner; a light source, typically burning oil or gas; gas pipes; a slot for slides; and a base board.[39]

Magic lanterns and their slides have had a long history, and are varied in design.

Slides

Little is known about the images projected in the earliest magic lantern shows. However, it can be surmised that the first slides used silhouette effects created by figures painted in black—in the seventeenth century Athanasius Kirchner used jumping jacks, cutout letters, devils' heads, and even living flies in his primitive device. As lantern shows became an established form of entertainment, the slides themselves became progressively more sophisticated, and the best were truly works of art, containing clear, subtle images; the historian Deac Rossell describes them as, "superior to those in the illustrated books of the day and often comparable to the genre paintings, woodcuts, and engravings that could be seen in galleries and museums."[40]

The first lantern slides were mounted in wood frames, and include images that were painted on glass. Images might be protected by a layer of transparent lacquer or a second glass that functioned as a cover. In most cases only one image appeared on each slide, but sometimes long strips of glass contained up to six images. Another variation, the single-image "panorama slide," was typically between 12 and 14 inches (30 and 35 centimeters) long, though one existing example is more than 3 feet (1 meter) in length.[41] It was moved slowly across the slide holder to show action over a wide space. "Dioramic" slides involved two pieces of glass: the background panorama and a foreground object that could be pulled across it[42]—just one form of simple "animation" available to the enterprising showman.

Mass production became possible during the 1820s, in part through the introduction of decalcomania, a process that employed transfer-like pictures; it allowed for the use of color, unlike early photography. After the mid-1850s, photographic slides were produced in great numbers. Commercially available sets typically ranged from 15 to 125 slides.[43]

The success of a magic lantern performance depended largely on tricks and effects. Some of these, like smoke and sound, were external to the lantern. However, modifications were also made to the equipment itself. Following is an overview of the various technologies used to create effects.

Dissolving Views The dissolving views technique, which was first used around 1840, entailed the transition of one picture into another by closing down the shutter on the first one while simultaneously opening up the shutter on the second; in other words, one image disappeared while another appeared in its place. A typical example would involve one slide showing a house during winter and another depicting the same house in spring. Through the process of dissolving, the storyteller effected a transition between the seasons. The most common method of creating dissolving views employed a "biunial" lantern with two lenses (one mounted above the other) and a special diaphragm that controlled the closing and opening of each.

Chromatrope Developed by the Scottish physicist Sir David Brewster in 1846, the chromatrope involves two round pieces of painted glass that can be rotated in opposite directions by a handle. As light shines through them, they create abstract images in a kaleidoscopic effect that could be used to simulate fireworks or other dazzling visuals.

Slip Slide The slip (or slipping) slide contains a movable piece that blocks out one part of a slide while another is exposed; an example is an arm that is lowered in the first instance, but raised in the next, due to the masking and unmasking of the arm positions on the slide. Slip slides allowed for rapid transitions and were often used for humorous or fantastic effects—for instance, when a man's head is replaced by that of a pig.[44] This is a type of "two-state" animation, a simple form of metamorphosis that involves only two positions.

Choreutoscope Developed by L.S. Beale in 1866, the choreutoscope allowed an increase in the number of still frames that could be animated. Charles Musser describes it as employing "a ratchet device with a front shutter that allowed [for example] six images of a skeleton to be projected in rapid succession.… The result suggested a moving image."[45] The choreutoscope fitted into the gate of an ordinary magic lantern, with images sitting in a horizontal rack.

Zoopraxiscope In about 1879, Eadweard Muybridge invented the zoopraxiscope, a device that allowed images from his motion studies to be projected with a magic lantern, so a series of stills could be reconstituted into a single moving figure. This first design of the device used a biunial magic lantern to project images from 16-inch (40.5-centimeter) rotating glass discs. Drawn images of Muybridge's series photographs appeared along the edge of each disc.

Phantascope John Arthur Roebuck Rudge created a number of magic lantern apparati, and often gave them similar names. His phantascope, developed in the mid-1880s, employed four converging lenses and a single shutter. It projected images from a slide that contained four sequenced portraits, resulting in changes in the subject's facial expression.[46]

Bi-phantascope Rudge continued to develop projecting equipment through the 1880s. His bi- (or bio-) phantascope used the principle of dissolving views to create continuous movement with a minimum of lost light. It employed two lanterns, each of which held a disc containing seven images that were projected in alternating order (one, three, five, seven on one side, and two, four, six on the other). The lens of each lantern was focused on the screen in exact superimposition, and an image in one was projected while an image in the other was being changed. Dissolvers were used to gradually cover and uncover images in alternating lanterns, so the transitions were smooth.

William Friese Greene, a pioneer in the field of cinematography, was intrigued by Rudge's invention and worked with him to create animated sequences, including one in which a man removes his head and places it under his arm (strangely, the head belongs to Rudge and the body is Friese Greene's).[47] The seven photographic slides that make up the sequence were posed individually and photographed with an ordinary still camera, so the projected movement was somewhat jerky, probably like a rudimentary pixilated stop-motion work.[48]

Two-state Devices

Two-state animation devices employ the simplest form of incremental movement: an A pose and a B pose that alternate back and forth to create the appearance of change.

Thaumatropes
A thaumatrope is a disc or rectangle with images printed on both sides. Using strings that extend from the device, the two images are spun around until they merge into one. For example, if a bird is on one side and a cage is on the other, turning the thaumatrope creates the illusion that the bird is in the cage.

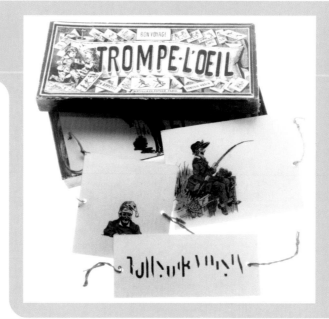

Thaumatropes from the collection of Andy Voda.

This device was first marketed in 1825 by Dr. John Ayrton Paris, a prominent figure in English medicine, who promoted it as an educational device.

Historian Richard Leskosky explains that Paris and others experimented with the basic thaumatrope model until well into the twentieth century, incorporating frames and different turning mechanisms. Some modifications were made to try to regulate the rate of spin, and at least one type of thaumatrope was spun vertically not horizontally.[49] Even simple design changes affect the way the device works. For example, if string is threaded through both sides and twirled using the four extending strings, the spin will be even and the two images will be aligned in space. If the threads are knotted on one end, so only two extending strings (one on each side) are used to spin the disc, one of the images will be a little closer to the viewer during rotation. As a result, the effect will be slightly three-dimensional.[50]

A lenticular, or winky, is a toy with a ridged surface on which two images appear—one on the right side of the ridges and the other on the left. When it is tipped to one side, one of the images is visible, and when it is tipped in the other direction the second image appears. Moving the device from one side to the other causes two-state animation.

Kaleidoscopes

Invented by Sir David Brewster in 1816, a kaleidoscope is a tube-like device containing objects at one end and mirrors that reflect them in random, abstract patterns. Since his time, kaleidoscopes have evolved into an art form practiced worldwide—a form of expression that can be related to abstract animation.

There are four distinct types of kaleidoscope: the teleidoscope, wheelscope, marblescope, and, most common, cellscope. The teleidoscope has no endpiece, only a clear lens that turns everything in its range into a kaleidoscopic image. It has been said that "the ultimate value of the teleidoscope is the potential each viewer has to see the artistic value of his own environment."[51] The other three have varying types of endpiece. One, two, or more wheels of various sorts comprise the endpiece of a wheelscope. The marblescope, in contrast, holds one or more marbles. The endpiece of the cellscope is an enclosed case that contains colored objects. These cells can be dry-filled with tumbling pieces, liquid-filled with floating materials, or they can be empty to allow a personal choice of items; commonly used objects include stained glass, dried flowers, agates, clear or colored oils, beads, marbles, semiprecious stones, or any transparent, colored objects. The cell itself can be clear, frosted, or etched; recessed, flush, or protruding; or sidelit with a black backdrop.[52]

Kaleidoscopes of various designs (above) and phenakistoscopes (right).

The interior of a kaleidoscope contains two, three, four, or more mirrors that run its full length. Their number, type, and the angles at which they are placed are of central importance to the formation of imagery. The number used determines the patterns that are formed, which can range from circular to rectangular or other symmetrical shapes. The best type of mirror is a first-surface or front-surface one; it has silvering on the front of the glass. Back-surface mirrors produce duller and sometimes blurred images. Angles play a part because they determine how many reflections or points there will be within the imagery.[53]

Multiframe Animation Devices

Multiframe animation devices demonstrate animated movement in short segments, sometimes projected onto a screen.

Phenakistoscope

A phenakistoscope is a disc, fixed at its center so it can spin freely, that contains a cycle of animated action. The images are drawn or painted around the edge of the disc on the side that will be turned away from the viewer when the device is operated; each image is positioned between a slit in the outer edge of the phenakistoscope. The viewer stands in front of a mirror, spins the disc, and looks through the slits at the reflected images, which form an animated loop. The device was invented by the Belgian physicist Joseph Plateau in 1832;[54] the Austrian Simon Ritter von Stampfer around the same time created a similar object, which he called the stroboscope.

A projecting version of the phenakistoscope was developed in 1847 by Ludwig Leopold Dobler, who was considered to be the finest magician in Europe at the time.[55] The kinesiskop, also a projecting form of the device, was developed during the mid-1850s by Jan Evangelista Purkinje, a noted eastern European physiologist. It employed a disc that held nine photographs. In 1861, he used it to demonstrate the workings of the human heart and circulation of blood.[56]

While technology has changed, phenakistoscopes continue to inspire. An example is the kinetic sculpture *Man With Flowers* (2004) by the American artist Steve Hollinger. A large copper spinning wheel contains a loop of sequential images that depict a silhouetted man bending onto one knee while presenting a bouquet of flowers to an unknown recipient. His image is cut into the wheel and is seen through a small piece of glass at the top of the sculpture as light from a small strobing LED passes through it.

Zoetrope

Invented by William George Horner in 1834, a zoetrope employs a spinning drum that has narrow slits placed equidistantly. A long strip of paper that contains a cycle of images is placed inside the drum. As it rotates, the images, seen through the

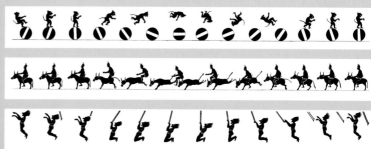

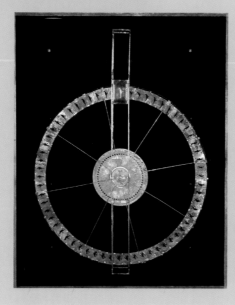
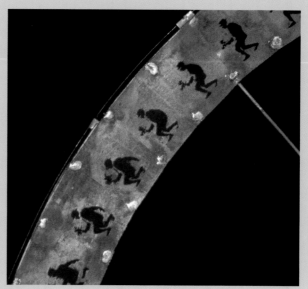

Zoetrope and three zoetrope strips (above).

Steve Hollinger's *Man With Flowers* (right) utilizes a phenakistoscope design. The detail shot (far right) shows the images cut into a metal wheel which are illuminated as they pass by an LED at the top of the sculpture.

slits, appear to be moving. In a variation dating from 1887, Etienne-Jules Marey placed 3D plaster figures of a bird in flight inside the spinning drum to reconstitute their movement[57] (see page 120).

Praxinoscope

The praxinoscope is similar to a zoetrope, but there are no slits in the drum; instead, mirrors are placed in the middle of the device. When the drum spins, viewers look into a mirror and see the images reflected in it. Frenchman Emile Reynaud invented the praxinoscope in 1877, and within two years he had developed a further innovation, the Praxinoscope Théatre, which has a scenic proscenium that makes the moving image appear within a miniature theatrical set.[58] In 1888, Reynaud incorporated projection into this device so that it could be seen by a group of people.

Flipbooks

A flipbook is linear in form, in contrast to phenakistoscopes, zoetropes, and praxinoscopes, which are cyclical. Consisting of a paper booklet, each page contains one in a series of sequential drawings or photographs. When the pages are flipped through from start to finish, they depict animated movement. John Barnes Linnett is said to have invented the flipbook—also known as a kineograph or flick book—in 1868.

In 2005, Kunsthalle Düsseldorf put the spotlight on this art form when it held an impressive exhibition, Daumen kino

[Thumb Cinema]: The Flip Book Show, which was accompanied by an equally impressive book and DVD. It included such diverse works as *A Movie of Me* (ca. 1933), featuring the child actress Shirley Temple; *Cyclopedia of Drawing* (2004) by William Kentridge (see page 198), created with charcoal images placed over text; and Laercio Redondo and Birger Lipinski's *Final Cut* (2004), which has razor blades placed along the flipping edges of its pages. All genres can be found in flipbooks, from pornography to comedy to self-aware analyses of the medium itself.

Flipbooks have inspired a number of animators to create works that explore the nature of cinema and its frame-by-frame examination of the real world. For example, *Circulation* (2002) by the Japanese animator Shizuko Tabata shows a girl in a field who changes position as photographs of her are gradually removed from a stack; these are moved about a tabletop in a circular pattern until they have all cycled through the path, gradually rebuilding the stack in the final position, next to where it began. Another Japanese animator, Maya Yonesho, has made a number of flipbook-influenced films using sketchbooks, including *Üks Üks* (2003), a complex work that depicts animated forms moving around first one open sketchbook, and then a series of them arranged close together, so the forms can flow from one to another. A multiplane camera setup was used so books could be placed on various levels.

Praxinoscope (below).

Maya Yonesho utilized a multiplane setup (left) to animate flipbooks for her film *Üks Üks* (above).

Case Study: George Griffin

George Griffin has been a role model for many animators, helping to unify, define, and promote independent production within New York City and its environs; he is also a leading figure in commercial animation. *Frames*, an anthology he organized and edited in 1978, is the most significant publication to document the free-spirited, artistically vital 1970s in American animation history.[59]

The late 1970s were a high point of independent animation in New York; as Melissa Chimovitz writes: "With Griffin as the driving force, animators ... redefined animation with their unique personal approaches to filmmaking. Aligning themselves more with the art world than with the traditional animation establishments of the time, these filmmakers were decidedly anti-

commercial, often irreverent, sometimes even superior, but always expressive."[60] She further explains that his work has reflected "two of the major characteristics of the independent movement: a responsibility to himself as an artist and to his own style, and the freedom to experiment and change that style as often as he wishes." Two of Griffin's most interesting works, *Trikfilm 3* (1973) and *Head* (1975), reflect a mid-1970s concern with structuralism (that is, structuring systems), which manifests itself in a critical view of the creative process of animation and the way in which animated imagery operates. Both films were featured in the 2005 Daumen kino exhibition.

Griffin grew up in Tennessee and earned a degree in political science from Dartmouth College in New Hampshire, where he worked as a cartoonist for a literary magazine. His political interests led him to produce antiwar posters, and eventually into the realm of

experimental film. Griffin explains that he was influenced by the local film society, where he was inspired by visiting artists Stan Brakhage (see page 156) and Jonas Mekas, and the films of Robert Breer and Stan Vanderbeek. He says, "These film explorers were my introduction to animation as an experimental form, which might include drawing, photography, scratching, burning. Though not particularly ideological, they were revolutionary, perfect analogs for the defiant anarchism of the counterculture."[61]

Griffin's early freelance jobs included work on commercials, an aborted series, Ralph Bakshi's *Fritz the Cat* (1972), and "The Electric Company" (an offshoot of the Children's Television Workshop's [CTW] "Sesame Street" series). Griffin notes, "At that time other animators [e.g., Eli Noyes, Don Duga, Fred Mogubgub, Al Jarnow] were also balancing their output of independent

films by producing spots for CTW, following the principal example of John and Faith Hubley. Their studio hired young apprentices (including me, only for a weekend, to draw a storyboard for a commercial), who learned much of their spirit of creative play in both theatrical and commercial work."[62] Griffin strongly disliked the hierarchical system of most studios; he realized that the freedom he desired was contingent upon his ability to control all the elements of production. To do so, he had to reduce the animation process drastically—it had to be simple enough for him do everything by himself. He explains, "As I learned more of the history of animation, I began to formulate a critical analysis of the studio system and recognized the need for another production model. The most important first step was simply 'doing my own thing.'"[63] In 1971, he and three other individuals set up a collective, Metropolis Photoplays, which by 1976 had evolved into Metropolis Graphics, headed by Griffin alone.[64]

Within this small studio context, Griffin began to take on jobs that contributed to his development as an artist and commercial animator. He explains:

Crossing the line between the studio system and the independent mode of production had stylistic and economic consequences. Without a conventional cel animation team, I (and others) discovered more reduced graphic strategies like working directly on paper, cutouts, unconventional coloring techniques. And working directly with an agency or producer meant that you became a subcontractor, a supplier, not a salaried employee: more money, more responsibility, and a closer relationship with those who commission and edit mass media content.[65]

Griffin's first independently produced films reflected his anarchic vision, reacting against the excess of studio works as well as the conservative tendencies of commercial production. His youthful idealism is apparent in an essay he wrote at the time, "Cartoon, Anti-Cartoon," which includes discussion of his own films. In it, he laments the separation of artist from work that occurs within the assembly-line process of big studio animation production. As examples of alternative practices, he discusses several of his own films and what they achieve, including the "unmasking of illusion" that occurs in *Trikfilm 3* and *Head*—works that directly challenge the "invisible" nature of cinema and the frame by frame recording process. He writes that *Trikfilm 3* "is one of a series of flipbook films set to sections of Bach's *Well-Tempered Clavier*, in which I explore variations in shooting small-scale sequences drawn on dime-store memo pads. The title, referring to the German word for animated film, contains an appropriate connotation of magic."[66]

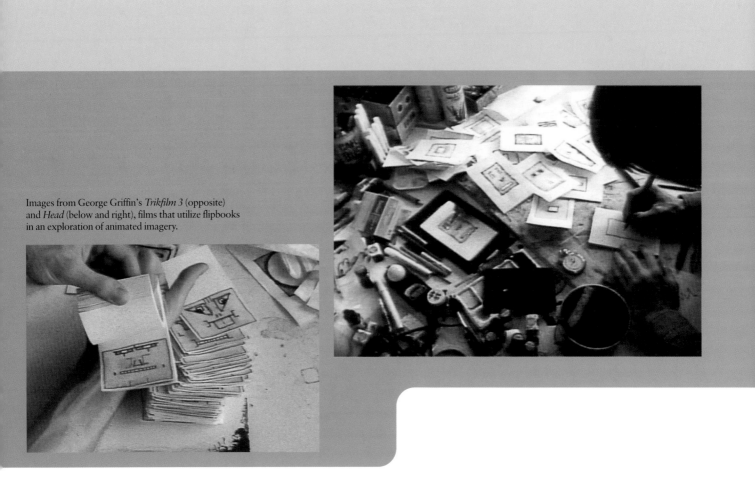

Images from George Griffin's *Trikfilm 3* (opposite) and *Head* (below and right), films that utilize flipbooks in an exploration of animated imagery.

In this film the unmasking of reality occurs through the contrast of two environments: "The flipbook's 'art' is embedded in a larger field which we associate with 'reality,' though both zones are actually recorded frame by frame. The organized flow of lines is recapitulated smoothly, while the documentary photography appears jerky and unreal. Many of us [Eli Noyes, Jane Aaron, Al Jarnow] were intrigued by this paradox and used it in our work."[67] In the late 1970s, Griffin wrote, "Live photography or reference to process was used in … early animation as a framing device. Today it is a key to understanding self-referential animation" of the sort he and other filmmakers were creating at that time.[68] In such works, artists explored the borders between the real and the fabricated, and the ways in which an artistic expression is created.

Griffin also sees his films as addressing issues related to the origins of animation. He explains: "Flipbooks represent the pre-cinema roots of animation: synthetic motion instigated by the hand, a peep show without the gears and cranks. Even though I often call the flipbook a machine, a primitive technical apparatus without which animators are no different from other artists, it really is a book, an art object with a rich history stretching back to cylinder seals and papyrus."[69] In *Head*, Griffin pays homage to the earliest copyrighted motion picture, *Fred Ott's Sneeze*, filmed by Edison employee W.K.L. Dickson in 1894; he does this not only "to remind us of our pre-movie roots, but also the spontaneous, irrational element of animation (one thinks now of [the experimental animation pioneer] Emile

Cohl…)."[70] The film involves renditions of Griffin's own head going through the sneeze as well as various other actions.

In both *Trikfilm 3* and *Head*, the tools Griffin used to create the animation are clearly visible (again, unmasking the means of production, usually kept out of view). In *Trikfilm 3*, Griffin wanted to reveal how easy it is to animate, and to encourage others to take the tools of production into their own hands. To emphasize the ordinary nature of animation, Griffin drew images using inexpensive, readily available materials, and worked within a fairly unremarkable environment. This fact, he says, is "clearly indicated by the documentary lens focused on my kitchen table, surrounded by dirty dishes and squalor. I wanted to suggest that animation, despite the mystique engendered

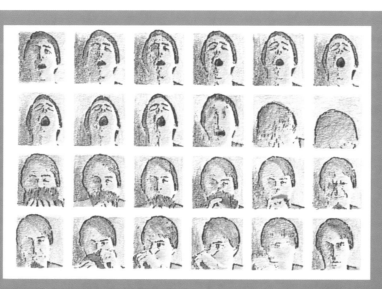

This series of frames from George Griffin's *Head* (above) is an homage to the Edison film *Fred Ott's Sneeze* (right), dating from 1894.

A "Schematic Storyboard" (opposite) was used to organize the nonlinear structure of George Griffin's *Head*.

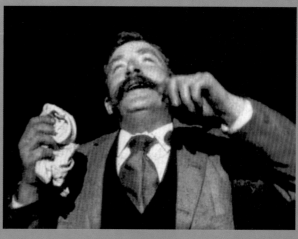

countless times by Disney, was in fact a rather simple process and required no particular specialized, professional equipment. A child could do it. Everyone doodles!"

Most of Griffin's films are planned and executed in a relatively traditional manner from conception, through storyboard, layout, animation, and artwork rendering, to final shooting. *Head*, however, developed differently, with a nonlinear structure built around small independent parts. Griffin writes: "The numerous strategies employed in *Head* (variations in scale, temporal direction, shape) were originally conceived as unrelated experiments. From the postage stamp-size self-portraits, made by automated photo booths, to the full-size room containing a real human holding a Xerox of a filmed frame enlargement of his self-portrait, the eye must continually travel back and forth to establish context and impose order."[71]

He explains how the images of the artist work to achieve different objectives. *Trikfilm 3* contains:

only images of the animator's hands, while *Head* reveals his face as well, setting up a system of mirrored self-images. A sync-sound, live headshot of the animator at the film's beginning, explaining that his drawings have become simpler in style as his face has aged into complex "character," is contrasted to an animated self-carica-ture who delivers the same monologue at the end. *Head* then is self-referential in its double focus on the mediating process of art and the image of the artist. Both gain meaning most when seen in relation to one another.[72]

Griffin linked the separate parts of *Head* together using a chart he created to visualize the structure of the film. He stitched scenes together "according to a well-defined plan balancing drawing, photography, and xerographic copies of photos. The editing

strategy allowed me to offer some comparisons between machine and handmade art; between original, unmediated gestural strokes and the decay of reproduction; between different time zones, particularly the passage of linear time that cinema conventionally proposes: beginning, middle, end."[73]

In the thirty years since Griffin made *Head*, many aspects of the animation industry have changed. With fellow animators Paul Fierlinger and David Ehrlich, he has discussed the role of drawing on paper in animation. He says, "Paul alone feels it can be dispensed with, except for doodling while chatting on the phone. As an echo of the 'paperless office' he touts himself as a 'paperless animator.' The term would apply equally to Flash animators, CGI, in fact anyone who relies exclusively on the digital tablet instead of marking on paper." For Griffin—commercial animator, independent filmmaker, and flipbook creator—paper continues to provide the foundation for animation practice in its various forms.

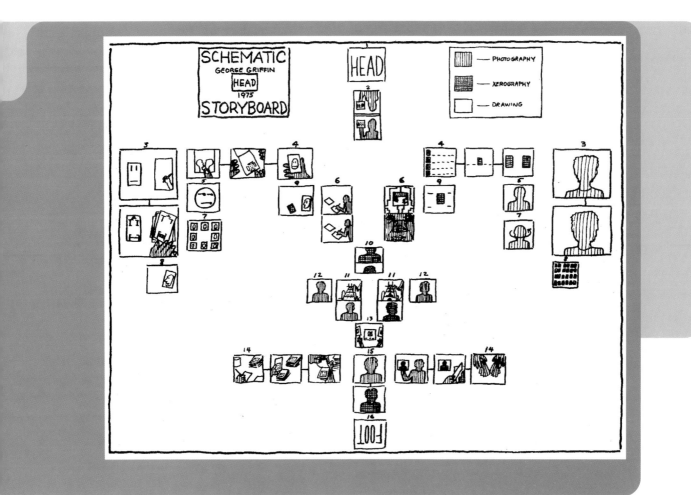

Applications III
Thaumatrope

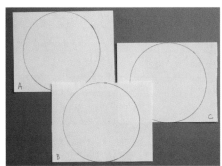

Step 1

The process of creating a thaumatrope allows animators to explore the most basic level of intermittent movement: a series of only two frames that overlap to form a combined image. This project illustrates that interest can be generated at the level of the frame, through careful attention to detail and the way in which one image relates to the next in a sequence.

Objective:

The creation of a thaumatrope, demonstrating the perception of sequential images as a unified whole.

You will need:

- Circular stencil or object for drawing circles, approximately 2¾ inches (7 centimeters) in diameter
- Drawing media, including a pencil
- Lightweight drawing paper
- Scissors
- Light table
- Clear adhesive tape
- Glue stick
- Lightweight cardboard
- Single-hole punch
- Heavy thread or lightweight cord

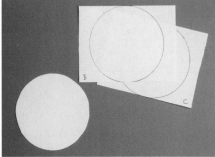

Step 2

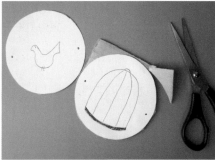

Step 6

Step 10

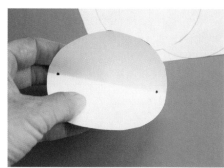

Step 4

Step 7

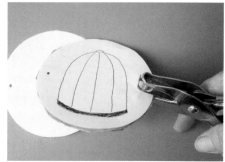

Step 11

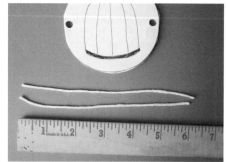

Step 13

Step 15

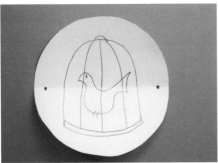
Step 5

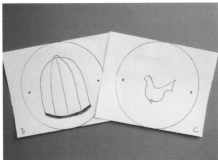
Step 8

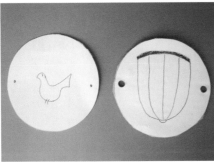
Step 12

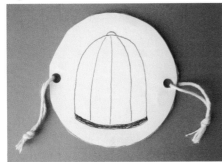
Step 16

1

Use the circular stencil to draw three circles (A, B, and C) on lightweight drawing paper.

2

Cut out one of the circles (A), and set the other two (B and C) aside to be cut out later.

3

Gently fold circle A in half and make a slight crease in it.

4

Make a dark pencil dot in the crease, ¼ inch (0.6 centimeters) from each side of the circle; these two marks indicate the sides of the images, where holes will be punched in the final figures.

5

On circle A, draw a simple figure containing two parts (for example, a bird and a cage, the sun shining over ocean waves, or a butterfly fluttering around a flower); remember to keep the pencil dots at the sides of the images.

6

Place circle A on a light table and tape it down.

7

Place (uncut) circle B over the drawing and draw half the image from circle A (for example, the cage); trace the two pencil dots indicating where holes will be punched.

8

Place (uncut) circle C over the drawing and draw the second half of the image from circle A (for example, the bird); trace the two pencil dots where holes will be punched.

9

Cut out circles B and C.

10

Glue circle B onto lightweight cardboard, and cut it out.

11

Punch holes in circle B, using the two pencil marks at the side of its image for registration.

12

Turn circle B upside down and flip it over.

13

Glue circle C onto the back of B, using the punched holes as guides for placing the pencil marks. You can use a light table to see the holes through the paper of circle C more easily.

14

Carefully register the single-hole punch over circle B's punched holes, and punch the area again to remove the circle C paper. You should now have a cardboard circle with images on both sides (one right side up and the other upside down), and two punched holes. Trim any cardboard that shows through on either side.

15

Cut two 6-inch (15-centimeter) lengths of lightweight cord or heavy thread.

16

Place one piece through a hole and knot the two ends together. Repeat on the other side with the second piece.

17

Twist the cords back and forth, using your thumbs and forefingers, until the thaumatrope spins rapidly and combines the images on both sides.

Flipbook

Flipbooks are useful for helping animators to consolidate ideas, and to get an entire story, or aesthetic objective, expressed within a short period of time. If they can be easily reproduced, they also make interesting calling cards to give to potential employers or clients. This project provides the opportunity to draw animation by hand within a limited context: the two or three seconds of action provided by a flipbook.

Objective:

To create a fifty-page flipbook that explores the aesthetics of incremental movement, metamorphosis, and movement on three axes (x, y, and z).

You will need:

- Spiral sketchbook no bigger than 4 x 6 inches (10 x 15 centimeters) and no smaller than 2 x 3 inches (5 x 7.5 centimeters); it must contain at least fifty pages and the binding holes must be on the short side of the book
- Light table
- Drawing media or other creative materials
- Writing utensil
- White paper (for storyboard)
- Large needle
- Thread
- Lightweight card stock paper
- Scissors
- Glue stick
- Ribbon or cord, approximately 1 foot (30 centimeters) long

Step 1a

Step 1b

Step 7

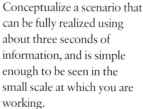
Step 8

1

Remove the spiral binding that holds the sketchbook together. The holes in the paper will be used to bind the flipbook, so be sure to leave them intact.

2

Only the outer two-thirds of the pages can be used, since the inner one-third (the hole side) is covered when the pages are pinched together for flipping. Take one sheet of the sketchbook paper and mark out the inner one-third. The remaining area will be used as a guide to create windows for the storyboard.

3

Conceptualize a scenario that can be fully realized using about three seconds of information, and is simple enough to be seen in the small scale at which you are working.

4

To create dynamic movement, consider how the scenario can maximize incremental movement (moving around, rather than remaining in one spot), metamorphosis (changing shape), and movement on all three axes (x, or left/right; y, or up/down; and z, or foreground/background).

5

Create a rough ten-frame storyboard to guide the overall development of the book. Use arrows to indicate how figures will move from one frame to the next. The first window (1) should contain the first image of the flipbook and the last window (10) should contain the last.

6

Now make a more refined storyboard. On a blank sheets of paper, create ten windows, each one the size of the two-thirds area on the sketchbook paper guide you created.

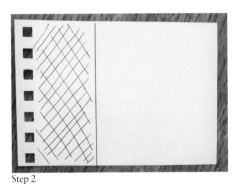
Step 2

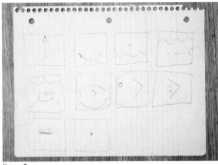
Step 5

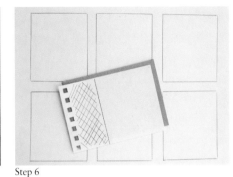
Step 6

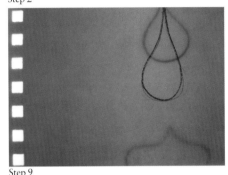
Step 9

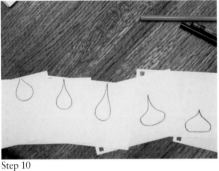
Step 10

7

Translate the rough storyboard sketches into images that are almost exactly like the ones for the flipbook. You can add color to this storyboard to test the look before committing yourself to the final artwork. Number the windows with the following frame numbers: 1, 5, 10, 15, 20, 25, 30, 35, 40, 45, 50.

8

Trace each storyboard window onto a separate piece of flipbook paper. Write the number that corresponds to the window number in the inner (spiral-edge) side of the paper. This will help you to keep the images in order as you work.

9

Begin animating by placing flipbook frame 1 and flipbook frame 5 on the light table, directly over each other. Place a clean sheet of flipbook paper on top of them to form a stack of three papers. Draw an image in the middle of the two reference images to represent the halfway point (in this case, frame 3). Use only a pencil or pen to outline the image; coloring will come later. Number the frame on the spiral edge of the paper.

10

Repeat this process, creating frame 2 as an in-between of frames 1 and 3; then create frame 4 as an in-between of frames 3 and 5. Continue this process until all the in-between images have been drawn.

11

When you have completed all the primary sketches, begin the coloring process. It is best to color one figure from start to finish (on every page), and then to move onto a second figure, and a third, and so on. This keeps the colors consistent.

12

Check that all the flipbook pages are in order. You might like to place the pages back to front, to allow flipping from bottom to top so the pages fall flat (when pages are flipped from front to back, they arch and the images are harder to see).

13

Add five blank pages to the front and end of the flipbook, to aid with the flipping process and with assembly (the first and last pages will be glued to the cover, so they cannot contain images).

Flipbook

Step 14

Step 15

Step 16

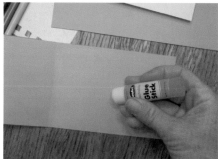
Step 17a

Step 17b

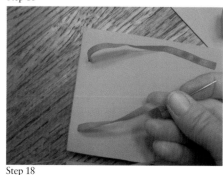
Step 18

14

Use needle and thread to stitch the pages together, using the holes of the spiral binding. Be sure that the thread binding is very tight, and that the pages are stitched so that the flipping edge is evenly aligned. If it is not even, the book will not flip properly.

15

Using card stock paper, cut out a cover for the book. It must be the same height as the book, and twice its width, plus the depth ("spine") of the fifty pages. For example, the cover for a 4 x 6-inch (10 x 15-centimeter) book with a ½-inch (1.25-centimeter) spine must be cut to 4 inches (10 centimeters) high and 12½ inches (31.25 centimeters) wide.

16

Fold the cover so that there is a central part that can be fitted around the flipbook spine area. Gently scoring the inner side of the spine edges with scissors helps to make the creases look sharp.

17

Generously coat the front, back, and spine areas of the cover with glue. Insert the bound flipbook pages into the cover, pushing it deep into the spine. When the pages are in place, press the first page against the glue on the front cover, and press the last page against the glue on the back cover.

18

For extra reinforcement, thread a needle with ribbon or cord and, working from back to front, pull the ribbon or cord through the cover and one spiral hole at the top of the book and one hole at the bottom. Tie or knot it firmly.

19

Design your cover. Create an image based on the content; include a title for the book and your name. Glue them on the cover. Trim the cover so that it is just slightly narrower than the pages of the flipbook, to help with the flipping process.

Step 19

Tips and Cautions:

— Start planning early; the project will probably take longer than you think.

— Consider how the book will be bound before you begin drawing; if pre-punched paper is not used, it is vital to punch the paper as a first step, to ensure flipping will be possible when the book is completed.

— It is important not to hand-trim the flipping edge of the book as any irregularities will impede the flipping process; shorter pages will be bypassed.

— Remember to draw only on the outer two-thirds of each pages (leave the one-third on the binding edge blank).

— You probably should not attempt to use "cuts" in the action to depict two or more scenes; these common cinematic transitional devices do not translate to flipbooks, in part because the total running time of the action is too short.

— Remember that an image by itself might look awkward, though it works when flipped in the sequence of other images.

— Remember to include a few blank pages at the beginning and end, so that all parts of the action can be seen easily.

— While any technique (stamps, photocopies, etc.) can be used, be aware that items pasted onto pages tend to impede flipping and/or fall off.

6

Direct Filmmaking: Practice and Presentation

Direct—sometimes called "cameraless"—filmmaking is a vast area. It may be narrative or non-narrative in content; figurative or abstract in form; synchronized or nonsync in sound (or silent); black-and-white or color in imagery; gag-oriented, dramatic, or meditative. Additionally, its images and sound can be created in a range of ways: scratching on dark (usually black) film, drawing or painting on clear or white film, working on "exposed" film (sometimes "found" footage), and even applying objects to the film itself. Some individuals who work directly on film consider themselves to be experimental filmmakers more closely connected to live-action productions than animation. Others see their work as an extension of photography, printing, painting, or even performance art. The realm of direct film work also extends to post-production, where hand-developing processes can be manipulated to create a wide range of effects.

Related Art Practices

The production of direct film is closely allied with many arts in addition to drawing and painting, some of which are described as follows.

Miniatures

Artists working directly on the surface of film deal with frame sizes as small as 8mm, 16mm, 35mm, and 70mm, which links them to the long-standing practice of miniature art. Although various criteria are used to identify a work as a miniature, a common requirement is that it be created at one-sixth actual size (of the depicted figure) or less. A fine miniature has been described as one that "can be magnified many times and it will still hold together as a fine work of art of much greater size."[1] Certainly this is true of animation made directly on film— when projected, its imagery will be viewed at many times the size of the original frame.

Batik

The art of batik—using a "resist" method to create designs on on fabric, or even leather, paper, wood, or ceramics—has been practiced for many centuries, in the Far East, Middle East, central and southeastern Asia, central Africa, and India. Today, the finest examples are associated with Java, Indonesia. Typically, wax is applied to the fabric in a pattern, using a pen or stamp,[2] and when the cloth is immersed in dye the color soaks in everywhere except where the wax was applied. After the dye has dried, the fabric is boiled to remove the wax. Many direct filmmakers have used similar techniques to create patterns on film. Hot wax is likely to damage the

Rose Bond (above) creating the miniature art used in her films by drawing directly on film stock, using a fine pen to trace images from a paper guide.

Helen Hill (left) developing film by hand.

film, so it cannot be used. Petroleum jelly works well, if color is applied over it carefully, so it doesn't rub off. Small stickers also can be used in a resist process.

Stencils

A stencil is created by cutting a shape out of paper or some other material. It is then placed over a base and paint or other media is applied within the cutout area. Like batik, stencils have been used for centuries; examples have been found in prehistoric cave paintings. They are convenient to use in direct animation to create consistent shapes from frame to frame.

Airbrush

A relatively recent innovation—invented at the end of the nineteenth century—the airbrush is an atomizer device that uses compressed air to spray a liquid, such as paint, onto a surface. It has been used extensively in commercial animation production, particularly to create backgrounds. The paint can be applied transparently or opaquely, depending on the thickness and the type used. Typically, designs are developed from background to foreground, using "frisket" film (sheets of clear, self-adhesive material) to cover areas that should not be sprayed. The airbrush and other spraying devices effectively apply a random mist of droplets on film stock.

Engraving

The term "engraving" describes both a procedure and the product resulting from that procedure. This practice involves creating a design by cutting into a material, coating it with ink or paint, and using it to print onto a base surface. "Scratch films," made by drawing on black film with a sharp instrument, are its equivalent in the context of animation, but the lines are not reproduced with ink or paint; instead, light is used to "print" them onto the screen. Another related practice is the use of engraved stamps to apply images to film, which is then projected.

Collage

The art of collage—gluing different materials together to create a composition—takes its name from the French *coller* ("to glue"). It first gained respect as a modern art form between 1907 and 1925, within Cubism, when Pablo Picasso and Georges Braque became known for incorporating cloth, newspaper, and other objects into their largely abstract works. Though the surface area of a film frame is tiny, many direct animators have created imagery through collage.

Photograms

To create a photogram, an object is placed on a photosensitive surface (paper or other material), which is then exposed to light. The technique is ideal for direct filmmaking, as an

Bärbel Neubauer's *Firehouse* (below) was created using a photogram technique, placing objects on unexposed film in a darkroom and then making exposures frame by frame with a small light source.

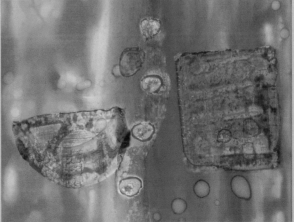

Bärbel Neubauer used a variety of stamps (left) to create her direct film *Algorithmen* (below).

unexposed filmstrip can be imprinted with the images of objects placed on it. These objects are illuminated with a small flashlight or other light source, with the resulting image dependent on the length of exposure, the placement of the objects, the way in which the light is moved over them, and other variables.

Probably the best-known creator of photograms is the American photographer, painter, and filmmaker Man Ray, who moved to Paris in 1921 and became a major figure in Dada and Surrealism.[3] Ray was so influential in this art form that "rayogram" is the term often used to describe direct-film projects of this sort.

Presentation Strategies

The English artist Stuart Hilton, who became well-known for his use of Letraset and other stick-on materials in direct-film station identifications for MTV during the early 1990s, has said he did not concern himself with narrative or even principles of animation. Rather, he used "a plan, a simple system to dictate the structure of my work."[4]

Within the general category of direct film, various structuring practices have developed, so that we can describe these works as visual music, narrative storytelling, and compilations involving found footage, for example. Like Hilton, most direct filmmakers do not see their works as falling within simple categories of conventional animation.

Visual Music

Visual music describes an exploration of direct correspondences between sound and image (form, color, and movement) in painting, animation, and other arts—the pursuit of an equivalent to music in visual form. The painter Wassily Kandinsky articulated his theories related to visual music in *Concerning the Spiritual in Art* (1911), a text that has influenced many artists who have explored such concepts using motion picture media. Visual music artists are often inspired by the possibilities of synaesthesia, an "overlapping of the senses" found in some individuals who have a long-term, consistent secondary sensory experience when they perceive a "normal" primary sensation. For example, a person will "hear" particular sounds when confronted with individual colors; over time, the one-to-one correspondence between the color and the sound remains the same. Visual music artists have also been inspired by Kandinsky's belief that some colors and sounds have a mystical or spiritual dimension, and have investigated this possibility in direct films as well.

Harry Smith The enigmatic Harry Smith was among the direct filmmakers who explored the mystical qualities of form and color, as well as the aesthetic of chance. An award-winning ethnomusicologist who recorded folk music, a collector of Fabergé eggs, and a vital member of the Beat community in San Francisco during its 1950s heyday, he was a complex and mysterious figure. He studied alchemy, experimented with a wide range of mind-altering substances, and seemed to delight in fabricating stories for interviewers, making his work somewhat difficult to document.

"Genetic information about historical stages in evolution is carried simultaneously with organic information, such as information about antibodies, protein structure, and cells as they exist now. Symbols of the past and present can be imbued with this truth of evolution which our cells carry."[5]

Len Lye

Smith's direct films, *No. 1* (1946), *No. 2* (1946–48) and *No. 3* (1947–49), run two to three minutes each. All are in color, on 35mm film stock, and silent, though he would run them with the accompaniment of various recorded soundtracks. The first was hand-drawn, while the other two employ a batik process. Smith experimented with various means of creating his multicolored imagery, using a resist process that has been described by Henry Jones: "He sprayed the film with colored inks out of an atomizer, randomly and with an even stroke. Then he put a piece of tape over each frame, and the tape was in a shape. He would cut little shapes out of Scotch tape—then animate them across the frames by referencing them to the above frame. Then he would cover it with Vaseline [petroleum jelly], remove the bits of tape with a needle, spray another color with the atomizer, then use trichloroethylene, or dry cleaning fluid, to remove the Vaseline and that would be his first two-color step."[6] Smith claimed to have many inspirations for the patterns in his work, including body rhythms (such as respiration), color and sound correspondences, and patchwork quilts.[7]

Len Lye Relationships between form, movement, and sound were central to the creative process of New Zealander Len Lye, whose work spanned direct film, documentary film production, kinetic sculpture, painting, and written prose, as well as art theory.[8] He worked for John Grierson at the General Post Office Film Unit in England, where he created the cameraless *A Colour Box* (1935), which includes colorful designs painted on film in synchronization with "La Belle Creole," performed by Don Baretto and his Cuban Orchestra. Lye's

Kaleidoscope (1935), also a direct film, makes use of stencils and is accompanied by Baretto's "Biguine d'Amour."

One of Lye's most interesting direct films is *Free Radicals*, which was first released in a five-minute length in 1958, then shortened by a minute and re-released in 1979. It was made by scratching onto black film and is accompanied by the music of the African Bagirmi tribe. Organic in form, it reflects Lye's belief in what he called the "old brain," related to our primal origins; he believed the scratched, squiggling figures which made their way into the film are bits of information that function as "representations, illustrations, and illuminations" of what was lodged within his subconscious.[9] The notion is similar to Carl Jung's concept of a collective unconscious that unites all humanity—genetic information that affects human behavior now, though its origins are in our earliest ancestry.[10] Lye recognized a certain ineffable quality in his work, as though it represented a dense, complex record of internally held secrets of life, linked at the same time with biology and magic.

Norman McLaren The achievements of Norman McLaren (see pages 204 and 269) in animation spanned a variety of techniques, including many types of direct work; he is among the most influential animators in history. Like Lye, he was hired by Grierson to work at the General Post Office Film Unit in England. When Grierson moved to Canada to establish the state-supported National Film Board (NFB), he then asked McLaren to lead its animation unit. At the NFB, McLaren was able to experiment with the form and content of his work, though many of the films he created there addressed specific issues of concern to the government. For example, *Hen Hop*

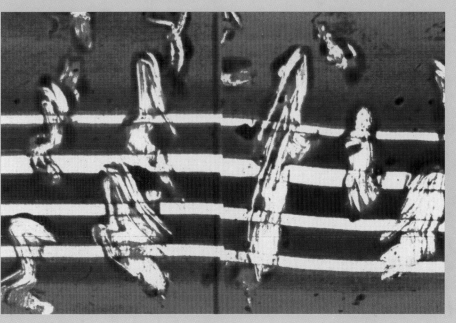

Len Lye's *Free Radicals* (left) was created by scratching onto the emulsion of black film. His *A Colour Box* (below) was painted directly on film stock.

(1942) and *Mail Early for Christmas* (1959) are fun and lively animations that provide useful messages about the war effort (for World War II) and the postal service.

However, not all his work was promotional. *Lines Vertical* (1960) and *Lines Horizontal* (1962) are thoughtful formal experiments that demonstrate McLaren's mastery of direct animation techniques. *Lines Vertical* was made by engraving straight lines onto 6-foot (1.8-meter) strips of black leader, using a sharp knife and a stainless steel draughtsman's rule, also 6 feet (1.8 meters) long.[11] Using tape to anchor the film to a solid base and three knives of varying widths, McLaren worked on only very fresh film taken out of the can as needed; emulsion exposed to air for too long became brittle and was impossible to scratch cleanly. After internegative and positive prints had been made, the film was optically printed. The negative was run with color filters to create background colors, and the positive was then used to burn in the white lines of the film. The same frames were used to create *Lines Horizontal*; each image was flipped 90 degrees and reprinted with new colors and sound.

Finally, both films were printed together to create yet another derivative work: *Mosaic* (1965). This is composed of patterns of light—the dots formed at the intersection of *Lines Vertical* and *Lines Horizontal* when the two films were overlapped in printing. Aside from a human whistle at the beginning and end, *Mosaic*'s soundtrack was created by hand,

by scratching onto the emulsion and adding echo and reverberations to fill some of the sound space.[12]

To create *Blinkity Blank* (1955), McLaren engraved on black film with a penknife, sewing needle, and razor blade, and colored the clear portions with transparent dyes, using a sable brush. He considered the film to be an experiment in the "spasmodic nature" of direct animation, caused by the difficulty of exactly registering images when working frame by frame. McLaren did not work in a linear way, from start to finish, but rather he engraved "a frame here and a frame there, leaving many frames untouched and blank—sprinkling, as it were, the images on the empty band of time; to the spaces between, to the music, to the idea that emerged."[13] Though there are no engravings on most of the frames, in places McLaren worked on three, four, or more adjacent ones to create a frame-cluster; sometimes it "would have related and continuous images within it and would thus solidify some action and movement; at other times the frame-cluster would consist only of a swarm of disconnected, discontinuous images, calculated to build up an overall visual 'impression.'"[14] He also included some longer groups of frames animated in a more traditional way, to vary the visual flow. Maurice Blackburn scored the music.

Steven Woloshen Canadian animator Steven Woloshen has carried on the traditions of McLaren's direct film work, though he also credits Stan Brakhage (see page 156), Michael

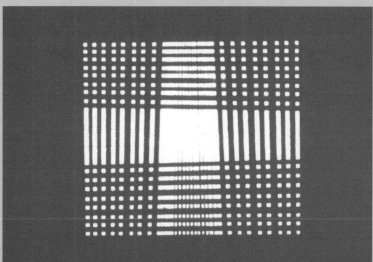

Norman McLaren's *Mosaic* (above) was created by combining the images of two films, *Lines Vertical* and *Lines Horizontal*.

To create *Blinkity Blank* (left), Norman McLaren scratched some frames of film and left others black. The resulting images are somewhat stroboscopic in nature.

Snow, and Len Lye (see page 143) as significant influences. He works in various aspects of the film industry in the Montreal area to finance his independent film productions. Woloshen has used the widescreen CinemaScope format in several of his films, including *Get Happy* (1999), *Ditty Dot Comma* (2001), *Cameras Take Five* (2003), *Snip* (2004), *The Curse of the Voodoo Child* (2005), and *Changing Evan* (2006)—while it is a costly format, the resulting work is visually impressive. He traces his decision to work in this format to the impact of McLaren's films. He explains, "McLaren had such good ideas," but they got reduced "to a small idea,"[15] because he used confining aspect ratios.

The three-minute *Ditty Dot Comma*, which has been described as "a musical tribute to visual punctuation," employs a variety of marks: lines, hatching, and dots. *Bru Ha Ha* (2002) runs only two minutes and features color fields and white lines (sometimes abstract, sometimes almost recognizable forms) that accompany a bebop jazz score by Erik Satie. *Cameras Take Five* is a visual exploration of Dave Brubeck's cool "Take Five" jazz score; its images suggest smoky loops in the air, as well as neon lighting, evoking the atmosphere of a nightclub. Woloshen relies on a fairly standard range of drawing and engraving tools, but most important to him is his synchronizer block, a device film editors use to move several pieces of magnetic sound stock and workprint (visuals) quickly in unison. He writes, "When you are able to move through a film quickly, it is possible to create more spontaneously."[16]

Woloshen approaches his films as technical experiments, but is also committed to creating a pleasurable experience for viewers. He achieves these objectives by following a "mission statement" composed of four parts:

(1) I believe that each handmade is an event (much like a fireworks display) and within each event is a subdivision of many other events.

(2) Synchronicity between the sound (music that we recognize) and the abstract image (a visual that is unrecognizable) can create a perfect balance for the observer.

(3) The creation and presentation of a handmade film has to attempt to meet the audience halfway. This is achieved by utilizing point no. 1 and point no. 2 together.

(4) I approach a film like a science experiment. It is necessary to bring a maximum of three or four basic elements together throughout the length of the film. A short form of film (three or four minutes) can easily serve this function, as well as can have logical depth or no depth at all, depending on how much thought the viewer cares to donate to the experience.[17]

Direct filmmaker Steven Woloshen (right) at work.

Steven Woloshen's *Cameras Take Five* (below) was inspired by a Dave Brubeck jazz score.

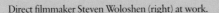

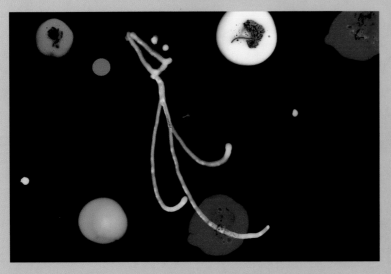

Caroline Leaf scratched into 70mm color film to create *Two Sisters* (right).

Narrative Storytelling

The relatively small working space for creating direct film imagery makes it difficult to tell detailed stories. Nonetheless, some artists have taken on the challenge of working directly to present characters involved in narratives.

Caroline Leaf A renowned American animator, Caroline Leaf has experimented with various animation techniques throughout her career, and has also created documentary and narrative live-action films, as well as set designs and kinetic sculptures.[18]

Her acclaimed scratch film *Two Sisters* (1990) tells the story of women who live on an island, hiding from the world within their shadowy home. One sister, an author, has a facial disfigurement; she spends her days at her word processor, and is cared for by her domineering sibling. One day a visitor swims to the island and asks to speak to the writer, causing much upheaval. The key moment of the film occurs when she walks outside and faces the man in the light of day. The black film surrounding the scratched images suits the story well: The characters appear to emerge out of the darkness as sketchy, roughly defined figures.

It took one-and-a-half years to complete the thirteen-minute production, which was made on 70mm color film stock. Leaf employed a useful system for working on this material, which is small as drawing surfaces go, but large when it comes to film stocks. She used two strips simultaneously, scratching the odd frames (1, 3, 5, etc.) on one of them and the even frames (2, 4, 6, etc.) on the other, fitting their sprocket holes on pegs attached to a metal plate. This tool allowed her to lay consecutive frames on top of one another; when she completed frame 1, she placed frame 2 from the other filmstrip over it. As a result, she had a reference when she modified each frame. Color was achieved by removing various amounts of emulsion. She explains, "If I scratch a strip of color film and scratch just a little bit, the red emulsion comes off and you get the green, and if I scratch more I get to the yellow and when I scratch all the way down, it is white. As for the blue, I used blue film."[19]

Paul Bush Like Leaf, English animator Paul Bush uses various techniques. In 1998, he completed a remarkable fifteen-minute scratched animation, *The Albatross*, an adaptation of Samuel Taylor Coleridge's "Rime of the Ancient Mariner," using nineteenth-century engravings. He had already completed two

Paul Bush created this chart (right) to explain his scratch film production technique.

Paul Bush's *Still Life with Small Cup* (below) is a scratch film exploration of an etching by Giorgio Morandi.

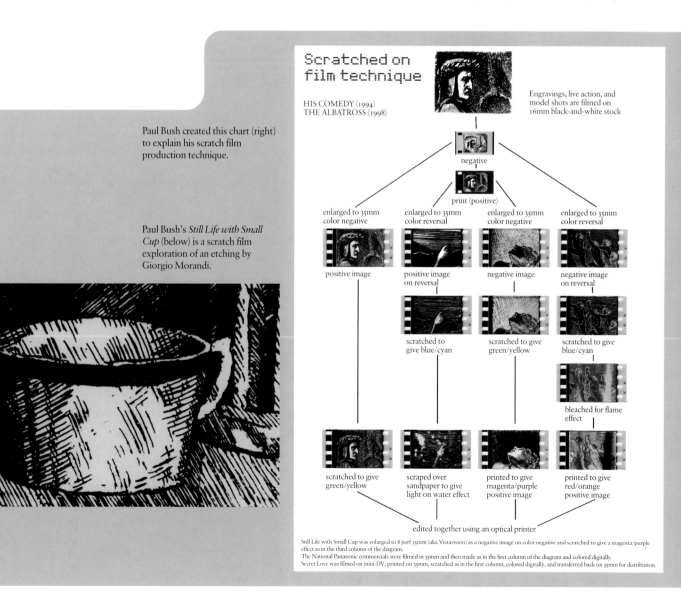

Scratched on film technique

HIS COMEDY (1994)
THE ALBATROSS (1998)

Engravings, live action, and model shots are filmed on 16mm black-and-white stock

negative

print (positive)

enlarged to 35mm color negative — enlarged to 35mm color reversal — enlarged to 35mm color negative — enlarged to 35mm color reversal

positive image — positive image on reversal — negative image — negative image on reversal

scratched to give blue/cyan — scratched to give green/yellow — scratched to give blue/cyan

bleached for flame effect

scratched to give green/yellow — scraped over sandpaper to give light on water effect — printed to give magenta/purple positive image — printed to give red/orange positive image

edited together using an optical printer

Still Life with Small Cup was enlarged to 8 perf 35mm (aka Vistavision) as a negative image on color negative and scratched to give a magenta/purple effect as in the third column of the diagram.
The National Panasonic commercials were filmed in 35mm and then made as in the first column of the diagram and colored digitally.
Secret Love was filmed on mini-DV, printed on 35mm, scratched as in the first column, colored digitally, and transferred back on 35mm for distribution.

shorter scratched works. *His Comedy* (1994), an eight-minute film, is based on nineteenth-century woodblock engravings illustrating Dante Alighieri's *Divine Comedy*. The four-minute *Still Life with Small Cup* (1995) is a reworking of an etching by the twentieth-century Italian artist Giorgio Morandi. Viewers are taken through ambiguous images to arrive finally at the artist's finished work; the visuals change over sounds he might have heard while working.

His Comedy and *The Albatross* were made the same way, using black-and-white 16mm film images of live-action actors, some stock footage (for the sea at the end of *The Albatross*), and wood engravings.[20] The images were printed onto 35mm stock and scratched so that the original figures disappeared underneath; as a result, parts of the film employ a variation on rotoscoping, as they are closely based on live-action footage.[21] Bush's scratching equipment includes primitive dental-style sculpture tools, scalpel blades, and mini rasps.

The wood engravings used in *His Comedy* are all by the French book illustrator Gustav Doré. In *The Albatross*, everything except the man, the sea at the end of the film, and a couple of shots of birds is based on still engravings from newspapers and books, animated by a moving camera and

with cutouts. In both films, the colors came from scratching into color film stock, similar to Caroline Leaf's technique in *Two Sisters*. Bush has detailed his method in a diagram that shows how he created color using negative and positive prints that were scratched (sometimes with sandpaper underneath) and bleached.

Although Bush has begun using computers for his productions, the films retain his distinctive style. *Secret Love* (2002), which is based on a traditional Nordic song, is created from live-action images shot with a MiniDV camera, which were transferred to 35mm film for scratching; this footage was shot frame by frame off a computer screen to keep costs down. When scratching was complete, the work was telecined back to video, then into the computer for coloring and some compositing of foreground figures onto backgrounds. The film was output to 35mm for theatrical release.[22]

Rose Bond Canadian-born Rose Bond is one of the most experienced of the storytellers working with direct film. She has used direct techniques in six works, including a trilogy based on Celtic mythology: *Cerridwen's Gift* (1987), *Mallacht Macha* (*Macha's Curse*, 1990), and *Deirdre's Choice* (1995).[23]

Images from Rose Bond's *Deirdre's Choice* (above) and *Macha's Curse* (left), as well as her technique of tracing paper guides onto film (right).

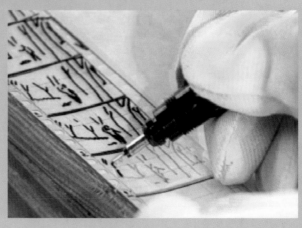

The first two films run ten minutes each, while the third is quite lengthy at twenty-three minutes. In addition, she has used painted film in a museum installation, *Sacred Encounters*, which was exhibited in Los Angeles, Bozeman, Indianapolis, Tacoma, Vancouver, and Portland, where she lives.

A short documentary, *Celtic Trilogy Intro* (1997), details the origins of the narratives she used in the three films, as well as her production process.[24] Taken from the Irish oral storytelling tradition, the tales refer to real people and locations. Bond says she was attracted to them because they feature strong female characters and also because the Celtic belief in shape-shifting provides opportunities for morphing.

The trilogy was created on 35mm film, using reference images sketched onto small pieces of tracing paper that could be flipped in flipbook form to check timing and movement. An image was placed underneath each frame of the film and traced using black ink. Colors were then added with a brush and felt pens. This technique appealed to Bond in part because she sees it as a way of asserting her "signature," much as storytellers in the oral tradition individualized each telling with added details and voice inflections.[25]

Films within Films

In 1937, Len Lye made the direct film *Trade Tattoo* for the GPO Film Unit in England, incorporating documentary footage to get across a message about efficient mailing procedures. This is but one example of a direct filmmaker who has chosen to work on film stock that already contains images (as opposed to being clear or black leader, for example). This footage falls into two general categories: found film (any marginal material, such as out-takes and industrial footage, that is somehow "found") and other types of exposed film (perhaps from mainstream features or footage shot specifically for the project at hand). The distinction between these categories is not particularly significant, except in that they suggest the range of film materials used in direct animation.

Vincenzo Gioanola Italian animator Vincenzo Gioanola is the founder of La Lanterna Magica company and has taught at the Scuola Nazionale di Cinema in Turin. During the mid-1990s, his *Fight da faida* (*Fight the Feud*, 1994) was a favorite with film festival audiences. Using images of war and other footage, the film illustrates a popular song of the same name released in 1993 by the Italian rapper Frankie High-NRG. To create his direct imagery, Gioanola employed reference drawings prepared on bits of paper that were traced onto film.

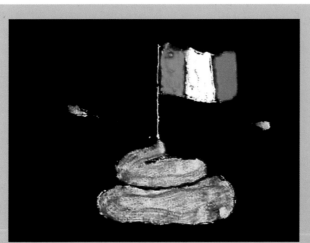

Vincenzo Gioanola's drawn-on film work includes *Fight da Faida* (above) and *Garybaldy Blues* (right).

He worked on black and clear 35mm leader, as well as film found in a flea market.

Gioanola has used found footage since he made his first animated work, *Boogie*, in 1981; the film illustrates an accompanying song by the Italian singer-songwriter Paolo Conte. It was drawn with permanent markers on 16mm film, including found footage, clear stock, and scratched black leader. The control that Gioanola maintains over this imagery is all the more impressive because he did not magnify the small 16mm frame as he worked on it. He used similar techniques in his early 35mm films: *Garybaldy Blues* (1982, illustrating "Viva," sung by Bruno Lauzi) and *Russian Roulette* (1985, illustrating a Jim Page song performed by Moving Hearts).

Naomi Uman Found footage and direct techniques are also employed in Naomi Uman's provocative *Removed* (1999), a film that explores sexuality and the onscreen representation of women. Uman uses pornographic film footage of a woman going through a series of sexual acts near some men. The entire surface of the film, except the portion containing the female figure, was coated with nail polish of various colors; the polish was colored because clear lacquer is difficult to see, which makes it hard to determine whether the film is adequately covered.[26] The lacquered film was then dipped into buckets of bleach. As a result, the woman is blotted out, or removed from the scene, while the remaining imagery is colored in some manner, depending on practice nail polish used. The original soundtrack remains on the film.

Hand Eye Coordination (2002) begins with a close shot of a human eye, then focuses on a variety of images of hands, some taken from found footage, such as a female secretary demonstrating proper business use of a telephone (accompanied by the original voice-over). It also includes original 16mm footage (by Adrian Garcia), such as a hand being tattooed with the word "hand," and a series of small hands that were filmed, cut out, and linked with thread. Uman placed this "string of hands" onto fresh film stock and exposed them through contact printing, as a rayogram. Throughout most of the film, the visuals surrounding various hands have been obliterated by applying nail polish, scratching off emulsion with a blade, or inking with a fine-point pen.

Uman also has explored direct filmmaking in terms of post-production. Her film *Leche* (1998) focuses on a family in rural Mexico, employing live-action images shot by Uman. It was handprocessed in buckets and hung on a clothesline to dry. As a result, the footage is flecked with particles and scratches.

> "Most of my screenings unfold from the position of the projection booth. They are performances of a film screening proper and make use of the properly cinematic variables that accumulate in that highly specialized apparatus called cinema."
> Luis Recoder

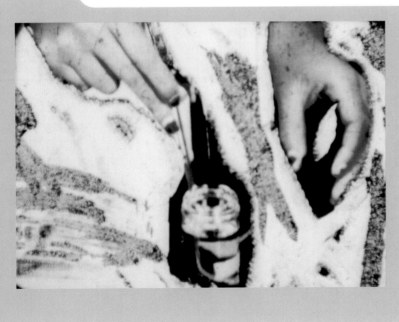

In *Hand Eye Coordination*, Naomi Uman uses such techniques as scratching, inking with a pen, and painting with nail polish.

Luis Recoder The work of Luis Recoder is conceptual, and often involves an element of performance art. His presence and active participation were integral to the realization of *Ballad of …* (1999), *Magenta* (1999), and *Moebius Strip* (1998). These works were created by bi-packing a filmstrip onto itself (double-threading it through the gate of the projector) or feeding the same print through two projectors. They employ both direct film prints created by Recoder and found footage. *Ballad of …* uses scenes from a B-movie western feature; *Magenta* involves a film on first aid, which shows close-ups of hands; and *Moebius Strip* employs a sports footage reel of runners, boxers, skiers, and other athletes.

1977 Leader (1999) is based upon a found 16mm soundtrack. Recoder took out all the magnetic track, which contained sound elements, so only the silent fill leader (or "slug") remained. The soundtrack had been damaged by rough use, leaving the relatively clear surface flecked with dirt and scratches. When run through a projector these imperfections create ambient sounds, releasing the suppressed noise of the slug acoustically as well as visually. Recoder further utilized this footage when he created *Space* (2001), which consists of a positive print of *1977 Leader*. Recoder explains, "It turns all those scratches and dust particles into cosmic space."[27]

For his 2001 film *Pour-trait*, Recoder shot a Super 8mm film of himself from the shoulders up, looking expressionlessly into the camera. He processed the footage by hand using outdated chemicals, then bi-packed it through the film projector running at 6 fps. The resulting image is "apparition-like, a transparent veil that slowly evolves in unexpected ways." Flecks of unknown material flicker past during the ten-minute production, adding to the unusual aura of the work, which is given dimension through the recognizable sound of an amplified projector.[28]

For Recoder, the direct approach extends beyond the treatment of the film's surface to the presentation of the work. He feels that "the strip of film traversing through the projector—visible to the projectionist—is the site of an unacknowledged performance and/or installation that we so recklessly call the 'movies.'" While the projectionist maintains the precarious illusion of the cinematic object, Recoder creates a wedge that exposes precisely that precariousness.

Luis Recoder's *Ballad of...* (left) and *Magenta* (below) include found footage along with direct film images.

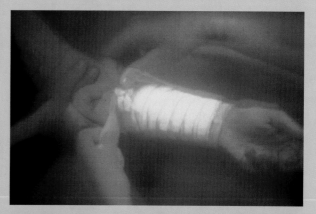

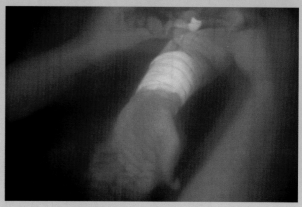

Case Study: Peter Tscherkassky

Austrian filmmaker and theorist Peter Tscherkassky began making films in 1979. He has organized festivals and co-founded Sixpack Film, a film distribution company based in Vienna. He also teaches filmmaking at the academies of applied arts in Linz and Vienna. Like his productions, Tscherkassky's critical writing—which is extensive—is concerned with the boundaries of the film form, which he explores from both historical and theoretical perspectives. His work includes a series of three films—*L'Arrivée* (1997/98), *Outer Space* (1999), and *Dream Work* (2001)—that is referred to as the CinemaScope Trilogy. As the title suggests, all three employ a CinemaScope format. In them, the filmmaker has utilized footage from live-action films, contact-printing excerpts from his source material to create entirely new imagery through a form of collage. All three works defy easy description.

L'Arrivée begins with two identical strips of film (mirror images) that gradually enter from either side of the frame, depicting the scene of a train station. Slowly, the image of a train arriving at a station emerges into center frame, appearing to be pulled in front of the projector's gate, out of registration. As the two strips of film merge, the trains on them collide violently—at least symbolically, as the image is obscured and the borders of the film emerge, creating a chaotic visual scene. The two-minute work is a homage to film pioneers Auguste and Louis Lumière, referencing their *L'arrivée du un train* (1895). It ends with a woman emerging from the train and embracing her waiting lover. This footage was taken from *Mayerling* (1969) by British director Terence Young. The soundtrack consists of assorted "noise." Tscherkassky writes, "In *L'Arrivée*, the original material was copied past the edge of the unexposed film strip so that the projector's pickup reads parts of the image as sound, thereby making them audible"; he explains, "The result is vaguely reminiscent of the Italian Futurists' *intonarumori*—'noise instruments.'"[29]

Outer Space and *Dream Work* both employ footage from American director Sidney J. Fury's horror film *The Entity* (1983). *Outer Space* begins with a night shot of a house with a bright light flashing on it. A bit of music, distorted and broken, can be heard as a woman (played by Barbara Hershey) enters the home and starts walking around. Soon her image is being fragmented and, as she moves her lips, we cannot hear her words. Sprocket holes, the optical soundtrack, and other components of the filmic material appear and add a violent effect as she panics and tries to escape from some invisible force within the film. Eventually, the woman's face is broken into parts and shown in small portions of the frame, and we see her being accosted by something that remains unknown. Finally, we are left with her face duplicated within the frame, her defiant gaze looking out at the audience.

Peter Tscherkassky (left) works in a darkroom, exposing images on film through the use of a small hand-held light source.

Sets of consecutive frames (above and right) from Peter Tscherkassky's *L'Arrivée*. The missing framelines reveal how he works across the film rather than in separate frames.

Dream Work has a relatively more recognizable soundtrack. As in *Outer Space*, it was composed of contact-printed fragments from the original soundtrack. However, the material was then submitted to composer Kiawash Saheb Nassagh, who compiled bits and pieces in a nonsynchronous fashion. Score, effects, and dialogue pulse as images of the original film are distorted and pass rapidly before viewers' eyes. At one point, hands (not part of the found footage) enter the frame and are silhouetted as they touch and cut pieces of the film that have just been seen, emphasizing the manipulation the material has undergone. Overall, the amount of distortion in *Dream Work* is greater than in the other two films in the series, though there are consistencies in the way viewers are tantalized—promised a spectacle but prevented from actually viewing it. Using a horror film, Tscherkassky has heightened the viewer's feeling of helplessness. The woman is clearly in distress, but the audience cannot understand the nature of the threat she is facing because the scene is presented in pieces. What viewers see is a collage of raw materials, rather than the clearly defined, orderly images they have come to expect from traditional movies. Tscherkassky made *Dream Work* in appreciation of the cinematic art of Man Ray, the father of cameraless darkroom films. The films also relate to the artist's interest in film theory and ideology, or the underlying, relatively invisible, forces shaping our society, including the production of film. Structurally, The films reflect the irrational logic of dream states.

Technically, production of the three films was quite complex. The director explains that the original film footage was viewed on videotape:

> ... and the film was studied closely, virtually learned by heart: All of its shots, the elements of each frame and the sequences of images provided a kind of vocabulary for the new film. The new work's dramatic structure was then set down on paper in the form of notes.
>
> A second plan resembling a musical score was worked out for the darkroom work: The precise micro-structure of each strip of film was determined before it was exposed, and all the changes it was to undergo were noted; the result resembles graphic notation for each film strip.

Tscherkassky used unexposed orthochromatic (desensitized to red light) 35mm film stock in strips of 48 frames (approximately 40 inches [1 meter] long), equal to two seconds of projection time. Working in a darkroom, the strips were attached to a board of the same size by pins that protruded through every fourth perforation on both sides of the film, allowing

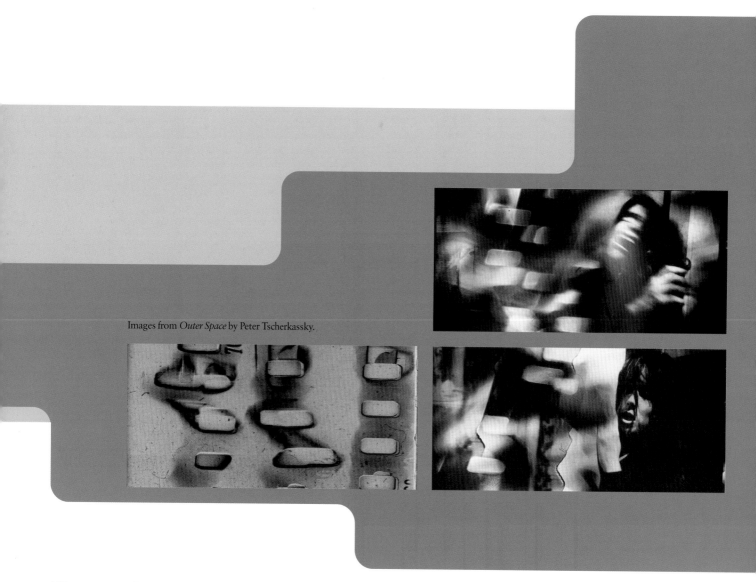

Images from *Outer Space* by Peter Tscherkassky.

the divisions between frames to be visible. Once the unexposed film stock was anchored, the source footage was placed on top of it and the contact-printing process began.

Two light sources were used to expose the images:

The first was a conventional enlarger. The brightness can be adjusted at its lens, and a timer was used to ensure a precise exposure time. Approximately 18 frames can be exposed in the enlarger's cone of light at one time.

Most of the film was exposed frame by frame. In this case I made use of a laser pointer to copy portions of the original frames. The duration of the exposure can be varied in each case according to previous experience. The act of exposing the film stock is reminiscent of the work of a painter, as the laser pointer is guided manually in a way similar to a brush.

After the initial exposure, the director continued the process on the same filmstrip, adding to the complexity of the copied images by layering visuals from different parts of the original film. Tscherkassky writes:

Portions of frames from various positions on the strip can be combined and assembled into collages … Parts of *Outer Space* have undergone as many as five exposures, the material taken from different parts of the original film, either layered on top of one another or inserted side by side. There are frames that underwent seven passes in *Dream Work* (*L'Arrivée* was produced with an enlarger in its entirety. The collage effect was produced by stacking various sections of the found footage on top of the unexposed film stock).

It took the director between forty-five and seventy minutes to create the multilayered, frame by frame exposures for two seconds of projection time. After the exposed film was developed by hand, it was checked visually on a light table. To create the sound elements of his film, Tscherkassky used a similar process of copying and collaging various components of the original film onto the optical sound area of the unexposed film stock.[30]

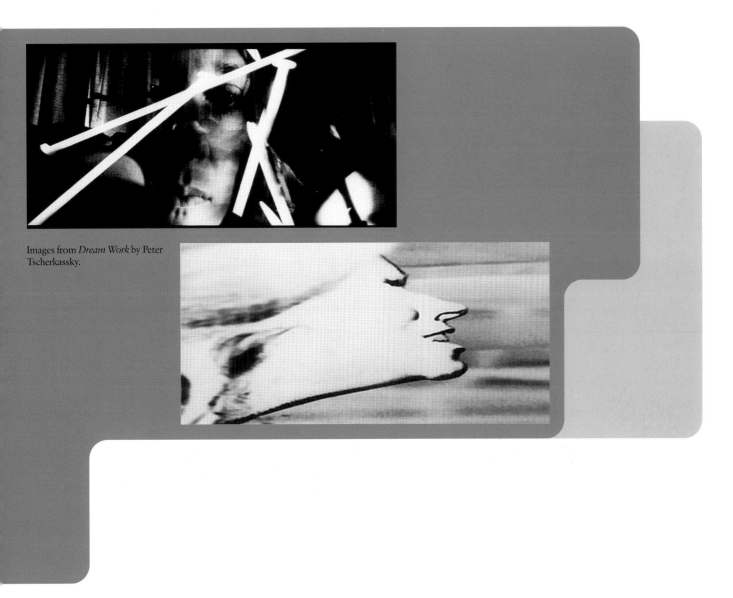

Images from *Dream Work* by Peter Tscherkassky.

Direct Filmmaking: Vision, Sound, and Collective Experience

Direct filmmaking is an accessible art practice, allowing even beginning artists to make work that is engaging in the creative process and interesting to watch when done. However, direct cinema can also be technically and theoretically complex. Bypassing the need for technology, it allows us to take the means of production into our own hands, which has powerful implications for the democratization of the artistic process.

Expanding Vision

Direct cinema provides opportunities to envision and understand the world in unique ways, magnifying elements applied to film stock and removing technological intermediaries in the creation of images on film. Many direct filmmakers have engaged in this pursuit as part of a larger concern with perceptual processes, which can be explored on both practical and theoretical levels.

Stan Brakhage Stan Brakhage was perhaps the single most important figure in American avant-garde cinema. Between 1953 and his death from cancer in 2003, he was an active and highly influential filmmaker, theorist, and teacher; in that period of fifty years he made more than three hundred films

and wrote extensively on film-related topics.[1] Among his most famous works is *Dog Star Man*, a five-part "epic" 16mm film running for more than an hour, which many consider to be his masterpiece.[2]

One of Brakhage's primary concerns throughout his career involved the phenomenon of "seeing," extending past the physiological processes of eyesight to the ideal of expanded vision and the development of consciousness well beyond day-to-day awareness. His "Metaphors on Vision," published as an entire issue of *Film Culture*, asks readers to "imagine an eye unruled by man-made laws of perspective, an eye unprejudiced by compositional logic, an eye that does not respond to the name of everything but which must know each object encountered in life through an adventure of perception."[3] In his films, Brakhage created environments where the viewer is unable to perceive images using standard modes of seeing and understanding. To do so, he modified the surface of exposed and clear film in various ways. For example, he painted clear film and bleached, scraped, and gouged black and exposed film; he also coated film stock with molds and crystals. His numerous direct films include some of the last works he created: *Panels for the Walls of Heaven*, *Ascension*, and *Resurrectus Est*, all completed in 2002.[4]

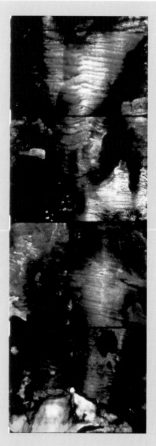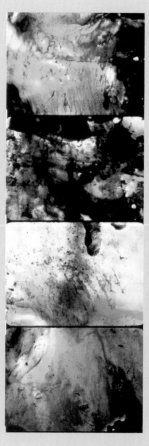

Images from Stan Brakhage's *Panels for the Walls of Heaven* (above). Brakhage anchored natural materials in splicing tape to create *Mothlight* (opposite). Estate of Stan Brakhage and www.fredcamper.com.

Natural objects play a dominant role in Brakhage's films. His three-minute *Mothlight* (1963) was made by adhering bits of moth and other natural materials to 16mm splicing tape, and placing a second layer of splicing tape on top. This "collage" was run through an optical printer to make a copy, from which release prints were made.[5] When viewing the film, it is not possible to recognize the origin of every particle passing before the projector lens, but the overall sense is of witnessing some essential quality of the materials.

Jennifer Reeves One of the most significant aspects of Brakhage's career is the enormous amount of work he motivated others to produce. The Brooklyn-based filmmaker Jennifer Reeves is among those inspired by Brakhage, particularly in respect to his aesthetics, which challenge passive viewing and our expectations of what a film should be. She has written about his *Stately Mansions Did Decree* (1999) and *Coupling* (1999), explaining that they explore "our relation to time and perception"; his work calls "for active participation and openness from viewers," at the same time offering "new forms of pleasure."[6] She acknowledges that Brakhage's work can be challenging to viewers, who are asked to abandon so-called normal ways of seeing the world around them. With their "heightened awareness of color, texture, and detail," the films can be overwhelming.[7]

Reeves's *Fear of Blushing* (2001) was inspired by a screening of Brakhage's handpainted films, which reminded her that "abstract forms of light and color could excite complex thought and emotion, while offering a pure beauty to be held only for an instant."[8] As in much of Brakhage's work, her film contains glimpses of images, but otherwise is primarily nonrepresentational and distorted visually. She created the film by applying bleach and paint to 16mm film and using an optical printer to manipulate it.

Fear of Blushing opens with sprays of color falling across the screen, soon shifting among the intense primaries blue, red, and yellow, along with bright white and black. At times, viewers glimpse an object or patterns like those of a plant or feather, as well as other natural images, perhaps rocks, starbursts, and fire. The soundtrack is similarly structured; though a human scream and a few repeated lines of dialogue are heard, in general the sound amounts to abstract "noise." At times it is natural, like that of an avalanche or other destructive force, but in other instances it has a more mechanical quality.

Like most independent filmmakers, Reeves controls virtually all aspects of her media production. She writes, shoots, directs, sound designs, and edits her work, using optical printing, direct animation, and sound manipulation. However, she also has worked collaboratively, creating the

Jennifer Reeves at work (right). Images from *Fear of Blushing* (far right).

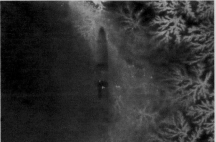

projector performance *Light Work Mood Disorder* (2006) with musician Anthony Burr. Shown on up to four screens, pulsating electronic sounds, bass clarinet, and organ accompany Reeves's visuals of abstract imagery combined with educational found footage, including detailed images of synapses, dendrites, electromagnetic waveforms, and other enigmatic content, coated with melted pharmaceuticals.

Thorsten Fleisch Like Jennifer Reeves, German filmmaker and musician Thorsten Fleisch counts Stan Brakhage as a strong influence. His *Blutrausch* (*Bloodlust*, 1999) is similar to Brakhage's *Mothlight* in that it was created by placing natural objects on the surface of film. Brakhage used bits of moth and other natural materials, such as leaves. In *Blutrausch*, Fleisch applied his own blood to the film, to create "a very direct and immediate man–machine dialogue… I give the machine (the film projector) my blood (fluid of life, secret of life, color of life) for digestion/analysis and am rewarded with a new perspective on life itself (the projection), the perspective of the lifeless machine."[9] Among many other influences on this project are the Austrian painter Hermann Nitsch's blood paintings, as well as Italian horror/splatter films, *Weissfilm* (*White Film*, made by a college friend, Goh Harada, which features clear leader with silicon on it), computer games (particularly first-person shooters), and natural formations such as clouds.[10]

To create *Blutrausch*, he first fixed the blood on the film leader with splicing tape. It remained liquid for a few days, and Fleisch originally wanted to conserve it in this state. He then experimented with applying blood to the leader without splicing tape, and it not only stuck perfectly to the leader during the drying process, but it also produced cracks like very old paint. He immediately liked the images and tried different ways to create interesting structures with his blood, dropping it on the leader, using Q-tips to spread it over the film, pressing the leader on his cut skin. He also found that blood in a test tube would clot after a few hours, which resulted in different structures on the leader. For the finished film, he left the chronology of the different stages unaltered, starting with the splicing tape method and progressing through the techniques in the order he tried them.[11]

Other projects by Fleisch also employ direct film processes, though they can be considered "expanded cinema" productions (film employed in a context beyond a typical screening) rather than films per se. His *Der Antifilm* (*The Antifilm*, 1997) was created using Super 8mm black leader composed in ways that make projection impossible; for example, sprocket holes have been cut away and the stock is spliced together in opposite directions. Fleisch explains, "It's the film that cannot be screened, that doesn't want to be screened. It has nothing to show anyway since it's only black

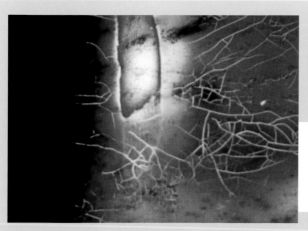
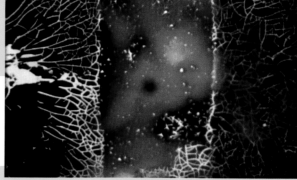

Images from Jennifer Reeves's *Fear of Blushing*.

leader."[12] To create his 16mm film *Feuer frei* (*Open Fire*, 1998), Fleisch burned black and clear leader, also applying ashes to some of the celluloid (for example, to a shot of his burning guitar). This film has never been projected, as it is too deformed to run through equipment properly. Rather, it exists as a piece that is observed as film itself.

Sandra Gibson American filmmaker Sandra Gibson sees herself as being between a filmmaker and a painter. For her, the surface of film is a canvas, a raw base upon which to build her moving paintings. She says, "The joy of filmmaking for me is in the initial surprise of projecting the elaborately hand-labored work on a large screen. This is the moment of letting go and of experiencing one's personal imprint on a completely different level." Her film *Edgeways* (1999) "was composed as a tapestry of film strips, woven and stitched, reflecting the warp and weft of the cinematic fabric."[13] Gibson was inspired by such direct filmmakers as Len Lye (see page 143), Stephanie Maxwell (see page 310), and Richard Reeves (see page 164). She says, "I was lured by the direct, unmediated, and tactile nature of working with the actual plasticity of the film material." She followed *Edgeways* with *Soundings* (2001), which she describes as an "afterword. A continuation of ideas," and elaborates:

> My films explore the physical material of moving images, disrupting the flow of cinematic illusion by applying painterly, sculptural, and other handmade techniques. *Soundings* is a sound-image collage. It is a journey from the abstract to the concrete. Images flash by, flicker, come into focus, only to disappear; a soundtrack offers a way to grasp these pictures that pass by in the blink of an eye.

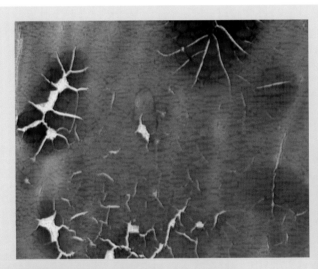

In her work, Sandra Gibson explores the fabric of film. Below is an image from her *Soundings*.

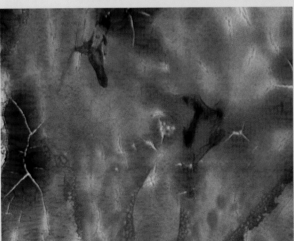

Experimental filmmaker Thorsten Fleisch used his own blood to create *Blutrausch* (above). His *Der Antifilm* (right) is an unprojectable direct film work.

Case Study:
Donna Cameron

Direct film production presents a unique opportunity for close examination of materials, to move beyond surface detail by magnifying them and filtering light through their forms, in search of some essential quality of being. New York-based filmmaker Donna Cameron has engaged in this pursuit using a method she devised, "cinematic paper emulsion," which she patented in 2001. On photographs and other paper-based materials, she marks areas that are equal in width to a piece of 16mm film. She then lays clear sticky 16mm editing tape over the marked-out portions of the images and peels them off. Excess paper on the sides of the tape is trimmed off and the strips are then printed onto film.[14]

Cameron discovered the technique when she decided to attend a university screenwriting course. She recalls:

My instructor did not share my views of what made a good film script, and took to publicly humiliating me by harping loudly on its shortcomings ("You'll never make a film with that script!"). For a final project, I ripped that script into 16mm size shreds and then projected each one through a Bell and Howell 1920s open wind projector (which I still own). I called my project *A Film Made with a Script*. Of course, *A Film Made with a Script* had a scrappy running time. But—amazingly—in those tiny intervals of screen time I SAW the gesture of TREENESS. I was surprised by those flashes of fibrous light.[15]

Another breakthrough came when she was printing photos and accidentally left one in its fix bath. When she returned some days later, she found the fixer had gone and that the dried image, peeled away from its paper base, had adhered to the plastic fix pan.

One of her earliest cinematic paper emulsion works is the silent 16mm film *Newsw* (1979), which was made with a variety of art papers and *Newsweek* magazine. Using a stencil, Cameron exploited the true-life aspect ratio of the 16mm frame as a measure and a guide for "lifting" information from the magazine. For example, the title is taken from the footer on every page; "Newsw" is all that fits into the 16mm frame. Cameron writes,

This consistent measuring device holds the disparate materials of the film to one thematic vision. The 16mm stencil provides a gauge edit—35mm or 8mm

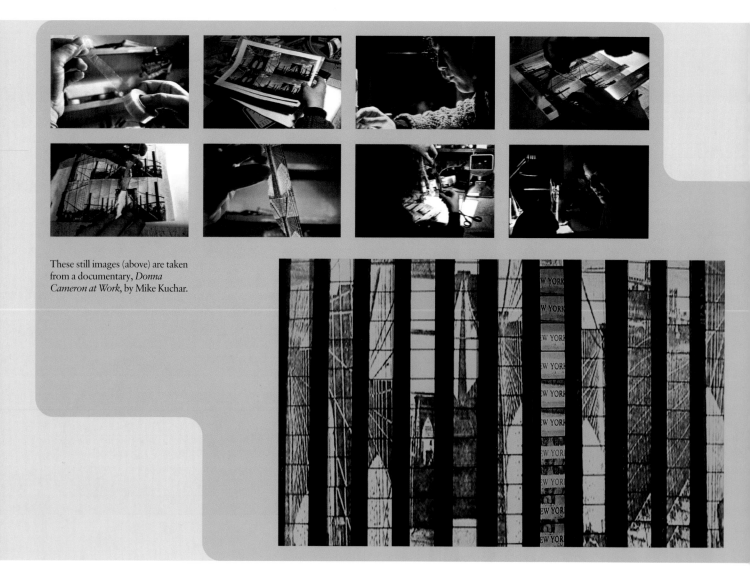

These still images (above) are taken from a documentary, *Donna Cameron at Work*, by Mike Kuchar.

stencils would never produce the same film. And it's the stencil that fragments the existing world of the papers, the paper elements are not fractured and broken to fit onto the 16mm gauge. This premise of gauge and viewpoint is consistent in all of my work. The film itself is seeing the world. You are seeing the world the film sees.[16]

Within the borders of the 16mm film frame, viewers see a date—January 1, 1979—and a few other words, plus some comic-book images. Mostly, though, the film displays abstract patterns of pixels from printing and paper fibers. It also contains some drawn-on-film images.

In films such as *New Moon* (1982), *Tyger Tyger* (1990), and *NYC/Joshua Tree* (1991), Cameron also employs photocopying, her own live-action imagery, found footage, ink animation on paper, filtered pigment wash (a combination of pigment, paper pulp, and liquid), and other techniques.[17] In 1993, she collaborated with filmmaker Shirley Clarke to create the experimental biographical *Shirley Clarke in Our Time*. The seventy-minute film incorporates the cinematic paper emulsion technique into home movies and popular film footage from when Clarke was growing up.

Cameron sees the cinematic paper emulsion process as part of her work as a photographer. She contends, "The physical sphere manifested in the cycle of my films begins and ends with the photograph. I create special photographs with the idea of making filmstrips from them. The process of photography dictates how to shoot each picture element of the shot. Each still frame is like a DNA structure, which, composited together, provides material for the film frame."[18] Her stated goal is to explore "the relationship of image to the frame, and the function of the frame within the framework of inter-media."[19] Cameron explores natural objects in close proximity, asking her audiences to see her photographic images in unconventional ways.

Her approach reflects her interest in the structures and origins of images projected on the screen. She writes,

Paper and pigments pass TO THE SCREEN through a photographic membrane. Paper, any paper—from the lowliest generic newsprint to the highest-grade exotic import—contains in its anatomy the history of its origin: the tree, the plant form. On the screen, luminous light embryos grow into dancing flora; gritty fibers speak eloquently of the life of the tree or the grasses from whence they came. The film membrane acts like a sieve, through which light flows, in lush color and with sensual textures.[20]

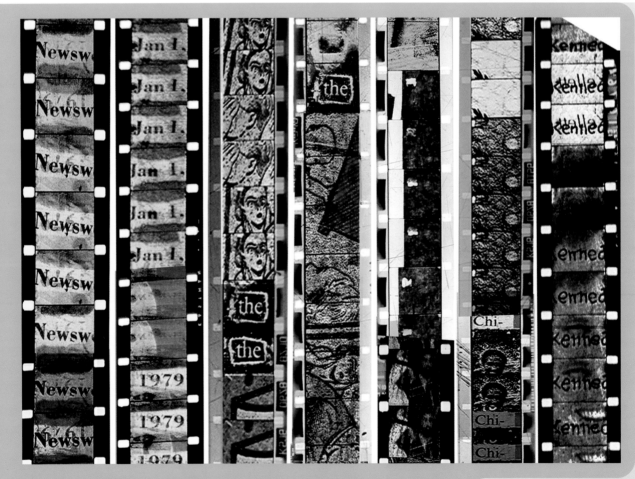

Donna Cameron uses a patented process she calls "cinematic paper emulsion," which allows her to conceptualize each frame as part of a DNA-like structure. Included here (opposite and above) are images from *Newsw* and *Tyger Tyger*. © 2006 by Donna Cameron. All rights reserved © Papercamfilms™.

Visualizing Sound

Direct cinema offers us new perspectives of the world around us—not only visually, but in terms of sound as well. Direct sound is the creation of aural elements by manipulating the surface of film or photographing images into the optical sound area of film stock. For example, in Thorsten Fleisch's *Blutrausch* the visual material of the film also provides its sound: His blood overlaps into the optical soundtrack portion of the film and is "read" as aural data. The result is abstract "noise," soft and fluttering. Norman McLaren's films provide the best-known examples of direct sound, but many other artists also have explored its possibilities.

Norman McLaren As head of the animation unit at the state-supported National Film Board of Canada, Norman McLaren received institutional support that allowed him to develop his many experiments in direct film—including drawn and photographed "animated" sound. He detailed his production work in a series of film notes, which are an invaluable resource for animators. Included are two sets of instructions for creating animated sound within the optical sound area of film: one for a photographed "Card Method of Optical Animated Sound," and another for what he described as a "Handmade Sound Track for Beginners," using drawing, painting, or scratching on film.[21]

For the first, McLaren and his colleague Evelyn Lambart created a series of "pitch cards" measuring 4 x 20 inches (10 x 50 centimeters) that were photographed into the audio portion of a filmstrip. McLaren's instructions are complex, taking into account such issues as avoiding "purr," creating envelopes for sounds, masking the cards, and controlling the volume and "attack" of the score.

The handmade approach employed clear film marked with pens, brushes, and ink, as well as black film that could be scratched. McLaren recommended the latter, as it does not pick up dust and dirt (which is read as "sound" along with any other images drawn on the film). He explained that black film "can be handled fairly carelessly as far as dirt is concerned. 35mm or 16mm film where the soundtrack is black and the

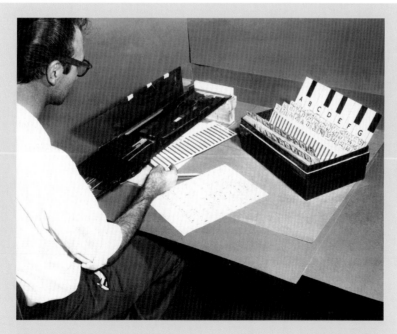

Among his many other accomplishments, Norman McLaren was also a pioneer of direct sound techniques.

picture area clear or in a different density from black is preferable, as it shows the exact width of the track."[22] He also recommended using recently developed film, as the emulsion is easier to remove.

McLaren created synthetic sound in ten films, including *Dots* (1939, the first one he made with animated sound), *Neighbors* (1952), and *Mosaic* (1965) (see page 144). On the whole, the sounds are mechanical in nature. Some people say they recall early video games, with lots of "blips" and "zipping" noises. A film like *Neighbors* works well with this type of track: Its two characters move as a result of pixilation and variable speed cinematography, which makes them look somewhat robotic, complementing the unnatural-sounding soundtrack.

Oerd van Cuijlenborg The Dutch animator Oerd van Cuijlenborg is among the countless artists who have been influenced by McLaren's work. He began experimenting with scratched sound on 35mm by consulting McLaren's

"Handmade Sound Track for Beginners," and closely examining the soundtracks on his films. The Netherlands Institute for Animation Film (NIAF), where van Cuijlenborg studied for two years, had some 35mm copies of McLaren's films, so he could see how various shapes on the soundtrack created different sounds.

In his film *Scratch* (1999), van Cuijlenborg employs scratched images for both the visuals and the soundtrack. He began by scratching on the sound area of film, and recorded the results on a computer. He noted the frame numbers of this audio information, and indicated where every sound on the soundtrack was located and how many frames each lasted. He then filmed a color background for the visuals on 35mm. The visuals were scratched on the negative of that background footage, resulting in dark images on color backgrounds that are synchronized with the scratched sounds. He used a wide range of tools to remove the emulsion without damaging the film's base, including sandpaper, needles, and engraving tools.[23]

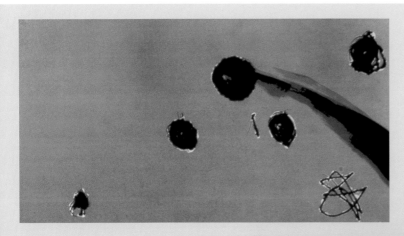

Oerd van Cuijlenborg used scratched imagery for both the visuals and the soundtrack of his aptly named film, *Scratch*.

Case Study: Richard Reeves

Canadian filmmaker Richard Reeves has also been inspired by McLaren's production notes, and the films behind them—particularly *Begone Dull Care*.[24] This inspiration has translated into a series of films concerned almost equally with direct production of visuals and sound. His first direct film, *GarBanZo* (1992), includes a traditional soundtrack, which he created himself, but he used drawn sound in *Zig Zag* (1993), *Linear Dreams* (1997), *Sea Song* (1999), and *1:1* (2001) (see pages 176–179 for Reeves's application and notes on creating drawn sound).

Reeves reworks the direct filmstrips he creates, manipulating them in layers to build complexity. He begins by drawing or painting on a piece of film, and when it is dry he goes back over it, adding more detail or increasing layers to saturate the color. He says, "This process—working along the film, then rewinding it, then working along it

again—helps create depth or texture that can be very dynamic. For example, painting on both sides of the film can create a type of depth of field because the projector will only focus on the top of the film's surface, leaving a slightly out-of-focus background."[25]

Reeves has accomplished much of his work in affiliation with the Quickdraw Animation Society (QAS) in Calgary, Canada, which supports independent animators working in the region.[26] He writes, "If the Quickdraw Animation Society in Calgary had not existed, I might have not heard about visual music, or realized animation was an art form. It was here that I was able to see films by Jordan Belson, James and John Whitney, Oskar Fischinger, Mary Ellen Bute, Walter Ruttmann, and others." Reeves made his second direct film, *Zig Zag*, in association with the QAS. Its imagery was created by precisely scratching into black leader, and adding color by marking Lumocolor pens over the scratched areas. He animated the film's sound in the optical sound strip by drawing shapes with a fine-point technical pen and black ink, and by

applying stick-on shapes such as dry letter transfers. The one-minute animated work took about six weeks to complete.[27]

Reeves's next film, *Linear Dreams*, is much longer—it runs seven minutes—and more complex. A handmade score is combined with both abstract and more representational imagery suggesting mandalas, planetary forms, humans, animals, and explosions of light or particles in space. Flashing images evoke the concept of memory, perhaps of a collective unconscious that unites humanity. At times, z-axis movement pulls viewers through space—for example, through a mountain range, the most representational imagery in the film. These sequences provide a perceptual break

Richard Reeves (above) at work.

Images from the films of Richard Reeves, including (left to right) *GarBanZo*, *Sea Song*, and *Zig Zag*, which includes its drawn soundtrack.

from the other nonstop, more abstract images. Viewers are also given a rest when Reeves pauses the information stream for a moment, with no sound or imagery.

He writes, "*Linear Dreams* was produced 'straight out,' in a linear format, the way dreams, visions, and thoughts are. The abstract imagery was intentional to shut down logical thinking of left-brain activity, which interrupts the creative flow. ... I have found that even the free-flowing films of cameraless animation produce a story or journey: It is the very nature of our thoughts."[28] The title is a play on words, suggesting the duality of the film. Reeves explains that the work employs "images from the mind's eye and music from the mind's ear.

The word 'linear' is composed of two words: 'line' as in drawing and 'ear' as in hearing. ... The line gives rise to the circle and explodes into the colorful universe of forms."[29]

Linear Dreams was in production for two years, beginning with more than seven months devoted to the soundtrack.[30] Reeves scratched shapes into the sound strip of 35mm film, recorded the sound into a computer, and added reverb to create a feeling of depth; he refers to the effect as a kind of "persistence of sound" that might be compared to the "persistence of vision" associated with continuous frames of images.[31]

The soundtrack was used to guide the creation of the visuals, which were primarily conceived straight ahead, starting at the first frame and progressing to the last. Reeves employed an airbrush, bleach, various scratch tools, markers, inks, and painting techniques to create textures, colors, and images on black, clear, and "orange" (processed negative) film stocks. Reeves worked on 200-foot (61-meter) strips of film. When they were finished, he draped them around his studio until they were dry. Finally, to protect the film's fragile surface, it was sprayed with ClearCoat.[32]

Processed Negative Film

Processed negative film, or negative that is developed without being exposed, has a distinctive "orange" cast. Direct film animators can mark on it and then have a positive (or screening copy) made from it. The resulting footage is black, except where images have been added. The tricky part is that everything on a negative is "opposite" to everything that prints to the positive. Black becomes white, white becomes black, and colors print as their complements: red and green, blue and orange, and yellow and violet. In other words, a blue line inked on this film stock prints as an orange line on a black background. Although it may present conceptual challenges, orange film offers the advantage of allowing black backgrounds surrounding drawn elements.

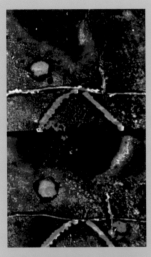

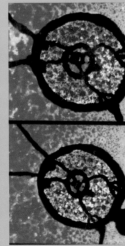
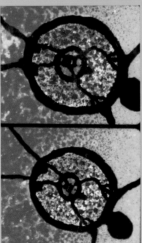

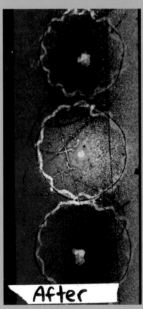

Images from *Linear Dreams*, by Richard Reeves, including (right) an example of his use of processed negative film, before and after printing.

Collaborative Approaches

Direct filmmaking often takes the form of intensely personal explorations, and gives animators the opportunity to become intimately engaged with the process, focusing on one small frame over long periods of time. However, it also lends itself to collaboration and social experience through partnerships or collective production. Norman McLaren, for example, often worked on his direct films for the National Film Board of Canada with a close collaborator, Evelyn Lambart. Three American filmmakers, Thad Povey, Devon Damonte, and Helen Hill, are among those who have advocated the production of cameraless film, as well as handprocessing, through workshops, creative groups, and writing.

Scratch Film Junkies

The Scratch Film Junkies are a San Francisco-based direct film collective established by Thad Povey in 1998. Among its ever-shifting members have been a variety of nonfilmmakers, including a sculptor, an architect, a painter, a digital designer, and, as soon as she was old enough to hold a pen, Povey's daughter Isabel.[33] Povey says, "We are a group of digital filmmakers—a spin on the term, since we truly use digits, the ones on the ends of our hands. We're making films by hand … with the purpose of exploring the possibilities of truly analog work in a digital world. This is a quilting bee with celluloid as fabric and sprockets for stitches."[34]

Group members sometimes collaborate on a single piece of film, but more often they generate their own work on individual strips, which are held for future manipulation by others and eventual use in a film—although some pieces never get used. *St. Louise* (1999), the first film created by the Scratch Film Junkies, was made to accompany a band, Soul Coughing, on tour. It includes such techniques as architectural appliqués and rub-ons, bleach-and-resist treatment of previously photographed images, scratched and cut-out black leader, and emulsion that was heated and burned with magnified sunlight. Some images were rephotographed onto print stock, reversing (or "inverting") the polarity of the original film.

The group experiments with all types of direct cinema, and doesn't limit itself to celluloid as a base. For example, Povey cut strips of mesh into 16mm widths and then punched holes in their edges so that they could be used as "film." The Scratch Film Junkies also use found footage. Povey is especially attracted to out-takes, with their awkward moments of humanity.

Thad Povey and family (above) creating films together.

Two stills from *St. Louise* (right), including a negative image of architectural appliqués on clear leader (top right).

When he prints the footage, Povey slows the films down so they run at 12 fps or slower, rather than 24; this makes them "a little more watchable. Cameraless films can be really hard on the eye after a while, just because they go so fast."[35] The effect can be seen in *Drink from the River* (2002), which Scratch Film Junkies made in response to the attacks on the World Trade Center in New York.[36] They worked directly on images filmed during a performance by a pyrotechnic group, Therm, which were contact-printed with handmade rayogram loops, as well as black-and-white footage of a woman and two children from a 1929 home movie found at a flea market.[37] This was the first of their films to be edited digitally, allowing for superimpositions and effects.

Getting back to analog basics, the group's *To the Beat* (2006) blends footage from *Drink from the River* with new material to create a playful toast to life, synchronizing the images with an improvised soundtrack by the German percussionist Steven Garling. Several long, continuous sections include bleached animations over streaked camera footage and handpainted, bleached found footage. One section was created by drilling into the face of a reel of film with a power drill to produce thousands of animated holes in a previously rephotographed handpainted sequence.

Crackpot Crafters

Crackpot Crafters (see page 19) is the name given to the direct film gatherings started by Devon Damonte in 2002. After many years teaching workshops at nonprofit media centers and at universities as a visiting artist, he decided that handmade filmmaking wasn't dependent on institutions, and was in fact somewhat antithetical them. So, somewhat inspired by Thad Povey's Scratch Film Junkies and the Sunday-night screenings held by Stan Brakhage (see page 156) he began free weekly work groups "to help empower both filmmakers and nonfilmmakers to get their hands dirty, experiment, and create movies in the most immediate direct ways imaginable."[38]

In addition to weekly meetings in Seattle and Olympia, Washington, Damonte has convened others in locations such as Boston, Massachusetts, and Providence, Rhode Island. Special twenty-four-hour versions have also been organized (the brainchild of fellow Crafter Jo Dery). At these marathon events, small groups of filmmakers make as many films as possible within twenty-four hours, using direct film techniques and handprocessing. At the end of the period, a public party is held to screen them. Sessions include a critique of loops made during the event, when participants discuss the results and

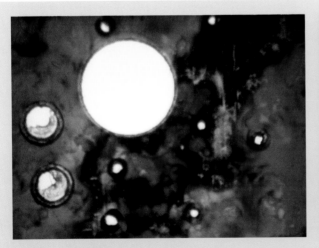

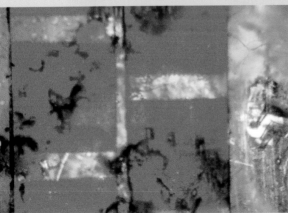

Three images from *Drink from the River*, including punched and handpainted clear leader (above left) and found footage (above right).

how they might be applied in his or her independent work. Damonte has shown selections of work produced by the Crackpot Crafters at screenings around North America.

As with the Scratch Film Junkies, the analogy of a quilting bee has been used to describe the way the Crackpot Crafters work; the collaborative experience is as significant as the filmmaking.[39] Damonte says, "The focus is not on group projects, nor on finished products, but on providing a space (usually an artist's live–work loft/studio) where normally solitary independent animators and friends can conjure up harebrained ideas to try out on film." Some of the most unusual techniques used by Crafters include growing salt crystals on clear film, using a soldering iron as a line tool on found footage, placing custom-made tiny temporary tattoos on leader, and packing a jar with found footage and rice and then pouring bleach over them to create a "rice resist pattern."

Since the late 1980s, Damonte himself has created numerous direct works on 16mm and 35mm film. One of his techniques, photocopying images onto clear film stock, can be seen in *Catcycle* (2001), *Rolling Man* (1999) (see page 120), and *A Barrel of Paul Klee* (1998). The last was inspired by Klee's seminal text *Pedagogical Sketchbook* from 1925, which contains a condensed version of his Bauhaus design lectures.[40] Made in black-and-white, the film combines text from the book with various images, juxtaposing them in interesting and sometimes amusing ways (for example, a portrait of the artist shown intermittently with a monkey figure).

In *Radio Active Spider* (2002) and other films Damonte uses ink transfers—specifically, a hot iron technique invented by San Francisco filmmaker Rock Ross. The process involves transferring ink from unnecessary pre-printed plastic items (like grocery bags, certain plastic tablecloths, lollipop bags, etc.) onto clear film leader by ironing the plastic onto the film; the iron must be hot enough to slightly melt the plastic, but not melt the film.[41] Damonte recommends using a sheet of Mylar (not acetate) or aluminum foil between the iron and plastic, to prevent the plastic from sticking to the hot surface. Ironing the transfer onto a rough surface (one that won't melt) creates interesting textures. After the plastic has cooled, it should be peeled carefully off the film to avoid flakes in the projector or lab equipment when film prints are made.

Recipes for Disaster

Helen Hill, of New Orleans, has made a number of interesting cameraless works, and has also created teaching materials for making handmade films. Her *Recipes for Disaster: A Handcrafted Film Cookbooklet* (2001) describes various direct film techniques, and also contains information on

Direct filmmaking at one of Devon Damonte's Crackpot Crafters meetings.

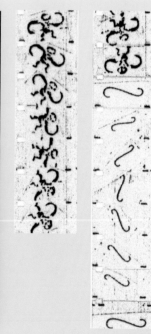

Filmstrips from Devon Damonte's *Catcycle* (left) and *A Barrel of Paul Klee* (above).

"Camera Tips and Projector Tricks" and "Handprocessing, Tinting, and Toning." The latter is covered in some detail: Many interesting effects can be made during processing and choices at this stage greatly affect a film's finished look. The possibilities are numerous and sometimes unusual. T.L. Frederick recommends using urine (combined with various chemicals), which boosts the contrast of black-and-white reversal film.[42] Maïa Cybelle Carpenter likes to soak nonhardener-fixed, developed film in dark red wine for a week.[43]

Hill demonstrates direct techniques in *Madame Winger Makes a Film: A Survival Guide for the 21st Century* (2001). The ten-minute production opens with a shot of a small pig, as the voice-over narration of Madame Winger notes that gelatin used in film manufacturing is made of animal bones—she hopes one day there will be vegetarian film stock. She goes on to explain that you don't need a lot of equipment to make a film, you just need a good idea. She also talks about film stocks and demonstrates ways to work directly on them. This lighthearted film includes appearances by Hill's husband and their pet pigs. Like a lot of her other work, it is made of mixed media, including pen on paper, cutouts, three-dimensional figures, and live-action footage (some pixilated).

Direct Animators in the Industry

It may come as a surprise, but direct film production can be found in the backgrounds of some individuals who have become successful animators in the industry—contributing to mainstream features, television series, games, and commercials. Following are a few examples.

Eric Swarthe

While enrolled in the animation program at the University of California, Los Angeles, Eric Swarthe created the Oscar-nominated *Kick Me* (1975). It begins and ends with legs kicking a ball, forms that evolve throughout the film. After graduating, he went on to have an immensely successful career in visual effects, working on *Close Encounters of the Third Kind* (1977) and *Star Trek: The Motion Picture* (1979), among other films.

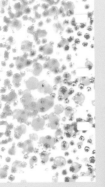

Helen Hill at work (below) and an image from her film *Madame Winger Makes a Film: A Survival Guide for the 21st Century* (right).

Images from *Radio Active Spider* (above) by Devon Damonte.

Steve Segal

An accomplished animator, Steve Segal has worked at Pixar on sequences for such features as *Toy Story* (1995) and *A Bug's Life* (1998), and also has credits for commercials, games, and short films. His non-CGI portfolio contains—among other direct films—*Russian Rooster* (1974), *Red Ball Express* (1975) (see page 21), and a contribution to a collaborative film, *Animation Has No Borders* (1986), directed by Peter Sweenen and produced by Cilia van Dyke in the Netherlands.[44] Segal also created direct animation sequences for *Futuropolis* (1984), a forty-five-minute film he co-directed with Phil Trumbo, which involves live action and a wide range of animation techniques.

Russian Rooster, set to the music of Nikolai Andreevich Rimsky-Korsakov, and *Red Ball Express*, which uses a bluegrass score, "Orange Blossom Special," reflect the influence of Norman McLaren, and particularly his film *Hen Hop*. In *Red Ball Express*, train imagery moves playfully across the screen, breaking into parts (such as spinning wheels) and abstract patterns, recalling the imagery of McLaren's film. Segal says *Hen Hop* was an even stronger influence on *Russian Rooster*, as he "deliberately chose a fowl and an alliteration title" to resemble *Hen Hop*.[45] His direct work was made by applying Dr. Ph. Martin's dyes on the emulsion side of the film (in *Russian Rooster* he used markers) and India ink on the other side.[46]

Direct Film Techniques

Recipes for Disaster, edited by Helen Hill, contains an array of interesting production tips, which were submitted by a wide range of filmmakers. The techniques described include:
– Using glitter nail polishes.
– Attaching negatives to film stock and using Letraset rub-ons.
– Using steel wool, blades, etching needles, push pins, and sandpapers over raised surfaces.
– Photocopying images onto film stock.
– Sewing directly onto stock with a sewing machine.
– Using curved knife blades to "sculpt" images on film stock.
– Working on the floor to attract random particles to the film.
– Using salt to create starbursts.
– Applying food from the refrigerator.
– Soaking live-action film in Fantastik cleaning fluid to soften the emulsion, so it can be lifted and transferred to another piece of film.[47]

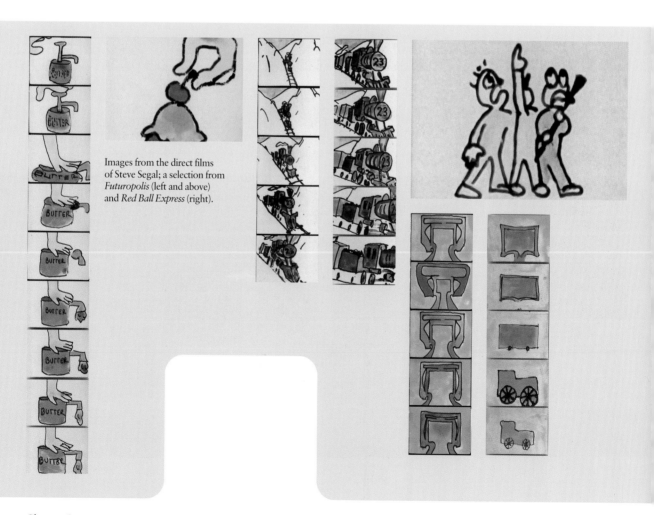

Images from the direct films of Steve Segal; a selection from *Futuropolis* (left and above) and *Red Ball Express* (right).

Eric Darnell

Co-director of the CGI features *Madagascar* (2005) and *Antz* (1998), Eric Darnell created the direct film *Grasslands* (1987) as his graduate thesis production at California Institute of the Arts. Using both documentary footage and live-action images he shot at southern California beaches, he painted on the film, frame by frame. Historian William Moritz described *Grasslands* as "an elegy and a protest for the erosion and loss of grasslands and the animals that traditionally inhabited them. Through the use of paint on film, [Darnell] sometimes 'closes in' on the desperate animals and sometimes restores to them the vanished wilderness."[48]

To some, the experience of creating hands-on direct animation may seem quaintly outdated in this age of high-powered digital technology. However, the immediacy of the form and the vitality of the imagery can invigorate artistic sensibilities, and the processes of creating direct visuals and sounds can bring immense creative challenges. Direct filmmaking strips the production process to its essential elements: film stock, a pen, brush, or blade, and the hand of the artist. Appealing equally to the beginning film student with a small budget and the accomplished artist seeking a "moving canvas" for his or her work, direct film has a long history and represents a distinctive, diverse animation practice.

Eric Darnell's *Grasslands* (below and right) was created as a student film, before he began his career in the field of computer animation.

Applications IV
Direct Motion Graphics
Loopology

Contributed by Devon Damonte
(see page 167)

Devon Damonte is a visual artist who has been specializing in making, teaching, and showing directly handmade, camera-free motion graphics since 1985. His films have screened internationally and he has been a guest lecturer at various institutions in the United States and Canada. Damonte currently abides in Olympia, Washington. His films include:
A Sense of Wonder (1987)
Catcycle (2001)
WonderPain (2002)
Explore the Endless Secrets of Nature (2002)
Duct and Cover (2003)
Website: www.devonimation.com

Objectives:
Instant filmmaking, immediate gratification, ultimate enlightenment! The following two exercises show how to make imagery by hand, directly onto film leaders, without a camera. They can be done by a group working on the same strip of film (group loops!) or individually.

Loopology A:
Seven-minute Warm-up

You will need:
- 16mm clear film leader: single- or double-perforations
- White paper
- Adhesive tape
- Permanent markers: extra-fine points and other widths
- 16mm guillotine tape splicer and tape: perforated splice tape or "press-tapes"; single splices could be used, but the guillotine splicer makes the exercise infinitely easier and more fun
- 16mm projector: preferably slot-load style or one with easy access to the film path; not self-loading. Certain models by Eiki and Singer are popular. Kodak "Pageant" is a little less yielding. Theoretically, any projector can be made to work, but you will probably spend more time fiddling with a non-slot-load one than doing anything else, and your creation may be destroyed in the first ten seconds.

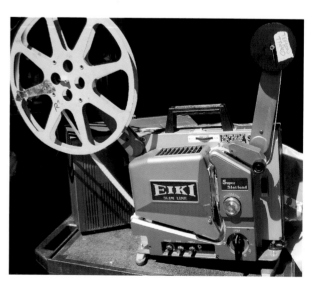

Devon Damonte (above) working on film.
Examples of single- and double-perforation filmstrips (right). An Eiki slot-load style projector (far right).

Filmmakers work from left to right.

1

Cut a length of clear leader. The length depends on the projector—for Eikis, the minimum is about 43 inches (1.1 meters) and the ideal about 68 inches (1.7 meters) The film can be longer, but you should remember that you'll have to hold a long loop by hand while it is running through the projector.

2

Put white paper around the edge of a table. Use adhesive tape to fix the film to the paper, running near the edge of the table with the top (starting frames) to your left. You will have to turn your body to the left to begin work on the film and then gradually shift your chair to the right as you move down the length of it.

3

Using permanent markers, quickly draw a succession of tiny pictures to animate a ball bouncing, a figure jumping, and your name moving.

4

Frames are defined by the inside corners of four sprockets. Try working within frames as well as making stripes across them to see different effects.

5

Try writing on every other frame, or every fourth frame, or using words and then letters on alternating frames, etc.

6

Splice the film together to make a loop.

7

Load the loop in the projector and run the film. Watch many times and note what works best and the results of different approaches.

Tips and Cautions:

— Some inks, paints, and solvents are toxic—always take precautions such as wearing gloves and working in a well-ventilated room.

— Do a few tests and watch the results before spending hours doing something that may turn out to be invisible (or self-destruct in the projector in the first .02 seconds).

— Most film runs at 24 fps. So if you draw one picture per frame, it will take forty-eight images to get two seconds' of running time. The number of frames needed so that something is readable is entirely subjective, so experiment—a single-frame word is surprisingly readable, even more so when white words are scratched into black leader (see Loopology B: Textured Scratch, pages 174–175).

— Respect film equipment that you share with filmmakers employing more traditional (and way cleaner) techniques. It's best to use your own and/or designate a particular projector/splicer setup as the "dirty" one. It's relatively easy to get equipment via eBay or buy it secondhand. To prolong its life—particularly if you are using someone else's—be very careful about the materials you use and make sure the equipment is clean after using it.

— Always clean projectors before and especially after use. Rubbing alcohol and Q-tips work well on most parts of the film path. A wooden or plastic stick might be needed to remove persistent bits—never use metal probes as they may scratch components.

Direct Motion Graphics Loopology

Loopology B: Textured Scratch

You will need:

- 16mm black film leader; make sure you can scratch through the emulsion side so that the scratched film is clear when held up to light
- Textured surfaces: metal speaker grille, lettered/textured glass, plastic, etc.
- Adhesive tape
- Hard smooth table/work surface that is safe to cut on
- Sponge
- Water
- Single-sided safety razor blade
- Assorted implements that can be used to scratch the film's surface
- Hair dryer (or hot lamp) to speed film-drying
- 16mm projector (see Loopology A: Seven-minute Warm-up)
- Guillotine tape splicer and tape
- Optional materials: Art/image-making supplies for additional coloring/layerings; permanent markers (or other suitable ink/paint); semitransparent ink/paint, or any material that marks/sticks on plastic, and is thin/smooth and flexible enough to flow gracefully through the projector gate and guides. Also try this exercise with colored leaders and found footage. Experiment with anything you can find!

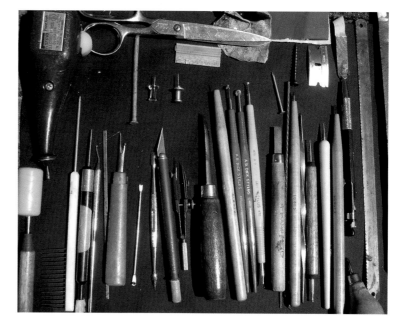

A selection of scratching tools used in this process.

1

Cut a length of black leader (see Loopology A, step 1).

2

Designate one end of the leader for "wet" methods and the other end for dry scratching.

3

Place the leader, emulsion side up, on your work area, over the top of a textured surface, and use adhesive tape to fix a section in place. To find the emulsion side of the film, put it on your wet lips—the kiss test. The emulsion side will stick because of the gelatin on it; the other side is slick and will fall off.

4

First work on the "wet" end of the leader; as you do so, moisten small portions of the film with one end of your sponge to prevent the film from drying out.

5

Carefully drag the edge of the razor blade across the film on top of the texture, applying enough pressure to scrape some emulsion off, but not so much that the film is cut or torn. The blade scrapes it clear/white wherever the texture is raised or bumpy.

6

Emulsion tends to readhere to scraped areas. Be sure to remove excess scraped emulsion trailings with the dry end of the sponge, and/or your fingers, as you work.

7

On the dry end of the film, repeat steps 4 and 5 and observe how the quality of the scraped image differs (and how much harder it is to scrape when the film is dry).

Step 5

8

Experiment with scratching letters and lines, both wet and dry, using different scratchy implements for different line qualities.

9

After the film has fully dried, splice it into a loop.

10

Load the loop in the projector and run the film.

11

Watch and note what works best, then repeat the exercise, adding more scratched layers to the loop.

Tips and Cautions:

— Keep sprocket holes and film edges intact. If you accidentally cut a hole or two, or the blade slices and breaks the film, the damage can usually be repaired with splicing tape, but this affects how smoothly the film runs, and how long the loop lasts; sometimes the only answer is to cut chunks out of the film.

— When scratching, the harder the work surface the better—if the film is on top of paper or some other soft surface it will get dented when you scratch letters or lines. This often makes it impossible to focus on the full image in projection, since the film is a dented or curved plane rather than flat. This can be used to good effect—literally "multiplane direct animation"—but if the dents are too extreme the film may be unprojectable.

— Razor blades are sharp—use caution, especially around youngsters.

— Because scratching takes more time than drawing with permanent markers, you might want to try a few things quickly, make the loop, and watch it, and then go back and do some more work on the film.

— If you are using single-perf black film, you can also create sound by scratching the sound edge (see Direct Sound application, pages 176–177).

Direct Sound

Contributed by Richard Reeves
(see page 164)

Richard Reeves continues to produce new works, exploring cameraless filmmaking as visual music and promoting animation as a time and space artform.
His films include:
GarBanZo (1992)
Zig Zag (1993)
Linear Dreams (1997)
Sea Song (1999)
1:1 (2001)
Element of Light (2005)

Objective:
To create sound by working directly on film. This exercise explores the components of volume, frequency, pitch, and tempo, as well as sound/picture synchronization.

You will need:
- Two 48-frame and one 240-frame (two- and ten-second) lengths of black leader—single-perf 16mm film
- Short length of any exposed 16mm film containing frame lines and an optical soundtrack
- Exacto blade or other tools for scratching fine lines
- Very small dry letter transfers or other sticky materials that can be adhered to the film
- Projection system for playback of optical sound

Take a 48-frame (two-second) length of black leader and place it on the table in front of you, running left (head) to right (tail), with the perforations on the side nearest you. Turn toward the left and work from top to bottom on the unperforated side of the film. Compare the leader to the exposed film to see how wide the sound stripe area is, so you know where to work (it is on the part of the film that would be covered by perforations on double-perf film).

2

First, experiment with volume by variable area. Scratch lines in the sound stripe area, beginning with thin and ending with thick (see page 178 for visual aids).

Richard Reeves drawing sound.

3

A second way to affect volume is with density. Scratch two small circles in the sound stripe area of one frame; just indicate the shape of each with a thin line and leave the circles black inside. Continue down the film, adding more lines inside the circles until they are completely scratched out (emulsion removed) and larger in size.

4

On a separate 48-frame (two-second) piece of film, experiment with frequency by varying the number of dots or lines per frame. The more dots or lines used, the higher the pitch when the film is projected.

5

On a 240-frame (ten-second) length of film, focus on tempo, which is created by repeating the same shape on frames in a pattern of some sort. For example, if a sound shape is placed on every 24 frames, the sound will occur at one-second intervals. Experiment with different types of shapes, using dry letter transfers or other sticky materials to see the sorts of sounds they produce.

6

For a more advanced project, if you wish to make visuals for your film that depict the shapes being used in the sound stripe area, remember that there is a separation between sound and picture. For 16mm film, the separation is 26 frames, with the sound coming before the image. Also remember that the visuals run across the film, whereas the soundtrack runs up and down. You will have to rotate your sound images by ninety degrees when they appear in the picture portion of the film.

Tips and Cautions:

— Working on 35mm film is helpful, since the sound area is very small on 16mm film; the larger-size film is not much more expensive than 16mm, but it can be more difficult to project (35mm projection equipment is not as easy to find in schools as 16mm equipment, for example).

— Be sure to scratch on the emulsion (gelatin) side of the film.

— It is generally recommended that the entire soundtrack is scratched first, so that it can be played back and timed out before the visuals are created.

— Be careful when using any sharp instrument, including knife blades, for scratching film stock.

— Gentle pressure will prevent cutting through the stock, but it is a good idea to work on surfaces that will not be damaged by the blade.

— Use caution when projecting film, as dry letter transfers and other materials can come off and damage equipment as it runs through sound heads. It is advisable to make a contact print of film stock containing extensive amounts of adhered objects, so that the print can be projected instead of the original.

16mm Animated Sound Notes:

Contributed by Richard Reeves
(see page 164)

Tempo
This is created by repeating shapes along a set pattern or number of frames apart. For example, a heart beating at 60 beats per minute would require a sound shape to be placed in one frame every 24 frames.

Dry Letter Transfers
These are mechanically made letters by companies such as Letraset. Once used in the graphic arts, they have now been mostly replaced by computer-generated lettering. Dry letter transfers are produced on a thin sheet of translucent plastic film. The letters are perfectly spaced and registered, and are applied to other surfaces by rubbing the back of the plastic sheet with the letters face down. If a long row of the same letter is applied to

the film, a musical "pure" tone can be heard. The letters are so perfectly spaced apart that they produce a pattern, which in turn is read as a tone when played through an optical sound reader. For example, a row of the letter A would create a definite-sounding tone. All of the letters have different tones. Also, small letter or point sizes make higher-pitched sounds, while larger letter or point sizes make deeper-sounding notes.

AAAAAAAAAAAAAAAA
(9 points)

AAAAAAAAAAAAAAAA
(14 points)

The 9-point letter A will sound higher in pitch (more lines per frame) compared to the 14-point A, which will sound deeper (fewer lines per frame).

35mm Sound + Picture Separation/ Synchronization
To make films that can be shared and viewed in all countries, the whole world agreed to make the universal standard for sound film 24 fps, and for silent film 18 fps. Therefore, the sound-to-picture separation was also agreed to be 20 frames apart from 35mm film. The reason for this separation is purely mechanical, as the distance between the projection bulb and the excitor bulb (optical sound reader) in all projectors is exactly 20 frames apart. By following the film path through the projector in the illustration, the visual frame being projected has its sound for that frame 20 frames ahead at the optical sound reader bulb. Sound therefore comes before picture.

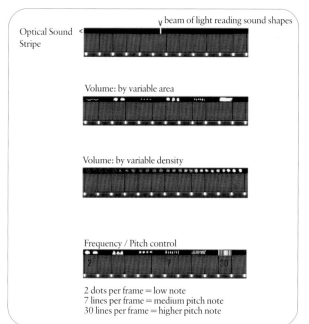

Optical Sound Stripe

beam of light reading sound shapes

Volume: by variable area

Volume: by variable density

Frequency / Pitch control

2 dots per frame = low note
7 lines per frame = medium pitch note
30 lines per frame = higher pitch note

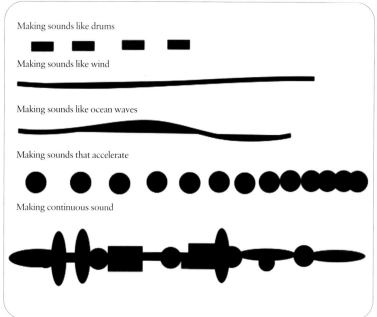

Making sounds like drums

Making sounds like wind

Making sounds like ocean waves

Making sounds that accelerate

Making continuous sound

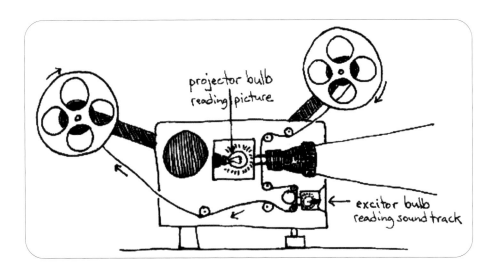

projector bulb
reading picture

excitor bulb
reading sound track

Synchronized Picture and Sound Separation

35mm = 20 frames
16mm = 26 frames
*always sound before picture

sound speed = 24 fps
silent speed = 18 fps

Emulsion Side Up/
Sound on Right-Hand Side

This will ensure the picture will be projected the right way up, and the sound will synchronize with the picture.

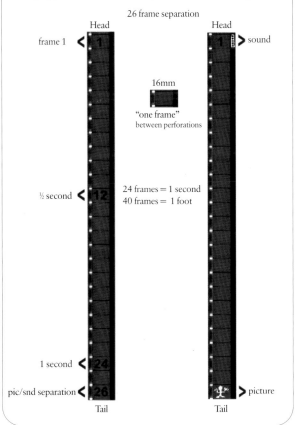

26 frame separation

Head · frame 1 ◄ 1 ·· Head · 1 ► sound

16mm
"one frame"
between perforations

½ second ◄ 12

24 frames = 1 second
40 frames = 1 foot

1 second ◄ 24

pic/snd separation ◄ 26 ·· ► picture

Tail · Tail

Mixed Media and Drawing

During much of the twentieth century, cel techniques dominated the commercial animation industry worldwide, and the "Disney style" was considered to be the ideal for 2D animation. However, the aesthetics of animation have varied throughout its history, and artists always have employed a wide range of media to create animated images.

Mixed Media

A mixed-media approach allows animators to work with varied materials as they develop storytelling possibilities and the overall aesthetic of a work. Sometimes mixed media combine 2D and 3D materials, including mixtures of drawn and painted images in conjunction with live-action, stop-motion, or 2D and 3D CGI.

Simon Pummell English artist Simon Pummell provides an example, as he works across a continuum of live-action and animation practices, creating productions that are enigmatic and sometimes disconcerting. Historian Jayne Pilling has described his work as challenging "all conventional definitions of animation through its complex, technically innovative

production techniques. … Though highly diverse in subject matter and look, the films all deal with anxieties around the human body, technology, and one's place in the self and in the world."[1] *Butcher's Hook* (1995) illustrates both of these themes and Pummell's preference for a mixed-media approach. It employs objects (sometimes to create shadows), charcoal, graphite, and other media to tell the story of a taxidermist who is attacked by his preserved animals and becomes a specimen himself. Ant Walsham was responsible for the compositing and digital manipulation, which was used to create translucency in the images and integrate the taxidermist into his environment.[2]

Many of the techniques used in *Butcher's Hook* grew out of Pummell's work on *The Secret Joy of Falling Angels* (1992)—and developed from experiments in drawing the body for an earlier film, *Surface Tension*, which he made as a student at Royal College of Art and Design, London, in 1986. *The Secret Joy of Falling Angels* was inspired by fifteenth-century depictions of the Annunciation, and depicts a confrontation between a woman and a winged figure that ends with a sexual liaison.[3] In the film, Pummell explores the ways in which complex forms can be moved in a type of squash-and-stretch animation style, and contrasts

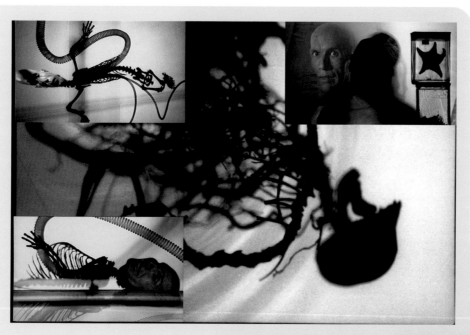

Images from Simon Pummell's *Butcher's Hook* (above).

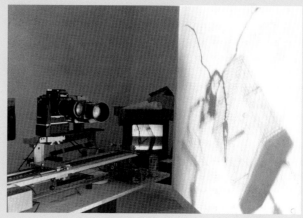

the structure of a firm skeletal figure with that of a fleshy outer covering.

For parts of the work, he used a shadow puppet made from a real bird skeleton fitted with tiny flexible brass joints that were inset into each bone. The shadow was shot through translucent paper capturing the grain and texture. Each frame was printed onto photographic paper and pegged with holes so it could be aligned with other images created for the film. These images were drawn on 90-micron 15-field animation paper using charcoal and graphite. Under the camera, the heavily reworked drawings were layered so that multiple images could appear simultaneously through backlighting. These forms were shot with a traditional 35mm rostrum camera modified to incorporate a backlit multiplane setup. The lower-level drawings appear to be softer than those on top, with the fiber of the paper providing a cloudy texture that adds to the dream-like quality of the images.

Wang Shuibo A mixed-media approach also suited Wang Shuibo's objectives for his *Sunrise over Tiananmen Square* (1998), a documentary of his life in China before, during, and after the Cultural Revolution. It was created largely through "kinestasis," moving a camera over still artwork, though some segments animate in relatively limited ways. The artwork is Wang's own; thus he traces his evolution as an artist, from a young child creating pencil drawings to a propaganda poster artist in the Red Army, and on to an award-winning university student who absorbed the influence of western culture after the Cultural Revolution ended. These images are interspersed with photographs documenting not only Wang's life, but also "the journey of his generation from the Red dream to American dream."[4]

Wang trained as a painter, studying both traditional Chinese and European classical techniques, so, he says, "I could draw like a European and also like a Chinese."[5] Some sequences from *Sunrise* demonstrate his Chinese approach. Scenes from his hometown were created on silk in the tradition of scroll painting, using a kind of watercolor made from natural sources, such as flowers and leaves. The silk was only about one yard (one meter) long, whereas scrolls are often much longer. To create images of his village, he employed a multi-angle perspective traditionally used in China. He explains that in Chinese painting, "you can draw from your imagination and draw from your heart, your brain. You can play with different angles of perspective or even ignore perspective. It's very free and full of imagination."

As the images of the village dissolve to a boy reading, Wang shifts to an academic European drawing style, based on a portraiture approach that favors realism; he used Prismacolor pencils on frosted cels, a technique also employed in other sequences. Other media and stylistic choices appear throughout the film. For example, paper cutouts were used in a sequence featuring Coca-Cola bottles juxtaposed with Karl Marx, and a photocopier was used to make many different-size color images of Mao Zedong pointing at the camera.[6] Traditional Japanese rice paper appears behind a sequence showing a dead baby in a box. A headmaster who has been hanged is depicted in a Chinese style using a cel; the atmosphere is Zen-like, a scene of death under beautiful pear blossoms. An image of a Buddhist temple is created on silk stretched over a wood panel, using a technique Wang invented for the project. He first applied watercolor and ink to the material, then varnish, and, finally, oil.

Simon Pummell created some images for *The Secret Joy of Falling Angels* (above and opposite) using a shadow puppet made from a bird's skeleton, which was photographed through paper.

In *Sunrise Over Tiananmen Square* (above), Wang Shuibo used mixed media to depict the changing culture in China.

Case Study:
Michael Sporn

Michael Sporn is a New York animator who has created a number of made-for-television and independent projects through his studio, Michael Sporn Animation, Inc. These include *The Hunting of the Snark* (1989), an adaptation of the Lewis Carroll poem; *The Talking Eggs* (1991), a folktale involving children and a mysterious old lady set in a modern context; *Whitewash* (1994), based on the true story of a black girl who was assaulted and spray-painted white; and *Champagne* (1997), an animated documentary about a girl growing up in a children's home because her mother is in prison. All the narratives were developed by Sporn's writing partner, Maxine Fisher.

The rich visual look of Sporn's animation is the result of a technique that employs cutout paper figures pasted to cels and used in combination with treated paper backgrounds (in addition to traditional "ink and paint" cel animation). Typically, figures are animated on Hammermill Copy Plus 25 lb., which is cut to match the paper used in the studio's photocopier. Final production art is printed onto the same paper in some cases, but often it is rendered on other paper, which varies in color, style, and thickness. Sporn favors paper with a lot of tooth, since it shows more texture when colored.

The production process generally involves animating characters on the bond paper at an 8-field size, then overlaying each drawing with the selected production paper and outlining the image on it with the aid of a light table. Outlining might be done with colored pencils, markers, or a Rapidograph pen; in some cases only a light pencil tracing is made, so no outlining appears. The drawing is colored with whatever media have been selected—mostly markers with Prismacolor pencils on top for added detail, accentuating the tooth and texture of the paper. Because Kraft paper was used to create characters for *The Talking Eggs*, that film's production process was slightly different.[7] It was hard to see through this dark, thick paper, so animated images drawn on white paper were photocopied onto Kraft that had been cut to size for use in the film. The images were then colored with Prismacolor pencils.

On projects using paper cutouts and markers, it is sometimes challenging to combine colors on a figure, as Sporn explains:

We use alcohol-based markers, which will make other alcohol-based markers bleed (i.e., Eberhard Faber markers will cause Sharpies to run). Hence outlines of characters have to be done with water-based markers (Pentel, Razorpoint, and Penstix are the most frequently used). If the style demands that alcohol-based markers have to be used for the outline, coloring of the character could be done with a water-based marker, but they are problematic for larger areas: there's no consistency of tone, they wear out quickly, and they are difficult to blend. In these cases, we've colored from the back of the paper, counting on the alcohol-based marker to bleed through the paper and not cause outlines to run. However, we usually try to avoid blending the same type of markers. We try to design a style around the problems.[8]

Animator Michael Sporn (above), collaborates regularly with writer Maxine Fisher (pictured right with Champagne, of whom they made a film of the same name).

Champagne remained in a red shirt throughout the film, to make it easier to follow her character as she developed from a small girl to a teenager.

Outlining and coloring are the first steps in the completion of Sporn's artwork. After the figures have dried overnight, they are prepared for adhering to the cel and, eventually, cutting. First, the bond paper with the original drawing is placed on the back of a clear cel so it can be used for alignment. The character's area on the cel, as indicated on the drawing, is then covered with rubber cement. The back of the character on the production drawing is also coated with cement. When both are dry, the production art is aligned to the model shown on the original drawing and they are pressed together to make sure the production art has adhered to the cel's surface in its proper location.

At this point, the cel (with production art attached to its front) is flipped over and objects that extend beyond the character's central figure, such as the whiskers of a cat, are inked on the back. The cels are also numbered in order at this stage. When inking has been completed, the cel and art are turned frontward again and placed on an illuminated light table. A knife is used to cut around the edge of the figure, just outside its borderline, and Prismacolor pencil is used to darken the

edge of the cut figure, to avoid white paper appearing at its edge. Sporn explains, "This white edge can show on film, or oftentimes glow because animation camera lights are placed on 30-degree angles from the table top. The light reflects back into the lens of the camera off this white edge. Using Prismacolor pencils and edging the paper to black (or a dark color) prevents this problem."

Up to five levels of cels can be combined under the animation camera. However, less light reaches the ones on the lower levels, so a color used on the bottom layer of cels will be darker than the same color on the top level. As a result, if an element appears on a low level and then on a higher one, the colors will appear to be a different. To solve this problem, known as a "color pop," Sporn keeps separate animated elements—perhaps a head and a body—on their own levels throughout a scene. It is possible to compensate for the varied layers by using different tones of cel paint, known as "let downs," but that is much more difficult to do using markers, colored pencils, and other media.

Backgrounds, like characters, are handled differently in each of Sporn's films, though texture is always significant. Staedtler Lumocolor pens have often been employed to color background elements on paper. They were used to create backgrounds in *Doctor De Soto* (1984), *Mysterious Tadpole* (1986),

Lyle Lyle Crocodile (1987), *The Hunting of the Snark*, *Abel's Island* (1989), and *Nightingale* (1992). They were also used on backgrounds for *Little Match Girl* (1991), but with the addition of airbrushing on a cel above them. Backgrounds for *Champagne* and *The Emperor's New Clothes* (1991) were made with watercolor and Prismacolor pencils on Wachtman Arches watercolor paper. Chalk pastels on pastel paper were used for *The Talking Eggs*. Although a fixative was applied to the completed backgrounds, the color remained delicate and was easily scarred, so during shooting it was protected with a clear cel overlay.

The backgrounds for *The Red Shoes* (1989), *The Marzipan Pig* (1990), and *Whitewash* were created with oil sticks. These images took about four days to dry, so they prolonged the production process. However, the oil sticks complemented the character design in *The Red Shoes*, which involved thick layers of colored pencil. First, the characters were colored with a marker that was nearly black but allowed black outlines to show through. Next, different colors, in order from darkest to lightest, were added with Prismacolor pencils. Sporn says, "If you were going to color flesh tones, you'd color the skin tones 95 percent black, then add dark brown Prismacolor pencil, a lighter color on

Lumocolor pens on paper created backgrounds for *The Hunting of the Snark* directed by Michael Sporn.

The documentary short *Champagne*, directed by Michael Sporn, used cutout paper figures, cels, markers, and other media. The staging and lighting of this scene enhance its visual appeal.

top of that, and then on top of that the final flesh color. Essentially, like an impasto, you'd build to the color. This gave us very rich, dense colors, and you needed equally dense backgrounds. Oil stick gave us that."

A similar technique was used for the backgrounds in *Whitewash* to create a "dirty look" that suggested the backdrop of New York City. In this case, the oil sticks were layered. Once the bottom coat was dry, it was covered on top with more oil stick. While the top layer was still wet, the end of a paintbrush or other sharp object was used to scrape through to the bottom layer, or sometimes to the paper itself, giving the backgrounds a rough look that simulated the dirtiness of the streets. The backgrounds were overlaid with cels containing photocopied layout lines.

Sporn draws inspiration from artists working in a variety of media and styles. For example, he based the title sequence of *Whitewash* on the titles of the live-action feature *West Side Story* which were designed by the graphic artist Saul Bass. Sporn also cites the influence of Robert Rauschenberg on the film, as well as the look of the New York School of painting. He wanted backgrounds that included texture and lots of grit; little flakes and bits of paint were welcomed as part of the desired look.[9] In some instances, the appearance of a scene is the result of particular in-studio talents, such as Bridget Thorne and Jason McDonald, who are Sporn's primary storyboard and background artists. For example, *Champagne* was greatly influenced by McDonald, who designed and storyboarded the second half of the film and painted its backgrounds. The first half was animated straight ahead by Sporn himself, without the use of storyboards.

More and more, Sporn has incorporated digital tools into his production processes, though not wholeheartedly. He states candidly, "Given the current state of the film industry, given the current state of the animation industry, there is no way any animator could continue producing animated films using past methods—cels, Oxberry cameras, film." He says, too, that clients increasingly expect digital technology will be used. Considering his strong attachment to intricate, handmade films, it is not surprising that he laments the changes; however, he also recognizes that computers offer a number of advantages.

As desirable qualities, he cites:

- The unlimited number of levels available digitally.
- The available effects that can be easily added to a piece.
- The immediacy of pencil tests and color tests.
- The ability to immediately correct mistakes or problems in an animated piece, and the ability to alter field guides and camera moves.
- Slow down, speed up, twos to threes to ones—all changes that can be made relatively quickly.
- Firm, absolutely solid tracebacks[10] are easy to produce.
- No color pops, no shadows, no cel flash.

However, in same breath as he says "These are all positives," he adds:

They're also all negatives. Because you are able to have all of the above, you

Doctor De Soto (above and right), released in 1984, is among the early films of Michael Sporn Productions.

Texture adds a great deal of visual interest to these two images from *The Red Shoes* (below and opposite) directed by Michael Sporn.

do. Unlimited cel levels can be easily disorganized. Effects can override a simple piece. All those changes keep going on to the point where they push the end back and back. It takes a lot of discipline to say, "This is not all that I wanted, but I have to stop changing it and accept the limited piece I have in hand." Compromises existed all those years on film—it's hard to remember that they should exist in a piece you can so easily change… and change … and change.

Sporn stresses the importance of restraint when using digital tools. He feels the "amateur" status of directors is often apparent in the extent to which they overuse digital effects, just because they can.

Sporn's first contact with digital tools was during the production of *Goodnight Moon* (2000), which was adapted for the HBO cable network from the Margaret Wise Brown story of the same name. Although the film was storyboarded and animated by hand, Sporn was not satisfied with the resulting pencil test and decided to try computer enhancement of the imagery. After they had been colored, animated figures and backgrounds were scanned into a computer. The 2D backgrounds were arranged into a 3D setup and small camera movements were created. A kind of multiplane effect was achieved when the 2D characters were placed in the 3D background using Animo. Sporn also taught himself to use Photoshop and After Effects.

Dissatisfied with the "readymade" filters provided by Photoshop, Sporn has learned to create some of his own. For example, he sometimes uses the "canvas" filter to create texture, but also imports his own paper weaves. But whether a filter is part of the package or an "original" he developed, the results share a problematic feature: They always look the same. Sporn says, "The weave or the patterns are always placed in the same position on the art. You have to move it about so that the texture replicates the randomness of working on handcolored paper. It has to move." To create the look of watercolors, he has scanned in a sheet of watercolor wash, which he cuts and pastes into the art. He has done the same with colored pencils, oil paints, and chalks. In all these cases, says Sporn, the texture "has to be moved around the character at random or it will look like the character is moving through the field of texture and the texture treatment will be annoyingly obvious."

Sporn continues to work at "sound film speed," creating 24 fps. To avoid large pixels, he works at very high resolutions, only bringing the resolution down to normal DV 4:3 standards, 720 x 480 pixels, during the last step of After Effects compositing. At this point, he adds camera movements and shifts to 30 fps. While Sporn continues to conceptualize his work in terms of his past production techniques, he has come to accept computer animation. He explains, "My goal was that hand-drawn look, which I had developed on cels. I've reached the point where I'm content with what I *can* do. I prefer the actual handcolored, hand-drawn artwork, but I can't have it. This will do."

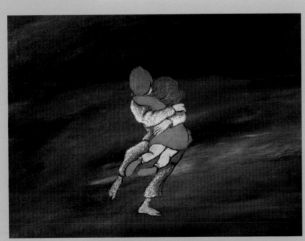

The backgrounds for *Whitewash* (above and left), directed by Michael Sporn, were created by layering different colors of oil stick on paper and then scraping down to the various levels.

Drawing

During the 1950s, the United Productions of America (UPA) and Zagreb studios created stylized figures and backgrounds for cel animation that contrasted greatly with classical Disney-style aesthetics. Since that time, many animators have used cels to create innovative animation. However, a drawback of the cel process always has been the laborious, costly work of inking and painting hundreds if not thousands of cels. The development of digital ink and paint systems has streamlined the process, making it possible for individual artists to create the look of cel animation using their home computers.

Variations on Cel Animation

Cel animation generally involves tracing images onto clear celluloid sheets using acetate-adhering inks. When the ink has dried, the cels are painted on the back with acrylic paints formulated to stick to the surface. Using "frosted" acetate (a cel that is clouded on one side to give it "tooth") allows the application of a wide range of media—pencils, ink pens, watercolors, pastels, and so on—that would not stick to the slick surface of regular cels. Some animators have used cels in traditional ways to create images that are quite stylized and distinctive, far from the norm of Disney-style animation.

Others have used cels in innovative ways to create wholly new techniques. Today, digital ink and paint systems have largely taken over the processes of inking and painting cels, creating work that achieves a similar look using software rather than pens and brushes.

Frédéric Back German animator Frédéric Back used colored pencils and frosted cels to combine the look of drawing on paper with an ability to layer images. He sometimes sprayed varnish over his images to make the frosted look disappear, so the area around the colored pencil drawings became clear. It was important to get this sort of transparency in scenes where he layered up to six cels, including elaborate landscapes and water imagery,[11] for *L'homme qui plantait des arbres* (*The Man Who Planted Trees*, 1987).

This beautiful film was produced by the Canadian Broadcasting Corporation (in French, Société Radio-Canada). It is based on Jean Giono's story of Elzéard Bouffier, a shepherd who planted thousands of trees to reforest a stretch of barren land in southern France, reflecting Back's love of nature and environmental concerns. It is the most famous among the animator's well-known works, which also include *La fleuve aux grandes eaux* (*The Mighty River*, 1993; see page

Environmental issues play a significant role in the animation of Frédéric Back, who works with colored pencil on frosted acetate. Pictured here are *L'homme qui plantait des arbres* (above), *La fleuve aux grandes eaux* (above right), and *Crac!* (right).

16), an environmental history of the St. Lawrence River, and *Crac!* (1981), a story of a rocking chair and the family it belongs to, reflecting the industrialization of Montreal. Back has drawn these works primarily on his own, with the help of an assistant animator. He is also an accomplished illustrator and painter.

Ivor Kovalyov Ukrainian animator Ivor Kovalyov became well-known for a trilogy of stylized ink and paint cel animation films he directed over a period of seven years: *Hen His Wife* (1989), *Andrei Svislotski* (1991), and *Bird in the Window* (1996). The last was produced after Kovalyov moved to the United States to work for the Klasky Csupo animation studio. At the studio, he directed the mainstream feature *The Rugrats Movie* (1999), the first non-Disney animated feature to break a $100 million box office gross within the United States. Alongside a successful industrial career, Kovalyov has continued to create his own films, including the highly acclaimed *Milch* (2005), a virtually wordless film that runs over fifteen minutes in length (see pages 26 and 84).

For this film, Kovalyov (who is credited as writer, director, and animator) utilized digital technologies to scan and paint the images. In addition, Toon Boom Opus was used to composite backgrounds designed by Dima Malanitchev,

which were created using Adobe Photoshop. Pre-production planning involved a great deal of work on paper and two tests of the animation carried out by Steve Mills. After that, three key scenes from the film were tested using Toon Boom Opus, to better prepare for full-scale production. After the tests proved satisfactory, *Milch's* production proceeded in this manner: scenes scanned; scenes painted; backgrounds pulled in; first pass "best guess" composite done; art direction notes on this composite; changes made based on art director's notes; director's notes; changes made based on director's notes; final approval received; sent to Avid; and sent to film recorder for output onto film. This production process took approximately six months, a speed made possible because of the efficiency of the digital media.[12]

In all his work, Kovalyov's character designs are distinctive; figures are usually somewhat grotesque, with plump bodies, angular faces, and pocked skin. His sketchbook images, from which he draws inspiration, reflect skewed perspective (sometimes completely flat characters) and a sordidness that pervades the gritty milieus of his films, which typically examine obtuse interpersonal relationships and the psychological complexities of life. Kovalyov's films are set within backgrounds that are visually rich, including patterning and detail that provide interesting environments for highly

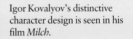

Igor Kovalyov's distinctive character design is seen in his film *Milch*.

personal and evocative stories that are semi-autobiographical in nature. His influences include the legendary Russian animators Yuri Norstein (see page 239) and Fedor Khitruk, whose style was influenced by the Zagreb School of animation, and the live-action filmmakers Ingmar Bergman, Carl Dreyer, and Andrei Tarkovsky. However, the greatest impact has come from the Estonian animator Priit Pärn and the French live-action filmmaker Robert Bresson, both of whom were painters.

Priit Pärn The distinctive style of Priit Pärn includes highly stylized, flattened characters with little emphasis on physical beauty. They appear throughout his body of work, including *1895* (1995), a revisionist history of the birth of cinema, co-directed with Janno Poldma, and *Night of the Carrots* (1998), a surreal investigation into the effects of technology on our lives. His cel-animated film *Breakfast on the Grass* (1987) tells the story of four characters whose lives intersect as each searches for something they need. The title refers to Edouard Manet's painting *Le Déjeuner sur l'herbe* (1863), which met with public hostility for its depiction of a nude woman amid clothed men, but became a major influence on emerging young Impressionist painters. Pärn's film is a pointed commentary on the Soviet system; the characters in *Breakfast on the Grass*

know all too well how to maneuver through the dense bureaucracy complicating even the simplest of aims. For example, one of the female characters desires only some apples, but this costs her dearly. Pärn's work as an artist extends to other media such as etching and charcoal drawing, and these sometimes provide inspiration for his animation.

Rachel Bevan Baker Cels also were used to create *Beelines* (1999) by Scottish artist Rachel Bevan Baker, co-founder of Red Kite Productions.[13] However, Bevan Baker used the cels in an innovative way—as the base for an etching process. Using etching needles bought from a Bulgarian master printer, she scratched on cels that were relatively thick—about 100 microns in weight—and could therefore withstand the process. She also roughed up the surface of the cels using sandpaper and steel wool, which provided "tooth" and allowed her to rub in various media to create a cloudy layer of color. The media she used included oil pastels, oil bars, china markers, and oily colored pencils that would adhere to the cels. She also used some colored tissue paper.[14]

Bevan Baker says making *Beelines* was time-consuming. "I'd line-test each sequence sometimes up to ten times, and the coloring process was very complex. I would etch the color into the cels by scratching lines in the acetates and rubbing it

Pictured here are four images by Priit Pärn: a painted-cel image of Jean-Paul from *1895* (above), a painted-cel image of Anna from *Breakfast on the Grass* (left); a charcoal sketch, *El Sur* (right); and sketchbook drawings (below).

into the lines, sometimes using six layers of acetates at a time.... It gives a very rich, earthy look."[15] A similar technique was used for *The Green Man of Knowledge* (2000), but the coloring process was slightly different. The cels were also etched, but in this case only oil bars were used, applied very liberally. Bevan Baker explains that the excess color was rubbed off "more like you would clean ink off a monoprint, i.e., using a rag to 'draw' in the ink. There was a layer of paper underneath, too, where we rubbed chalk pastel (which we ground up with a pestle and mortar!). The scene was really like an old artist's studio, with rags and inks and pots of pigment, all coded to match different characters' coloring! It was mad."[16] More recently, Bevan Baker also has embraced digital technology, including Adobe Flash.

J.J. Sedelmaier Productions Within an industrial context, production studios often are limited in the range of media that can be used. However, studios specializing in advertising tend to have some leeway. Clients wanting to create strong visual impressions in animated advertisements are generally attracted to interesting techniques. At J.J. Sedelmaier Productions (JJSP), located in White Plains, New York, artists have used a wide range of drawing and painting media to deliver the desired results—varying approaches from

project to project or sometimes combining media within a given work. The decision to use cels—or not—has rested on a variety of factors, including the aesthetics of the piece, the complexity of the visuals, and the current state of technology.

J.J. Sedelmaier started JJSP, with his wife Patrice managing the business, in 1991. Among its first projects was the "Beavis and Butt-Head" series, which was animated at the studio during its first season (beginning in 1992) and sent to USAnimation (later known as VirtualMagic) for digital ink and paint. The series backgrounds, which were created with chalk pastels on paper and color-scanned into a high-resolution computer, also were made at JJSP. Subsequently, the studio has been involved with other made-for-television animated series: Sedelmaier created "The Ambiguously Gay Duo," "The X-Presidents," and "Fun with Real Audio" with writer Robert Smigel for the "Saturday TV Funhouse" segment of the "Saturday Night Live" series. The studio also has been involved with productions like "Captain Linger" and "Harvey Birdman, Attorney at Law" for Cartoon Network's "Adult Swim" block.[17]

JJSP's television commercials have been created for a variety of clients, and many—Sedelmaier estimates 80 percent—require animated images in the style of artists, cartoonists, and other designers from outside the studio.

Rachel Bevan Baker (above) at work, etching and checking cels. Images from her films *The Green Man of Knowledge* (right) and *Beelines* (below).

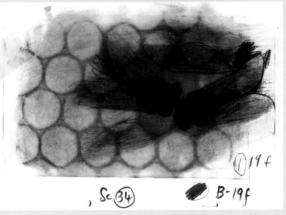

Sedelmaier says, "We have to figure out how we can take this artist's style and make everyone think the artist did the animation. We can't have preconceived ideas of how the animation would be done."[18] When Gary Baseman provided the character design for "Bed" (1996), a cel-animated commercial for Celebrity Cruise Lines, Sedelmaier had to find a creative way to reproduce the quality of his work—in particular, its texture. Texture can't be achieved by painting on the bottom side of a cel (in the conventional way), so Sedelmaier put the paint on top. When complete, the setup for photography consisted of three layers. The first was a cel containing a photocopied outline of the figure; underneath it was a cel painted with the character's color and texture on its topside; and finally there was the background, made with cel paint on paper.

Though the studio produced a great deal of cel animation, a significant amount of its work was animated on paper—for example, a thirty-second Brown & Co. commercial, "Buy Low" (1995). Images for the commercial were based entirely on a single print advertisement for the company drawn by David Levine. For inspiration and visual reference, Sedelmaier videotaped the company's founder, George Brown, who appears in the advertisement giving investors the advice to "buy low." To reproduce Levine's style, artists had to create very fine lines using India ink in a Pigma Micron pen with a 001 tip, drawing on bond paper. Unfortunately, the lines were so fine that they could not be photocopied without significant image loss—normally, the studio uses photocopies rather than original drawings under the camera.

It might seem preferable to photograph the originals, but Sedelmaier believes it is easier and psychologically better for assistants and in-betweeners to have the opportunity to correct any errors that may crop up. If a line is covered over with opaquing fluid, it will not appear on the photocopy. The copies are also easier to paint on; original ink lines will bleed when watercolors are applied over them, but photocopied lines will not. On the down side, photocopies do not reproduce the artwork exactly. Sedelmaier explains, "We adjust the Xerox machine with each job to retain the line quality. The biggest danger is the 'stretching' that occurs during the photocopying process. When the copies are pegged, we have to make sure we're taking the stretch into consideration."[19]

Photocopies also were used to film "Spider" (1996), a Converse Wild Things spot. A jittery, unsettling quality was achieved through the studio's choice of technique. Throughout the spot, they used only one level was used, which contained the background, figures, and color rendering. The advertisement was animated on twos, so everything was redrawn for every other frame. Original drawings were photocopied onto bond paper and watercolored, then filmed. They shimmer because of the small registration shifts in the background that result from redrawing and repainting.

Images from "The Ambiguously Gay Duo" (above), and "Buy Low" (right), animated by J.J. Sedelmaier Productions.

From the mid-1990s onward, digital media became more pervasive at JJSP. In 1995, Levi's "Factory" became the studio's first digitally rendered advertisement. Drawings on paper were done at the studio, and digital ink and paint was carried out at USAnimation. Sedelmaier was motivated to use digital ink and paint because traditional methods would have required something like twenty levels, and would have included extensive optical printing work. By about 1998, JJSP had stopped producing cel animation; anything that looks like it is now done digitally. However, different types of animation continued to be created at the studio, typically through a combination of handwork and digital production.

While software by itself can be used to create a drawn or painted look, the result is not always satisfying. Sedelmaier says:

We've done productions in watercolor, airbrush, pen and ink, cellotak, cel paint, digital ink and paint and compositing, Flash animation, 3D CGI, and various combinations of the above. With the replacement of acetate and cel paint by computer ink and paint, we've had to find ways to re-create techniques in a digital domain. The problem can sometimes be that the computer isn't the most ideal tool for executing work that consists of human inconsistency. The fluctuation of airbrush, the undulation of watercolor, and even the wiggle of a line, will all struggle against the formulaic tendencies of the digital production realm.[20]

Sedelmaier sometimes looks for a project just so he can learn a tool, experimenting with software to get it to do more than it is supposed to. In fact, his studio's first use of Flash occurred in that manner. In 2003, he was asked to create fifteen thirty-second spots for the Oxygen cable network, and he saw this as an opportunity for his studio to learn the software. They approached the experience from a problem-solving point of view, rather than just following the manual. In the end, traditional animation was mixed with Flash by scanning in drawings, tracing over them to vectorize the images, and further manipulating them with the software. Sedelmaier explains, "This allowed us to incorporate human inconsistencies into the drawing and animation."

During the early and mid-1990s, the studio outsourced its digital work, but today more of it is done in-house. Sedelmaier explains, "There are now fewer facilities you can go to for digitizing, compositing, or other work. I used to work with USAnimation/VirtualMagic in Los Angeles, but it got out of the service industry." Today, Sedelmaier sees digital methods as essential to his studio. He says, "There's absolutely no way to justify producing films in the same way we used to, even shooting on film. But that's true in terms of a production studio, not for independent filmmakers. I'd still recommend working on film to a beginning animator because it's easier to grasp the process. You can see the frames while using film, as opposed to video, where you can't."

J.J. Sedelmaier's studio began using Flash when it worked on a series of spots for the Oxygen cable network, pictured here.

Pencils

Pencils are fundamental tools for creating animation. Regardless of the media used to render the final images, almost every production begins when an artist puts pencil to paper. However, as many animators have proven, the role of the pencil—whether it is a standard no. 2, a pared-down stick of graphite, or colored—need not stop at preliminary artwork. Like other forms of dry media, including charcoal, Conté crayons, and pastels, pencils have been the medium of choice for many animators across the world.

Debra Smith English animator Debra Smith used pencil for her graduation film, *Touch* (1990), at the Royal College of Art, London. The work depicts a life from birth to death through a series of meetings and partings. The 16mm film was animated in pencil straight ahead (with some in-betweening to adjust timing), using 12-field animation paper. To create textures, Smith did rubbings over varied surfaces, such as hardboard and sandpaper; the finished, cleaned up animation drawing was placed over the selected surface, and then a pencil was rubbed over it to create patterning in the desired area (such as a character's dress). Because the pencil marks were fairly light, the sheets of paper were photocopied (using 11 x 17-inch [28 x 43 centimeter] or A3 paper). The resulting images were

darker, but retained the original pattern of the rubbings. Each sheet was registered and repegged for alignment. The photocopies were colored using Dr. Ph. Martin's inks.

Smith's next film, *El Caminante* (1997), features a tightrope walker and the crowd that has gathered to watch him. It, too, was animated straight ahead in pencil, this time using 12- and 15-field animation paper, which was eventually filmed on 35mm. In this case, Smith rendered the final animation drawings by hand, mainly using Charisma colored pencils (also a bluish-purple chalk pastel in two interior scenes, and cels for two scenes at the end of the film). Due to her choice of media, in all but two scenes only one level was used. As a result, the backgrounds for images had to be redrawn. Smith preferred redrawing, rather than exclusively using cels, because she liked the feel that characters were anchored to the backgrounds—as opposed to images on cels, which she feels shift and slide to some extent.[21]

Bill Plympton American Bill Plympton has a signature style that is recognizable throughout most of his work (see page 91). The caricatured faces and figures that are typical of his films, such as *Your Face* (1987) and *25 Ways to Quit Smoking* (1989), grew out of his early work as a political cartoonist for the *Soho Weekly News*. Plympton's humorous animation,

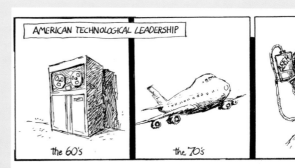

Images from the work of Bill Plympton: *Mondo Plympton* (top left), *Your Face* (left), and one of his political cartoons (above).

which is characterized by bizarre, sexual, and/or relatively violent content, has been influenced by the work of such figures as Roland Topor, R. Crumb, Tex Avery, Eugene Ionesco, Rene Magritte, and Winsor McCay.[22]

For the most part, Plympton's animation has been rendered using one of two methods: highly metamorphic color pencil drawings (sometimes combined with watercolor) found in *One of Those Days* (1988), or ink and paint on cels, as in his feature *I Married a Strange Person* (1997), for example. Plympton's colored pencils of choice are Prismacolor, which he values for their ability to blend and layer. He explains, "You can use yellow as a base, add blue to get green, then add brown to layer it further, and the color keeps getting richer. It's almost like an oil effect, with kind of an impressionistic look. You get a lot of depth because you can see the undercoloring. The more colors you put on top of it, the more depth you get. The subtle coloring effects result in a fine-art look." For general drawing purposes, Plympton uses a regular no. 2 pencil. Typically working at 10 field, he animates his figures on ordinary bond paper.

For his film *Drawing Lesson #2* (1985), Plympton developed a "scroll" method of drawing. He took a big roll of white butcher paper, approximately 18 inches (45 centimeter) wide and 30 feet (9 meters) long, and laid it on top of a camera bed.

A camera and lights were set above the paper and a light source was placed below. In the film, a drawing line tells the story of its life through a series of vignettes. These illustrations emerge from out of the line itself. Plympton explains that he drew the several tableaus that tell the story of the line's life on separate pieces of paper. Individually, the tableaus were placed under the butcher paper so that each could be referenced at the appropriate frame. When the underlighting was turned on, a drawn tableau would appear. Plympton then traced over a small portion of it using black and colored felt markers. After he turned off the light, he recorded the image on film. Turning the underlight back on, the guide reappeared, allowing him to draw in more and more of the image, until it was compete. At that point, he rolled the paper to the left, so that the line could continue with its story.

The Tune (1992), the first of several successful feature-length films he produced independently, is about a man who has to compose music to save his job and his girlfriend. Plympton approached each section of the animation differently; using a range of techniques, he was able to treat each part as a self-contained work. He created one section by drawing figures on bond paper and photocopying them onto another sheet of bond paper. His assistants painted these images with watercolors, cut them out, and pasted them onto cels. Plympton

Images from the films of Bill Plympton, including: *I Married a Strange Person* (above), *Drawing Lesson #2* (above right), *One of Those Days* (right), and *25 Ways to Quit Smoking* (far right).

himself drew over the watercolors with colored pencils to create additional shading. In other parts of the film, Plympton used pen and ink on cels in relatively traditional ways, but still achieved varied effects. With acetate-adhering ink, he traced figures onto cels using a Rapidograph pen to create a smooth line. In another section, he used a brush to outline figures for a bolder look. In both cases, Cel-Vinyl paint was applied to the back of the cel for color. Plympton also used frosted acetate cels; he drew on them with colored pencils, and painted their backs to prevent background images showing through.

For a long time, Plympton avoided the use of computers. In the mid-1990s, he explained to interviewer Mark Segall, "If I used computers it would take forever and cost a fortune. By doing it by hand, it goes so much faster, and is more similar to what I see in my brain."[23] However, beginning with *Guard Dog* (2004), Plympton began to incorporate digital media into his work "reluctantly." The film includes characters and backgrounds created with colored pencils on bond paper, in Plympton's typical style. However, by scanning the images into a computer, he was able to effectively composite backgrounds behind the moving images, thus avoiding the need for extensive redrawing of each environment. The digital work was performed by assistants using Photoshop, After Effects, and Final Cut Pro.

David Ehrlich American animator David Ehrlich (see page 22) is also known for using colored pencils. He uses Prismacolors because he feels they provide superior results to other colored pencils; he says their sharpened points don't break when pressure is applied and they can also be used to create subtle shading effects. Though Ehrlich teaches his students at Dartmouth College how to use digital media, for his own work, he prefers to make each image by hand. He values the constant movement that results from redrawing each frame in its entirety. Ehrlich wants his backgrounds to move and transform as much as his foreground images because, as he points out, nothing in nature remains static.

For Robot (1977), *Vermont Etude, No. 2* (1979), *Point* (1984), and *Dissipative Fantasies* (1986), Ehrlich worked on 9 x 12-inch (22.5 x 30-centimeter) pads of Artmaster tracing paper cut in half, which provided a working area of 6 x 9 inches (15 x 22.5 centimeters). Within this space, he drew at 6-field size. The pads worked well because he animated straight ahead and therefore had no need to separate the pages. The adhesive aligned the paper, keeping his images in registration. Ehrlich traveled frequently, and the pad structure kept his drawings organized and accessible while he was on his way to some destination. It was easy for him to take out his pad and work while he was on a plane or train, for example.

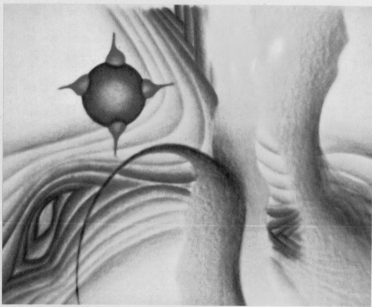

Images from David Ehrlich's *A Child's Dream* (above), and *Vermont Etude* (left) were made using Prismacolor pencils on both sides of tracing paper (lines on the front and shading on the back), and were shot in layers for receding after-imaging.

The use of drawing pads was not just convenient; this practice ultimately impacted Ehrlich's aesthetic sensibilities. He writes, "Working on pads like these caused me always to be looking at all the receding layers of image seen through the paper and obviously influenced my use of visual layering when it came time to film the drawings."[24] This layering fueled his interest in the visual effects of fades and dissolves. These effects play a significant role in his work and link to his interest in themes related to life cycles and metamorphosis—inspired by his earlier studies of eastern philosophies. Eventually he moved to the mountains of Vermont. Living there for many years has strengthened his ties to nature and the cyclical patterns of life.

For some films, Ehrlich purchased pre-punched animation tracing paper, which allowed him to work at the size of 10 field. This is what he used for *Vermont Etude*, which was completed in 1977. Using the tracing paper, Ehrlich continued to animate straight ahead, but he began to draw on both sides of the paper. He created solid lines on top of the paper with the tip of a Prismacolor pencil and shaded on the underside with the side of the pencil.

The sheer quality of the paper allowed Ehrlich to develop additional effects. To create the impression of fades while he was filming, he placed successive layers of blank tracing paper over a drawing until the image went white; to "fade in" to an

image he removed blank layers from the top of drawings as he filmed frame by frame. Ehrlich explains an even more complex effect: "By the time I got to *Precious Metal* (1980), it occurred to me that … I could also show a distinctly different image on a lower layer—in fact creating a visual retrograde canon with the image on the bottom layer moving in the reverse direction from the image above it. And it followed that I could also move the bottom layer further away from the top layer by placing successive sheets of blank tracing paper between the two. I could bring the bottom layer forward by removing those sheets, and even move the bottom layer above the top layer, in effect criss-crossing the two layers in depth."

In some of his next films, including *Precious Metal Variations* (1983), *Dissipative Fantasies*, and *Pixel* (1987), Ehrlich underlit four to five layers of tracing paper simultaneously for more intense color saturation and atmospheric effects. However, underlighting accentuated the "rag" texture of tracing paper. To avoid this effect, beginning with *A Child's Dream* (1990), he made a permanent move to more expensive tracing vellum. Ehrlich began ordering 24 x 36-inch (60 x 90-centimeter) sheets, which his local printer cut into twelve 8 x 9-inch (20.25 x 23-centimeter) pieces. Eventually, paper of this size was used to create *Robot Rerun* (1996), *Radiant Flux* (1999), and *Current Events* (2002). A mistake made during trimming left Ehrlich with a lot of excess paper at a size of

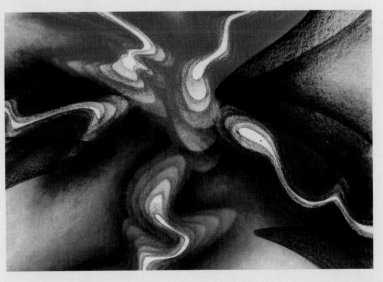

A series of images from *Interstitial Wavescapes* (left) and *Radiant Flux* (below) by David Ehrlich also illustrates the use of layers to achieve after-imaging.

4 x 7 inches (10 x 17.5 centimeter). Rather than throw it out, he decided to create an animated work with a widescreen aspect ratio of 1.85:1, *Interstitial Wavescapes*, which was released in 1995. He used the 4 x 7-inch sized paper again when he made *ASIFA Variations*, a widescreen work released in 1997; however, that time he had the tracing vellum purposely cut that way. While Ehrlich's core artistic sensibilities carry over from film to film, his creative process has continued to evolve based on the materials he has used and the opportunities presented by them.

Charcoal

Charcoal is an ancient drawing material. It is made of partially burned wood (generally, willow is used for artists' materials), which is heated in a restricted supply of air and converted into carbon. Artists' charcoal comes in various sizes and densities: thin, medium, thick, and an even larger "scene painter" size, ranging from soft to hard. This medium works well with paper that has some texture, which charcoal dust can cling to. If it is lightly applied to the paper, charcoal can be lifted off with a kneaded eraser or other type of erasing device. A more permanent line can be achieved by wetting the charcoal stick in some manner. Animators have used charcoal in various ways, attracted by its soft look, its ability to be lifted off the paper, or the fine-art appearance it produces. However, this is one medium that can be challenging to use in conjunction with digital animation processes.

William Kentridge Johannesburg-based William Kentridge is one of South Africa's best-known artists. His working context involves the residual history of apartheid and colonialism, and his art is informed by their effects on society. Kentridge extends beyond the realm of experimental animation to drawing, prints, collages, and theater. Much of his animation is created with charcoal on paper, though he also works with other media.

Kentridge's charcoal animations are created using a drawing and erasing method, utilizing approximately twenty to forty "base drawings" for a typical short film. He generally draws on Velin Arches blanc (occasionally crème) paper, chosen for its toughness under repeated erasure; less resilient papers would disintegrate. He uses all sorts of charcoal: soft to hard, from fine to large chunks.[25] In Kentridge's work, a single charcoal drawing is used as the basis of numerous frames of films. It is filmed, partially erased, modified with additional drawing in charcoal, and then filmed again in a repeated cycle of erasure, drawing, and image capture. Philippe Moins describes the subtle lines remaining after the charcoal has been "erased" as "rather fragile images, all in nuances, quite in the manner of a man obsessed by the idea of traces, or reminiscences."[26] Kentridge deals with historical memory in his work, not wanting to let it escape, as he develops "a process of unveiling the act of drawing. ... One can sometimes see his hand or his entire body appear in certain films."[27]

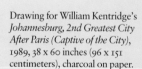

Drawing for William Kentridge's *Johannesburg, 2nd Greatest City After Paris (Captive of the City)*, 1989, 38 x 60 inches (96 x 151 centimeters), charcoal on paper.

For many years, Kentridge resisted the use of computer technology, but recently he has begun to incorporate digital media in his work; he "has made extensive use of a MiniDV camera, though more as a sketchbook or as a way of viewing immediately what is happening than for final product—which is still shot 95 percent on 35mm film, with occasional inclusion of other media."[28] He also edits digitally, working with a professional editor. Kentridge feels that adopting digital tools more widely would require too much pre-conceptualizing of his work, whereas his charcoal method allows for spontaneity and gradual development. He writes, "Charcoal and paper has imperfect erasure as an ineluctable part of it. In a digital medium it would simply be a digital effect, one of any number, all gratuitous."[29] The drawings he makes, and the traces left upon their erasure, suggest "a history of purpose, the purpose of not forgetting," in contrast to the impression of digital art, which is clean and ahistorical in nature, "a degree zero of perfection without a past."[30] Kentridge's use of charcoal allows a focus on process, which is revealed as an essential element of his work's totality.

Through a series of films, including *Johannesburg, 2nd Greatest City After Paris* (1989), Kentridge follows two white protagonists, Soho Eckstein, a factory owner, and Felix Teitlebaum, an artist; alter egos of each other, both are based in part on the visual reference of himself. Kentridge also includes himself in the charcoal animation *Ubu Tells the Truth* (1997). In this case, the animated work is based on a puppet performance, *Ubu and the Truth Commission*, which Kentridge directed in 1996, and a series of related etchings he made. The stage play, adapted from Alfred Jarry's satirical *Ubu Roi*, deals with testimony given at the South African Truth and Reconciliation Commission on the country's history of apartheid.[31]

Michael Dudok de Wit Dutch animator Michael Dudok de Wit worked with charcoal to create his eight-minute film *Father and Daughter* (2000), which tells the poignant story of a woman going through her life always longing for her father, who left her when she was a girl. It was made over a period of four years, but the project was frequently interrupted by Dudok de Wit's commitments to teach and do commercial work. As a result, actual "in-production" time was about twenty-four months, including four months when he worked with animator Arjan Wilschut.

Dudok de Wit conceived the storyline relatively quickly, but followed up on it with a lot of research. Sources of inspiration included Rembrandt's etchings, Hergé's "Tintin" books, Akira Kurosawa's films (for the way he uses space and the weather), some of Madredeus's music, Yuri Norstein's animated films, and the actual subjects he wished to depict. He says, "I watched clouds, landscapes, and birds in real life and on video; I filmed Dutch people on Dutch bicycles; and a friend even made me a wooden miniature model of a rowing boat for the end scenes. All the landscapes in *Father and*

Two film stills from William Kentridge's *Ubu Tells the Truth*.

Daughter are imaginary, based on a distillation of my childhood memories in Holland and on research photos."[32] Eventually, these environmental details became important to the storytelling. For example, birds are used "to soften the flow of the story, to introduce a certain timeless quality, and to lift the action up into the sky."

One of Dudok de Wit's biggest challenges was "to make the story work and to create an attractive visual rhythm." It took him several months to draw the film's storyboard, partly because of the way he works during the pre-production process. Dudok de Wit's approach to this first stage of animation provides him with flexibility in structuring his film and finding ideas that "feel right." He explains that he begins by drawing the storyboard in small sections:

> I sketch about six to eight individual simple drawings in one go, cut them out, lay them in sequence on the table, experiment a little with their chronological order, and maybe add some extra drawings. After this, I sketch the next lot of pictures. Eventually the whole story lies exposed on the table or the floor (the *Father and Daughter* board had about a hundred and sixty pictures) and I keep rearranging the drawings until the story and the visuals feel right. I then redraw everything and I add the text. At this stage the project is at its most vulnerable. I don't welcome too many opinions, but nevertheless I show the storyboard to my wife and children, my producer, and possibly some friends, and I ask them questions. Ideally this storyboard phase is followed by a month or more of work on another project, allowing me to get some distance from the storyboard and to come back to it with a fresh mind. Before I start animating, I hang all the storyboard pictures in sequence on the wall and leave them there until the end of the production. This serves as an essential visual support for me and for my collaborators.

Father and Daughter's musical score played a large role from the start. Dudok de Wit worked with Canadian composer Normand Roger, asking him to use as inspiration a nineteenth-century waltz from eastern Europe, "The Danube Waves," composed by Iosif Ivanovici. The first version of the music was written halfway through the production, and the final version was completed after the animation was done. Dudok de Wit writes, "As with my other independent films, I felt no need for any dialogue. The story is simple and I hoped that the visuals and the soundtrack would speak for themselves. I felt very strongly about telling a story clearly and unambiguously, while paradoxically leaving room for interpretation. For instance, whether a person may think that the lady dies in the end may depend on that person's feelings about death."

Images from Michael Dudok de Wit's *Father and Daughter*.

Father and Daughter was made using a combination of analog and digital media. It began with pencil and charcoal on paper. Dudok de Wit drew the film's images with 2B and 3B pencils on 12-field animation paper, mostly animating on twos, and these images were pencil-tested using Take Two software on an Amiga computer. After the line art was scanned into a computer, Animo was used to give the line contrast and a sepia color, and also to color and texture images. Originally, Dudok de Wit was going to make green the dominant color, but he decided on browns because they seemed to be more suitable for portraying the specific moods in the film.

Dudok de Wit used the coloring process to give the film more texture. He explains:

> Instead of coloring the animation with flat colors, the Animo operator would insert textured colors that I had prepared (charcoal smudged on paper, scanned into Photoshop and colored digitally, as in the backgrounds). The characters had to look grainy like the backgrounds. Each character usually had a body shadow on a separate level and a cast shadow, again on a separate level. The shadow drawings, like the animation drawings, were drawn with a pencil line and filled in with a textured color on Animo.

Backgrounds were drawn using both charcoal and pencil on inexpensive animation paper, which had the most suitable grain. Typically, Dudok de Wit created the sky first by smudging a large charcoal surface with the palm of his hand; he used an eraser and his (clean) fingertips for the clouds. He drew in the details with charcoal, smudging it with his fingers, and used thinner charcoal and 3B pencil for the finer ones. After a while he realized that he was "emulating the transparent quality of watercolor. As a result, the film has a slightly painterly look." The backgrounds were scanned and, using Photoshop and a Wacom graphics tablet, the black and gray of their charcoal imagery was turned into the browns, ochers, and other colors that appear in the finished film. Dudok de Wit enjoyed using charcoal because, as he says, "It's an honest and fast tool, and pleasingly messy."

Animo was used to composite the various components of the film. Dudok de Wit provided the Animo operator with the animation drawings, the background, a color model, and some color texture samples, as well as an exposure sheet with instructions for both the animated images and the camera movements. Eventually the film was edited with Speed Razor, using a very high resolution so it could be printed to 35mm film. The film was originally made in the standard 4 x 3 television screen format, but just before completion this was changed to 16 x 9 television widescreen. This meant the layout of almost every scene had to be individually altered on Animo.[33]

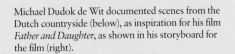

Michael Dudok de Wit documented scenes from the Dutch countryside (below), as inspiration for his film *Father and Daughter*, as shown in his storyboard for the film (right).

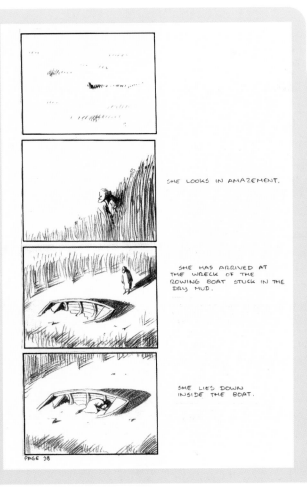

SHE LOOKS IN AMAZEMENT.

SHE HAS ARRIVED AT THE WRECK OF THE ROWING BOAT STUCK IN THE DRY MUD.

SHE LIES DOWN INSIDE THE BOAT.

PAGE 38

Case Study: Philippe Vaucher

Charcoal media and digital technology are intertwined in Canadian animator Philippe Vaucher's *Chasse papillon* (*The Song Catcher*, 2001), a film about lost love that he made at the National Film Board of Canada.[34] By working digitally, he was able to achieve effects that would be impossible using charcoal on paper alone. For example, when using paper, it is not possible to create selective focus on various planes (the foreground, middle ground, or background) and it is relatively difficult to "see through" to lower levels. However, digital imagery makes that possible in *Chasse papillon*, beginning with a kind of multiplane effect at the film's opening, when the background is out of focus. Digital media also made it possible to keep parts of an image still while other parts move; for example, when the old man in the film is shown sleeping, his head is immobile as his chest goes up and down with each breath.

Techniques used in *Chasse papillon* developed out of three previous films, which Vaucher made as a student at Concordia University, Montreal: *La plume* (*The Feather*, 1996), *The Color of Morning* (1997), and *The Maskarade* (1998). For all of them he used charcoal and pencils on frosted cels, as well as on paper, which he either used in a "slash and tear" cutout style to surround images on cels (avoiding the density of another cel and its effects on lower images) or in some cases as cutouts that were pasted onto the middle of a cel. These films were made using charcoal and pencils on regular and frosted cels, as well as paper. Vaucher sees *Chasse papillon* as "the digital perfection of the traditional techniques and media I used to make them."[35]

In fact, the film's production process was multifaceted, including use of not only a variety of charcoals, but also drawing pencils, Conté crayons, dry pastels, and India ink.

Modeling clay was employed during pre-production to create a life-size model of the old man's head (see page 85). Vaucher used it as an anatomical guide to ensure a realistic and consistent rendering of the character, and to help him with difficult lighting setups.

Many of *Chasse papillon*'s images were created on paper using Staedler 2B pencils for underdrawing, with willow and compressed charcoals on top; white and kneaded erasers were employed when it was necessary to lift these media from the paper. However, it was not possible to use charcoal for all the images. For example, it was too dusty for areas such as the pupil or jaw, which had to be well-defined. In such cases, Vaucher used Conté de Paris sticks in 2B black, medium gray, and white.

Black charcoal does not produce interesting grays when smudged, so Vaucher used Rembrandt dry pastels. He found they were not as dusty as other high-end brands of dry pastel, and says:

Chasse-papillon

Acte III Scène 1

Caméra: Nuit - EXT - nuit

Action: Maison du vieillard. Une lumière diffuse émane par les fenêtres

Son/Musique: vent / vague

Minutage: 4 sec.

Acte III Scène 2

Caméra: MLS - intérieur

Action: Le vieillard descend les marches menant au sous-sol.

Son/Musique: bruits de vieux bois / vent distant

Minutage: 4 sec.

Acte III Scène 3

Caméra: INT / HA

Action: L'ombre du vieillard disparaît en bas des marches.

Son/Musique: bois / vent distant (hurlant)

Minutage: 4 sec.

Page 12 de 24

A storyboard from Philippe Vaucher's *Chasse papillon* suggests the complexity of charcoal images used within the film—images that could only be achieved using the layering capabilities of computer software.

They smudge like butter and one therefore has an amazing control of shading. Through layering of tones (starting with the lightest), I was able to render subtle shadows. The film's slight undertones of blue come from the fact that I used bluish grays. You can actually notice the difference if you compare the final scenes which I did at the end of the production, done in pastels, with the rest of the shots, done with charcoal and Conté.

Vaucher welcomed the opportunity to create a film using digital technology. Because he had created a number of charcoal- and cel-based films as a student, he understood the restrictions of these media: A limited number of layers and the need to backpaint cels (to prevent lower levels showing through) were among the key problems. After drawings for *Chasse papillon* were completed, he worked with Pierre Plouffe, a digital artist at the NFB, to develop a "digital recipe" for creating his film. He explains, "First we cleaned the drawings done on paper in Photoshop using an automatic action. Then through another series of actions, we created alpha channels in Photoshop; Plouffe was able to create mattes to separate the character from the background. In After Effects, we assembled the two layers." Initial tests were disappointing because the character stood out from the background and did not look like a charcoal drawing. The major problem, Vaucher and Plouffe determined, was that a computer's images are sharp and clean, while charcoal drawings appear soft and dirty.

It was determined that Vaucher's drawings could not be cleaned automatically because that process erased the soft edges around the characters and whitened the natural "dirtiness" that creates visual interest in charcoal and pastel drawings. Instead, Vaucher used a Wacom drawing tablet and a computer mouse to generate mattes. He explains:

Using the lasso tool combined with a generous feathering, we first selected the character. Then we inverted the selection and filled it in white. The mattes, we realized, couldn't be done automatically (by using Actions in Photoshop) because the resulting edges were sharp and consequently only heightened the undesirable cutout look. So, we made the mattes and alpha channels using the airbrush tool; feathered edges softened the outlines of the scene's elements and blended them into one another.

Doing some work by hand also helped create a more natural look. For color elements, such as a butterfly wing, Vaucher used diluted India ink and a *sumi-e* brush to create a wash that was scanned in and used under computer effects.

9

Images from *Chasse papillon* by Philippe Vaucher.

Drawings were imported and composited in After Effects as "pict" sequences, and every element in a scene was separated, so each could be animated as an individual series of drawings; all moving parts were imported as layers, and as a result Vaucher was able to move elements autonomously. Vaucher explains, "Every shadow and highlight was animated independently. My old man was divided into a series of drawings, and so were his shadows (*ombres propres* and *projetée* in French), his glasses' highlights, and the reflection of light in his eyes (key light). The background and its elements were treated the same way; the sky was separated from the background or horizon and the clouds were animated separately." He admits the process was long and tedious, but by "treating every element in a shot as a distinct layer, we gained absolute control over cycles, camera effects, and camera moves." Shadows and highlights were cycled in After Effects with the "frame blending" option activated. The speed of cycling was determined by proximity to the camera, the nature of the light source, and the object being animated. Shadows and highlights in the foreground were cycled faster (from 12 fps down to 6 fps) than those in the background (1 fps). Outdoor shadows from the sun were cycled more slowly than those lit by a candle indoors.

In the process of filming his three student productions, as well as *Chasse papillon*, Vaucher employed a chain of mixes technique used by Frédèric Back in *L'homme qui plantait des arbres* and other films. Norman McLaren (see pages 143 and 269) also used the chain of mixes technique in his work—for example, in *Là-huat sur ces montagnes* (1946), a film created using black and white chalks. On a piece of board, McLaren drew a landscape that measured about 24 x 18 inches (60 x 45 centimeters). This picture was modified through the addition of lighter or darker tones. Each image was held for a 48-frame (two-second) fade in and a 48-frame fade out, which in turn was overlapped by the fade in of the next image.[36]

In *Chasse papillon*, because the frame blending option is constant (for example, 1 fps), Vaucher found it unsuitable for character animation "which is often erratic. For the longer chain mixes/staggered mixes involving a character, such as the woman giving birth or the young man becoming old again, the drawings were imported individually and animated as a series of cross-dissolves (drawing 1—fade out: layer opacity 100 percent to layer opacity 0 percent; drawing 2—fade in: layer opacity 0 percent to layer opacity

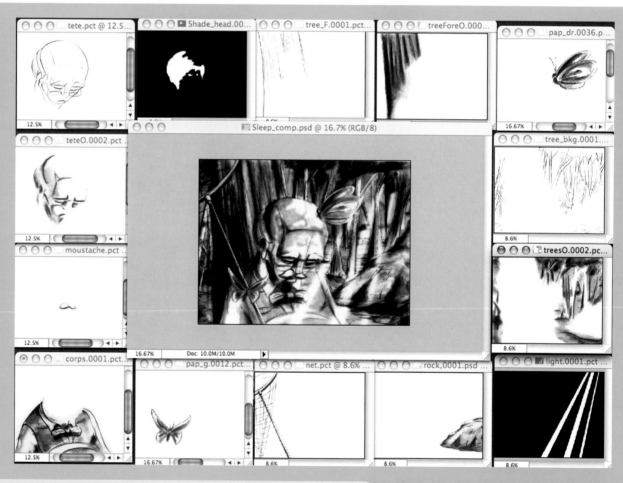

This screen capture indicates how layers were used to create a single image in *Chasse papillon* by Philippe Vaucher.

100 percent)." In cases where a character wasn't animated with dissolves, the sequence was imported without frame-blending as a "pict" sequence at 24 fps if on ones and 12 fps if on twos. Vaucher adds, "The dope sheet for the character and its mattes had been done manually in the 'Finder' by renumbering the files and duplicating them if there were holds." All but one of the film's dissolves were done in After Effects.

Vaucher was enthusiastic about using After Effects in part "because you can superimpose as many layers as you desire. Coming from a traditional cel animation background, this was for me the most interesting aspect of digital technology." An average scene in the film was composed of at least ten layers—but some were up to sixty. Layers allowed him to create the illusion of a "rack focus" by fading out the blur on the background as a blur on the foreground was fading in. He also could create dolly shots by adjusting a layer's speed in relation to its proximity to the camera, so "objects that are closer move faster than objects that are further away. The dolly-in shot in the basement provides the perfect example of this technique." Vaucher credits Pierre Plouffe with masterminding techniques that allowed the film to retain the organic look of charcoal, procedures perfected by Vaucher's technical assistant, Jihane Geadah. She also developed the dolly effect, fine-tuned the chain of mixes, and established the formula for highlights (such as reflections on glass).

However, *Chasse papillon* ultimately was a product of both digital and traditional approaches to animation. Despite the film's heavy reliance on computers, at the end it was edited without digital media, using a Steenbeck. Its scenes were printed onto 35mm film and edited together by Natasha Dufaux, using an animatic made in Premiere as a reference. From the experience of making the film, Vaucher learned that After Effects offered many advantages, but there were down sides to using it—and using a computer in general. Vaucher says, "very few final drawings from the film are complete in themselves, since they only illustrate a minute portion of the complete scene. This can be quite disheartening for the animator because it is only after a very long digital process that a scene comes to life." More generally, Vaucher warns that computers can take a physical toll on an artist. He developed tendonitis and therefore is a strong advocate of "posture, proper computer/ mouse positioning, and stretching exercises."

Philippe Vaucher used a "chain of mixes" technique similar to that of Norman McLaren in *Là-huat sur ces montagnes* (pictured left).

Water- and Oil-based Media

Two-dimensional animation can be created using media that is dry, as described in the previous chapter, or liquid, including water- and oil-based paints and inks. For many years, special animation inks and paints were used in conjunction with cels. Now that cels are used relatively infrequently, artists typically use ink and paint on paper, often in conjunction with digital media. This chapter will survey some uses of inks and paints, including complex work facilitated by the capabilities of animation software.

Water-based Media

Water-based inks and watercolors can be drawn or brushed onto paper to create hard and soft lines, solid areas, and semitransparent pools of color. These media have long been popular among animators all over the world.

Ink

"India ink," as it is known in the United States, or "Indian ink," as it is known elsewhere, is the most common type of ink used in the realm of art. It is made from black carbon pigment derived from burned wood, which is suspended in aqueous glue. The origins of India ink are in China and Egypt; recipes for its manufacture existed prior to the twelfth century. Chinese painters and calligraphers typically use ink that comes in dry form. To use the ink, a painter grinds the ink sticks slowly onto a special slate, dissolving them into a small amount of water. Preparation of ink is part of the art-making process; the routine of grinding ink and arranging paper helps prepare the painter for the creative process, by clearing the mind of stray thoughts. When applied with carefully selected brushes, the ink brushstroke reveals subtleties of movement and tonality that reveal the artist's skill.

Te Wei In China, the fine-art practice of brush painting carried over into the production of animation. Animators at the Shanghai Animation Studio, including one of the studio's founders, Te Wei, used a type of brush-painting technique to produce a series of films that has been internationally acclaimed.[1] One of them is *Where's Mama?* (1960), directed by Te as a homage to the works of the twentieth-century Chinese painter Qi Baishi. Using the aesthetics of traditional ink brush painting, it shows a group of tadpoles searching for their mother and meeting up with such creatures as a shrimp, a fish, a crab, and a turtle. The methods used in the film were further developed in Te's other work, such as *Feeling from Mountains and Water* (1988), which is the story of a musician and the protégé who takes care of him. One remarkable aspect of the film is its depiction of scenery, which dwarfs the human characters, in keeping with the *shan shui* ("mountains and water") tradition.[2]

Te Wei's *Feeling from Mountains and Water*, which employs ink brush-painting techniques.

Claude Cloutier The Canadian animator Claude Cloutier demonstrated the wide range of possible ink drawing techniques in his film *From the Big Bang to Tuesday Morning* (2000). At the National Film Board of Canada, Cloutier created more than three thousand India ink drawings with Winsor & Newton series 7 brushes. The images were animated under the camera, then colored digitally. The film tells the story of evolution, with a range of creatures poking out the neck of a man's suit collar throughout much of the film. The varied techniques used in it, including cross-hatching and sprays of ink, as well as the style of the imagery, reflect Cloutier's background in cartoons and illustration. His first film, *The Persistent Peddler* (1988), was inspired by his two strips, "Gilles la jungle" and "La légende des Jean-Guy," which appeared in the Quebec-based satirical magazine *Croc*.

Gil Alkabetz Israeli artist Gil Alkabetz (see page 81) has also used ink in a variety of ways. For *Swamp* (1991), which shows a battle between two armies suspended by balloons over a swamp, he traced his images onto photocopy paper, using a sable watercolor brush to apply black Winsor & Newton ink. He then colored the images using red and blue Ecoline watercolor. He also employed a brush and ink on photocopy paper for *Yankale* (1995), which relates details of a store clerk's life through an almost stream-of-consciousness approach, as

information about his mother and his childhood flow and cycle. To achieve a totally opaque black in the film, he photocopied all the ink drawings. For the colored portions of the work, he again used Ecoline watercolor in addition to gouache for the whites. The photocopy paper he uses is generally A4 (8¼ x 11⅝ inches [21 x 29.7 centimeters]) size—or A3 (11⅝ x 16½ inches [29.7 x 42 centimeters]) when a big camera movement is required.[3]

In *Trim Time* (2002), a story about trimming a tree, Alkabetz used colored pencils to sketch his animation. He worked with any color but black, preferring a soft pencil that allowed him to work fast and freely. When the images were properly positioned, he made the final lines with a graphite pencil, adding in-betweens as needed. He used ink to trace the images onto photocopy paper with a Pentel brush-pen, which created the relatively thick lines needed to achieve the simple graphic look of the film. For thinner lines, he sometimes used Geha felt pens.

Morir de amor (2004) tells the story of two old parrots who recall their past, using two different styles: one black and white, and the other colorful. The animation was created with the colored-pencil technique Alkabetz employed for *Trim Time*. For the black-and-white part of the film, he used Winsor & Newton black ink and a feather—the kind sold in art supply stores—to trace the images onto photocopy paper. He says

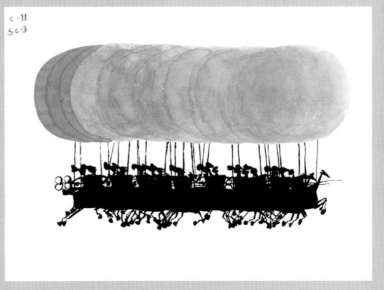

One of over three thousand India ink drawings from Claude Cloutier's *From the Big Bang to Tuesday Morning* (left).

Images from Gil Alkabetz's films *Yankale* (left) and *Swamp* (above).

this technique enabled him to "work a bit 'dirty' so one could see literally the fingerprints on the drawings." The other part of the film was colored on his computer, using the electronic pen of a Wacom drawing tablet and Painter software to give it a pastel-like look. More experimental still was his production design for *Travel to China* (2002), which was developed as a challenge to use only one picture for the whole film; movement is achieved through a form of kinestasis, or moving camera. As Alkabetz explains, "The movement was created only through differently positioning the camera on a still picture of one room containing five figures. This picture could be designed in many ways, so it took me some time to get to the final styling. Eventually I made a pencil drawing, colored it in Photoshop, and added photographed furniture elements, so it turned out to be kind of a collage."

Alkabetz finds an advantage of using digital media is that he can work quite freely. He says, "The change to computers was important to me because it released us (my wife, Nurit Israeli, who is my partner, and me) from being dependent on services from other studios.… The whole production can be done in one room with two computers and a light table."

Watercolor

Watercolors, sometimes known as "aquarelle" (in French), also have a long history, having been used by Egyptian, Greek, and Roman artists. Closely related is the medium of gouache, which is watercolor that has been made opaque through the addition of white pigments and possibly other substances. There are many factors affecting the quality and use of watercolor paints, including the substances mixed in with their pigments, the pigments themselves, the type of paper used, and environmental factors, such as heat or humidity. Although watercolors traditionally have been used to create backgrounds for animated productions, some artists have employed them more widely.

Michael Dudok de Wit In Michael Dudok de Wit's *Le moine et le poisson* (*The Monk and the Fish*, 1994), a monk discovers a fish in a reservoir outside his monastery and becomes obsessed with catching it. This wordless film was designed using a storyboard, rather than a script, which could explain why its visuals communicate the story so well. The film's images were created using a combination of liquid media: traditional techniques of ink line on the front of a cel, acrylic paint on the back, and painted watercolor

"The three main driving forces in creating *Le moine et le poisson* were the pleasure of animating the monk's chase after the fish, the pleasure of exploring light and shadow, and the challenge of expressing the ending in the right way."
Michael Dudok de Wit

Gil Alkabetz's *Travel to China* was made using only one image (left) by capturing various aspects of it sequentially (see detail below).

backgrounds on paper. Early in the production process, Dudok de Wit generally animated his characters with pencil on paper and copied the drawings onto cels, but he sometimes animated straight onto a cel with a brush. Rapid action was animated on ones and slower motion on twos.

Character outlines were painted on the cels using size 0 and 1 watercolor brushes and black Rotring Zeichentusche FL ink, a German product that can be applied like regular China ink, but will adhere to the slick surface of a cel. An advantage of this technique is that little errors can be corrected by scraping the lines off with a sharp piece of wood; disadvantages are that the ink takes time to dry, and, once they have dried, lines remain sensitive to scratching. Brushes are flexible and variations in pressure produce relatively thicker or thinner lines, allowing for creative outlining. However, as Dudok de Wit explains, "a brush meets with little resistance from the cel, which means that it has to be held with a very steady hand."[4]

Background lines were painted on their own cel layer to keep them in style with the animation lines; brush strokes on paper tend to have grainy edges, whereas brush lines on cel have sharp ones. For *Le moine et le poisson*, the watercolor backgrounds were painted on French watercolor paper with a medium grain NOT (cold press) surface and a weight of at least 200 grams. The sheets were first soaked in water and stretched onto boards, which ensures a flat surface when painting with a lot of water. Today, however, Dudok de Wit prefers to use Saunders Waterford watercolor board because it always stays flat.

Using different sizes of sable brush, with Rowney and Winsor & Newton watercolors in tubes, Dudok de Wit painted in a wide variety of ways—sometimes on very wet paper and sometimes on dry, but generally on wet paper that had nearly dried. He often tilted wet paper in different directions to move the liquid color around. He was not greatly concerned about keeping the paint within the background lines; he preferred to use loose strokes, knowing that the strong black ink lines on the cel would give the backgrounds definition.

He created aesthetic unity by using variations of ocher, ultramarine blue, and indigo throughout the film, with the exception of one scene where the monk stops chasing the fish—the turning point in the story. Here, he included some red. Throughout the film, the colors of the characters and the angles of their shadows change to create a sense of passing time, while the monk's shadow on the ground and his reflection in the water's surface integrate him into the landscape. There are no close-ups in *Le moine et le poisson*; Dudok de Wit preferred to "emphasize the characters' relationships with the landscapes—small characters in large, simple landscapes. The emotions were mostly conveyed

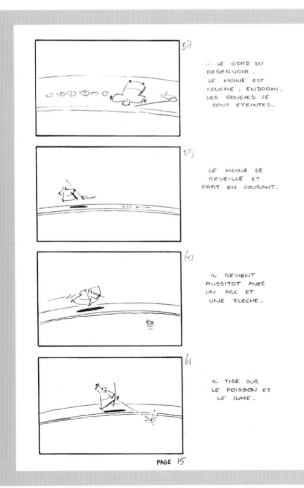

Michael Dudok de Wit's film *Le moine et le poisson* was designed visually, through storyboarding (far left) rather than a written script.

through body movements instead of facial expressions." Dudok de Wit was strongly inspired by traditional Chinese and Japanese art, in particular brush paintings by Zen monks. In contrast, he also found inspiration in Donald Duck comics written and drawn by Carl Barks.

Along with color, another unifying aspect of the film is its music. Dudok de Wit drew a detailed storyboard with the music he wanted in mind, and gave it to the composer, Serge Besset, along with the rough lengths of each scene and indications of different moods. The score was completed early in the production process and so provided a central reference for the creation of images; the animation was timed accurately to the music.

The entire production process, including storyboarding and 35mm photography on a rostrum camera, took only about seven-and-a-half months, with four months for the animation and the remaining time mostly on backgrounds and analysis of the music. Dudok de Wit worked with one animation assistant, Anatole Huynh Van Phuong, throughout the production, and for two months he co-animated with Guy Delisle, who later became a successful comic strip artist in France.

Elizabeth Hobbs The Scottish animator Elizabeth Hobbs employs a "wet watercolor" technique for her productions, using a single sheet of paper to animate an entire sequence; it can be compared with William Kentridge's modified-base charcoal process (see page 198). The process developed out of Hobbs's experiences in printmaking, particularly stone lithography and the use of tusche drawing fluid for making marks on the printing surface of limestone. She founded her own small press, Spellbound, in 1992 and used traditional printmaking techniques to produce her artist's books.[5]

Hobbs conducted experiments with tusche for *The Regret of the Grim Reaper* (1998), an animated work created during her postgraduate studies at Duncan of Jordanstone College of Art and Design, Dundee, Scotland. The film is based on a story she had published as an artist's book. In it, the Grim Reaper dances everyone on Earth to his or her death. Animated elements for each shot were painted in gray tusche on a single sheet of thick printmaking paper. They were filmed while they were wet, then lifted off the page and repainted in their next positions. Because the animated images soaked into the paper somewhat, a "vapor trail" of sorts follows moving objects across the screen. Hobbs felt the technique was well-suited to showing the destruction left in the protagonist's wake.

She began using watercolor instead of tusche for *The Emperor* (2001); the film, which depicts Napoleon Bonaparte's last moments on the island of St. Helena, was produced by Red Kite Productions in Scotland and commissioned by

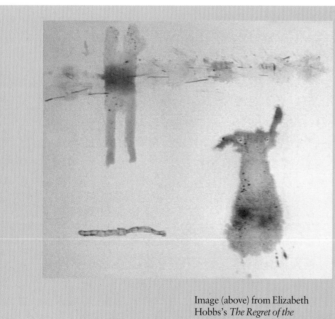

Image (above) from Elizabeth Hobbs's *The Regret of the Grim Reaper*.

Elizabeth Hobbs's "wet watercolor" technique involves painting and lifting images on a single sheet of paper. This image from *The Emperor* (below) shows Napoleon Bonaparte dancing on the island of St. Helena.

Channel 4 and the Arts Council of England. Hobbs painted backgrounds on smooth-surfaced 220gsm printmaking papers and, after they dried, painted the wet animated sequences on them. The pace of the production was relatively fast, but retakes were common and added to the overall production time. Even with its heavy weight, the paper was sometimes worn through during the process of painting, lifting color, and repainting. She had to film shots as many as six times in order to get them correct. Hobbs explains, "One of the limitations of this particular watercolor technique is that if too much pigment is used, the trace left on the paper is too dark and conflicts with the animation."

This problem was of particular concern in making *The Witches* (2002) because the film required a darker atmosphere than *The Emperor*. Commissioned by Cineworks, it tells the story of three witches trying to avoid a "dooking" (being submerged in water to see if they floated) during the reign of James VI of Scotland. It was written by Morag McKinnon, produced by Katja Anderson, and animated and directed by Hobbs at Red Kite. She solved the technical problem of animating dark colors by placing an overhead projector (OHP) adjacent to the camera's rostrum; light could be beamed through its projection head onto an angled mirror on the ceiling, which bounced it down to the A3 (11⅝ x 16½-inch [29.7 x 42 centimeters]) paper surface. Tusche was painted

onto a transparency that was placed over the glass surface of the OHP and animated while it was still wet. As a result, two animation surfaces were composited under the camera. The images made on the OHP transparency, such as the king's eyes and highlights of waves, were guided by the watercolor work on paper.

In *The True Story of Sawney Beane* (2005), a co-production between the National Film Board of Canada and Red Kite Productions in Scotland, Hobbs imagines the story of the infamous seventeenth-century Scottish cannibal from his mother's perspective. Images were drawn lightly in charcoal, over a watercolor wash on the same paper used in previous productions. Each one was captured on a Nikon D100 SLR still camera and edited in After Effects for transfer to 35mm film.

Hobbs animates by herself, and spends about seven or eight months under the animation camera, which accounts for most of the production process; *The Emperor* and *The Witches* each took ten months from development to completion. Images in these two films, as well as in *The Regret of the Grim Reaper*, were captured and edited digitally using Perception and Speed Razor, and transferred to Digibeta and 35mm film for screening. *The True Story of Sawney Beane* took two-and-a-half years from beginning to end, but the actual animation required only five months with very few retakes.[6]

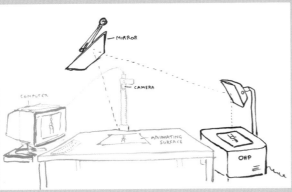

Image from Elizabeth Hobbs's *The Witches* (left) made using an overhead projector (bottom left) to reflect images on top of the surface she was filming.

Image from Elizabeth Hobbs's *The True Story of Sawney Beane* (below).

Case Study:
Iain Gardner

Scottish animator Iain Gardner has used both bi-packing processes of optical printing and digital tools to create complex, layered imagery in films such as *Akbar's Cheetah* (1999), *The Squire's Tale* (2000), and *The Loch Ness Kelpie* (2003). The aesthetics of these films grew out of Gardner's education in illustration at the Glasgow School of Art, which stressed personal artistic vision rather than a more technical approach. Gardner explains:

Our illustrations were to be as distinct as our handwriting, which is a training I appreciate. I could also appreciate it in Joseph Crawhall, one of my favorite former Glasgow Boys [a group of late nineteenth-century Scottish artists]. In his watercolor paintings, there is such an economy of line and incredible under-standing of form. The love of nature explored by many of the Glasgow Boys contemporary to Crawhall has always influenced me, with their confident brush strokes and impressionistic color. Crawhall always stood out for me because of his intimate under-standing of animals.[7]

Gardner was also greatly influenced by the 1998 Bristol Animation Festival. Its special guests included John Lasseter, Nick Park, Terry Gilliam, Oscar Grillo, and, most importantly for Gardner, Frédéric Back (see page 188), whose film *L'homme qui plantait des arbres* was screened there.

Gardner secured an internship with Oscar Grillo's company, Klactoveedstene, in London, and then worked on Richard Williams's *The Thief and the Cobbler* (1995) as in-betweener and assistant animator. From this experience he learned a great deal about commercial character animation. He later studied animation production on film, with little emphasis on digital techniques, at the Royal College of Art, London, where he learned about using a rostrum animation camera, covering such subjects as table moves, tracking in and out, fades, mixes, backlighting, high-contrast filming, and bi-packing; so great was his interest and ability in the last of these skills that he was dubbed the "bi-packing king" of the program.[8]

Bi-packing allowed Gardner to solve a problem that had bothered him for a long time: how to use watercolors for animation without the figures "boiling," or moving constantly, as they change from frame to frame. Using a series of mattes and multiple exposures, a sequence of images could be reproduced over multiple frames and dissolved to smooth the shimmering effect normally associated with watercolor painted directly onto animated images. He employed some of the process to animate a pink pigeon in his graduate film, *The Flight of the Dodo*

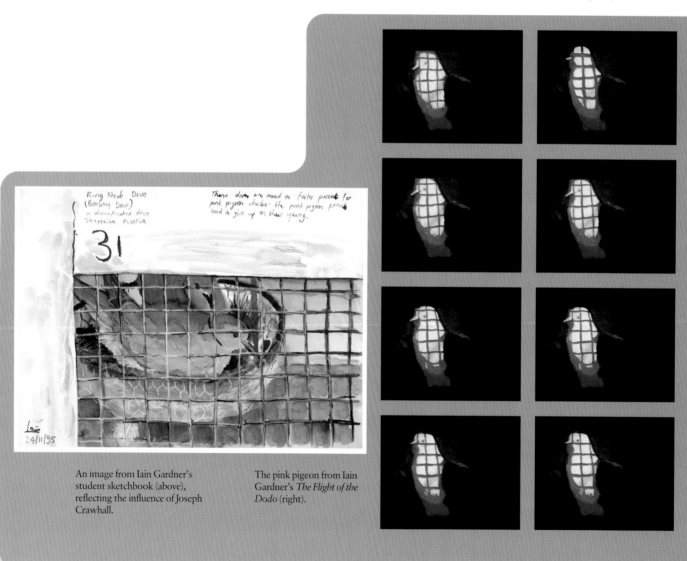

An image from Iain Gardner's student sketchbook (above), reflecting the influence of Joseph Crawhall.

The pink pigeon from Iain Gardner's *The Flight of the Dodo* (right).

(1996), which is a documentary-style account of conservation in Mauritius. He animated it "with all the control instilled by Richard Williams. Areas of the animation were rendered in black marker pen, and filmed on high-contrast film to make positive and negative bi-packing mattes from these images. Watercolor swatches were then cross-faded through these mattes."

Gardner realized the technique was too complex and expensive for large-scale works, so he replaced it with more conventional matte techniques in his next project, *Akbar's Cheetah*, which was developed through Channel 4's "Animation in Residence" program at the Museum of the Moving Image.[9] The film is about an Indian emperor who keeps a menagerie of wild animals. This project provided Gardner with an opportunity to utilize many of the animation techniques he learned when he was working with Williams. He observes, "His *Thief and the Cobbler* was full of standardized animation rules being broken, and my homage to Dick's vision was to make a film based around spots—an approach often avoided due to the necessity of animating on single frames and the complexity involved. The Asian source for the film was also a homage to Dick Williams, who drew inspiration from Persian miniatures for his feature."

The animals in the film, including the cheetahs, are defined by their markings rather than their outlines, a "less is more" approach influenced by Gardner's time at the Glasgow School of Art. A series of abstract watercolor swatches are used as backgrounds, with cross-dissolves giving an impression of paint mixing or spreading. The swatches were created with multicolored Diamine water-based drawing inks manufactured in Britain; they were waterproof when dry, but still luminous.[10] On top of these backgrounds he placed cels colored with china markers, cel paint (for baby crocodiles, the whites of peacocks' eyes, and mattes), aquarelle pastels, and mostly oil pastels.[11] All the animation was first drawn on paper, which was used as a reference for coloring cels and creating mattes.

Gardner's approach is demonstrated in the levels that he used to create the cheetah running through grass. At the bottom level was Fabriano watercolor paper. On it was painted a wash of water-based media (mostly Diamine drawing ink) that would define the cheetah only when it was seen through upper-level cels containing mattes; the color was applied almost randomly, and not painted to match an outline as in traditional cel animation. The watercolor images were cross-dissolved as the animation progressed; the inexact quality of the color alignment as the cheetah moved was part of the design. On the first (lowest) level of cel, Gardner used aquarelle pastels to create grass that appears to move

Iain Gardner's peacock in *Akbar's Cheetah* was created using a complex series of mattes.

behind the characters. On this layer, the combined silhouettes of two body shapes of the cheetah was left clear, to reveal the watercolor wash on the lower paper level. This level was animated on twos. On the top level of cel, Gardner used china marker to describe the spots on the cheetah's bodies and facial features; this was animated on ones. Green aquarelle pastel color was applied to cover any of the cheetah silhouettes not needed on the cel below. In effect, then, as Gardner explains:

It's all about holes in each level, to reveal the color on the background as a foreground element. The combination of holes and spots make up the illusion of the animal. I think that is the key to understanding what is going on—the background is the foreground color! The cel levels define the foreground shape, so in some cases they can be

defined as the background. It's not strictly a traditional animation!

Some of the animation sequences are very complex. Animating the cheetah was difficult not just because of its spots, but also due to its fast movement. Gardner studied footage of a cheetah running and determined there were 16 frames from the time the left paw touched the ground until the right paw touched the ground, or 32 frames for the complete cycle. He animated the sequence pose to pose, first creating the run on sixteens—in other words, drawing frames 1, 16, and 32. He then made frames 8 and 24, and finally drew the in-betweens. Most of the cheetah's run is animated on ones.

One of the most complex scenes created on camera is a peacock fanning its tail; mattes were used, requiring nine passes of the film. Gardner explains, "The peacock inherited what I had learned at college about bi-

packing. Due to the simpler nature of its design, I was able to create the illusion that the peacock had been painted with colorful inks by using several layers of mattes on cel, revealing different color swatches on each pass of the film through the camera."

Gardner abandoned the film camera, and instead composited images digitally, when he created *The Squire's Tale* as part of "The Canterbury Tales III: The Journey Back," an animated series produced by S4C in Wales. However, he says his method of working "changed little, except for the fact that all the rendered areas we had done before in *Akbar* with aquarelles on cel, we now did with gray pencil on animation paper, scanned and colored in the Animo system." There was not enough time to experiment with techniques involving digital media, so he had to restrain his use of textured areas; ultimately, many panels of color were "flat," with the look of cel animation.

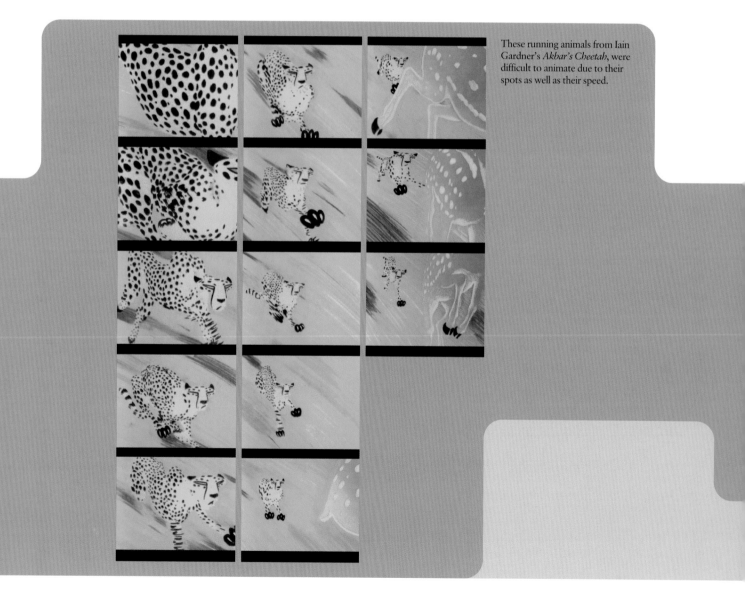

These running animals from Iain Gardner's *Akbar's Cheetah*, were difficult to animate due to their spots as well as their speed.

Gardner was introduced to Adobe After Effects when he worked with Bruce Alcock at Global Mechanic in Vancouver, where he lived for a time. He was asked to animate the titles for a documentary series, "Changing Currents," on the world water crisis. He began by creating his animated titles in pencil, and then he used Photoshop to paint the main areas black. He did this in order to use them as alpha channels:

There is a facility in Photoshop to select flat areas of color and create an alpha channel from them. An alpha channel does exactly the same thing that a positive and negative matte on cel would have done under the rostrum camera—mask off areas, leaving a region for re-exposure (demonstrated with the peacock illustration), except computers don't really think about it in terms of exposures. This allowed me to achieve the matting effects I had developed at college with a fraction of the time and cost! So, I did an entire thirty to forty second sequence of animation entirely based around alpha channels. I could also manipulate my watercolor swatches in After Effects to make them blend, swirl, and have an

energy that the static backgrounds could never have had with traditional 2D rostrum work.... The most exciting thing about After Effects for me was the facility to use mattes.

Gardner later used similar processes in making *The Loch Ness Kelpie*. This film is about a boy who stands up to a legendary Scottish beast that disguises itself as a horse and drags unsuspecting people to their deaths in the loch.

For *The Loch Ness Kelpie*, Gardner used Animo to create alpha channels from the original drawn animation. As a result, all the characters could have animated watercolor or pastel "movies" revealed through them. For example, the skin of the boy, Ewan, is made of a matte that allows subtle changes of color, while his clothes are made from one that reveals an oil pastel mixture created through a simple boil cycle on threes (that is, three slightly different images filmed in a cycle to keep a visual "alive"). To Gardner, the most exciting aspect of this approach was being able to put "3D animated characters into the mix—the final appearance of the kelpie was animated in Lightwave by Garry Marshall, following layouts I provided for him. In order to keep the 3D creature blended with the rest

of the film, and give it the watercolor textures, Garry rendered out his animation as a series of alpha channels."

Animated textures and elements were brought through the alpha channels and were combined with hand-drawn mouths and eyes that matched the computer-generated head to provide a movie of the monster. A "master matte" of the creature allowed the character to be combined with the rest of the scene. Next, other pre-animated elements, such as the rain and water splashing off the kelpie, were brought in. Gardner sees the process as similar to what he was doing in *Akbar's Cheetah*, but with the use of digital technology; he combined computer-generated animation with drawn animation to achieve a sophisticated blend of two different techniques.

Gardner continues to experiment with technology, explaining, "I haven't as yet pushed my designs to their limits—that is yet to come! It has always been my ambition to design animations that would echo the fantastic work of Joseph Crawhall. Now that I am beginning to understand CGI animation, I believe I can see a way to create films as beautiful as his paintings."

For his film *The Loch Ness Kelpie* (right), Iain Gardner used Animo to create alpha channels that function as mattes (below).

Oil-based Media

Oils have been the dominant media of fine-art painting since the early fifteenth century. In the realm of animation, traditionally they have been employed in the creation of backgrounds. However, some animators have used oil-based paints of various types—from tubes, in stick form, or even as mixtures of their own making—to render moving images. Oil-based paints are distinguished by their thickness, or viscosity, as well as the variety of tools used to apply them, including brushes, of course, but also palette knives, cloth, sponges, and often hands.

Oil on Glass

Alexander Petrov Probably the best-known practitioner of the oil-on-glass technique is Russian artist Alexander Petrov, who won numerous awards for his twenty-two-minute *The Old Man and the Sea* (1999). Before making it, he had already established his reputation with other award-winning works that used the technique, including *The Cow* (1988) and *The Mermaid* (1996). Petrov is also known for television advertisements, such as "Classic Sundblom" (2001), an oil-on-glass work made in the style of Haddon Sundblom who, beginning in 1931, created thirty years of print advertisements featuring Santa drinking Coca-Cola. Petrov's working method is to deposit oil paint on glass with a brush, and then manipulate it with his fingers. He explains, "It enables me to work rapidly and it is also the shortest and fastest link between my heart and the image I am creating."[12]

The Old Man and the Sea was produced by Productions Pascal Blais and made in IMAX format,[13] a condition stipulated by the three Japanese firms—IMAGICA Corporation, Dentsu Tec, and NHK Enterprise 21—that financed the film. As a result, Petrov created oil paintings that were much larger than usual, ultimately using a surface that was about 30 inches (75 centimeters) wide. It took him two years to complete the film.

Martine Chartrand The production of *The Old Man and the Sea* came about in large measure because of the devotion of Martine Chartrand, a Canadian artist inspired by Petrov's work when she saw a screening of *The Cow* during the 1990 Ottawa International Animation Festival. She received a grant from the Canadian Council for the Arts to study with Petrov in Russia, and while there she helped him put together a proposal for the film. It was embraced by Pascal Blais, who is Chartrand's brother-in-law, and further producing efforts yielded support from Japanese firms that provided financing.

After she returned to Canada, Chartrand began work on her own oil-on-glass film, *Âme noire* (*Black Soul*, 2001). Focusing on a young boy and his grandmother, who wants him to be proud of his heritage, the film deals with the history of black culture in various contexts, including the pharaohs, the degrading effects of slavery, and music, both gospel and jazz. To create her images, Chartrand used Rembrandt and

Martine Chartrand's *Âme noire* (right) was made using oil paint on glass.

Image from *Strings* (bottom right) by Wendy Tilby.

Image from Alexander Petrov's *The Old Man and the Sea* (below).

Holbein paints, due in part to safety concerns; they do not contain the cancer-causing chemicals found in some brands of oil paint. She limited herself to blue, brown, sepias, green, and red to avoid the muddiness that comes when multiple colors are mixed, and added bicycle grease to prevent the oil paint from drying.[14] Chartrand made more than 14,000 modifications to her paintings, working under the camera with her fingers as Petrov does.

The oil-on-glass technique allowed Chartrand to create metamorphoses throughout the film. Much of the opening scene—the woman in a room with her grandson—is still, but movement of the paint creates a transition into people working in fields. Within this scene, paint is again shifted to depict the moving arms of laborers picking cotton, while scraped paint suggests crops growing. From scene to scene, images are linked in these kinds of ways.

Oil Sticks
Wendy Tilby and Amanda Forbis

Wendy Tilby used an oil-on-glass technique in her first two films, *Tables of Content* (1986) and *Strings* (1991). However, she took a different approach in making *When the Day Breaks* (1999), the story of a happy-go-lucky character who witnesses the death of a stranger, a film she co-directed with Amanda Forbis. This film was made using oil sticks and other media over photocopies of live-action images.

The animators, both Canadian, began by shooting video footage of various objects and performers (including themselves). A video printer was hooked up to a VCR and used to capture and print selected frames onto 3 x 4-inch (7.5 x 10.25-centimeter) thermal paper. This enabled them to extend, abbreviate, and otherwise manipulate the motion. The results were tested for movement and photocopied onto regular bond paper.

Working with Oil on Glass

These are Wendy Tilby's recommendations for animators who want to use the oil-on-glass technique:

— Preserve your health and well-being by using nontoxic, nonsmelly water-based paint such as Pelikan gouache mixed with glycerin to create an oily quality.

— Limit your palette. Too many colors quickly turn to mud!

— Top or bottom? Lighting from the top will give your colors more brilliance, while bottom lighting will mute them. Ask yourself if you would prefer to spend countless hours in a dark room under hot lights or countless hours in a dark room staring at a light table. If you choose to bottom light, I would recommend color-balanced, nonflickering fluorescent tubes (incandescent bulbs are too hot).

— If you are bottom lighting, use milky Plexiglas or opal glass so the lights beneath are not visible to the camera. If you are lighting from the top, thin, clear glass on top of paper (white or your color of choice) can be used.

— Add and subtract paint with brushes, fingers, Q-tips, small sticks, strong tissue. Textures can be created with sponges, lace, or rubber gloves with patterned grips.

— Small field sizes (i.e., 5 to 7) are more manageable than big ones unless you are moving only parts of a larger tableau.

— Paint on glass is very forgiving. In other words, if where you start and where you are going are clear, you can get away with a lot of fudging in between.

— Don't treat each frame as though it's your last.

— Never destroy your last frame until you've sketched in the next.

— Paint on glass is ideal for metamorphosing, animated scene transitions, dream sequences, and fish.

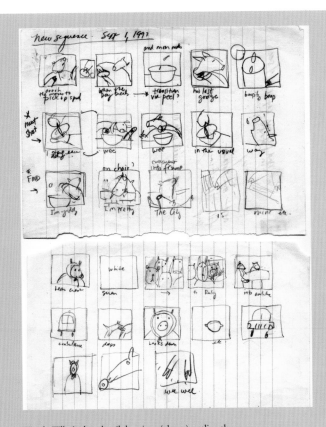

Wendy Tilby's thumbnail drawings (above) outline the action of *When the Day Breaks*, a film she co-directed with Amanda Forbis.

These photocopies provided the basis for the film's animation art. Tilby and Forbis used pencil, Shiva Artist's Paintstick oil colors, and rubber-tipped color shapers to draw and paint characters following the images on the paper; in other words, the animals in the film were created on top of live-action references that resulted from the videotaping and printing processes. Extra animated imagery was added to the scenes, while unwanted details were painted over.

Some improvisation led to interesting effects. Tilby explains, "Sequences such as the 'moving postcard' images of the city and chicken ancestors were paintings on photocopies which we moved under the camera somewhat willy-nilly. Images of bones, cells, and blood vessels were derived from *Gray's Anatomy*, while the pipes and wires were line drawings by collaborator Martin Rose that we squashed or stretched using the photocopier (if you move an image while the light is passing over it you can get interesting results) then inverted digitally to create the blueprint look."[15] Eventually, all the images were shot under a 35mm rostrum camera.

Because the oil stick color could be applied in a thin layer and was relatively "dry" (in comparison with tube oil paints), bond paper provided a strong enough support for the application of the color. The main challenge was to control

the "boiling" (moving texture) by painting as consistently as possible. Tilby and Forbis would smear a dollop of paint onto a plastic palette, then apply it to the image with a paint pusher. If it seemed a little thick, they thinned it with a clear blending stick. For animation purposes, oil sticks were a good alternative to oil paints because they are nontoxic, convenient to use, easy to clean up, and provide control over even tiny details, particularly when used with paint pushers. Oil pastels did not blend well enough.

Tilby and Forbis's recent work has increasingly incorporated digital media. An example is a commercial for United Airlines, which uses a variation on the technique employed to create *When the Day Breaks*. They began by shooting video footage of neighbors who were recruited to be actors. This was imported into iMovie, so that good takes could be selected, and then into After Effects, where shots were thinned out and timed to the animatic, to fit the desired length of the production. The next step was to import the resulting QuickTime files into Flash, where characters were redesigned by drawing on top of the live-action images. Sequences were then printed out frame by frame onto paper, so that they could be painted using oil sticks. Finally, the painted images were scanned, assembled, and colored using After Effects.[16]

In *When the Day Breaks*, animated figures (left) are based on photocopies of live-action images (right), which are covered in oil stick. Sketchbook images (below) suggest the development of action and complex links between objects in the film.

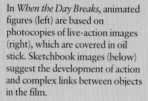

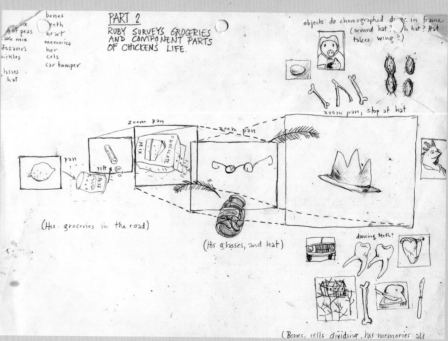

Case Study: Clive Walley

Clive Walley is a Welsh animator who specializes in oil on glass. His work on the six-film "Divertimenti" series (1991–94) is profiled in a documentary, "Space, Time, and Paint" (1995), made by BBC television's animation unit in Bristol, England. The program includes footage showing Walley's unique multiplane setup, which he invented himself.[17] His rig holds a camera over a stack of glass sheets on rests that are placed 1 inch (2.5 centimeter) apart. These sheets can be removed and replaced at any level. The rig allows for three types of camera movement—two horizontal and one vertical (that is on the x, y, and z axes). Using this equipment, from the camera's perspective images created on several levels appear to be combined.

Walley uses two-millimeter-thick display glass that has been treated to reduce reflections. The various levels are attached to links of a chain that can be used to raise or lower all the sheets at once to create an elevator effect. Moving them upward results in a forward move into the image, so the art appears to go past the camera. In *Brush Work* (1993), the third film in the "Divertimenti" series, the images move away from the camera. Images of a woman reclining on a chair, abstract shapes, and other figures recede into the background, continually disappearing, and being replaced by foreground images.

The lights on the rig are on faders (which allows them to be relatively brighter or dimmer) and can be manipulated along with other variables. To enhance or reduce the texture and saturation of the color under the camera, Walley uses a variety of devices, including "flags" (opaque obstructions in front of lights to limit the illumination to specific areas) and "scrims" (translucent sheets of material in front of lights to spread the illumination and create soft shadows). Both the "Divertimenti" series and *Light of Uncertainty* (1997) were filmed using an optical splitter with the camera; video images were recorded at the same time as the camera captured frames of film. This "video assist" system allowed Walley to monitor his work as it was filmed, so he could see if it was progressing satisfactorily.

Walley's oil paint is usually applied thickly to emphasize its "actuality," or presence. He mixes it with transparent Loctite 8105 grease (based on mineral oil and normally used to lubricate food-processing equipment) to "keep it wet and buttery under the lights. That is a secret ingredient I searched for years to find."[18] To assist with its application, he sometimes makes animation drawings, which are copied onto the glass sheets, one frame at a time. When there are a lot of variables, he creates cue sheets with every parameter charted for every frame of film.

Walley says the brand of oil paint he uses is relatively unimportant because "video (and film, but in a different way) doesn't register colors very accurately. With video shoots it is important to get the contrast and color scheme the way you want it on the monitor. The quality of the paint doesn't help much with this." He finds acrylics are useful for creating backgrounds or images that must be dry before photography—for example, if an object will be moved across them and wet oils might smear. Because acrylics easily peel off glass when they are wetted, they clean up nicely. However, they do not really suit his animation technique, which involves building the paint up into thick layers. He explains:

> When making high-relief textures, there is a tendency for acrylic media to shrink and crack. And they can look very plastic because some of the tooling marks smooth out as the color dries out. The quality of the media used to make up impastos matters more in acrylics because of this

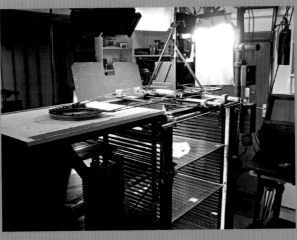

Clive Walley (right) created a special multiplane rig (above) that allowed him to paint on several planes of glass and combine them into a single image (far right).

tendency. In oils, my secret ingredient is the perfect impasto medium, but then the color never sets; different materials for different ends.

The oil paints are mixed in small containers, one for each color, and applied to the glass with a wide range of tools. He uses brushes "ranging from flats, through floppy rounds to seriously compromised long bristle brushes that happen to make excellent marks," but adds, "I use palette knives and rags, sticks, and fingers, in fact anything you might use to make a painting."

When the painting is completed and assembled under the camera, a single exposure is taken. Walley is then ready to create the next image, so he removes the affected sheets of glass from the rig and works on them. Sometimes there is only a partial erasure between frames, which speeds up the production process; he uses rubber-ended paint pushers and squeegees to move paint to the next position. Otherwise, the paint is completely removed with a palette knife covered in parcel tape to ensure it does not scratch the expensive glass surface. Most of the paint is recycled back into its container—Walley mostly works with a single color on any given piece of glass. Each time paint is removed, the glass is thoroughly cleaned with a water-based product he developed for this purpose; it contains grease solvents, protein solvents, methylated spirits, and detergent.

The many influences upon Walley's style include Oskar Fischinger's *Motion Painting No. 1* (1947), in which viewers watch a painting evolve from one state to another across a "canvas" (actually a sheet of Plexiglas). Walley says:

The film made me wonder if a painting could be made that was always just being made without clogging up its own surface. I always felt with Oskar's wonderful piece that he kept getting stuck for space on the picture surface. I wanted to remove the history of the work in a satisfying mechanical way to keep the road ahead unobstructed, so I built the now well-known rig. The "elevator" removed the history of the always-being-made picture in *Brush Work*.

Walley's film *Adagio* (2002) and a series of related paintings also focus on the process of a work being created. He explains, to make the film he "poured paint mixes down very shallow slopes and time-lapsed the results. Very slow, complex, and scale-less effects resulted. I have just done the same thing to a series of paintings about chaos theory because of what I could see going on during the long hours waiting for the paint to creep its way through my video frames."

Walley also counts the artist and animator Robert Breer among his greatest influences, because "he bridged from fine art to film in such a knowing way and made me realize just how easily the pieties of animation/film as entertainment could be dissolved away, and how, for animation's sake, they really did need dissolving away and still do." Other influences include the Canadian animator George Dunning, Len Lye, Norman McLaren, Man Ray, and Pablo Picasso— particularly as he is shown working in *The Mystery of Picasso* (1956), directed by Henri-George Clouzot.

In general, though, Walley's creative process has been most greatly affected by Abstract Expressionism and its associated artists of the late 1940s and 1950s such as Franz Kline, Willem de Kooning, and especially Jackson Pollock, as he is portrayed in film documents by Hans Namuth. Walley also cites the examples of the English abstract artists and sculptors Henry Moore, Ben Nicholson, Barbara Hepworth, and Howard Hodgkin. He explains, "The pioneers in my susceptible years, forty years ago, were using intuition, gesture, and movement, in a sense seeking meaning through connection with the body, which I took to heart. My own work reflects the changes that have affected the fine arts in the intervening decades, but the root of my inspiration remains more visceral than cerebral."

In recent years, Walley has incorporated digital techniques into his working process in "carefully judged increments." His first experience with digital media was an advertisement he made for Proctor & Gamble, for a detergent called Vibrant. It shows a series of bright colors of paint moving energetically across the screen in mostly abstract patterns. A voice-over narration emphasizes that

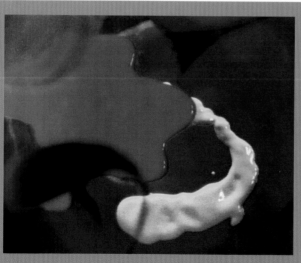

Images from Clive Walley's "Divertimenti" series.

the product will keep colors as bright as the day garments were purchased. To create the commercial, Walley explains, "I made a drawing first. Then for each frame I copied the drawing in high-relief oil paint (with the food grease as impasto medium) using a brush to get the outlines more or less right. Then just before putting the paint under the camera I gave it a quick, high-risk stroke, with a palette knife. This made the scene look like it had all been painted with a knife."

Digital media were used to complete the film, beginning with shooting on a hired digital video recorder. Walley says he watched this post-production process carefully and learned that there were good reasons to have such a system on a more permanent basis. When he saw high-end compositing techniques applied to the advertisement, he realized they could be used to create effects he had previously made under the camera—without a loss of quality and more quickly. However, the cost remained prohibitively high for his budget.

More commercial work followed as Walley created two advertisements for AIM Funds in the United States. These show his characteristic painting style, including the receding layers achieved by lowering the glass sheets on the multiplane rig. Images reinforce the narrator's comments, as he asks about investments in the future—five, ten, and thirty years from now. Question marks and

dollar signs appear on the screen. After completing these commercials, Walley won another film commission from a Welsh short film competition, "Short Shorts," sponsored by the television network S4C and Sgrin, a Welsh media agency. He used much of the money to buy uncompressed digital acquisition and post-production gear for his studio.

Walley wanted a professional animation capture system, and decided to purchase a DPS Reality video card, along with Velocity, Fusion, and Animate software for editing, post-production, and capturing images, respectively. The Animate capture program, which has been used by Aardman Animations as well, gave him the ability to follow reference video frame by frame; this capability allowed him to place his handmade "paint in space" into photographed environments, including synchronized camera movements on both. He used the system to make *Adagio*, but with mixed feelings. He was relatively happy with the included software; he says, "The Velocity editing program and the compositing program Fusion have proved to be wonderful extras and allowed me to bring the majority of the post-production of *Adagio* in-house." However, he was not so happy with the final results. He had hoped that uncompressed video images would print up well to 35mm film, but found that his work looked better

when it was enlarged from 16mm to 35mm, the process he had used for his previous film *Light of Uncertainty*. Walley says he has not yet found an effective system that combines instant video feedback with the high-resolution pictures produced by a still camera, so he has gone for the "best video-only option" he could find.

He has determined that there is a limit to the extent to which he can depend on computer technology. He says, "It is not possible to replicate the 'look' of my film work in CGI—I mean the lit paint under the camera—because ironically it would take too long texturing every frame, etc. Real painting is quicker and fresher." He has less of a problem substituting digital means for other parts of his technique—for example, compositing digitally instead of using the rig to layer images—because the difference is not visible on the screen. However, he regrets "the loss of quality, because even 16mm film is not clear enough for my taste. All my working life, I have tried to raise the money to go 35mm and never made it. I have always needed video feedback and converted 35mm cameras were always too expensive. Now I go the other way down to TV resolution."

Walley faces a challenge experienced by many fine-art animators working independently—he has the freedom to do as he pleases, but is limited by economic realities. Nonetheless, he has carved a niche for himself as an artist, creating distinctive work that has earned the respect and praise of colleagues and the critical establishment.

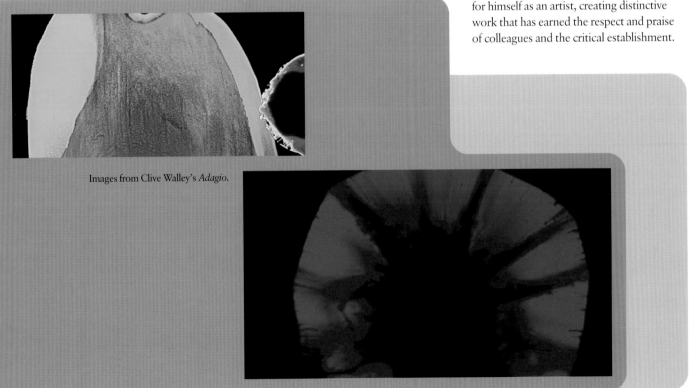

Images from Clive Walley's *Adagio*.

Applications V
Texture Book

One way to increase the vitality of a drawn image is by adding texture. This can be achieved with rubbings, stamping, or adding digitized patterns that have been scanned or photographed with a digital camera.

Objective:
Create a book containing a series of textures created with rubbings and surface treatments, as well as digital photography.

You will need:
- White bond paper
- Stick of graphite
- Inks or watercolors
- Ink or watercolor brush
- Materials that can be used to lift or apply wet media in patterns: for example, small-size bubble wrap, plastic wrap (cellophane), sponge, aluminum foil, coarse rock salt
- Digital camera
- Computer
- Image-processing software
- Printer
- Glue stick
- Sketchbook

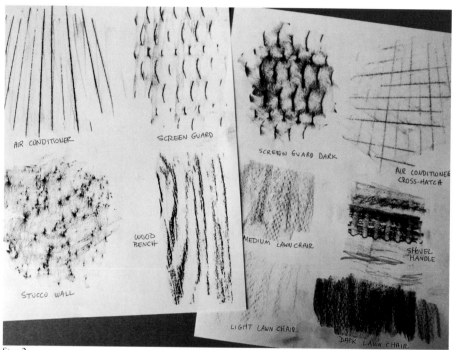

Step 2

1
Locate surfaces that represent variations in texture: fine, coarse, linear, bumpy, etc.

2
Place a sheet of bond paper over the surface of each texture area and rub the graphite stick along it, using the side to make broad strokes. Experiment with different levels of pressure (pushing lightly or firmly) on separate areas of the paper. Near each rubbing, write a descriptive title that includes the surface being rubbed.

3
Now create textures using the ink or watercolor and a stamping or lifting material—for example, a sponge. Create positive images by dipping the material into the ink and placing it on a sheet of paper. Make negative images by applying a wash of color to the paper and lifting part of it off with a clean dry sponge, rock salt (which draws liquid to it), or other material. Near each sample, write a short descriptive title that includes the media you used.

Example shots of a variety of textured surfaces.

4

Walk around your environment and use a digital camera to take close shots of interesting textured surfaces—perhaps some of the ones you used to create rubbings. Print the images onto paper.

5

Use the glue stick to paste the images you have created and photographed in a sketchbook. Note the kinds of object that might be made with the textures you have created.

Characteristics of Media

The wide range of available 2D media allows images to be developed in diverse ways. Sometimes the same medium can be used in various manners to result in a range of effects. Different types of paper also can be used to create varied results.

Objective:

To explore the characteristics of different media when they are applied to a range of paper bases.

You will need:

– White bond paper
– A variety of creative media in the same color (primary red or blue, for example) or black: colored pencils, aquarelle pencils (can be used with water), water-based markers, watercolors (student- and/or artist-quality), dry pastels, oil pastels, Conté crayons, wax crayons, hard charcoal, soft charcoal, graphite sticks
– Papers that are different in weight, tooth/texture, color, and composition (for example, newsprint, Kraft, cold press watercolor, tinted watercolor paper, colored card stock, etc.); the sheets must be large enough to accommodate approximately ten applications of media
– Sponge for dampening paper
– Watercolor brushes
– Cloth
– Spray fixative (optional)
– Tissue paper (optional)

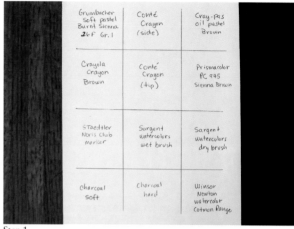

Step 1

1

This project involves making marks on a sheet of paper with each of the media being used. It is therefore important to determine the amount of space each medium can occupy and where it will be situated on the page to create consistency throughout the project. Begin by making a grid on a piece of ordinary bond paper, and write the medium to be used in each space. Specify all details, possibly including the medium's brand name, quality (if applicable), name of color, item number, and place purchased.

2

Be sure to include variations within each medium. For example, colored pencils can be used on their points, or on their sides for shading; they can also be used with light or firm pressure. Aquarelle pencils can be used on wet paper, after being dipped in water, or with water added after they have been applied to dry paper; dry pastels can be used on dry paper or paper dampened with a sponge, or water can be brushed over them after they have been applied to paper.

Step 5

3

Write details about the papers you will be using on the back side of each sheet. You can indicate paper type, color name, item number, and place purchased, for example.

4

Applying one medium at a time, move through each of these papers. Strive for consistency from application to application—for example, in the pressure used with a colored pencil or the amount of water used with a brush.

5

Use a clean cloth to slightly smudge the bottom of each patch of color to see how it spreads on the paper.

6

Note the differences between student-quality and artist-quality watercolors, if used. Do the pigments settle differently? Comparisons can also be made between the qualities of colored pencils, dry pastels, oil pastels, and so forth, if a range of these materials from different manufacturers is selected.

7

Write additional comments in your grid as necessary. It also useful to record your reactions to specific medium/application/paper combinations that are promising for future work.

8

If desired, move to a ventilated area and spray fixative onto the pastel and charcoal areas on the paper to prevent smudging.

Tips and Cautions:

— If pastels are used, it is best to apply them dry to all your sheets of paper before they are dampened to avoid changes in consistency.

— When applying water, take care not to affect media that already have been applied.

— Always use spray fixative in a well-ventilated area away from heat sources.

— Place tissue paper between the sheets of paper in storage to prevent them from sticking together and to stop the medium from transferring to the sheet above it.

Coloring Test

Wendy Tilby, Amanda Forbis, and other artists have created impressive animations using frame by frame live-action references under their work. Interesting effects can be achieved by covering the original source with various media, sometimes allowing the black-and-white of the reference images to remain in portions of the frame. Testing different media on a small range of images will give you a sense of which ones appeal to you.

Objective:

To test the use of different media on the same image sequence.

You will need:

- Digital still camera
- An actor
- A printer (and computer, if necessary)
- White bond paper
- Three media in a selection of colors: for example, colored pencils, aquarelle pencils, chalk pastels, oil pastels, colored markers, watercolors
- Digital pencil test unit or other recording system allowing variable speed playback

Step 2

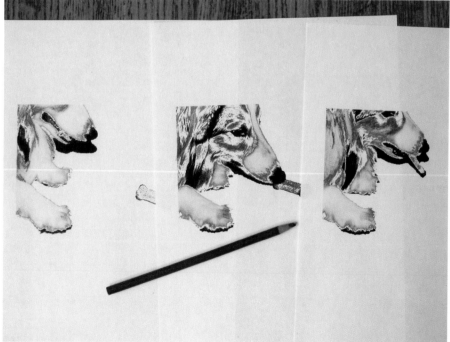

Step 5

1

Use a digital camera to record three to ten images of an actor going through a very simple action.

2

Print three grayscale (black-and-white) copies of the images onto bond paper. You should have a total of up to thirty images: three to ten in set A, three to ten in set B, and three to ten in set C.

3

Select one medium to use for set A. On the back of the first page of A, provide detailed information about the medium: brand, colors, product numbers, place purchased, and so forth.

4

Select one part of the image in set A and color it on all the pages in the set.

5

Return to the first page in set A and select another part to color from start to finish of the sequence. Repeat this process until all the pages in A are colored to your satisfaction. Parts of the image can be left without color.

6

Using another medium, continue this process with set B. The parts of the image you colored on set A should also be colored on set B.

7

Use a third medium to color the same parts of the image on set C.

8

Record the images from the three sequences and play them back, using varied speeds, if possible.

9

Make notes about each sequence. Which media were easiest to use? Fastest? Which ones make "boiling" (constant movement of the color) more apparent? Which results are the most appealing?

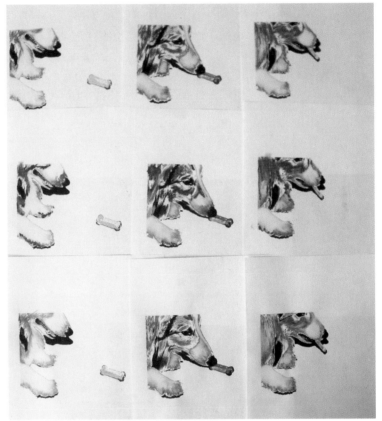

Step 7

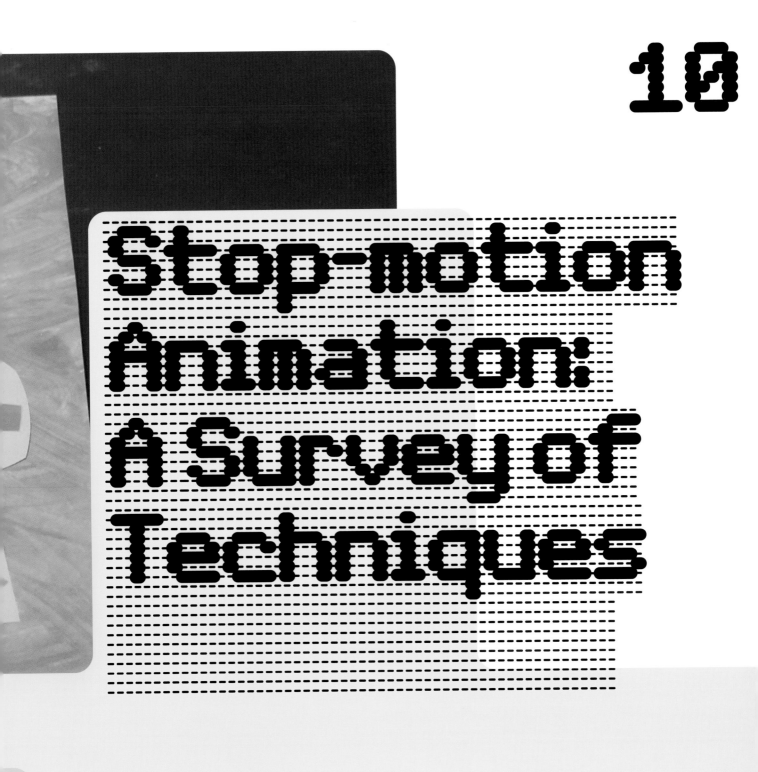

10

Stop-motion Animation: A Survey of Techniques

Stop-motion is a term that describes a wide range of animation techniques involving frame by frame manipulation of objects in front of a camera. At the beginning of film history, stop-motion animation appealed to enterprising filmmakers such as Georges Méliès, whose "trick films," including *A Trip to the Moon* (1902), featured a host of visual effects to entertain viewers. Though digital technology now produces two- and three-dimensional virtual images that can hardly be differentiated from material reality and has greatly expanded the realm of visual effects, there has been continued—actually, expanded—interest in the production of stop-motion animation. Animators still love to work with objects by hand, and audiences still love to see the results. Approaches to stop-motion are almost limitless, encompassing both 2D and 3D media.

2D Stop-motion Media

Mention "stop-motion," and most people probably think of clay, puppets, or other three-dimensional objects. However, there are some well-established practices involving two-dimensional art made with sand, modeling clay (e.g., plastiline or Plasticine), cut paper, and other media.

Sand and Other Particles

There are many types of particles that can be used in animation—for example, the colorful beads used by Ishu Patel in *The Bead Game* (1977). The Polish animator Aleksandra Korejwo uses salt in her animations, such as *Carmen Habanera* (1995). The salt is colored by mixing it with gouache watercolors, setting it in the sun to dry, and then grinding the mixture with a pestle and mortar. Korejwo lays the colored salt on a 28 x 20-inch (71 x 51-centimeter) black canvas, using frame by frame guide pictures made with pastels on cardboard. She moves the salt around the canvas with condor feathers, which she gets from a Polish zoo, and usually creates between 80 and 150 images a day.

Sand is the most popular form of stop-motion involving particles. It is economical, of course, but it is also an expressive and fluid medium that lends itself to metamorphosis. Generally sand is backlit to produce silhouettes with soft edges, and as a result, sand animators often work in black and white. However, color can be added by placing gels on lower levels of glass or even on the underside of the glass on which the sand is animated.

Beads are used to form the images of Ishu Patel's *The Bead Game* (right).

Gisèle and Nag Ansorge working under the camera (far right).

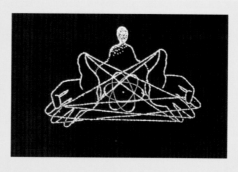

Aleksandra Korejwo specializes in using salt for her stop-motion films, as seen in this still from *Carmen Habanera* (below).

A rocket lands on the moon in George Méliès's early special effects film *A Trip to the Moon* (above).

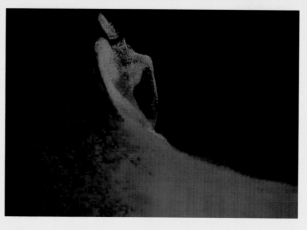

Gisèle and Ernest "Nag" Ansorge   The Swiss wife-and-husband team of Gisèle and Ernest "Nag" Ansorge are among the most accomplished artists in the field of sand animation. To create films such as *The Ravens* (1967), *Fantasmic* (1969), and *The Chameleon Cat* (1975), Gisèle worked with sand on one or more panes of opalescent glass, on a camera stand Nag built for the process. In the case of multiple planes, she created stationary components of a scene on the lowest one, so that an upper level of sand could be animated without disturbing them. When she used only a single level, which contained both background and foreground elements, the background was altered as a moving figure passed through it, and was reconstituted only by memory after the figure had progressed further. Although the resulting imprecision could be seen as a defect, Gisèle used it to create energy in the scene. In fact, such imprecision is a significant component of sand animation as a whole, adding a secondary level of action to every movement.[1]

Gisèle employed a range of relatively simple tools to move the sand, including brushes, combs, bits of cardboard, and cloth, and never reworked a line, but rather followed her "impulse of the moment." To achieve extreme fluidity she used a very fine sand, quartz, which she washed and strained "to get a powder as uniform in quality as possible, without dust." Control was elusive because the powder was not perfectly even; rather it was a pile of grains, each of which retained some autonomy.[2]

Caroline Leaf   Sand is among the animation media used by the accomplished animator Caroline Leaf (see page 146). She used it in some of her early works, including *The Owl Who Married a Goose* (1974) and *The Metamorphosis of Mr. Samsa* (1977). Leaf used white beach sand on a 24 x 18-inch (61 x 45.75-centimeter) glass surface; she recommends using opal or milk glass and avoiding Plexiglas, which builds up static electricity that makes the sand cling. The best way to achieve underlighting, in Leaf's opinion, is to put lights on the left and right sides of the animation table, and point them down toward a curved piece of white cardboard, which bounces the light back up; this setup is much gentler on the eyes than lights pointed directly up.[3]

Pinscreen Animation

The pinscreen, or pinboard, is made of a white surface set in a large vertical frame. It holds thousands of pins that can be pushed in and out, depending on the shapes and patterns

Sand animation by Gisèle and Nag Ansorge. Images from *Fantasmic* (above) and *The Ravens* (above right).

Image from *The Metamorphosis of Mr. Samsa* (above) by Caroline Leaf.

To achieve complex backgrounds for her sand animation, Gisèle Ansorge used more than one pane of glass. Pictured here is *The Chameleon Cat* (above and left).

desired. When all the pins are pushed in, the light-colored surface of the board is clearly visible. If pins are extended outward and lit from the side, shadows cause areas of black and intermediate gray to appear. This specialized medium has not been widely used, but examples can be found in the work of Jacques Drouin at the National Film Board of Canada, in such films as *Mindscape* (1976) and *Imprints* (2004).

Alexandre Alexeieff and Claire Parker

The pinscreen is the invention of Russian animator Alexandre Alexeieff and his American wife, Claire Parker, who used it to make some beautiful, critically acclaimed animation—as well as book illustrations. Among their best-known films are *Une nuit sur le mont chauve* (*Night on Bald Mountain*, 1933) and *Le nez* (*The Nose*, 1963). Alexeieff pushed pins into the front of the pinscreen, while Parker worked at the back, responding to his directions.

Stratacut Animation

In 1948, Douglass Crockwell patented a "Method of Producing Animated Motion Pictures" that included modeling an elongated body out of clay, slicing the form, and filming the resulting images in sequence. Essentially, he was describing what came to be known as the strata-cut technique—a

process that combines two- and three-dimensional processes. It is two-dimensional in that it involves a series of flat images, but three-dimensional because those images are modeled in depth, creating a "brick" of clay that is gradually sliced away to reveal the images within it. Animators can choose to shoot only the surface of the strata-cut figure, or dimensionality can be achieved by revealing the entire mass of the molded object.

David Daniels The best-known practitioner of the complex strata-cut technique is David Daniels. He creates his bricks by compressing long strips of variously colored modeling clay into the desired forms, anticipating how the figures transform themselves through space, over time. A flipbook-like storyboard is useful to guide the development of the bricks.

Buzz Box (1985), Daniels's first and longest film in the technique, runs fifteen minutes and involves more than 32,000 slices.[4] After completing that film, he went on to create animation for the television series "Pee-Wee's Playhouse" (1986–91). His work also appears in the music video for Peter Gabriel's "Big Time" (1986), as well as numerous commercials. For a Clearasil spot, he helped design and build a 3-foot (90-centimeter) motorized razor-blade guillotine to slice through the clay bricks.[5]

Alexandre Alexeieff and Claire Parker at the pinboard (above), and an image from one of their films, *Le nez* (top right).

An image from David Daniels's *Buzz Box* (bottom right).

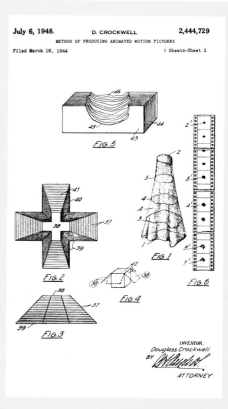

This 1948 patent (above) by Douglass Crockwell suggests how the strata-cut method works, by slicing away layers of a thick clay object.

Clay Painting

When modeling clay is softened in some way, it can be applied to a flat surface to create two-dimensional images. These "clay paintings" can be lit from the top or underneath.

Joan Gratz The American animator Joan Gratz is known for inventing the process of clay painting, which she developed as early as 1966. Gratz heats colored clay and mixes it with mineral oil. After it cools, she uses her fingers and small tools to spread the clay–oil mixture across a solid surface, creating images much like those made with oil paints. Her best-known work, *Mona Lisa Descending a Staircase* (1992), runs seven minutes and took ten years to complete. She has also made a variety of award-winning television commercials for clients such as United Airlines and Coca-Cola. She says film and painting come together in her work: "I am able to bring movement, sequence, rhythm, and process to painting and bring abstraction and stylization to the film image. Within the realm of animation I am most interested in the metamorphosis of images…. I am interested in creating a 'visual onomatopoeia' in which line, color, movement, and rhythm create the feeling of a particular experience without illustrating it."[6]

Lynn Tomlinson Animator Lynn Tomlinson has made a number of films using variations on clay painting techniques, backlighting her images to create a luminescent quality. She uses Modeling Pal, a French clay, because it spreads well and maintains its consistency regardless of the temperature, and—as opposed to many oil paints—it is nontoxic. Although Tomlinson largely works with her hands, various tools have proven useful, including erasers, because the clay won't stick to them. Because muddiness can result from the blending of colors, Tomlinson likes to use monochromatic color schemes—for example, in her 1999 productions *Simile* and *Onomatopoeia*, both commissioned by the Independent Television Service (ITVS) as interstitial spots for children's public television.

Out of her Summer Kitchen Studio, Tomlinson also has created, among other things, shorts for "Sesame Street," a logo and spot for MTV, and numerous spots for WHYY-TV12 in Philadelphia. Among her independent works made with clay on glass are *I Heard a Fly Buzz When I Died* (1989), which interprets an Emily Dickinson poem about a woman's last moments; *Paper Walls* (1993), which blends clay and live-action to explore the experience of a woman who becomes detached from reality while on a "rest cure"; and *Cauldron* (1994), a creation story that involves a swirling pot of boiling brew.

Pictured (top left) is clay animator Joan Gratz and three details of her work, including *Mona Lisa Descending a Staircase* (above and right).

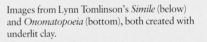

Images from Lynn Tomlinson's *Simile* (below) and *Onomatopoeia* (bottom), both created with underlit clay.

Cutouts

Any type of material can be used to create cutout animation—for example, Elizabeth Hobbs (see page 212) used fuzzy felt material for her two short films *Glenda* and *Over-Excited* (both 1998), which were based on flipbooks she had designed. However, it is probably not surprising that paper is a common choice. It can be cut and folded, lit from behind or in front, and appreciated in many textures and colors—all reasons why it is very useful as a medium for animation.

The diversity of approaches to cutout animation is evident in a survey of several animators using the technique. In China, with its long tradition of paper cutting and folding, cutout techniques have found their way into a number of productions, including classic works from the Shanghai Animation Studio. Wan Guchan—whose family made China's first short and feature-length animated films—was an early practitioner.[7] He modified his cut figures by adding tape hinges to create puppets that were moved under the camera with the aid of long tweezers. His *Zhu Bajie Eats Watermelon* (1958), released by the Shanghai Animation Studio, was followed by other films employing the technique, including *The Golden Conch* (1963). The studio also produced such award-winning paper-cut works as *Fox Hunts the Hunter* (1978), directed by Hu Xionghua.

Americans Larry Jordan and Harry Smith have produced esoteric, surreal, and mystical works using a range of found images. From the late 1950s through the early 1960s, Jordan studied and collaborated with the collage artist Joseph Cornell; later he made a series of cutout animations, including the short *Our Lady of the Sphere* (1969) and feature-length *Sophie's Place* (1984). Smith used cutouts extensively in mystical productions that reflected his interest in the occult. The most famous is his feature-length *Heaven and Earth Magic*, created in the early 1940s and edited several times through 1962. The Polish animators Jan Lenica and Walerian "Boro" Borowczyk collaborated on several films, including *Dom* (*House*, 1958), using cutouts in addition to other techniques to explore the absurd and grotesque. Lenica directed a number of cutout films of his own, often incorporating strong political subtexts. Among the most famous are *Labirynt* (*Labyrinth*, 1962), about an oppressed individualistic man who is brought down by social forces and eventually obliterated by totalitarian rule, and *A* (1964), in which a man is harassed by letters (suggesting language) that invade the privacy of his living space.[8]

Absurdist imagery is also characteristic of the work of American Terry Gilliam, whose cutout animations became famous as part of the "Monty Python's Flying Circus"

Images from Lynn Tomlinson's clay films, *Paper Walls* (above), *I Heard a Fly Buzz When I Died* (left), and *Cauldron* (below).

Felt cutouts were used by Elizabeth Hobbs in her film *Glenda* (above).

television series, which first aired in the United Kingdom from 1969 to 1974. His work is perhaps the best-known cutout animation in the world. The popular Comedy Central television series created by Trey Parker and Matt Stone, "South Park," is probably even better known, but its images only look like cutouts. When the concept was conceived as a student project in 1992, Parker and Stone did in fact animate paper figures, but that approach was not practical for full-scale production. Since the concept moved to television in 1997, Maya 3D software has been used to animate it, though the 2D cutout look has been retained.

These are just a few examples of prominent animators who have used cutouts. Following are more in-depth descriptions of this type of stop-motion production, including highly complex works using approaches involving silhouettes, found images, photographic figures, and frontlit 2D puppet designs.

Lotte Reiniger When cutout figures are lit from behind so they become dark objects on a light background, they are known as "silhouettes." The best-known and most prolific silhouette animator is Lotte Reiniger, who began working in her native Germany and later also made films in England and other countries. *Die Geschichte des Prinzen Achmed* (*The Adventures of Prince Achmed*), an adaptation of tales from *The Thousand and One Nights*, was completed in 1926 after three years in production,[9] and is a landmark in cinema history as perhaps the first-ever feature-length animated film. The art of

scissor cutting had been around for centuries and was popular in Europe for years before Reiniger began making her films. In fact, since the mid-nineteenth century, the folk art of scissor cutting commonly was taught to young women in Germany.[10]

Reiniger animated more than seventy silhouette films. Along with short narrative works largely based on traditional stories, she also made a number of animated advertisements. She used scissors, rather than a knife, to cut her figures and determined that a combination of thin metal and cardboard was ideal for making them both stable and flexible. In *The Silhouette Film*, Pierre Jouvanceau writes that Reiniger solved problems of scale by creating primary characters in multiple sizes, ranging from 1 to 24 inches (2.5 to 61 centimeters); the average size, for shots where the background was larger than the character, was about 5 inches (12.75 centimeters).[11] Some of her characters were extremely detailed; for example, the head of the ogress in *Prince Achmed*, used for a close-up, "has sixteen different joints: six parts for the mouth, three for the chin, one for the nose, four for the eyebrows, and two for the hair, not to mention a mobile pupil."[12]

Backgrounds in silhouette animation are created by using different types of paper: opaque for completely black elements, and cellophane or tracing paper for mid-range tones. Jouvanceau explains that, in Reiniger's work, darker and lighter mid-tones were created through layering sheer papers, rather than using a single sheet of relatively opaque material to block more light. To guide development of these

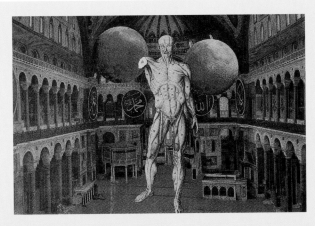

Larry Jordan's enigmatic cutout film *Sophie's Place.*

Lotte Reiniger used silhouetted cutouts in her work, such as a shadow theatre performance of *The Marriage of Figaro.*

layers, a sketch of the background is shaded to indicate its relative densities, which are reduced "to four or five zones of uniform tone. Each zone is then cut out from a layer of translucent paper, starting with the darkest. For Lotte Reiniger, five layers constitute a sufficient range for an elaborate set. … Thus, four superimposed layers form the darkest gray, three the intermediate tone, and two the lightest."[13] One layer of the material being used is set on top of the composition to prevent it getting entangled in the jointed silhouettes placed on it.

Frank Mouris American animator Frank Mouris saved images from magazines for many years before he completed his best-known work *Frank Film* (1973). It tells the story of his life from childhood through graduate school (which was when the film was conceptualized). The complex collage of images is complemented by a double dialogue track that provides an aural stream of information as dense as the visuals. After three years of pre-production, Mouris filmed the project over a seven-day period, working ten hours a day on a 16mm Oxberry animation camera at Harvard University.[14] Titles for the film were created with Letraset on typewriter paper, which was placed on red Color-aid paper; they were shot on the floor of Mouris's SoHo loft (in New York City) using a Bolex camera on a tripod.

Mouris cut identical images from different-size magazines (for example, small from *Reader's Digest*, medium from *Newsweek*, and large from *Life*), allowing him to create the effect of an object growing or shrinking in size. He discovered another effect by accident, after he attached images to cels using one-coat rubber cement and stacked them during test filming—he realized that the layering of the sheets created a fading-out effect that looked like complicated cross-dissolves. He explains, "Even cels are not completely transparent … so by the time you stack several dozen up, the images toward the bottom of the pile tend to go away into blackness—not to our sensitive eyes, but to the less-sensitive movie film."

About a year after the filming was complete, Tony Schwartz agreed to work on the soundtrack. Mouris had thought of it as containing only a list of words that defined his life, but at the recording session Schwartz insisted on hearing what all the imagery meant. The story soundtrack was, in Mouris's words, "a one-take wonder done under pressure, totally unprepared ('just tell me what it all means,' he said). I left his studio unhappy, but then the next week, we got back together and we came up with the idea of trying to combine the two different soundtracks, because by then he agreed that neither track by itself could stand up to the onslaught of the animated imagery."

Frank Mouris's autobiographical *Frank Film* (above, left and right) was created using cutouts gathered from magazines over many years.

Yuri Norstein at work on *Shinel* (right).

Yuri Norstein The great Russian animator Yuri Norstein is famous for his use of intricate 2D puppet figures in films such as *Yozhik v tumane* (*Hedgehog in the Fog*, 1975) and *Skazka skazok* (*Tale of Tales*, 1979), which have resonated deeply with viewers across the world. Because of his desire for spontaneity in the production process, Norstein generally foregoes scripts in favor of storyboards, which he feels "can be read like a musical score, instantly."[15] However, for many years strict censorship in the Soviet Union meant he was compelled to submit precise documentation of his work before production commenced. Straying from these plans resulted in many problems, including a lack of funding, despite the fact that his work was highly acclaimed internationally—*Skazka skazok* won the hard-to-top title "Best Animated Film of All Time" at a Los Angeles animation festival in the early 1980s.

At a five-day seminar, "How to Animate the Norstein Way," in October 1995, Norstein discussed the figures used in *Yozhik v tumane*. The hedgehog was about 6 inches (15 centimeters) long and made of layered pieces of celluloid covered with acrylic or oil paint. The first head layer was created to look spiky and rough, and was overlaid in part by another piece, which also contained spikes, giving "a sense of depth and 'prickliness' to the hedgehog's fur. The hedgehog's main body section [was] done in the same way."[16] In contrast, its arms and legs were made from single pieces of thin metal held in place by painted straight pins.[17] A similar technique was used for a fish that swims in a stream: Roughly cut circles of sepia-painted cel material in gradually reduced sizes were held together with screws, which provided movable joints. This group of body circles was overlaid with a smaller string of circles to add nuance in terms of changing light quality and depth.[18]

Like the figures in *Skazka skazok*, these cutouts were designed and created by Norstein's wife and principal collaborator, Francesca Yarbusova—"arguably the most talented Russian animation designer of her generation."[19] Both Norstein and Yarusova are well versed in the language of painting, which is often used in their discussions of film designs. Historian Clare Kitson notes that Norstein talks about "texture" and "scumble" in his work, and often refers to particular paintings to demonstrate specific effects. He insists, "Individual artwork elements should be executed swiftly and not finished off in perfect detail. His ideals in this respect are Picasso and Pushkin … as Norstein says of them, 'speed of execution allows a lot of feeling to flow into the line.'"[20] To allow for depth of field and shifts in focus, Norstein animates on a multiplane camera setup he developed with cameraman Alexander Zhukovsky. Currently he is working on *Shinel* (*The Overcoat*), a film that has been in production since the early 1980s.

Images from Yuri Norstein's films
Yozhik v tumane (above) and
Skazka skazok (right and far right).

Case Study: Lynn Tomlinson's Cutout Workshops

Lynn Tomlinson has found that cutouts are an ideal medium for the animation workshops that she leads with students of varying ages. For a number of years she has taught college-age students in Ithaca, New York, at Cornell University's Summer Session, but recently she also began working with schoolchildren. In 2004, she collaborated with a mixed-age (first through fourth grade) class of eleven children to create *Shopping for Utopia*, a cutout animation depicting their ideal societies. Tomlinson has also worked with a group of five fifth-grade girls, supported by a professional development grant from United Arts of Central Florida, to

make a series of films, "Girls of the World." The narratives focus on each of five girls in diverse contexts who made an impact on the world.

Tomlinson describes her role in *Shopping for Utopia* as "director," and explains that the children's work was primarily limited to designing scenarios and creating figures to illustrate them. Participants were also able to try moving the cutouts under the camera. However, because of time and technical limitations, and the number of children involved, Tomlinson did much of the under-camera animation and editing on her home studio computer, a Macintosh G5, with the help of her first-grade son, who was one of the children in the class.

She was invited into the classroom twice a week over a period of eight weeks. The

children were studying utopian societies and, in groups of two or three, had already written scenarios describing their perfect worlds. Tomlinson had each group elaborate on its utopia by creating a "tour," including a script for a tour guide. Within their groups, the children decided whether one or more of them would be recorded as the guide; they also created sound effects and played simple bits of music. Sounds were recorded using an external microphone plugged into the video camera, resulting in two types of usable material—the soundtrack itself and extra footage that could be incorporated into a "making of" documentary of the production process. The children also designed a simple storyboard to depict locations in their tour, and its images guided their creation of cutouts. To link the various utopian visions, they

Images from "Girls of the World" (left and below), a series of films designed by fifth-grade girls participating in a workshop led by Lynn Tomlinson.

Lynn Tomlinson at work with underlit clay (right).

came up with the idea of channel-surfing on television—with different utopias being described as channels are changed.

For both *Shopping for Utopia* and "Girls of the World," students were introduced to the work of children's book illustrator Eric Carle, whose renowned illustrations (for such books as *The Very Hungry Caterpillar*, 1969) are created with painted paper. The children used his technique to develop materials for their cutouts. They first coated sheets of card stock paper with tempera paint and acrylics; Tomlinson encouraged them to go for streaky, irregular effects rather than attempt to coat the sheets evenly, and to use a lot of water, creating a wash rather than a thick coat of tempera paint, which might crack. The painted papers were used for the cutout figures in the films. The children focused on the faces of their tour guides, making multiple eyes, eyebrows, and mouths. Tomlinson also asked them to create eyelids, emphasizing that the use of occasional blinks would make their characters come to life. Although colors and styles differed from figure to figure, and scenario to scenario, the

distinctive look of the painted paper provided continuity. Backgrounds were created with painted sheets of poster board, also streaky and dribbly.

Every task was divided into manageable chunks that would not test the children's patience; for this reason, cutouts were ideal for them. They could easily make a single figure that Tomlinson later brought to life through simple animation. The key to keeping them interested in the project was bringing updates to each meeting, so they could see its progress and be motivated to accomplish the next step. Equally important was the "wrap party" she coordinated at the end. Parents were invited, and the film was screened, along with a "blooper reel" of out-takes in a documentary about how the project was made.

Tomlinson employed a digital still camera mounted on a copy stand to record the images for the animated films. She placed the children's cutouts on the bed of the stand and moved them according to the general pacing of the dialogue. The images were stored on the camera's CompactFlash card, and transferred to her computer to be imported

into Final Cut Pro. Using the "timeline" of this software, Tomlinson manipulated the visuals to align them with the dialogue. She says this system "makes 'frames per second' irrelevant because it allows me to go backward and forward in timing. If something is moving too fast, I can go in and adjust the frame rate."

The participants in Tomlinson's Cornell workshops ranged from young college-age to older returning students. They used other techniques in addition to cutouts, since they were predisposed to making animation and so were able to handle the complexity that comes with varied ways of working. Here, too, Tomlinson employed a still camera in conjunction with Final Cut Pro. She liked working this way with the older students "because it involves both tactile processes and digital. The students may go in and out of the computer several times—for example, one Cornell student shot his film on digital video, printed it out frame by frame, painted on the images, rescanned them, and edited it digitally."

18

Images from Eric Carle's book *The Very Hungry Caterpillar* (below) were used as inspiration for the style of the children's work.

Images from *Shopping for Utopia* (above and left), a workshop for schoolchildren led by Lynn Tomlinson.

3D Stop-motion Media

In the realm of stop-motion animation, two-dimensional media tend to be shot from overhead, using a rostrum camera. In contrast, three-dimensional media usually are placed on a horizontal surface and shot from the side.

Folded Paper

Paper folding is an ancient art form that provides interesting opportunities for stop-motion animation. Pressed flat, folded paper forms can be filmed two-dimensionally, as cutout paper images would be. However, when positioned upright on a horizontal set, these figures can be placed within three-dimensional environments.

Virgil Widrich Austrian animator Virgil Widrich uses a range of folded and cut papers within *Fast Film* (2003) to provide a rapid, highly kinetic tour through film history. The film's "story" is built around a mixture of action/adventure, romance, and other genres, and is created with about 65,000 images from 300 feature films that were captured as screen grabs using Adobe After Effects. About 12,000 euros (approximately US$12,000) in worth of toner was required to print the images on DIN A3 (11⅝ x 16½ inches [29.7 x 42 centimeters]) and A4 (8¼ x 11⅝ inches [21 x 29.7 centimeters) 80gsm paper.

Over a year, twelve animators ripped, sawed, and occasionally cut out images that were used flat or folded into origami-like forms or three-dimensional models. The filmmakers used a paper-folding tool to create sharp edges, a saw to give the paper an interesting rough edge, and—perhaps most importantly—lots of hand cream for the individuals doing the work. The images were animated using traditional stop-motion techniques, shot with a digital still camera (sometimes with a green screen to facilitate compositing), and then imported into a computer to process complicated shots (see page98). Widrich employed a Canon EOS D30 digital still camera with 2.048 x 1.536 pixel resolution to allow for an eventual high-quality (2K) exposure on 35mm negative film. Images were edited with After Effects and stored to Maxtor disks using a FireWire interface, requiring about one terabyte for the entire movie.

The film has done well internationally, in part because of its sound design. As Jon Davies has observed, Frédéric Fichefet's soundtrack, which consists of fragments taken from the source films and remixed, "contains no dialogue, allowing it to travel internationally—without subtitles—across linguistic barriers."[21]

Altogether, the fourteen-minute film was in production for about two years, beginning with research that included the

Images from *Fast Film* directed by Virgil Widrich (above).

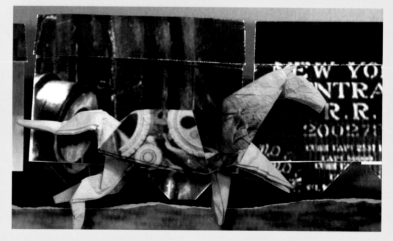

viewing of 1,200 potential feature-film sources (see page 14).[22] Widrich documented the production process in *Making of Fast Film* (see page 79), which he placed on his website (www.widrichfilm.com/fastfilm), along with a large number of still images.

Brickfilms

The World Wide Web has provided opportunities for independent and small-scale animation creators to promote and exhibit work that previously would have languished with little or no distribution, seen only by a few people at best, or that would never have been produced at all. Karin Wehn is among the first animation scholars to write about the phenomenon of brickfilms, which have flourished in the wake of the ever-growing Web[23]—a website, www.brickfilms.com, displays the wide range of these works made by individuals across the world.

Brickfilms are made with toy building materials—primarily from LEGO sets, but bricks by other manufacturers also are used. The small "minifig" people that come with such sets function as prefabricated characters; most have perpetually smiling faces, though a wider variety (smiling on one side/frowning on the other, or variously detailed) are available. Productions made with these materials are

sometimes called "LEGO films," but the name brickfilm is functional. It avoids legal battles with the LEGO company, which understandably is protective of its name and reputation. Many brickfilms are created by novice animators in their spare time, using webcams to record images. Although there is a certain amount of roughness in their animation, there is also a great deal of charm. Some works are actually quite impressive in terms of cinematic shooting, set design, visual effects, storytelling, and use of sound.

Lindsay Fleay People were using bricks to create animation long before the Web boosted their popularity. *The Magic Portal*, a sixteen-minute production by Australian Lindsay Fleay, was completed in 1989, and remains an impressive example (see page 44). This brickfilm is about an astronaut, called L, who discovers a magic portal onboard his giant spaceship. The portal transports him and the rest of the "LEGOnaut" crew to strange worlds where they have a series of adventures. In recent years, Fleay has documented the film's four-and-a-half year production process on his Magic Portal website (www.rakrent.com/mp/mp.htm). It includes extensive production notes, as well as storyboards, and the film can also be downloaded.[24]

A lot of hand lotion was required for artists folding the many paper objects used in Virgil Widrich's *Fast Film*.

Fleay's characters tend to look similar in overall profile, and are distinguished primarily by the facial expression they wear most often. At the time *The Magic Portal* was made, LEGO did not produce the range of faces it does today, so Fleay created his own using Rotring ink. However, he soon found that using special heads for different expressions was not always practical. Fleay writes, "Within the spaceship interiors, even a simple blink involved ripping apart the set, gingerly replacing a head without moving the character and then rebuilding everything." One of the film's characters, Plasticene, was made out of clay, which was problematic because of the small scale at which Fleay worked. He describes animating "a LEGOnaut-size glob of putty" as "sheer torture."

Animation and shooting, which he did in his parents' basement, took between nine and twelve months. His homemade stands were fashioned from old tables and crates, and sets were illuminated by photographic lights he inherited from his grandfather. A brigade of fans were used to try to prevent the plastic pieces from overheating. Fleay typically began work at 10 A.M. and finished around midnight, taking three weeks to expose a hundred-foot (thirty-meter) roll of film (about three minutes of footage). Most of the work was animated on ones (24 moves per second), though some parts, including many of the walking movements, were animated on twos. Images were filmed with a wind-up Bolex.

Fleay began by trying to compose his own music, which he called "a disaster," but then was introduced to Thomas Kayser, who was eventually responsible for most of the sound effects and ambient noise. Together they explored many facets of sound production, including field recordings with Nagras and electronic sound generation. The voices were played by four experienced actors. Fleay devoted two-and-a-half years to sound production, which culminated in a one-day (mono) sound mix by Kim Lord at the ABC-TV studios in Perth.

The film's titles (see page 103) were shot professionally by John Tollemach, using an Oxberry animation stand. Fleay felt it was important to get the best titles he could, considering how long he had worked to make the film itself look good. He says, "I can see how designers fret and worry over the smallest of details in fonts and logos. It really *does* matter with type. Opening titles set the tone and establish audience expectations and aren't to be underestimated." He drew inspiration from other impressive films, such as *Citizen Kane* and *2001: A Space Odyssey*, and selected Futura Medium, which he saw as "serious and arty, but not so aggressive; sharp-edged, but not quite horror-show. Its squared-off edges

Lindsay Fleay at work (above) and production shots from *The Magic Portal*.

and perfect circles complemented … LEGO geometry rather well, I thought."

The finished film was transferred to one-inch broadcast video and aired on television; it appeared on Australia's SBS Television's "Eat Carpet" six times. But the film was never made into a release print that could be shown in a theater, and festival screenings turned out to be a disappointment—in large part due to legal issues surrounding his right to use LEGO products in a film. Although Fleay had gone so far as to get informal approval from a company executive in the form of a letter, he had not signed a contract, and a change in management caused him to have to undergo a round of new negotiations. Today toy bricks appear online in large number, so the hobbyist probably has little worry about using them. However, Fleay's experience underscores the general importance of contracts giving pre-approval, whether it be for trademarked images, sound elements, or any other component of the work that another party might claim to own. Contracts are especially important if the production will be shown at festivals, on television, or in any other context in which a profit may be made.

Chris Salt For many years, Chris Salt was a fan of animation, but did not make his own films because the process seemed to be expensive. However, at the end of 2002, he saw someone at his workplace fooling around with a digital camera and a toy, and he decided to do a few test animations himself. That experience led to the production of *Out of Time*, a short brickfilm that tells the story of two friends who come across space travelers and their time machine.

Salt refers to himself as a "brickfilmer," a term that has been widely adopted by people who make stop-motion films using LEGO-type materials. Salt says he and most other people in the brickfilms.com community "do this as a hobby, so no one really takes themselves too seriously." Competition is friendly and there is a lot of commentary from fans and practitioners alike. The tone is one of equality, rather than hierarchy; even the work of award-winners is subject to public discussion and debate by other brickfilmers.

Salt's films usually begin with a script that includes a lot of stage directions and description. If he has trouble visualizing a scene, he might try to storyboard it, but in most cases he sets up the characters in front of the camera and moves them around until he is happy with the composition. His shooting ratio is usually 1:1—for every one image shot, one is used (in other words, there are no out-takes). He works with a Logitech QuickCam Pro 4000 webcam. Its good points, he says, are that it is "cheap, has a good-quality image, is small

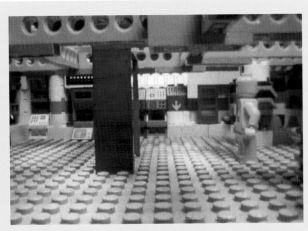

Images from *The Magic Portal*, directed by Lindsay Fleay.

enough to film LEGO figures close up, works well in low-light indoor conditions, and has a manual focus. Its bad points are that depth of field is pretty limited when you get up close and the manual-focus mechanism makes it difficult to shift the focus within a shot—turning the focus ring physically moves the lens within the camera and creates a shaky effect when you do it over a series of frames." Images are captured to a dedicated hard disk because the raw footage he shoots is stored uncompressed, so it takes up a lot of space.

The baseplates that are a feature of LEGO make it ideal for stop-motion. Set pieces and characters can be easily anchored by fitting them onto their pegs. In creating *Out of Time*, Salt shot mostly on a 48 x 48-stud baseplate (about a 16-inch [40.5-centimeter] square), with typical walls rising eight bricks in height. Some people within the brickfilm community adhere to the philosophy "keep it pure" by utilizing only LEGO products for their films. Salt also uses other materials, in particular colored card for backdrops—sky, hillsides, and so on. However, he tends to use LEGO parts for his sets because they are designed to fit together. In general, he finds bricks are appealing because "the sets are almost infinitely recyclable. Also, once they're put together, they stay together—they don't move about in the middle of a shot." Salt's sets are lit with three halogen desk lamps—two are in the foreground, and the third in the background. He sometimes employs sheets of white card stock to diffuse the light, a technique he finds especially useful for creating reflections when he is filming all, or mostly, black figures.

The first step in the production process is recording a voice track. Salt performs most of the voices, recording himself on a Sony microphone that he plugs directly into his sound card.

He says that when he reads lines he tries to make them sound "as close to natural conversation" as he can. Salt records various takes of the dialogue being delivered in different ways, including changes in emphasis and timing; when they are all recorded and he begins to assemble the audio track, he then picks the ones that work best. The editing software allows him to make adjustments in timing, creating pauses for comic effect, speeding or slowing the delivery, and so forth.

After setting up his soundtrack, Salt decides exactly how long each shot must be and where gestures have to be placed. He then animates his figures and captures images, and begins editing simultaneously. Small changes in animation timing can be made with the computer. For *Out of Time*, Salt employed an easy-to-use freeware application, Anasazi Stop Motion Animator, but he moved to Stop Motion Pro for subsequent projects. He likes its additional features, like frame averaging (a mathematical process that reduces graininess and visual defects known as digital artifacting) and audio sync, as well as the overall increased quality of the picture. His brick films have been edited using Sonic Foundry's Vegas 4.0 (now owned by Sony).

Although the LEGO company is less contentious about the use of its figures in animation than it has been in the past, the shadow of the rights owner continues to hover over the brickfilm community. At brickfilms.com, discussions about content standards touch on suitability for children, and any effects on LEGO's reputation. While violence is not uncommon (one brickfilms.com tutorial gives advice on how to create the effect of spurting blood), many brickfilmers aim for content that is suitable for a wide range of viewers—this group includes Salt, who tries to keep his films "family-friendly."

Chris Salt and his brickfilm set.

Clay Figures

Clay animation dates back to the early years of cinema, and has maintained a regular presence since then. One of its first uses was in Edwin S. Porter's *Fun in a Bakery Shop* (1902), in which a huge slab of dough (actually clay) thrown against a wall is quickly transformed into shapes by a baker-sculptor (see page 41). Gumby, the lovable green character created by Art Clokey, appeared in a television series beginning in 1957, and was certainly among the highlights of clay animation during the twentieth century. Also notable were a series of works produced at the Will Vinton Studio, including the first clay animated feature, *The Adventures of Mark Twain* (1985). During the late 1990s, clay animation broke new ground in one of the most outrageous series ever seen on television: "Celebrity Death Match." This American series pitted celebrities against each other in fights to the death that featured ever-larger weapons, a smorgasbord of deadly stunts, and an extravaganza of spurting blood. These examples are only a small sampling of work created within an American industrial concept—of course, clay has been widely used internationally, and in more experimental and independently produced work as well.

Aardman Animations Many young stop-motion animators have been inspired by the successes of the Aardman Animations studio in Bristol, England. The studio's popularity largely has been built on the directing accomplishments of Nick Park,

such as the "Wallace and Gromit" series of short films, including *The Wrong Trousers* (1993). Aardman's feature *Chicken Run* (2000), co-directed by Park and Peter Lord, made history in the United States as the first animated feature created outside the country to become a "blockbuster," earning millions of dollars. This accomplishment was all the more impressive because *Chicken Run* was made with clay—which has rarely had a presence in feature production. Topping this accomplishment, Aardman's *Wallace & Gromit: Curse of the Were-Rabbit* (2005), co-directed by Park and Steve Box, won an Oscar for Best Animated Feature.

In *Creating 3-D Animation: The Aardman Book of Filmmaking*, Lord and Brian Sibley describe basic principles of modelmaking, and they provide details about the construction of characters created at the studio.[25] For example, they explain that Aardman's canine star Gromit begins with a ball-and-socket armature and a body made of fast-cast resin, which is built up with modeling clay to create the character's features.[26] The book offers many helpful tips for clay animators. For instance, the authors recommend that clay should be built up in two layers, since armatures tend to give off a black oil; the first layer absorbs the oil, and the second (top) layer is used for sculpting.

Adam Elliot An independent animator, Australian Adam Elliot uses clay figures for what he calls "mock-documations"—fiction films that are loosely based on people he has known

The Adventures of Mark Twain (above), animated by the Will Vinton Studio, was the first clay animation feature.

Wallace and Gromit, seen here in *The Wrong Trousers* directed by Nick Park, helped launch the international success of the Aardman Animations studio.

and that are structured like documentaries, including voice-over narration to give details about the characters. They deal with individuals who are outcasts because of some physical and/or mental condition that causes them to do things that are not socially acceptable. With a balanced hand, Elliot studies his subjects, and presents poignant stories that are humorous and, in ways, sad. His trilogy of short films—*Uncle* (1996), *Cousin* (1998), and *Brother* (1999)—were popular within the festival circuit before his twenty-four-minute *Harvie Krumpet* (2003) won an Oscar and made him one of Australia's most famous animators. The victory was all the sweeter because he won against multimillion dollar films from Pixar (*Boundin'*), Twentieth Century-Fox (*Gone Nutty*), and Disney (*Destino*). In comparison, *Harvie Krumpet*'s budget was AU$377,000 (under $300,000 in US dollars and under £200,000 in UK pounds) and it was filmed in a storage shed.

Elliot sees the appeal of his productions, and stop-motion in general, partly in terms of the "history" of the process. He explains, "I use a very old Bolex camera and I like to think I'm making films the same way they did fifty years ago. The technique is exactly the same. We do use a video-assist camera linked to a laptop, just to see what we're doing. But it's still done the traditional way, and audiences like that. … Audiences like to see fingerprints on the modeling clay—it proves that what they're seeing is tangible."[27] Certainly, Elliot's films also have benefited from the professionalism of the voice actors he

has worked with—William McInnes, Geoffrey Rush, Kamahl, Julie Forsyth, and John Flaus.

Elliot approaches both the writing of scripts and the animation process with less emphasis on technical perfection than a sense of what feels right. The characters in his films are somewhat still, yet they clearly reflect an understanding of the qualities that make a person human. Subtle movements—for example, facial and hand gestures—rather than nonstop motion bring them alive. In his three early films, the models and sets were painted black, white, and gray, to suggest old black-and-white photographs from an album, but were recorded on color film, allowing one shot of spot color in each (for example, Fluoro Orange for a lizard's tongue in *Brother*). *Harvie Krumpet* was colored to suggest the Harvie character's various moods. For example, when he fell in love the scenes were "bright and colorful, and when he went into a nursing home, they became sepia again."[28]

Generally, Elliot follows a relatively strict production schedule, waking up at 6 A.M. and working during the early part of the day. He draws inspiration from biographies, the work of Michael Leunig and Barrie Humphries, and in part from his own life. He says, "My films are about people with disorders. And I've got a disorder myself." Elliot's condition causes tremors at times; as a result he made his characters (and especially their eyes) relatively large, so he can work with them more easily. His figures stand about one foot (thirty centimeters) in height.

Adam Elliott (above) on the set of
Harvie Krumpet (right).

Harvie Krumpet was in production for more than three years. The script was completed in about three months, after Elliot got a bank loan that allowed him to do nothing but write for the whole time: "I did seventeen drafts of a twenty-eight-page script. *Harvie Krumpet* took a lot longer to write than anything else I'd done, because there was so much I wanted to tell about this character. Just with all the facts and trying to get everything accurate: researching Poland and the language and so on." After two years of securing financing, it took fourteen months to shoot the film and four more months in post-production. Elliot's producer, Melanie Coombs, was a vital resource throughout the film, providing not only moral support, but also assistance with securing financing, scheduling, and logistics. Elliot's parents also played a role, as his mother knit clothing for the figures and the hot, unventilated storage shed where the film was shot had been rented by his father.[29]

Before Elliot won an Oscar, he downplayed the overall effects of his success at festivals, even the Academy Awards. He said, "Winning mainly means we get into more film festivals: We'll now be invited to screen as opposed to having to submit (and we'll save a fortune in courier costs). When I first started making shorts, I thought that winning a prize meant that someone would give me a check to fund my next film. But it never happens like that. Even if we get nominated for an Oscar, it doesn't really make life easier. It opens doors a little but you still have to push your way through." Part of the problem, he concedes, is the fact that short-format films are relatively difficult to distribute.

However, actually winning the Oscar seems to have impacted Elliot quite a lot. A few years later, he was saying, "The post-Oscar circus continues, especially here in Australia! My producer and I have done over five hundred pieces of media and are still bewildered by the interest in us (especially as we have never in the last decade actively sought publicity)." He felt "the biggest change is the 'fame' thing and being recognized in the street and at traffic lights; but that will all fade (hopefully!)." The more important thing for Elliot as an artist was that doors did open, and open widely, presenting opportunities for collaborations as well as financing for other projects. However, Elliot rejected most offers. In 2005 he said, "Life for me has changed considerably but in many ways is still the same since the Oscar. My producer and I have been determined to continue to make our own films despite the various offers from Hollywood and the commercial sector. We are in development for my first full-length feature claymation, which I have written and will direct here in Australia. It will be like my other four films, but will be longer and of course have a much bigger budget (between five and ten million Australian dollars). I have refused all offers to collaborate with other writers or directors, and so I suppose that is one thing that has not changed."[30]

Winning an Oscar opened many opportunities for animation director Adam Elliott and producer Melanie Coombs, though they decided to continue working independently, rather than accepting offers for collaborations with larger studios.

Case Study: Charles daCosta

At the University College of the Creative Arts in Farnham, England, Charles daCosta created a five-minute clay and silicone graduation film, *School Dinners* (2007), in conjunction with doctoral research exploring social structures and the experience of black senior citizens in England (see page 102). The Ghana-born animator based this short on an interview with an elderly woman about everyday life. To represent her experiences, he created the female character Nana Efua—the name of a Ghanaian woman born on a Friday, which is the day of the week on which daCosta had the idea for the film and, later, the day when the figure's cast was completed.[31] This short is the first in a series, "One Out of Many," that he plans to develop for television.

DaCosta says his work was motivated by "a basic question: Why are blacks often portrayed in 'entertainment' or 'problem' contexts and not in ordinary circumstances?"

He spent time watching and listening to old black English people, "the unseen citizens. Those people who've known no country—ever—but England." He adds, "This production was in line with my thinking, research-wise. Social inclusion can be discussed at length, but a picture says more than a thousand words, and so this goes hand-in-glove with my theoretical work."

As a young boy, daCosta won awards for his artwork, and seemed destined for a career in media arts. Unfortunately, in Ghana resources for production were limited, and it was difficult to get access to supplies and facilities. After high school, he worked for a year as a teacher's aide at the Lincoln Community School—an American international school in Accra—where he used drawings and cartoons to help first- and second-grade students with mathematics. Next he enrolled at a regional training academy, the National Film and Television Institute (NAFTI), which had been established in 1978 by the Friederich-Ebert

Foundation. He graduated with a diploma in animation and graphics, then worked for a year as audio-visual officer at the W.E.B. duBois Center for Pan-African Culture in Accra. DaCosta went on to obtain degrees in film and video production, computer animation, and media technology administration. For the media degree, he focused on leadership and management within new media organizations. He explains, "I argued that the new media manager/leader had to be one who was 'equipped' (prepared) to demonstrate how things worked in practice. It was not his mission to simply strategize, but to 'activize,'" by demonstrating issues in engaging ways. DaCosta's training in computer animation helped him determine that it would take too long to produce a substantial work using computer-generated imagery, so he turned his attention to clay, which he felt could be animated more quickly. He also was attracted to what he sees as its inherent allure: As a medium that is normally associated with "kid stuff," he says, it tends to attract people's attention.

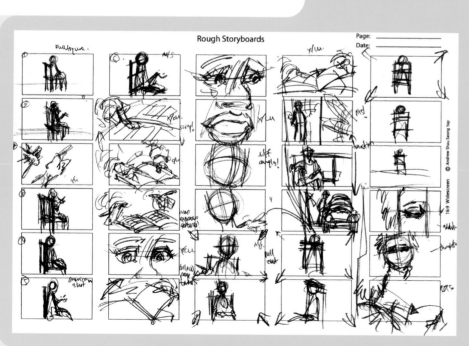

Rough and finished storyboards from Charles daCosta's *School Dinners* show the development of visuals within the film.

He began production by writing scenarios for three five-minute productions. After selecting *School Dinners* as his first project, he recorded a series of interviews with the woman, and then edited them, did a dialogue breakdown, sketched the character, determined the look of production, and storyboarded. Working with a budget of £2,450 (approximately US$4,500), daCosta economized by featuring only one character, who remains seated throughout the production—as the woman on whom it is based did during the interview. Because she is elderly, the scenario is convincing, and it saved money, since the figure did not require a full armature. DaCosta explains, "Due to budgetary constraints I was only able to construct an upper-body armature. This allows what I call 'conversational mobility.' Seated, we tend to make mostly upper-body movements when we talk. It is still possible to get shoulder shrugs, waving, etc. The fingers were constructed separately to enable flexibility." He created the 11-inch (28-centimeter) figure

in four sections, some of which were made in multiple copies: he made one body and one head, but several hands and faces. However, he did not have the budget to create figures in various sizes (for the effect of a close shot, for example). To save time with animation, the character was given sunglasses to cover her eyes. Camera angles and visual effects also were prohibited by production constraints— time as well as budget—and his desire to use a realist documentary aesthetic. Instead, he used movement of the figure and editing to create visual interest.

DaCosta made a model of his figure out of Newplast, an English modeling clay he purchased from Chromacolour. After the model was finished, he cut it into pieces in preparation for casting. He explains:

I had to detach its head from its body; next slice its face off; then its hands had to be chopped off. The head and body were both (separately) placed in containers filled with latex. When the latex hardened, it was sliced open so the

clay could be taken out. This is how the molds were made. Next the armature was placed in the body mold; silicone was poured around it, and the mold was clamped tight and left to dry. When it dried it was simply taken out—carefully—and bingo, out comes our lady, nicely cast.

The faceless head was also cast in this manner. The face was handled differently because it was made of clay, not silicone. In fact, daCosta made several faces, using a fiberglass mold as follows:

After the face was sliced off the initial modeling-clay cast, it was placed in a fiberglass solution. Once the fiberglass hardened, it formed a sort of cup. Clingfilm was placed in the fiberglass mold, and modeling clay was pressed onto it, forming an impression of the face. To extract the face, I pulled the

11

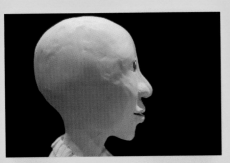

A clay figure provided the foundation for casting the finished figure used in Charles daCosta's *School Dinners.*

clingfilm from the mold. This provided some consistency, while allowing me to manipulate the face. Because it was modeling clay, I could modify the mouths by hand to match different visemes [visual phonemes]. So, for example, I have a face with the mouth shaped to match the letter "A" (as in "AH" and "AY") and so on, which I used in a replacement technique to execute lip synchronization.

As well as Newplast and silicone, daCosta used various other materials, including Modela, a Swiss modeling clay. Each product was chosen for its particular strengths: "Silicone can withstand the heat of lights, and treated properly it still has a clay-ey look. The modeling clay allows me to tweak facial expressions more easily (but it also melts pretty easily, so I had to construct several heads). Modela is almost like oil-based modeling clay but does not melt under

the lights. Also, it's not so messy. However, there wasn't enough of it, and it was difficult to find. I got it five years before the production. I used it for the hands— and nothing much else." Different colors of clay were blended together to achieve the desired palette.

On the body and head, silicone base paint was applied in several layers. He used silicone paints mixed with Silicone Paint Base No. 2 to harden them. Both were manufactured and distributed by Jacobson Chemicals, a company based in Alton, England.[32] Because the paint was noxious, daCosta had to wear a respirator mask while it was being applied.

Silicone was the perfect choice for the figure's body and head due to its flexibility. However, because clay does not stick to it, daCosta had to find a way to attach the figure's clay face to the head. The solution was to attach the looped side of a Velcro strip to the front of the head, adhering it with wet silicone (which will stick to other synthetic material).

The back of the clay face was then pressed into the Velcro loops to hold it in place.

Twisted wire anchored in a brass tube placed within the neck supported the figure's head, and allowed for turns and nods. It was also used in the fingers, in conjunction with brass tubes that ran through the wrist to fit into the character's sweater. However, daCosta determined that a stronger, professional armature was needed under the figure's silicone body, so he had one machined by John Wright, who has worked with Aardman Animations. It was made of brass and aluminum, and contained both single and double joints, in 5-, 6-, and 9-millimeter sizes.

For the background materials, daCosta chose a simple "no-cost" concept, not only to save money but also because he believed elaborate sets would be inconsistent thematically. His wanted to use shadowed backgrounds or a simple felt painting rather than a detailed set fabricated out of clay, in order to create an "ordinary" scenario to

The unpainted silicone figure (right) used in Charles daCosta's *School Dinners*.

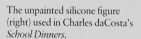

Charles daCosta used Velcro (above) to adhere the clay faces of his figure to its silicone head (right, above and bottom).

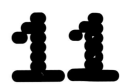

contextualize the realistic experience portrayed in the film. He says, "Ordinariness—that's really the motivating factor for my background. I'd sooner have 'the everyday' than 'the special.' Remember, I'm interested in ordinary (unseen) black citizens." To create the visual impression he desired, daCosta decided to use a range of Cokin filters he got from a second-hand bin in a store. He felt it was more economical to alter the visuals through the camera lens, using filters, than through extensive work on the set itself.

To prepare for the interview on which the project was based, daCosta started talking to the woman long before the day when the recording was made, to ensure she felt comfortable with him and that he had a good idea of what she liked to talk about. He kept a notebook listing what they had covered each time they met. During the interview, he recorded the woman's comments using tape, which he believes has a "warmer" quality

than a digital recording. He says that minidisc players are good for atmospheric sounds like birds, but their propensity toward higher frequencies makes them a poor choice for interviews because"you'd have problems with 'S-es,' 'TCH-es,' 'DG-es . . . as in 'edges,' etc."

Animation took place in daCosta's attic, which he partially converted into a studio, using a digital SLR still camera setup that was bolted to the floor to stabilize it. He selected a Canon EOS 350D camera for several reasons: interchangeability (it has a wide range of available lenses); adaptability (it allowed him to use a lot of different filters); weight (it's fairly light, not bulky); its ability to work in manual mode; and its "nice price." When animation was completed, daCosta used Pinnacle Studio 9 for editing.

Charles daCosta (left) wore protective gear as he used silicone paints. A still from Charles daCosta's finished film, *School Dinners* (below).

Stop-motion Tips

Charles daCosta has the following advice for would-be stop-motion animators:

— Think anthropology, not technology. Think behavior, not the big story (that will come one day). Pay attention to the little things that make people "people," their quirks and human foibles.

— Avoid tungsten and, worse still, halogen lamps. When working with the former make sure you have good correctional filters. In the case of the latter, they will soften clay characters quickly and make your work look a bit messy.

— Make sure your key lights aren't too hot—bounce them a bit, and use reflectors to redirect them on your subjects. It's just a bit cooler—temperature-wise—that way.

— If you can, have a little fridge nearby for cooling your characters, and chill them prior to shots.

— Nothing happens by chance, except disaster—so plan, plan, plan!

11

Animation in Real World Contexts

Animation has a complementary relationship with the "real world," each realm seeming to define the boundary of the other—though often seamlessly. The impulse to combine the animated and the real has always been strong in the hearts of animators, who practice this magic in various ways, within stop-motion puppet films set in realistic environments, pixilated work involving human actors, and installations or performances that bring animation into gallery and everyday settings.

Puppet Animation

Traditions of live puppetry include hand puppets, marionettes, silhouette figures, theater of objects, masks, full-body puppets, and even physical theater using the human form. Many of these practices have equivalents in the world of animation. Often modeled on humans, anthropomorphic animals, or symbolic figures, puppets in motion easily conjure strong associations with the real.

Wooden Puppets

Some of the world's greatest stop-motion animators are from eastern Europe and Russia, where there is a long history of toymaking. An early highlight of Russian animation dates from 1935, when animator Alexander Ptushko released an elaborate stop-motion film, *The New Gulliver*, in which a boy falls asleep over a copy of *Gulliver's Travels* and begins to dream. Some scenes incorporate more than a thousand wooden figures as well as a live actor within a shot—a special effect created on stage, not during post-production.

The Hungarian George Pal and Czech animator Jiří Trnka are also well known for using wooden puppets. Pal eventually moved to Hollywood, where he not only made his "Puppetoon" series of stop-motion shorts for Paramount studios but also produced such memorable special effects films as *Destination Moon* (1950) and *War of the Worlds* (1953). Trnka remained in his native Czechoslovakia. He primarily made entertainment-oriented films such as *Arie prerie* (*Song of the Prairie*, 1949), a satire on American westerns, but his most famous work is *Ruka* (*The Hand*, 1965), a commentary on oppressive political regimes, which was rebuked by censors. In this film, an animated puppet interacts with the hand of a live performer, telling the story of a simple artist who is forced to work for an oppressive ruler. At first, the little figure shows his happiness by spinning around like a dancer with a confident, upright posture, while despair becomes evident later when his head and body slump downward. Trnka uses the movement of his figure's body to show emotional shifts, rather than relying on replacement heads to reflect them through various facial expressions.

The artist from Jiří Trnka's film *Ruka*.

Mixed Media Puppets

Fabrics, furs, and metals are among the materials used in creating puppets made of mixed media. There are innumerable instances of this type of puppet being animated within settings meant to suggest the "real world." An early example is found in the work of Polish animator Ladislaw Starewicz, *Mest kinematograficheskogo operatora* (*The Cameraman's Revenge*, 1912), which features fabricated husband-and-wife beetles who have extramarital affairs and pay the price. This production grew out of Starewicz's interest in entomology, and a failed attempt to make a film using live beetles.

Of course, the history of cinematic special effects is filled with examples of animation occurring in "real" contexts. American animator Ray Harryhausen made his name creating spectacular effects for such live-action features as *Jason and the Argonauts* (1963) and *Clash of the Titans* (1981). He did so through a rear-screen process he invented, "Dynamation," which involved frame by frame projection of live-action footage onto a screen, animation of objects in front of this footage, and a sheet of glass used to create foreground and background mattes. Harryhausen was greatly influence by Willis O'Brien, who created animation for *King Kong* (1933); the two worked together on *Mighty Joe Young* (1949). Though the figures used by these animators were clearly fabricated, they were manipulated in ways that made them seem to be alive, and that appealed to the imagination.

The films made by Jane Aaron combine animation and real environments in other ways. For example, her *Traveling Light* (1985) shows the pattern of "light" (bits of shredded paper) traveling across an actual room. Her film *Set in Motion* (1986) takes on a larger area; it also moves outdoors, where a variety of objects come to life. Aaron's films celebrate domestic spaces, imbuing them with fantasy created through stop-motion animation.

Kihachiro Kawamoto Historian Brian Sibley sees the work of Kihachiro Kawamoto as uniting "the European approach to puppet filmmaking with the long tradition of puppetry in Japan, which dates back to the Bunraku puppet plays first presented in the seventeenth century."[1] This is partly because Kawamoto trained in eastern Europe—he went to Prague to study with Jirí Trnka after seeing the great Czech animator's *Cisaruv slavík* (*The Emperor's Nightingale*, 1949), and spent some years working in Hungary, Poland, Romania, and Russia. He returned to Japan in 1965, where he produced animated films using puppets and other techniques. In his films, puppet figures take on the mannerisms of live performers from the stage.

Insect puppets appear in Ladislaw Starewicz's *Mest kinematograficheskogo operatora* (left).

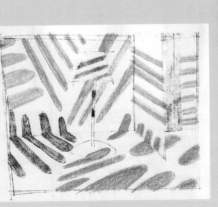

This drawing (left) visualizes the use of colored paper strips in Jane Aaron's *Set in Motion* (above).

His short films include *Oni* (*The Demon*, 1972), *Shijin no Shogai* (*A Poet's Life*, 1974), *Dojoji* (*Dojoji Temple*, 1976), and *Kataku* (*House of Flame*, 1979). Creating a puppet for these films took about ten days. Particular care was taken with its head, which was made using a plaster mold and, as Kawamoto explained, "an agglomerate of Japanese paper, which is then covered with a fine, supple leather and subsequently painted; thus it is light but solid. Eyes, mouth, and eyebrows are movable, and the ears, in plastic, are made from molds. . . . Teeth are fashioned from a type of paraffin, the chests from rigid paper; the hands, in supple rubber, are easily moved. For ten minutes of animation, one year of preparation is required."[2]

Barry Purves Barry Purves is among the animators who have passed through Aardman Animations. Like Kawamoto, Purves specializes in theatrical plays involving human characters acting in the manner of real performers. *Next* (1989), which features William Shakespeare auditioning for his own works,

was made at Aardman for the British television network Channel 4. Other films, such as *Rigoletto* (1995, for SC4/BBC2 television) and *Achilles* (1996, for Channel 4) were made at his own studio, Bare Boards Productions. Purves is remarkable in part for his ability to simultaneously animate large groups of characters through complex actions.

Found objects

Found materials include everyday items that create a sense of ordinary spaces, which can become extraordinary through the powers of animated motion. Some artists have employed found objects as a way to explore the psychic impact of objects around us that are all too often overlooked. The result may be a greater appreciation for the varied aspects of our physical environments or the sometimes disconcerting experience of entering into a surreal landscape.

Images from the films of Barry Purves: *Achilles* (top right) and *Rigoletto* (above and bottom right).

Hermína Tyrlová One of the first women to work in the field of animation, Hermína Tyrlová is another of Czechoslovakia's celebrated stop-motion animators. She began to animate in the 1920s and had a long career making children's films, using everyday objects such as yarn, pieces of wood, and toys.[3] As historian Giannalberto Bendazzi observes, "By using new materials, she managed to achieve the dual goal of avoiding creative stagnation and showing children the hidden lives of common, close-at-hand objects."[4] Her productions include *Ukolébarka* (*The Lullaby*, 1947), which combines live actors and animated objects, and *Uzel na kapesníku* (*The Knotted Fabrics*, 1958), using animated pieces of cloth.

David Anderson David Anderson is one of a number of interesting stop-motion filmmakers who emerged during the 1980s, working with found or commonplace objects in a variety of ways. His series of macabre "Deadtime Stories for Big Folk," made for British television, included *Door* (1990), a film about a mysterious key, two people who contemplate using it, and the end of the world.

Brothers Quay Americans Stephen and Timothy Quay, known as the Brothers Quay, live in London, where they have made short and feature-length films using animation and live-action production methods, designed theatrical sets, and directed television commercials. Their best-known film is *Street of Crocodiles* (1986), which director Terry Gilliam has listed in his selection of "the ten best animated films of all time."[5] It depicts a puppet figure who inhabits the inside of a dusty old machine, which he shares with eerie dolls, screws that come to life, and a range of other disturbing creatures— a visualization of author Bruno Schulz's short story of the same name.

Jan Svankmajer The most famous Czech animator today is Jan Svankmajer. In addition to live-action and animated films, he has been involved in the production of puppet theater, sculpture, poetry, still images, and cabinets displaying objects. A member of the Prague Surrealist Group, Svankmajer has an interest in the "inner life" of dreams and childhood memories. He is also centrally concerned with the history of objects, and

11

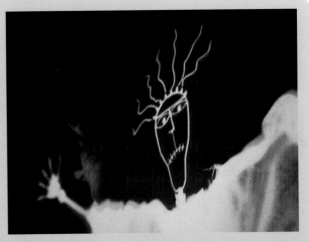

The stop-motion films of David Anderson include *Door* (above left) and *Deadsy and the Sexo=Chanjo* (above right).

Street of Crocodiles (right) directed by the Brothers Quay, is a visualization of a story by Bruno Schulz.

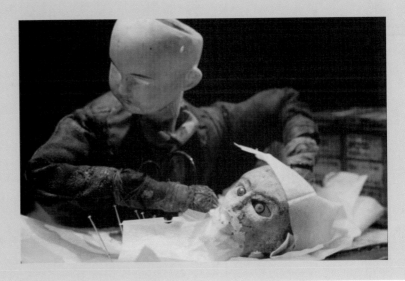

the energy they store from their years of use. The items that populate Svankmajer's films tend to be old, apparently worthless things, yet he feels they are instilled with the memory of everything that has happened around them—that "a life was put into them by people who had contact with them." Also evident in the artist's work is the influence of mannerism, including the art of Giuseppe Arcimboldo, who created portraits with images of fruit, vegetables, and other items. Other strong influences have included the political regimes under which Svankmajer worked and the art direction of his wife, Eva Svankmajerová.

Svankmajer creates scenarios that are often surreal or gory—for example, pig entrails and blood are used in *Konec stalinismu v Cechach* (*The Death of Stalinism in Bohemia*, 1990). He is interested in tactile experience, and his films connect with viewers in strong, possibly disconcerting ways. In one section of *Moznosti dialogu* (*Dimensions of Dialogue*, 1982), Arcimboldo-inspired human heads square off, one devouring the other and regurgitating matter into the form of a new head, which then eats its opponent, regurgitates another head, and so on. The heads are made from solid clay, food, sharp metal instruments, rocks, and other tactile materials that engage the eyes and also connect to other senses.

Roger Hawkins In 2003, the Annecy International Animation Festival screened in its competition the first animated feature from Africa—a Zimbabwan stop-motion film, *The Legend of the Sky Kingdom*. Directed by Roger Hawkins, it was made with a technique he has trademarked "Junkmation™," reflecting the African skill (a veritable art form) at recycling and reusing products, converting old objects into new forms. The film tells the story of three orphaned children and their friends, who escape from the enslavement of an evil emperor and have daring adventures on their way home to the Sky Kingdom. All the characters and each set were made from junk: The hyenas' bodies are scrubbing brushes, pruning shears are used for birds' beaks, and a vulture's wings are empty sacks. One scene features "sixty rusted boilers and drums, three hundred empty paint cans varying in size, and eight hundred crushed drink cans—burned to remove the trademarks and to give added texture."[6] The crew decided against using digital effects and instead animated everything frame by frame. For example, the effect of running water was created by attaching plastic to a roller that was moved for each exposure. Flaming arrows were composed of bits of mirror on the ends of darts; shining a light into them made it look as though the tips were on fire.

The influence of mannerism on Jan Svankmajer can be seen in this still from his film *Moznosti dialogu* (above).

Roger Hawkins (above) directed *The Legend of the Sky Kingdom* (right), the first animated feature from Africa.

Latex puppets

Christmas Films *The Miracle Maker* (2000) contains stop-motion animation from Christmas Films, in Moscow, created under the supervision of Stanislav Sokolov. Cartwyn Cymru, in Wales, was responsible for the film's 2D elements, and the work of the two studios was blended through effects created by Digital Film at the Moving Picture Company in London.[7] This film illustrates the industry practice of international co-production. To compete with the established American and Japanese industries, and to increase economic effectiveness, studios in other countries are uniting to produce work across borders.

To create *The Miracle Maker*, Christmas Films's team of about 250 people worked on the production for four years. Around 260 figures were needed, each about 12 inches (30 centimeters) in height. Lip sync was created using replacement animation, employing twenty or thirty different mouths for each figure. Because filming was done concurrently on six different sets, identical duplicates of the key characters were required. A studio publication describes how the figures were made: "Foam 'flesh' covered a skeletal metal frame, with armatures embedded inside the latex limbs to allow movement. Latex was used wherever skin would be visible, to provide a convincing texture. The finely detailed heads were made from dental acrylic, cast in a mold carved in clay by the Russian model sculptors. For close-ups, the modelmakers produced larger heads, which would even have moving eyelids."

The Miracle Maker (above), directed by Stanislav Sokolov, was created as an international co-production between studios in Russia and the United Kingdom.

Case Study: Tim Burton and *Corpse Bride*

Tim Burton's stop-motion features *The Nightmare Before Christmas* (directed by Henry Selick, 1993) and *Corpse Bride* (co-directed by Burton and Mike Johnson, 2005) represent landmarks not only in stop-motion, but also in the entire field of animation. When *The Nightmare Before Christmas* came out in 1993, no one could predict its popularity; Burton had a following of fans, but an industry-produced, fully stop-motion feature was an unknown entity. Could such a film be produced at all? And if it could, would viewers respond to it? The answer to both questions was most certainly "yes." *The Nightmare Before Christmas*—which tells the story of the pumpkin king of Halloweenland, Jack Skellington, who longs for something new—was not only successful; it also led the way to more diverse filmmaking by breaking the mold of classical Disney 2D animation.

Corpse Bride was cited as a "remarkable step forward in digital filmmaking" when it was released in 2005.[8] However, the story, based on a Russian folktale about a man who marries a zombie by mistake, was almost completely animated through traditional stop-motion techniques, using figures made from silicone over metal armatures. It was in its digital editing and camera technology that it broke new ground. Robin Rowe, reporting for *Editor's Guild Magazine*, explains, "Technologically, this is a movie of many firsts; it's the first feature-length, stop-motion film edited using Apple Final Cut Pro (FCP), it's the first feature shot using commercial digital SLR still photography cameras, and, perhaps most significantly, it's the first movie to choose digital cameras over film cameras based on the criterion of image quality."[9]

Using a digital still camera was not a simple decision. One of the major problems related to the process was registration: how to keep the images consistent from shot to shot. Rowe explains:

Director of Photography Pete Kozachik and his team had been considering digital acquisition, but not with off-the-shelf SLR cameras as [effects consultant Chris] Watts proposed. With the beginning of photography only a month away, digital SLR camera testing began. There were many unknowns:

- Are images from a digital still camera consistent frame to frame?
- Is the quality comparable to film?
- Is the image quality stable under different thermal and humidity conditions?
- Could a system be devised for previewing animations on set?
- Could a system be devised to keep track of all the frames?
- Could a live video tap be created for a digital still camera?[10]

To answer these questions, the crew acquired a wide range of still cameras and used each to record a scene, which was then

Corpse Bride, co-directed by Tim Burton and Mike Johnson, was shot using a digital still camera, which was a first for a big studio stop-motion feature.
TIM BURTON'S CORPSE BRIDE © 2005 Patalex II Productions Limited.
Licensed by Warner Bros. Entertainment Inc. All Rights Reserved.

printed to film. In addition, a "control case" was shot using motion picture film, to see how it differed from the still camera footage. To the surprise of those assembled in the screening room, the images that looked least appealing, due to relatively soft focus, were those shot on film—so the decision was made to use a digital still camera. Ultimately, the Canon EOS-1D Mark II SLR was chosen, and twenty-four cameras were purchased for production.

Another significant problem remained: how to preview each frame of animation. Some digital SLR cameras have a "video out" port, which can be used to generate images as they are recorded. Animators want to see an image before it is recorded—in sequence with preceding images—to ensure that the desired effect will be achieved. Crew members designed a small device that allowed a video camera to be attached to the back of the still camera, so it could feed images to the monitor. The attachment slid out of the way when the time came to focus the lens for the shot.[11]

One of the benefits of using the Canon still camera to record images was that the film's editor, Jonathan Lucas, could blow frames up by 30 to 40 percent without seeing degradation. He also noted that using digital images speeded up editing; he was usually able to begin the process within three hours of a shoot. He learned Final Cut Pro in about two weeks, and was pleased with its ability to handle high-definition footage. However, there were problems; in particular, the software was not equipped to manage the film's huge number of storyboard panels, and these had to be converted to QuickTime images to reduce the load.

Burton's preference for tall, thin characters with small feet made it difficult to design puppets capable of carrying out the actions in the script. Solving these problems fell largely to Graham G. Maiden, head of the puppet department at Three Mills, a facility set up for the production of *Corpse Bride*.[12] Maiden consulted with an expert, Merrick Cheney, an armature builder who had

worked on *The Nightmare Before Christmas* (as well as *James and the Giant Peach*, 1996; *Mars Attacks*, 1996; and *Chicken Run*, 2000). Cheney holds a patent on one of the joints used to make Jack Skellington; he had to come up with a completely original design in order to fabricate him.

Chinese silk without pile was used to create many of the characters' costumes because it lacked texture, which would have made it move and could be troublesome during the animation process. It was hand-dyed to match a strict color palette selected by art director Nelson Lowry. In some cases, forms were sculpted for the clothing. For example, the skirt worn by Emily, the Corpse Bride, had to look exactly the same on each of the fourteen puppets made of her, so a sculpture of it was molded to allow for mass duplication. Maiden explains, "Silicone was sprayed onto the shape and fabric applied on

11

The Nightmare Before Christmas, directed by Henry Selick, helped change the face of feature animation when it was released in 1993. © Touchstone Pictures.

top. Each skirt was individually wired or weighted depending on what the shot was like and which animator was using her."

One garment in particular was challenging: Corpse Bride's veil when it was blowing in the wind. It was ultimately animated with both fabric and CGI, depending on the shot. This was among the few instances where computer-generated imagery was used to create the animation, and the animators worked hard to ensure that differences between the stop-motion animation and the digital imagery were imperceptible. In some cases, a single shot of the veil took three to four weeks to complete.[13]

It was necessary to create figures in various scales, and sometimes in partial form, to get particular shots; for example, to capture images of just the legs or torso of Corpse Bride, a half figure might be used. There were twelve each of Victor and Victoria, the hero and heroine, and seven of Lord Barkis Bittern, the villain. It took about three years of full-time work to bring the figures from maquettes to puppets, plus additional time to make adjustments to them to fit the needs of animators once they began shooting. Because the standards were high, says Maiden, the time taken to build the puppets averaged a year and a half to two years. The figures were generally 16 to 18 inches (40.5 to 45.75 centimeters) in height, and were coated with silicone, which provided a good combination of durability and flexibility.

Facial expressions posed a challenge, as they always do, but the puppet designers at Mackinnon & Saunders were able to create highly emotive faces by using gears. Mike Johnson explains that the tiny mechanisms made it possible to get "a much more expressive performance than you could with replacement animation, which was used on *Nightmare Before Christmas*. You can get much more subtlety. ... Audiences are used to the superplasticity of CG characters—we aren't trying to compete with that, but we know that people expect expressive characters. We are just trying to bring stop-motion forward."[14] Maiden describes the construction of the heads, using the example of Victoria's, which had a hole in the bow in her hair and in her ears, as did the heads of the Corpse Bride and Victor. He explains, "You access the gearing system with an Allen key and turn the gears that open and close her mouth; that way they can make her smile or pout. The heads also have paddles in them to make the eyebrows rise or fall so they can look surprised, angry, or serious."

When asked if today's technology made animating the film easier, Johnson said, "No, not easier, but we've got better tools." Those tools only add to the animator's inspiration, creativity, and desire to achieve more, which in turn adds complexity to the production process and creates bigger challenges. Stop-motion is not about being "easy"; just the opposite. Since the earliest days of cinema, "trick films" have intrigued and enchanted audiences with their evidence of what human ingenuity can accomplish. This is a significant element of stop-motion animation's entertainment value—something computer-generated images might replicate, but won't replace.

Corpse Bride's long veil was particularly difficult to animate; at some points its image was computer-generated. TIM BURTON'S CORPSE BRIDE © 2005 Patalex II Productions Limited. Licensed by Warner Bros. Entertainment Inc. All Rights Reserved.

Pixilation and Related Techniques

Pixilation is animation that is created by moving a live human or animal figure incrementally. The actor is required to stop and hold a series of poses that make up a continuous movement, so it can be recorded with a digital still camera or a motion picture camera that operates frame by frame. Sometimes it is advantageous for the actor to move continuously, but slowly (or in some cases, rapidly); in this case, to create stylization of movement a motion picture camera may be operated frame by frame using variable speeds (slower or faster than normal) to record the movement. Pixilation and variable speed cinematography are unique aspects of motion picture production, requiring not only animation skills but also the ability to direct actors.

Variable Speed Cinematography

Variable speed cinematography entails the use of a motion picture camera for image recording at half-speed, double-speed, or any other nonstandard setting. If actors slow down or speed up their performances to match the variable speed capture (for example, acting at half-speed while being filmed at half-speed), playback at regular speed creates a normal pace, but stylized movements. The term "time-lapse" is used to describe one type of variable speed cinemagraphy; it involves the capture of normal-speed real-time images with a slow-speed camera, so that the motions are relatively fast when they are played back at regular speed.

Susanne Horizon-Fränzel For her fifteen-minute *Steinflug* (*Flight of the Stone*, 1989), Susanne Horizon-Fränzel used a sort of time-lapse process to create the impression that the camera is documenting the movement of an object—a stone that is picked up and thrown in anger, with enough force for it to travel around the world, passing through such countries as Germany, the United States, Japan, Thailand, and India (see page 42). To record the footage, directors of photography Dietmar Ratsch, Juraj Liptak, and Guido Frenzel went to the locations and, using a 16mm Bolex camera, shot one frame of film for every few steps they walked. A two-second sequence might have taken an hour or much longer to record, depending on the terrain. When the images are seen at the speed of regular projection, viewers appears to be traveling quickly through space, experiencing the flight from the stone's point of view.

Though most pixilation involves humans, animals sometimes can be animated in this way.

Images were shot around the world using a time-lapse technique to create *Steinflug* (right) directed by Susanne Horizon-Fränzel.

Pixilation in Feature Films

Pixilation is a very stylized technique and can be difficult to sustain in long-format works—from a production perspective, the actors may find it difficult to perform for such a long time and, in terms of exhibition, viewers may grow weary of the style after fifteen or twenty minutes. Nonetheless, the technique has been used in a number of notable feature-length films. Svankmajer's *Neco z Alenky* (*Alice*, 1988) employs live action, pixilation, and stop-motion animation of objects to create a surreal story that is true to the spirit of the original Lewis Carroll tale, as well as the animator's own aesthetic sensibilities. *The Secret Adventures of Tom Thumb* (see pages 79 and 80), a feature by the Bolex Brothers, tells the story of a tiny stop-motion baby boy born into a nightmarish existence filled with grit, sweat, insects, and trash; the quirky pixilation of the film's performers are suitably disturbing. *The Wizard of Speed and Time* (1989), a cult classic directed by Mike Jittlov (who is also the film's star), is more comical. With live action and animation, it tells the story of a man who wants to break into the Hollywood film industry, but meets many obstacles.

Variations in Pixilated Movement

Though pixilated features do exist, more often the technique has been used in short-format films, often in conjunction with other animation methods or variable speed cinematography.

Gail Noonan In her short film *Honey* (2002), Canadian animator Gail Noonan uses pixilation in a symbolic dance representing the work of bees.[15] The film was inspired, interestingly enough, by a fax she received from an unknown sender,[16] which contained a poem by Robert Morgan, "Honey." She loved the way it started with practical advice on beekeeping and culminated in "a gloriously literate and spiritual summation of what honey is made up of." As a result, she decided to make a lighthearted film exploring the relationship between the keeper and the bees, and parallels between their behaviors.

Honey contains various animation techniques and visual effects, including the pixilation of human actors who perform before the camera as a beekeeper and bees, stop-motion bees, animated still photos of a tree and field, and smoke coming from a hive. Noonan used a Bolex camera and Kodak 7248 16mm film to capture the film's dancers, who moved in both real time and pixilation, as well as the beekeeper and bees, who were shot completely in pixilation. Noonan projected the footage underneath the bed of a 35mm rostrum camera and refilmed the sequences on Kodak 5248 35mm film. This method allowed her to layer the stop-motion and handcolor the top images. Noonan created the visual effect of blowing smoke by dropping cel paint into a jar of water and filming it with the camera turned on its side. She says, "I filmed at something like 48 fps. When I was reshooting the 16mm of the

Gail Noonan used a combination of photos (top right), live actors (right), and various stop-motion techniques to create her film *Honey*. Troy Derrick (above) painted the honeycomb pattern for the set.

actors onto 35mm, I did a double exposure of the smoke billowing toward the 'worker bee' actors. I absolutely love in-camera effects."

At the end of the film, there is a collage of photos of a tree and the surrounding field. This sequence illustrates a variation on time-lapse, with still photos representing an intermediary step in the frame-by-frame capture of living things. For Noonan, "The overall pattern for the collage of the field was to move backward from hay season (analogous to storing honey) through summer, spring, and then winter." She had taken photos from the same spot for about two years. These images were aligned on cels according to the position of the tree and glued down. The photo-on-cel tree images were shot directly onto 35mm using a rostrum camera.

Paul and Menno de Nooijer Father and son Paul and Menno de Nooijer have focused on the human form in pixilation films, still photography, graphic art, installations, and performance pieces. Their productions are highly stylized, and often employ bold colors, performers who are clothed eccentrically (or not at all), and dramatic movements. They also tend to be analytical, exploring the nature of media, representation, and perception through visuals and words. The de Nooijers usually appear in their own films, partly due to the physical difficulty of pixilation and the type of performance skills required.

In Menno de Nooijer's film *At One View* (1989), Menno and Paul are seated side by side and struggle over a

Working With Actors

Usually, both pixilation and variable speed cinematography are challenging techniques for actors to learn. Animators Jeremy Schwartz and Musa Brooker have worked with young and mature performers in pixilated work and offer these suggestions for directing actors:

• Every performer works differently, and it is the director's job to determine whether rehearsals are needed or not, how much direction is needed, and the length of time that any performer is at his or her peak (how long he or she can work).

• The skills of regular acting do not necessarily carry over to pixilation, and performers benefit from being allowed to see tests of the action. Think of them as beginning animators, rather than performers, and allow them to see their work over and over.

• It can be difficult for actors to understand extreme expression and the way in which the face looks grotesque in various "in between" poses of laughter or fright, for example. There might be reluctance to contort the face into such "ugly" positions until the performer sees how these increments are absorbed into a continuous movement.

• Get in front of the camera and show them how to act for pixilation. Allow someone else to take the pictures, and demonstrate how to break down facial positions or relocate the body to achieve such effects as sliding across a floor or appearing to hover in air.

• Remember that the rules of animation generally apply in pixilation. Slow in and out actions, as well as holds lasting a few frames or more, accentuate a movement that otherwise will be absorbed into the overall flow of motion.

• Before production, explain to the performer how many frames he or she has to transition from one pose to another. Children generally will not be able to calculate how to move over a number of frames, as older actors can. As the actor performs, don't worry too much if he or she is a frame or two off; if you are working digitally, adjustments can be made in post-production.

• Staying in rhythm is important. If you give actors too much time between shots or don't keep the movement consistent, they will shift around and ruin the flow of the movement. Avoid bulky equipment on the set that slows the pace of production; video assist units can be distracting if they cause excessive noise or slow things down.

• Provide a supportive environment for actors. Avoid telling them that something is "wrong" or vaguely advising that something needs to be done differently. It is often best to let a scene play out and then do a retake. It is useful to say something like "This time, let's try it another way," providing additional information to help the actor interpret the scene or strive for other goals. As the director, make sure your facial expressions don't reflect disappointment or frustration.

• Perhaps most important, be sure pixilation is being used for a reason—why is it better than regular live-action performance?

photographed face held in front of their heads. They pull it back and forth, each one alternately covering his own face and leaving the other's face exposed, until a second photo of a face emerges from behind the first, allowing both actors to conceal their heads. The faces on the photos slide in and out of view and rotate, providing an interesting contrast to the performers' bodies, which remain in a forward, seated position. The action flows seamlessly in constant metamorphosis, obviously pixilated but developing a natural tempo of its own. As the images appear, a voice-over describes how the speaker perceives the nature of photography and film, and the way these media represent their subjects. At times the speaker seems to contradict himself—but in fact we are hearing a dialogue, Menno's and Paul's, in voices that sound similar.

Menno explains, "Film is close to photography; twenty-four film stills projected each second make a film reality. *At One View* talks about the differences and similarities between photography and film—when photos become film and when film becomes a photo. Of course, *At One View* is also about the fact that both film and photography are never the reality."[17]

The de Nooijers record pixilated images with motion picture film cameras, but they also use digital still cameras and have embraced digital technology in various aspects of production. Menno says, "In 1990, we had no computer. Now I spend most of my time behind the screen of my G4. For Paul it is the same. I work with Final Cut Pro to do the editing. Paul uses Photoshop to work on stills or video sequences that he or I want to have manipulated." In other ways, too, computers have impacted their work. Menno adds, "The computer has made our handmade photo (and other) animated films look rather normal. In 1990, *At One View* blew people away. Now it is less impressive," considering that artists can accomplish such techniques relatively easily with the aid of digital technologies.

Menno and Paul de Nooijer work with a relatively wide range of media and keep up a rapid production schedule. In 2005, for instance, they completed three animated films, a long performance for four dancers and three musicians, and almost seven hours of video projection. Their ten-minute video installation *100 Jaar Schoonheid* (*100 Years of Beauty*, 2002) contains images of individuals ranging from the age of zero to one hundred years old, in order from youngest to oldest. They say the work depicts "life as a cycle.... The aim of the project is to demonstrate the beauty of inner growth and the unique auras of one hundred individuals.... Everyone breathes in and then out again. On breathing in, the blurred image comes into focus, and on breathing out, it becomes blurred once again. The images are projected on a thin piece of fabric that moves and are accompanied by the sound of breathing."[18] Here, too, they deal with frame-by-frame movement of the human form: in this case, embracing the subtle rhythms of breath, the defining element of life.

"We like the audience to 'work' and think about what they see. We like to arouse an emotion, and hope that the viewer realizes that even a negative or uncomfortable emotion can be good sometimes. We try to look for the magic of film. The magic the audience felt while they were watching a film for the first time."

Menno de Nooijer

Paul and Menno de Nooijer are multimedia artists who display the human form in various production contexts. Shown here are images from *At One View* (left) and from their video installation *100 Jaar Schoonheid* (right).

Case Study: Norman McLaren

Probably the best-known examples of pixilation are in two films Norman McLaren (see pages 143 and 204) made while he was working at the National Film Board of Canada: *Neighbours* (1952), which depicts two men who battle over a small flower that has grown between their properties, and *A Chairy Tale* (1957), in which a man tries to subdue a renegade chair.

In his production notes, McLaren explained that, through the use of pixilation, "a new range of human behavior becomes possible. The laws of appearance and disappearance can be circumvented, as can the laws of momentum, inertia, centrifugal force, and gravity, but what is perhaps even more important, the tempo of acting can be infinitely modulated from the slowest speed to the fastest." He extolled the technique's ability to make actors capable of "spectacular feats of virtuosity" as well as "a caricature type of movement. In much the same way as a pictorial caricature can make comment on character and situation by distorting the static form of a drawing, so live action animation [that is, pixilation] can create a caricature by

tampering with the tempo of human action, by creating hyper-natural exaggerations and distortions of the normal behavior, by manipulating the acceleration and deceleration of any given human movement."

In his production notes for *Neighbours* and *A Chairy Tale*, McLaren elaborated on pixilation and variable speed shooting processes used in the films. In regard to *Neighbours*, McLaren wrote that he began production not with a "scenario, but only a skeletal idea of the theme and its rough development in my head. The detailed action was improvised from day to day as we shot. It was all filmed in natural sequence [straight ahead]. At the start of each day our team of four (two actors [Grant Munro and J.P. Ladouceur], cameraman [Wolf Koenig] and myself) discussed for about an hour how we should make the action progress for that day." *Neighbours* was filmed with one camera that could take single frames and also run at various speeds: 24, 16, 12, 8, 6, and 4 fps. Some of the most important decisions each day concerned the speed at which to shoot the action.

McLaren started filming *Neighbours* using pixilation, but realized the approach did not always yield the results he was seeking. As a result, he began to incorporate variable speed cinematography. He wrote:

We soon found a better method; a certain action being decided upon, the actors chose the best rate for clicking the camera; the cameraman then clicked at that speed (usually about a half, one, or two seconds), counting aloud the number of each frame (1, 2, 3, 4, etc.); the actors then moved very slowly and continuously, synchronizing their visual tempo, acceleration, and decelerations to the frame count. For instance, we decide to shoot them walking nine paces, the first pace to take 30 frames, the next 25, then 20, then 15, 10, 8, 6, 4, 2.... When the cameraman gets to the first thirtieth frame, he starts calling from one again and goes to twenty-five, etc., to make it easier for them. If [one actor] … was moving too slowly, we could always shout out to him to speed it up a little.[19]

Near the beginning of *Neighbours*, when the men walk back to look at the flower, the actors moved at half normal speed and the images were captured at 12 fps, which is half the standard running speed of the camera. Other movements were shot at various rates to choreograph the pixilation in interesting

Norman McLaren's film *Neighbours* was created using both pixilation and variable speed shooting.

ways. McLaren wrote, "Sometimes we would break a shot down and shoot different parts of it at different speeds. It might, for instance, start with some action at 12 fps, then require 4 fps, then a patch of single-frame work, with longish pauses between each frame for careful repositioning of the props (and therefore also the actors), and then the shot might finish with a stretch of single-frame, clicking a frame every half second, every second, or every two seconds." It was demanding work, and only performers familiar with the concept of incremental movement could understand what was being asked of them; as a result, McLaren stressed the need to use animators as the actors. He explained, "This was important; when it came to shooting single-frame sections (and also other speeds slower than normal) they knew exactly how to move themselves, for instead of making a series of drawings they made a series of postures."

Another important consideration of variable shooting speeds relates to the physics of a given movement. McLaren used the example of a woman twirling in a skirt, moving quickly before a camera filming at the normal speed of 24 fps. In this case, her skirt would rise up quite high at the edges, peaking as she reached top speed. In playing this

footage back, the viewer would see the woman spinning "normally." If the same woman were to spin at half her normal "full speed," and the camera recorded her at 12 fps, or half its normal speed, on projection at 24 fps she would still appear to spin at normal speed; however, because she did not move at full speed during recording, her skirt would not fly up as high as it did when she spun normally. In this instance, viewers would get the sense that the skirt was very heavy. As McLaren noted, "Many gradual or sudden modifications in the behavior caused by momentum, gravity, and other physical forces are possible by this technique."

Some parts of *Neighbours* had to be shot frame by frame, using pixilation. For example, when the actors slid across the grass they were shot in a series of single frames. Jumps into the air were filmed in the same way. To create these sequences the actor jumped as high as he could, at which point the camera was clicked to expose a frame of film. The actor then moved to the side and repeated the action. He could do twenty or thirty jumps before needing a rest, so shooting of jumping sequences occurred in quick bursts, with pauses between groups of several frames. At other points in filming there were long periods of waiting

between every new frame. For example, it took three to five minutes to animate the fence posts around the graves that appear at the end, with three or four people working on the set. In other parts of the film, it was quicker to make adjustments between shots: The men moving themselves as they slid along the ground took five seconds, while shots of sliding babies were set up in thirty seconds.

Because *Neighbours* was filmed outdoors, McLaren had to contend with environmental factors, most of which complicated the production. However, one seemingly problematic incident turned out to be a lucky accident. As he explains, "The fade in at the beginning of the film was done in the camera; and the fade out at the end was made by God. When we first filmed our last shot we began at 3:30 P.M. and were most annoyed that before we could finish the action the sun had set, and it was dark. But in the rushes, the natural sun fade out looked good in itself …" As a result, they ended up reshooting the action on another day, but started at 1:30 in order to end when the sun was setting. In this case, the loss of light was desirable, but it was usually harder to deal with such variations. Images shot on a cloudy day would not match those filmed when it was sunny. Sometimes a

Norman McLaren on the set of *Neighbours* (above), and the final scene from the film (right).

day would begin sunny and turn cloudy as they were filming. McLaren lamented, "a slowly passing cloud might block out the sun in the middle of a single-frame shot, just when the actor was balancing on one leg and holding a difficult position." His advice: "Shoot it indoors with artificial light."

That is exactly what he did when he made *A Chairy Tale*, a film that utilizes complex variable speed shooting. On an indoor set the two characters in the film—the man (played by co-director Claude Jutra) and the chair—both move at a range of speeds and are captured by the camera using frame rates to complement the action. Before shooting, McLaren devised a visual reference that allowed him to track the overall pacing of the production; it is less a storyboard than an abstract representation of the energy flowing through the film as it progresses (see page 71). McLaren described the chair as being moved in the manner of a "traditional string-puppet," manipulated through horizontally attached strings that ran off the left and right sides of the stage and were controlled by animator Evelyn Lambart. To get a full range of motion, the horizontal strings were tied high or low on the chair legs, depending on the desired effect. McLaren wrote, "For only a very few scenes did we use vertical threads.

The strings were fine black nylon fishing tackle, which was invisible to the camera."

McLaren found it was much easier to control the chair's actions if it was slowed to half-speed and filmed at 12 fps; likewise, the man slowed his actions to half-speed, so that he appeared to move at the same pace as the chair. When a difficult chair action was required, the speeds of the man and the chair were further slowed; in these instances, both were filmed at one-quarter sound film speed, or 6 fps. The technique allowed for interesting contrasts between their paces. McLaren explained, "In cases where the chair moved with supernatural speed and the man with normal speed, our formula might be: camera 8 fps, chair normal speed, and man one third normal speed. … When the man was dashing back and forth across the screen in search of the chair, he was running as fast as he could and the camera was turning at 2 fps, producing a blurred effect." Much of the action was improvised, including some effects. For example, "When the man was chasing the chair in circles, we tied thread from his knees to the chair-legs, and had him run backward, pulling the chair after him, while making gestures as if to catch the chair. This, when the action was reversed in the optical printer, gave a convincing effect of him racing after the chair."

McLaren indicated that he was attracted to pixilation in part because it allowed him to control the tempo of action on the set. Like many animators, he designed his films in a kind of musical pattern to complement a future score. Pixilation allowed him to "tie in with steady musical beats and phrases of the as yet unmade soundtrack." He wrote, "We often wished the actions to be of precise metrical lengths, so while shooting at slow speed we would count out the number of each frame as it went by in the camera, thus the actors could arrange to be at such and such a spot on the sixtieth frame, to have their arms raised at the eightieth frame, and their hands touch on the ninetieth frame, to start rotating on the hundredth frame, and to decelerate to a standstill over a period of sixty frames, etc."

In his production notes, McLaren wrote of pixilation, "The creative potentialities of this stop-motion live-action technique are quite considerable for a new genre of filmic ballet and mime." He was a visionary and probably would have been inspired by the opportunities that have come with the digital age—including motion-capture, which has added new dimensions to animation of the human form.

A Chairy Tale, co-directed by Norman McLaren and Claude Jutra, was filmed using variable speed cinematography.

Installations and Performance Animation

A background provides a space in which animated action occurs, creating the atmosphere for storytelling. However, installation artists go beyond the normal use of backgrounds, integrating animation into gallery settings or "everyday" locations. Instead of creating a world through animation, these artists animate the world around us.

Animated Environments

Installations are difficult to document, since they depend on the interactive element of the space in which they are placed, including the ambience of viewers walking by and through the area encompassed by the work. Also, they are generally meant to be ephemeral, and as a result they cannot be accurately recorded on film or video.

Jean Théberge In 1996, the multidisciplinary Canadian artist Jean Théberge created a "cinematographic installation" that explored environmental spaces through animated imagery. His work, Intuitu Personae, À deux pas de la chambre (Intuitu Personae: Two Steps from the Room), involved two 16mm projectors running two films in a loop. The images were projected onto two suspended translucent screens facing each other, accompanied by the ambient sound of the projection system, as well as the noise of the visitors in the space.[20] Théberge describes his installation this way:

In a long and narrow room, the visitor is free to walk around the installation. The entire film shows four pans shot frame by frame on 16mm film. Three of these pans are photographic documents of a room from dawn to dusk; two of them are lit by daylight from the window, and one is shot at night while animated projections from a slide projector lit the room. The fourth animated pan was executed in a dome made of branches and leaves and built in a forest: Only the walls were seen. This last footage was shot on a sunny day. The two screens were suspended six feet [two meters] apart in the middle of the installation at eye level. By using translucent screens, the viewer is able to see the projected image on both sides of the screen. The idea of a labyrinth guided the creation of the piece.

Théberge's installation was concerned with different aspects of image representation and production, as well as associations with youth and memory. Apart from the title, no narrative link and guidance were provided to the installation's visitors. Instead, they entered a space to confront photographic and cinematic images, including objects in a room and a slide projector with its light turned on. Within this general ambiance, individuals were able to create free associations while being in the moment of experiencing Théberge's work.

Jean Théberge's installation, Intuitu Personae, À deux pas de la chambre, involved a series of images on filmloops, projected on two screens.

Case Study: Miwa Matreyek

Miwa Matreyek specializes in performance animation. As a graduate student at California Institute of the Arts, she studied in the Experimental Animation department while also taking part in the Integrated Media program. Integrated Media is an interdisciplinary program available as a supplement to MFA students whose creative work is geared toward technology and digital media. Within this program, which provides a good forum for cross-disciplinary discussion and collaboration, Matreyek worked with a theater-directing student, Chi-wang Yang, on a variety of projects.

This relationship went well because, as they started working together, the two students realized they had very complementary interests and aesthetics and were able to truly collaborate throughout the process to create something that was interesting and significant to both of them. In combining

video and theater, they wished to create a hybrid form that represented both media at the same time. Matreyek specializes in creating digital images and animation through After Effects, Flash, and other applications, whereas Yang is accustomed to working with the physical—actors, sets, props. As a result, they each contributed different strengths.

Essentially, their performances involve a screen, several video projectors, actors, and some props. Matreyek approaches the performance as a live cinema, where the eye can collapse layers in the staging into a "film" that plays out in the "space" of the screen. Yang approaches the performance as a sort of new-media theater, to explore the ways in which digital media relate to "the body" and how they can challenge each other in the conventions of the theater. Through the intersection of each artist's intentions, the performance pieces constantly challenge the conventions and languages of film and theater—the tensions between 2D space vs.

3D space, pre-recorded/manipulated time vs. live time, projected body vs. live body, the ephemeral vs. the real, scale, transitions, and so on. Both Matreyek and Yang feel that through this enriching collaboration, their work opened up to new directions and approaches they probably wouldn't have thought of or explored had they not worked together.

On her thesis project, *Dreaming of Lucid Living* (2007), Matreyek decided to challenge herself to create a performance animation piece on her own. For this project, Yang only got involved at the end of the process in an advisory capacity to help fine-tune the staging before the show. Matreyek created the piece to be a one-woman show, though in the end she did need some minimal stage help to move props around.

Aside from herself, as actor, the components of Matreyek's show included a projection screen and two projectors (one

Miwa Matreyek is a performance animator, interacting with animated images and still graphics she projects onto a screen. Here she appears as a silhouette in *Dreaming of Lucid Living*.

placed 15 feet (4.5 meters) in front of the screen and one placed the same distance in back), a number of cardboard boxes, and a few props. All the other images were silhouettes or color images projected onto the screen. Typical of Matreyek's other work, this production combined a range of evocative visuals with her own performance, emphasizing the "magic" of combining animation and live action. Included in this work are images such as Matreyek using a large microscope, fantastical anatomies projected onto silhouettes of both her body and her hand, a silhouetted domestic space featuring a cat in a window and an oven, and a cityscape of buildings and vehicles.

Dreaming of Lucid Living was developed over a one-year period. Matreyek's efforts were aided significantly when she was awarded a Princess Grace grant. The grant allowed her to buy several items she had requested in her budget, including two digital projectors, a high-definition camera, external drives, a projection screen, a MacPro desktop computer, and a range of software, including After Effects, Final Cut Pro, and Flash.

Although she could have used these resources at school, having them at home meant she could easily and quickly test out her ideas at any time. Importantly as well, since she owned all these items, she could take them with her for performances in various locations, as she began to establish herself as a professional outside the borders of the campus.

Though Matreyek's project involved live acting, it had strong links to puppet theater—more specifically, silhouette puppets. She used a combination of real props and projected animation, in addition to her own body, to create silhouette images on screen, using the back projector. For example, in one part of the film, Matreyek walks to a silhouette of an oven (projected image), takes out a pie (prop), sets it on top (projected image), walks away, and returns to pick up the pie again (prop). The pie seamlessly changes from a silhouetted cardboard cutout to a projected image and back to a cardboard cutout as Matreyek moves her body in back of it, creating a larger dark area that hides the transitions. This choreographed movement has the effect of reinforcing the "reality" of the setting, so the viewer is certain that the oven is a physical prop and not just a projected image. However, a look behind the screen reveals that the only material items used in the performance were a chair, a spoon, an oven mitt, a milk carton, a cardboard cutout of the pie, and curtains defining the borders of an animated window. One of Matreyek's goals for the piece was to play with the viewers' perceptions, creating the

Images from Miwa Matreyek's *Dreaming of Lucid Living*.

dual sensation of believing and not believing that an event is taking place—intellectually knowing that the real and constructed images were not in the same space, and yet seeing them together.

Performance animation benefits from the dimensionality of space, creating a completely different sensory experience than watching animated works in a theater or on a monitor. In *Dreaming of Lucid Living*, Matreyek emphasized this dimensionality by projecting animation of city life onto a series of cardboard boxes, which she had retrieved from a dumpster and painted a neutral color. Comparing the original cityscape animation, created in After Effects, with the final projected images, one can see the great difference created by the textured and dimensional box surfaces. This sort of blended realism, the real box and the animated overlay, strongly appealed to Matreyek. A similar example is a close shot of her hand silhouetted on screen, which is overlaid with an animated image of veins and muscles. She notes that the audience perceives the shaking of her body, which occurs naturally through nervousness or slight tension. This "natural" effect could not be achieved through animation.

Having a great interest in collage, the material for Matreyek's animation came from various sources. Some things were animated in Flash, some images and videos were generated or shot on her own, and some images and videos were taken from online found-footage archives and manipulated or appropriated for use in the production. Often this imagery was framed through Matreyek's silhouetted body, which she made larger or smaller by walking toward or away from the projection light, aided by taped marks on the floor to indicate her stopping points. The screen, which measured 7½ feet (2.3 meters) in height and 10 feet (3 meters) in width, was made of professional-quality Rose brand projection material, which was vital because it prevented hot spots from the projection light—originally, she used only a sheet, which did not permit even lighting. This screen allowed Matreyek to see the front projected images as she was standing in back, so she could align her body as necessary.

Matreyek's work is a blend of digital and analog media and performance. It bridges the new world of digital (After Effects, Flash) animation with ancient traditions of silhouette puppetry, and recalls the magic of vaudeville stage performances by such pioneers as Winsor McCay, who interacted with his animated dinosaur, Gertie, on stage almost one hundred years ago.

12

During her performance of *Dreaming of Lucid Living*, Miwa Matreyek places boxes on the set to create 3D figures of projected 2D images.

Applications VI Replacement Animation and Lip Sync

Replacement animation is widely used to speed the process of cutout or other stop-motion animation; rather than making individual figures for every frame, only the moving parts are recreated, so they can be used in conjunction with static elements that are cut out only once.

Objective:

To create a short animated sequence using cutouts and the replacement method to practice lip sync animation.

You will need:

- An actor
- A chair
- Digital still camera
- Tripod
- Computer
- Equipment for uploading photos from camera to computer
- Printer
- Bond paper
- Pencil (regular and white)
- File folders or an expandable file, plus labels
- Felt in various colors, including a large piece for the background and smaller pieces for different parts of the figure
- Fine-tip fabric marker
- Precision craft scissors
- Rostrum camera or other means of recording frame by frame images of artwork

Step 2

Step 4

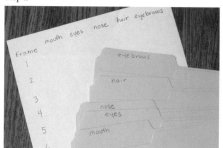
Step 8

Step 9

1

Ask the actor to practice a series of ten mouth movements to create the phrase "watch me move": 1—"w," 2—"a," 3—"tch," 4—"m," 5—"e," 6—"m," 7—"o," 8—"v," 9—"e," and 10—nonspeaking position.

2

Seat the actor in a chair. Set the camera on a tripod so it remains still, and take a close-up photo of the actor's head as he or she makes each of the ten movements.

3

Transfer the ten photographed frames to your computer.

4

Print two black-and-white copies of the frames onto bond paper (sets A and B). If you wish, you can also print a single color image to use as a reference when you select felt pieces to match parts of the face.

5

On the back of set A, lightly write the frame number of each image in order, one through ten. Do the same for set B. Put set A and the single color image (if created) aside.

6

Using set B, examine the series of images to determine which parts of the figure should be represented by a single cutout—for example, the nose—or by a series of

replacement parts—the lips, for instance, or the eyes if they blink or look around.

7

Create an exposure sheet on a sheet of bond paper. Write the frame numbers, one through ten, down the left side of the sheet. Then create columns headed with each of the major parts you are using, such as neck, head, lips, eyes, eyebrows, nose, ears, and hair.

8

Make labels for each of the major parts you are working with and attach them to individual file folders.

12

9

On your exposure sheet, indicate where each of the pattern pieces will appear. When there is a repeated movement, such as the "m" mouth shape, which appears in frames 4 and 6, you will need only one replacement part. You can write a 4 under "mouth" in frame 6 so you will know to reuse the previous part; in other words, mouth 4 will be used in frames 4 and 6. If the same eyes, nose, or other parts are to be used throughout the sequence, the cutout image from frame 1 is all you need. Indicate reuse of an image in consecutive frames by drawing a downward arrow on your exposure sheet.

10

Using set B, start with frame 1 and cut out the parts you need. As you do so, label the back of each cutout piece with the "frame number" of the sheet it came from. Use pencil and write lightly, so the numbers don't show through the paper. You can place each cutout on the exposure sheet to be sure you've created all the pieces you'll need for the finished animation. These cutouts will be used as patterns for the felt, but they also can be animated, so they should be handled carefully.

Step 10

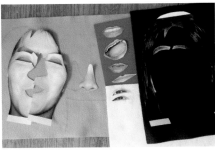

Step 11

Step 13

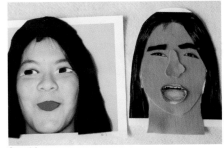

Step 16

11

After you've created your exposure sheet and cut out your paper pieces, you can begin cutting out the matching parts from felt. Use a pencil to lightly trace the paper patterns onto the fabric; dark felt might require the use of a white pencil.

12

Cut out the pieces. On the back of each one, write the same frame number you wrote on its pattern piece. Use a fine-tip fabric marker, but make sure it doesn't soak through the felt. Place each felt part in its appropriate section in your file, along with the paper pattern piece.

13

You are now ready to animate. A large piece of felt can be used as a backdrop—the other felt pieces will stick to it. Using the ten images in set A and your exposure sheet as guides, animate the felt pieces under the camera.

14

After you have finished with the ten felt frames, capture the photocopied frames 1 to 10 from set A, to animate the series of still photos.

15

View the footage of the felt cutouts and compare it with the sequence of photocopies used as the basis for the animation.

16

Film the cutouts again, and change the movements of the shapes—for example, add a two-frame eye blink or move the hair around a bit—or combine parts differently. You can also put the felt pieces on top of the set A images, or animate the paper cutout parts on top of the felt, to create animation that is part photocopy and part felt.

Cutout Figure Using Paper Pivot Hinges

Cutout figures have a long history in animation because they appeal to artists at all skill levels and can range from simple to elaborate, with budgets to match. Animator Mareca Guthrie learned of a special way to create hinged figures in a workshop held by animator Chris Sullivan, who in turn got the idea from a child in another course he had taught. Guthrie's illustrations accompany this exercise.

Objective:

To design a "paper pivot hinge" cutout figure that can be used in an animated production.

You will need:

- Bond or sketch paper
- Tracing paper
- Carbon paper
- Heavy card stock or lightweight poster board
- Temporary adhesive
- Precision craft scissors or knife blade and cutting surface
- Single-hole punch
- Liquid glue

1

Determine the sort of character you wish to create, perhaps using the "developing personality" exercise provided by Leslie Bishko (see page 60). Write down several qualities that define its personality.

2

Consider how you can create the impression of such a personality using form. Think about how facial features, body types, and proportions can communicate meaning. Also consider how color, patterns, and texture might be used symbolically in the figure. Write your ideas down and create preliminary sketches in order to evaluate the impact of the figure.

3

Draw the figure to scale on bond or sketch paper, including all hinged body parts attached to the torso or (in the case of an abstract figure) moving parts hinged to each other in their most extended position, so you can see each form clearly. Indicate where hinges will be placed.

4

Lay a piece of tracing paper over the sketch, and trace the complete outline of the torso or central part of the figure.

5

Overlay this with another piece of tracing paper and trace the attached body parts or outlying portions of the figure. Be sure to include room for overlapping areas, where hinges will be placed. The amount of overlap depends on the size of the figure, but you should consider what the "excess" by the hinge will look like when the part is rotated.

6

Cut the pattern pieces out of the tracing paper.

7

Overlay the pattern pieces and rotate them to make sure they will work properly when they are hinged; indicate which pieces will be on top and which will be on the bottom by writing on them, "t" for "top" and "b" for bottom. Modify and recut pieces if necessary.

8

Place carbon paper on top of the card stock or poster board, carbon side down.

9

Place the pattern pieces on top of the carbon paper; if you wish, attach the three layers—pattern pieces, carbon paper, and card stock or poster board—to each other with a temporary adhesive.

10

Trace around the edges of the pattern pieces with a pencil, so that the carbon paper transfers onto the card stock or poster board. On the bottom pieces only, be sure to include the points where holes for the paper pivots are to be cut.

11

Remove the pattern pieces and tracing paper, and cut out the body parts using precision craft scissors or a knife blade. When all the pieces are cut, decorate them as desired.

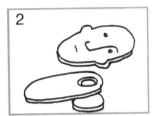
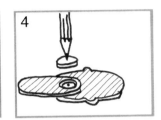
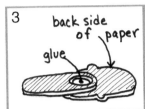

1 head →
neck →

2

3 back side of paper
glue

4

5 paper disc
glue head neck

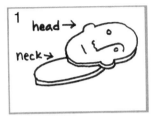
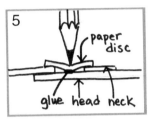
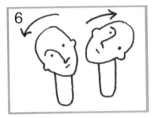

6

7 peice of paper with pupils drawn on sandwiches between two faces with the eyes cut out.

8 The eyes can be moved beneath the face.

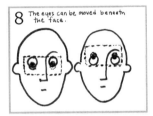
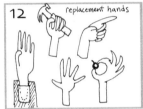

9 seperate mouth peices can fit in this pocket.

10 mouth peices can slide in and out of the head.

11 pocket for replacement parts.

12 replacement hands

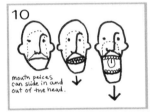
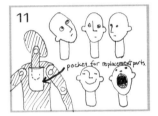

An alternative sequence for constructing a figure by Mareka Guthrie.

12

To hinge the figure, take each bottom piece and use the single-hole punch to remove a circle of paper around the hinge point. Do not punch the pieces marked "t" for top—they must be solid at the hinge area.

13

Count the number of holes you have punched on all the bottom pieces. Using bond paper, cut the same number of circular pieces of paper; they should be slightly larger than the punched holes. These circles will be used as the paper pivot hinges. Set them aside.

14

Use all the cutout body parts to assemble the figure upside down, so the top pieces are underneath and the bottom pieces with holes punched at the hinge areas are on top.

15

Put a small dab of glue in each punched pivot hole on the bottom pieces (which means the glue will be on the undersides of the top pieces).

16

Place one of the small pivot-hinge paper circles on top of each dab of glue. Push it into the glue with a sharpened pencil or other pointed object. Take care to make sure the glue doesn't get between the top and bottom pieces

17

Let the figure dry thoroughly before moving its parts.

Tips and Cautions:

— Avoid placing too much glue in the hinge holes; the top and bottom pieces might stick together. The parts of the figure with holes punched in them should move freely around the paper pivot hinges.

— Be sure to use a pointed object to push the paper pivot into the glue in one spot. A broad object (such as the eraser end of a pencil or even a retracted pen) will probably cause sticking.

Pixilation

The animation of living beings is similar to live-action filmmaking in many ways. However, in breaking movements down into 12, 24, or 30 fps (or whichever increments are used), directors and performers face many challenges—and learn valuable lessons. Dividing motion into minute parts helps animators to understand how in-betweens affect the overall impact of a given movement.

Objective:
To deconstruct, perform, and record a short sequence of movements using pixilation.

You will need:
- An actor
- Digital still camera
- Tripod
- Set lights (optional)
- Computer
- Equipment for uploading photos from camera to computer
- Animation software
- Printer
- Bond paper

1

Prepare a scenario for a three-second sequence of animation. It should include actions requiring extreme changes of body position and/or facial expressions. Imagine this material as three one-second parts: A, B, and C.

2

Discuss the scene with the actor, then demonstrate the one-second increments of the action to show where the body and/or face should be at the start (pose A1), roughly one-third through (pose B1), roughly two-thirds through (pose C1), and at the end (pose C12).

3

Ask the actor to strike and hold each of these four poses—A, B, C, and C12—in sequence, to get a feeling for the pacing of the piece. Explain that he or she has about twelve movements to shift from pose to pose. You might like to demonstrate how the incremental movements could look by acting them out yourself, though you should encourage other interpretations.

4

Next, ask the actor to run through the action. It might be helpful to count off frame numbers. If so, use the pose letter and numbers one to twelve. In other words, begin by counting "A1, 2, 3, 4, 5…" as the performer strikes the beginning pose and begins to move through the eleven remaining increments toward pose B. After reaching twelve, start with "B1, 2, 3, 4…", then "C1, 2, 3, 4…" ending with "C12." If counting inhibits the performance, allow the actor to count in his or her head. Rehearse this process until the actor feels comfortable with the timing and process.

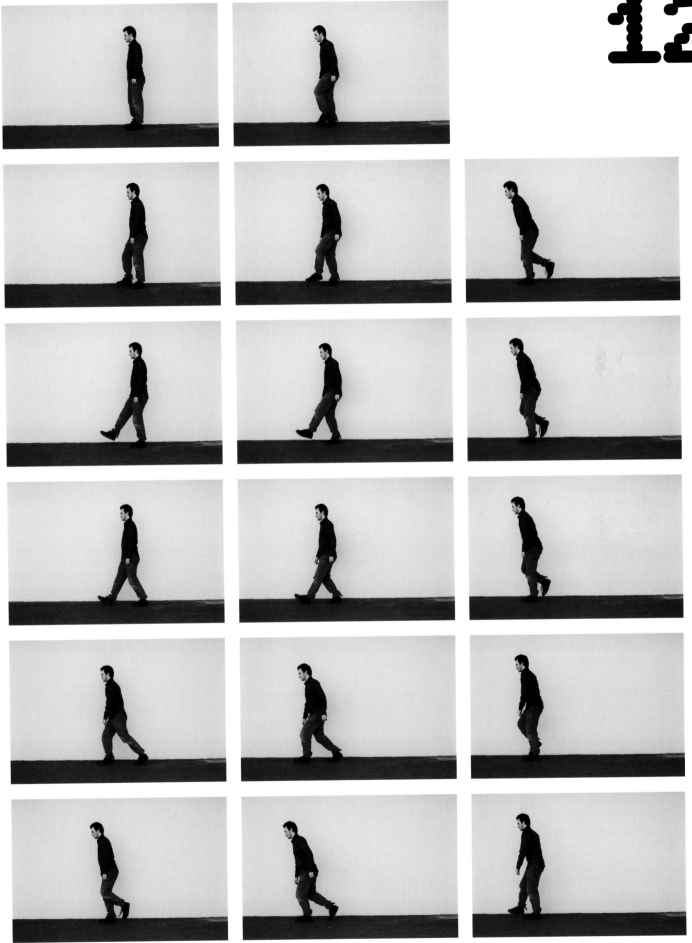

Pixilation

12

5

Set your camera on a tripod and prepare the set by adjusting the lighting and/or arranging objects, if necessary.

6

Film the sequence, exposing one frame of the digital still camera for each of the actor's poses. It doesn't matter if mistakes are made or the timing isn't just right. You can improvise, and also make adjustments in the computer after shooting. At the end of shooting, you should have about thirty-six images (twelve each for parts A, B, and C). Show the performer the sequence of images, and refilm if necessary. An actor's performance may be stronger (more animated) if he or she sees the results of a first attempt and can adjust his or her movements accordingly.

7

When you have achieved the desired performance, upload the sequence of movements to your computer's animation software and place the images into its timeline. You have filmed at 12 fps.

8

Print the images onto sheets of bond paper; number them to keep them in order.

9

Play back the images, and adjust the speed of the actions as desired. Manipulate the speed of playback to see how the images work at, for example, twice the speed of recording (24 fps) or half the speed of recording (6 fps). You can also use each image in two frames and run the sequence at 24 fps to see the difference between this playback and the original sequence at 12 fps. Images can be played in reverse or moved forward and backward, rather than in a purely linear way.

Tips and Cautions:

— Exaggerated actions work best for this exercise. Subtle acting tends to get lost in the pixilation process.

— An actor who has no previous experience with pixilation may feel uncomfortable about making extreme facial contortions or breaking movements down into small increments. It might be helpful to show him or her an example of a pixilated film before the performance.

Digital Media and Computer Animation

Since the late 1970s, computers have increasingly impacted traditional animation practices of the last century. Many artists have migrated to the use of digital technology in small or large measure, sometimes reluctantly and at other times wholeheartedly. A versatile animator uses digital media like any other, after considering its aesthetics, what it can do for him or her, and whether a particular approach will be useful in a production.

Digital Media

The terms "new media" and "computer-generated imagery" (CGI) are sometimes used interchangeably with "digital media." However, each has a different connotation. The term "new media" came about as the computer assumed more significance in society. Today digital media are more likely to be seen as standard, not new; thus "new media" is no longer an accurate term. The terms "computer-generated" is not too useful for describing animation produced with digital technology because it is vague. Digital media can be employed at just about any part of the animation process, from the early stages of development to the final steps in distribution. As digital technologies become more varied and

are embraced in creative ways, it becomes increasingly difficult to determine the exact meaning of the description "computer-generated film." In any case, computers do not generate the majority of animated productions—people do! Computers and related technologies are creative tools that artists can use, just as they use any other media. In some cases, digital media are a welcome addition to the production process; at other times they are clearly a hindrance.

The term "digital" refers to a method of recording and encoding information. Whereas analog recording techniques operate by creating information that is in some way analogous to the original, using infinitely variable patterns, a digital recording operates on a binary system of assigning ones and zeros in a manner that results in mathematical formulae. Analog recordings degenerate as they move from generation to generation away from the origin ("generational loss"), while digital ones can in theory be reproduced at essentially the same quality level for every generation of sound and/or image.

It is challenging to describe the scope of digital media or how an animator will use them. Each area—for example, gaming, visual effects, motion graphics, Web animation, performance art, television series, and animated features—may employ different digital media and approaches to meet

Digital media provide additional choices to artists creating art of any type or style, from abstract to representational.

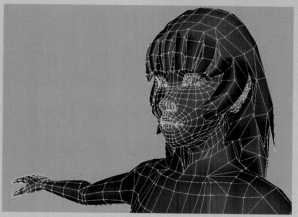

varying needs during the other stages of production, distribution, and exhibition. And digital technologies tend to be used differently depending on whether a work is a small, independently produced project or a large-scale studio venture. Independent animators can find themselves using a wide range of digital technologies, spanning every aspect of the production process, from creation to distribution. They might also work with different types of digital media from project to project, shifting to meet their current needs. In contrast, a member of a large animation crew at a major studio is likely to be involved with only one component of the animation process, using a limited set of digital media within a narrow job description; someone who focuses on lighting, for example, is unlikely to work with digital sound-recording media.

Software

The term "software" describes a set (or "program") of coded instructions that directs a computer to carry out some action. Anyone can develop software, but few of us do. Rather, we rely on commercially available programs, including several that have become standardized in the animation industry, creating consistent practices from studio to studio. As a result,

software sales are a gigantic business. Commercial manufacturers guard their products closely, licensing them for use by others without allowing the user to learn too much about how they are developed.

End users have the option to modify off-the-shelf commercially available software if it is built with an "open architecture" that allows them to personalize it by adding their own components. At big studios, computer programmers who can write code typically create these modifications; although they are not necessarily trained in animation, they can work closely with animation artists who make requests for specific capabilities, and drive the research and development process. Animation studios generally are secretive about "proprietary software" they create for their exclusive use, in an effort to differentiate their work from that of other studios. However, these modifications eventually may be offered to the public. An example is Pixar's Renderman, developed in-house but now sold to consumers.

Particularly during the early years of computer animation, in-house programmers were faced with the job of creating compatibility between applications that otherwise did not work together very well. However, more and more manufacturers today stress their ability to incorporate data

---

Animation Software

Below are types of software typically used for animation production, the features associated with them, and the names of representative programs.

Image design Processing, editing, and handling of digital images, sometimes in conjunction with a graphics tablet
Examples: Adobe Photoshop, Adobe Illustrator, Corel Painter

2D pipeline Scanning, line testing, ink and paint, layout, animation, and other aspects of the 2D production process
Examples: Crater Software CTP Pro, Cambridge Animation Systems Animo (also allows integration of 3D), Toon Boom products (at varying levels, including Harmony, Opus, Solo, Studio, and customized packages), Bauhaus Mirage, Adobe Flash (also includes interactive content development)

3D pipeline Modeling, rigging, effects, rendering, compositing, and other aspects of the 3D pipeline
Examples: Alias Systems Corporation Maya, Autodesk 3ds Max, NewTek LightWave, Softimage/XSI, Adobe After Effects (visual effects for both 2D and 3D images), Autodesk Combustion

Stop-motion production Image capture and manipulation for stop-motion productions
Examples: Stop Motion Pro, FrameThief

Image and/or sound editing Timelines for assembling footage, archiving elements, color correction, audio capture, and output
Examples: Adobe Premiere Pro, Apple Final Cut Pro, Digidesign Pro Tools

Operating system Underlies other software and controls the functioning of the computer
Examples: Microsoft Windows, UNIX, Linux, Apple OSX

Internet browsers Allows HTML (Hypertext Markup Language) and other compatible documents to be viewed on computer monitors, making possible the World Wide Web
Examples: Microsoft Internet Explorer, Mozilla Firefox, and Apple Safari

from a range of software sources and to work across platforms. For better or worse, another factor aiding the coordination of products and increased compatibility is corporate takeovers and buyouts, which reduce competition within the industry and result in products that are manufactured to work together in a "suite" that is well-synchronized (and guarantees profits stay within the parent firm). The animation industry has increasingly been consolidating around the products of leading manufacturers.

Shifts in the industry are sometimes evident in the names of software, which may change from time to time. For example, Flash became an animation program under the name Future Splash Animator in 1995, then changed to Macromedia Flash in 1996, and ten years later, in 2006, was renamed Adobe Flash, reflecting the evolution of its ownership. The nature of the software itself can also change as it adapts to the needs of the industries using it. Flash had started out as a drawing program, SmartSketch, but was adapted for animation in 1995 after its creators received public feedback requesting the shift. Its developers also wanted to take advantage of the Internet, which was beginning to grow at that time.

Ideas that become significant to the animation industry sometimes begin with students and independent animators trying to solve problems for their works and make a name for themselves by developing impressive products.

Bob Sabiston When Bob Sabiston was a student at the Massachusetts Institute of Technology (MIT), he developed software known as Rotoshop. He used the software for his own short works, such as *Snack and Drink* (1999), a slice-of-life narrative about an autistic boy. However, it became widely known after it was employed in the production of the feature films *Waking Life* (2001) and *A Scanner Darkly* (2006), both directed by Richard Linklater. Thus Rotoshop moved from the small scale of a college classroom to the much larger arena of theatrical film production, bringing the creator's original aesthetic sensibility to an industrial context.

Historian Paul Ward explains how the program works: "Rotoshop follows some of the same principles as ordinary rotoscoping, in that it traces over live-action footage. The key difference is that the process is computerized. Live-action footage is shot digitally, saved to computer and converted to QuickTime files. The resulting footage can then be viewed one frame at a time and transformed using the Rotoshop program."[1] Using a Wacom graphics tablet and pen, artists trace each live-action frame of film freehand in a process that Sabiston describes as "more about art and the artists' impressionistic sense than what is typical of CGI animation today.... There is no texture modeling or digital motion-capture." The process is labor-intensive; Sabiston estimates it took about five hundred hours to create a minute of imagery for *A Scanner Darkly*.[2]

Bob Sabiston developed his own software, Rotoshop, to create images for his films, such as *Snack and Drink*, pictured here.

Open Source Software Today's programmer-animators are assisted by the availability of open source (OS) software (such as the 3D graphics program Blender),[3] which is freely available online and can be modified and redistributed. Central to this effort is the Open Source Initiative (online at www.opensource.org), "a nonprofit corporation dedicated to managing and promoting the Open Source Definition for the good of the community."[4] Under this definition, OS applications have multifaceted requirements, guaranteeing that the products will continue to be accessible in their derivative forms.

File Formats

Anyone who works with computers should be familiar with various types of file formats, which are identified by extensions, the (typically) three-letter identifications that appear after a saved file name. Your choice of format for a file will vary according to the context in which the information will be used. For example, in respect to images, JPG, GIF, and PNG files are compatible with graphical browsers for use on the World Wide Web, while TIF files are not.

Image formats also differ related to the way in which picture information is compressed, reflected in their saved-file sizes. A JPG is considered "lossy" because after an image is compressed in this format some of the original picture quality is lost, though the loss is not particularly noticeable to the human eye. Generally, JPGs are recommended to save work with subtle color patterns, like photographs and naturalistic artwork. Because some data is lost, they tend to be small in file size. A "lossless" form of compression, which can be obtained with a GIF or PNG, for example, results in larger files, but these images can be reconstructed to their original form when they are decompressed. Generally, GIFs are recommended for saving images that are less intricate in terms of color: text, line drawings, solid color forms, and so on. Like GIFs and PNGs, TIF files are also lossless; they provide high-quality reproduction that appeals to print publishers. Their file sizes tend to be relatively large. Complicating things further, image files can be saved at various resolutions, described as dots per inch (dpi) for print and pixels per inch (ppi) for exhibition on monitors, which also affects their picture quality and overall file size. Print publishers usually work with 300 dpi or larger, while 72 ppi is standard for the Web.

Motion picture and audio file formats also vary in terms of compression and quality. In an audio context, MP3 files are lossy, which means MP3 players can hold many songs in a small space. In contrast, WAV files, which are lossless, are much larger. The loss of data in MP3 files is virtually undetectable if the data originally came from a lossless

"When programmers can read, redistribute, and modify the source code for a piece of software, the software evolves. People improve it, people adapt it, and people fix bugs. And this can happen at a speed that, if one is used to the slow pace of conventional software development, seems astonishing."

Open Source Initiative

compression, in a WAV file for example, or a CD. Loss of quality is more substantial when one lossy format is converted to another lossy format.

Compression of data is achieved with a "codec" (compressor/decompressor), which is software and/or hardware used to transfer sound, speech, and images to and from analog and digital states: Analog to digital is referred to as A/D, while the opposite transition is D/A. It is always best to record images and sound at the highest quality possible and downsize them as necessary for production, since it is impossible to work the other way. For example, images captured at 72 dpi cannot be improved by saving them at 300 dpi, since the actual process of saving does not add more visual data to the image.

Bitmap images are "raster graphics"; they are brought to life by a light beam scanning a screen, line by line, interpreting each pixel at a rapid speed. They are "resolution dependent" (they have a fixed resolution), so when they become bigger, so do the "bits" of information that constitute each pixel or dot. As a result, enlarged bitmap images sometimes look blocky, with jagged edges. However, because they are composed of a number of small bits of data, they are well-suited to displaying continuous tone images (such as photographs) that require subtle gradations of color.

Vector graphics are generally the choice for images that need sharp edges—for example, letters used in logos that will be scaled to various sizes. A vector graphic is made of lines and curves defined by vectors, mathematical representations of images according to their geometric characteristics. Not only are they infinitely scalable with no apparent change in quality (they are "resolution independent"), they also tend to be relatively small in file size compared with bitmap images. Illustrator drawings and Flash animation for the Web, for example, are displayed as vector graphics. In contrast, Photoshop and other paint- or image-editing software create bitmap images.

Hardware and Peripherals

The term "hardware" is used to describe the physical components of a computer system, including "peripherals," or attached devices, such as scanners and printers, which artists use in the production of their work. Of central importance, of course, is the computer itself, as it determines so much about the software and other tools available to its

File Extensions:

Text
The most common file extensions related to text documents include:
- **.doc** Microsoft Word
- **.rtf** Rich Text Format, which can be read across applications
- **.pdf** Adobe Acrobat Portable Document File
- **.txt** ASCII or simple text format
- **.wpd** WordPerfect
- **.ps** PostScript

Images
The most common file extensions related to image documents include:
- **.jpg** (also JPEG) Joint Photographic Experts Group, generally for use on the World Wide Web
- **.gif** Graphic Interchange Format, generally for use on the World Wide Web
- **.png** Portable Network Graphics, generally for use on the World Wide Web
- **.pict** Picture, Macintosh graphics
- **.bmp** Bitmap, Windows graphics
- **.tif** Tagged Image File Format, compatible with most image-processing software

Motion Pictures
The most common file extensions related to motion picture documents include:
- **.avi** Audio Video Interleave
- **.rm** Real Media
- **.mpg** MPEG
- **.mov** QuickTime
- **.fla** Flash (source files)
- **.swf** Shockwave Flash (rendered, playable images)

Audio
The most common file extensions related to audio documents include:
- **.aif** Audio Interchange Format, used for Macintosh platform
- **.mp3** MPEG-1 Audio 3, shorthand for Moving Picture Experts Group
- **.wav** Waveform Audio
- **.wma** Windows Media Audio, created for Windows Media Player as competition for MP3 players
- **.ra** Real Audio
- **.ogg** Ogg Vorbis, a free and unlicensed product

user. A surprisingly long-standing competition exists between Macintosh computers from Apple and the personal computers, or "PCs," made by such manufacturers as IBM, Sony, and Dell. Recently there have been efforts to bridge the divide through software that allows crossover between the platforms.

Monitors vary greatly in terms of image size, relative dimensions (or aspect ratio), and color reproduction. These considerations affect exhibition, especially if the work is shown online, as well as the production process. A relatively inexpensive monitor can be 15 inches (38 centimeters) wide or smaller, while monitors suitable for group presentations can be much bigger. Larger ones can help to avoid eyestrain and reduce the need to scroll in order to see an entire picture. There are two basic types of monitor: cathode ray tube (CRT) and liquid crystal display (LCD). LCDs are much lighter than CRTs and offer relatively good resolution even in smaller sizes, but they tend to be much more expensive. Neither type is inherently better; there are trade-offs in terms of resolution/ sharpness, color control, refresh rates (the number of times the screen is redrawn each second), convergence (alignment of the three electron guns—red, blue, and green—which affects the formation of lines), and other factors.

A computer's memory affects how much data can be stored and, as the memory fills up, how fast a computer can operate. There are two general types of memory: Read Only Memory, or ROM, which is permanently stored on the hard drive until it is erased, and Random Access Memory, or RAM, which is temporary and disappears when the computer is turned off. ROM is the place where essential operating information is stored on a computer. In contrast, RAM brings forth the applications and files being used at any given time; if it is not large enough, a computer does not have the "space" to carry out the necessary intensive calculations, so it may crash or operate very slowly.

Bitmap images get "blocky" when enlarged (below), whereas vector images (right) can be rescaled without a change in image quality.

The circuits of a computer include the motherboard, expansion cards, and the microchip that acts as the central processing unit (CPU), also known as the processor. The motherboard is the largest circuit board. It controls the overall operation of the computer, and houses both the processor and smaller circuit boards that act as co-processors, taking over some of the functions of the CPU. The speed of the CPU is an important factor in determining how fast a computer can operate.

Artists sometimes think that computers are not tactile enough to feel like creative media. As a result, some manufacturers have designed their products to replicate the experience of analog art practices, such as drawing and painting, in the digital realm. Graphics tablets used with special digital pen and brush tools are one example. Wacom has manufactured a range of these; its Cintiq interactive pen display enables animators to use handheld tools and work directly on an LCD monitor surface treated with a coating that makes it feel like paper. Haptic devices combine tactile sensations with computer use, allowing sculptors and model builders to "feel" the substance of the material they are shaping, though they are working virtually. ClayTools, a combined hardware and software system from SensAble, functions in this manner, allowing artists to feel like they are sculpting a figure out of clay.

Some artists continue to work in traditional ways, but eventually digitize their artwork using a scanner, digital still camera, or webcam, all fairly standard items in a home studio. Many 2D animators move back and forth between analog and digital images several times, alternately manipulating the work by hand and in the computer.

Relatively few artists use the expensive process of motion-capture. "Mocap" involves the use of a dedicated studio space and performers wearing data points that transmit information about their movements into a series of cameras. The data is transferred into a computer and becomes the basis for animated movement; it can be processed in real time and appear almost instantly, or it can be subjected to a great deal of post-production work, which is often the case for high-end stunt work. Though motion capture is widely employed for gaming and live-action film effects, it is also used for movement analysis, training, performance, and recording in such areas as dance, competitive sports, and medicine. Ascension Technology, Motion Analysis, and Vicon Peak are some of the leading manufacturers of motion-capture technology.

In contrast, the Web provides low-cost opportunities for all animators—for example, animation can be uploaded to a website such as Atomfilms or YouTube, which provide distribution for original work of any kind. The design of the World Wide Web is at once complex and simple. It boils down to two computers, some software, two modems, and lines connecting them. Websites are parked on a "server" computer that responds to requests for information (for example, a file

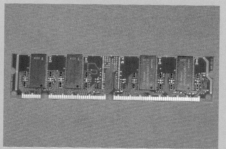

Some components of a computer (from left to right): motherboard, memory, and central processing unit (CPU).

transfer) from other computers, known as "clients"; this takes place through the workings of server-side software and client-side applications, such as Web browsers. Information is sent and received through a modem (modulator/demodulator), which converts data from one form to another so that it can be transmitted along the Internet. For example, data may change from digital to analog and from analog to digital as it moves out of a computer, along phone lines, and back into a computer.

The term "bandwidth" describes the speed at which data can be sent; for example, a modem using standard telephone lines typically has a bandwidth of 56 kilobytes per second (kbps), which can seem relatively slow for data-heavy websites. However, DSL, another type of phone line connection, runs much faster because it has a broader bandwidth—thus it is known as a "broadband" connection. Cable modems are also broadband. They operate with coaxial cables capable of sending multiple signals simultaneously, which speeds data transfer immensely. It is important for animators to understand the impact of bandwidth. While professionals in many parts of the world are accustomed to speedy broadband services, many viewers rely on much slower connections, which can present problems for downloading very large files and viewing complex websites.

Computer Animation

The earliest developments in computer media were largely funded by governments, working in conjunction with universities and large companies. However, artists also were involved in shaping its future.

Early Developments

The origins of computer technology are quite varied. Some say its beginnings lie in the abacus, and trace digital media to the mid-1700s, when automata creator Jacques de Vaucanson developed a punch card system to automate the manufacturing of weaving. Konrad Zuse, a construction engineer for Henschel Aircraft Company in Berlin, is described by some as the "inventor of the modern computer" for automatic calculators he first developed in 1938. In the 1920s Herman Hollerith perfected a punch-card system within his company, which later merged with others to form International Business Machines (IBM).[5] The resulting eighty-column "IBM punch card" became the standard input medium for computers until the late 1970s. At the University of Manchester, in England, Sir Frederic Williams and Tom Kilburn developed the world's

A webcam (left) is a small camera that can be used for simple stop-motion works.

Computer technology has become increasingly user-friendly with peripherals such as the Wacom Cintiq (above) and Graphire (right).

first stored-program electronic digital computer, the Small-Scale Experimental Machine (SSEM), nicknamed the "Baby," which worked for the first time in June 1948.

Many advances in computer technology came from projects largely funded by governments (especially the military complex): For example, early interactive computer systems were created for flight simulation training. We have the United States government to thank for the Internet, which it devised during the years of the Cold War as a complex information system with hubs across the nation that could withstand an attack on any one area. Naturally, a project of this scale took immense amounts of funding, unknowingly provided by American taxpayers, as well as specialized "brain power"—quite often supplied by university faculty, up-and-coming graduate students, and affiliated researchers. For example, with research partly conducted at Harvard University, Grace Hopper led development of programming languages in the early 1950s.

Beginnings of Computer Art

During the 1960s, Ivan Sutherland earned his place in history as the "father" of interactive computer graphics and graphical user interfaces. As a doctoral student at MIT, he worked on the Institute's TX-2 computer to create his dissertation around an interactive computer drawing program that he called Sketchpad; it was published in 1963, opening up the field of computer graphics.[6]

As new technologies emerged, they caught the interest of artists, including animators who struggled with the limitations of media at that time, helping to push it into new directions.

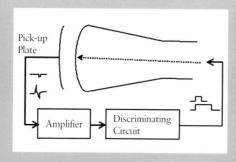

The Manchester "Baby" computer (above) and its circuitry (above left) formed the basis for half of the Manchester Mark I computer.

The internal mechanism of Konrad Zuse's Z1, a programmable machine that read instructions from a punched tape.

Lillian Schwartz Now internationally recognized for her role in validating the computer within art, Lillian Schwartz began working with computers in 1968, and later, with her son Laurens R. Schwartz, authored a seminal book in the field, *The Computer Artist's Handbook: Concepts, Techniques, and Applications* (1992).

During the mid-1960s, animation produced at American Telegraph and Telephone (AT&T) Bell Laboratories provoked Schwartz to think about using a computer to create abstract images in combination with some of the earliest examples of scientific visualizations. Bell Laboratories provided a site where multimedia art and electronic music could be developed after-hours, at night, and over weekends.[7] Schwartz became a consultant there, and then, she explains, "I created videos for the scientists and consulted on other scientific projects, and did my art at off-hours."[8] Eventually, she became a self-taught programmer, but earlier she collaborated with Ken Knowlton to create some of the first art-based computer animations.

These include *Pixillation*, *UFOs*, and *Mathoms* (all produced between 1970–71), productions that, in a way, catalogue the capabilities of computer animation at the time. Non-narrative in structure and largely abstract, some include forms that are boldly (even psychedelically) geometric and strobing, while others are more organic. For example, *Pixillation* includes images of crystals, while *Mathoms* has pulsing waveforms generated by electronic equipment, the computer-generated soundtracks for the films create a kind of "noise", more than music. In *Olympiad* (1971), Schwartz and Knowlton went far back in history, and drew inspiration from a running figure in the motion studies of Eadweard Muybridge (see page 120). Its sound, which is more melodic than in their previous works, accompanies the smoothly flowing image of an electronically rendered, highly pixilated man running across the screen in red, green, and blue. The strobing lines and color combinations of their 1972 films *Enigma* and *Googolplex* reflect not only the psychedelic aesthetic sensibilities of the period, but also the artists' interest in perceptual issues. Schwartz's crossover into scientific fields is evident in her 1972 film *Apotheosis*, with visuals created by using images of radiation treatments for cancer patients.

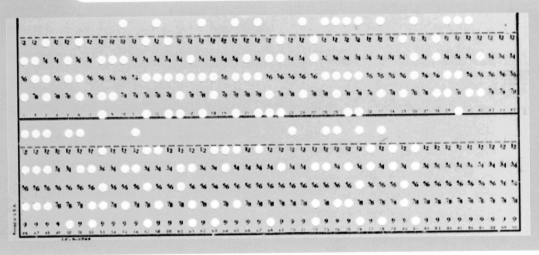

For many years, punch cards were the primary means of inputting computer data. Pictured here is a ninety-column UNIVAC punch card.

Case Study: Larry Cuba

In the early days of computer animation, programming skills were vital, since the small amount of available software was far from automated. As a result, artists and computer scientists generally worked together. Larry Cuba, in contrast, represents one of the first artists to embrace programming as the site of experimentation. He says he was motivated by "mathematics, rhythm, perception, and experimentation with the unknown" in the production of *First Fig* (1974), *3/78 (Objects and Transformations)* (1978), *Two Space* (started ca. 1976; completed 1979), and *Calculated Movements* (1985).[9] The abstract imagery of the films evolved within parameters set by Cuba during their programming phases.

Cuba's study of architecture in college reinforced his interest in form, function, and structure, which continued during his pursuit of animation in graduate school at the California Institute of the Arts. Because the Institute did not have sophisticated enough computer equipment, Cuba got access to the Jet Propulsion Laboratory (JPL) and taught himself how to program. The result was *First Fig*. It was made using FORTRAN on a Univac 1108 mainframe, and it opened the door to new experiences. The first was being hired as a programmer by John Whitney, Sr., who was producing *Arabesque* at Information International, Inc. (the Los Angeles studio known as Triple-I). Cuba was then hired to create an animated sequence for George Lucas's film *Star Wars* (1976), which took him to the University of Illinois at Chicago's Circle Graphics Habitat. There he worked with Tom DeFanti, who had developed a real-time animation system called GRASS.

After completing the *Star Wars* sequence, Cuba returned to Triple-I and began creating images for what would become *Two Space*. He programmed them and ran the footage through a moviola, thinking of it as test material. However, frustrated by the slow pace of production after working in real time with GRASS, he put *Two Space* on hold and moved back to Chicago to use the system again, this time to program the imagery for *3/78* (so named because it was completed in March 1978).

In this black-and-white film, "sixteen objects, each consisting of one hundred points of light, perform a series of precisely choreographed rhythmic transformations" accompanied by the sound of a *shakuhachi*, a Japanese bamboo flute; the work is an "exercise in the perception of motion and mathematical structure."[10] The film was critically acclaimed but Cuba felt that while GRASS had allowed him to see real-time results, there had been too big a trade-off in terms of processing—it limited his ability to perform complex calculations.

When he returned to California from Chicago, he was no longer able to work at Triple-I on *Two Space*, and the images he had considered test material became the basis for the film. However, they required post-production work, which was anathema to Cuba, who was striving for a "total programming" approach that involved the creation of a mathematical formula, testing it to see the results, and, based on what appeared, adjusting the formula to try again. He believed that his point of focus should not be the film "but the program that created the film; why edit film when you can edit the

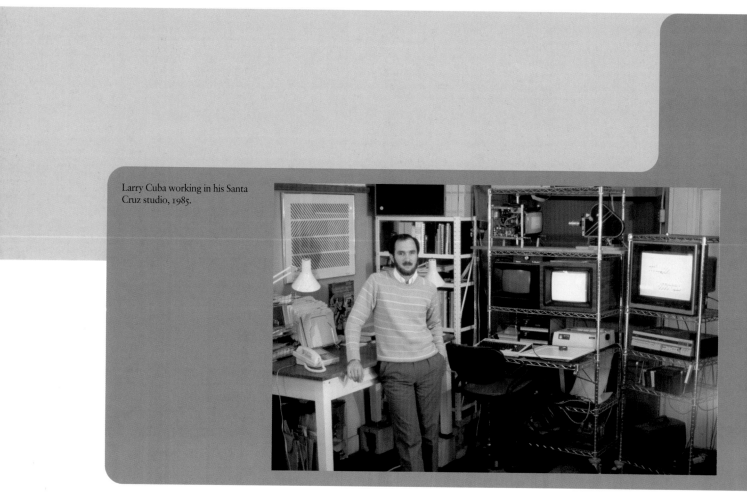

Larry Cuba working in his Santa Cruz studio, 1985.

software that generates it? I wanted everything to be in the program and driven algorithmically."[11] However, he did not have this option, so he evaluated the experiments and selected nine to form the eight-minute film. Optical printing was used to reduce the images from 35mm to 16mm, to make the patterns bleed off the edge of the screen (which his program wasn't doing), and to reduce the speed at the end to come to a slow stop with the music. While all the images were created using software, the segments were spliced together rather than generated from beginning to end.[12] Images in the film consist of a series of twelve two-dimensional patterns "generated by performing a set of symmetry operations (translations, rotations, and reflections) upon a basic figure."[13] They move to classical Javanese gamelan music, and create optical illusions through figure–ground reversals and after-image effects.

To create *Calculated Movements*, Cuba used the ideas that originated in his programming for *Two Space*, but implemented them using Z-GRASS, the personal computer version of the GRASS system; it allowed him to work at home for

the first time, rather than begging time from various institutions. Z-GRASS accommodated more arbitrary mathematical calculations, but it was relatively slow, taking approximately two minutes to draw each frame. After about two years of experimentation, his programming for *Calculated Movements* yielded approximately three hours of material. The experiments were recorded on a Lyon-Lamb half-inch video system for preview. The footage included strands of images selected to form the film as a whole; in some these were "overlaid into a two-dimensional composition in addition to a temporal one (think of voices singing different strands, coming in and out at different times, and sometimes overlapping)."

Whereas *3/78* and *Two Space* were constructed with dots of light that create curved and flowing lines, the visual design of *Calculated Movements* is much more angular. The film is made up of "a choreographed sequence of graphic events constructed from simple elements repeated and combined in a hierarchical structure" that range in complexity. It is the first work Cuba made

with a raster graphics system, which allowed him to create solid areas rather than use only dots of light.

At the end of the production process, the ideas, software, and data were distilled into a final "edit" of a program that drew every frame of *Calculated Movements* from beginning to end. The frames were shot onto 16mm film with no further editing or processing needed. As Cuba explains, "An animation camera was set up in front of the video monitor. After the computer finished drawing one image on the screen, it triggered the camera to shoot one frame. Since it took the computer two minutes to compute and draw each frame, the system ran twenty-four hours a day for two weeks to shoot the entire six-minute film."[14] He describes the result as "a realization of my desire to escape traditional film production technology (which seemed archaic), and move all creative activity to the computer. Twenty-five years later, we're *all* living this vision with personal computers and software like After Effects and Premiere."

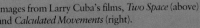
Images from Larry Cuba's films, *Two Space* (above) and *Calculated Movements* (right).

The First CGI Features

Perhaps it is no surprise that the Disney studio—always known for technological innovation—was at the forefront of the film industry's move to CGI with its release of *TRON* (directed by Steven Lisberger) in 1982. The primarily live-action feature film is about a programmer who is sucked into his computer and forced to play life-or-death games with the entities he created. Although it did poorly on its initial release, *TRON* has become a cult classic that has influenced many animators—not least John Lasseter, who went on to direct *Toy Story* (1995), a landmark film that has claims to being the first completely computer-generated 3D animated feature.

After seeing computer-generated footage from *TRON*, Lasseter left Disney, where he was employed as an animator, to pursue this new avenue for the animation industry. He moved to the production studio that became Pixar after it was sold by Lucasfilm, its parent company; there he worked on a series of animated shorts, including *Luxo Jr.* (1986) and *Tin Toy* (1988), leading research and development on Pixar's Renderman software and gearing up for the eventual production of *Toy Story*. Short films allowed Pixar to perfect its techniques in such problematic areas as facial animation, particles, organic forms, and liquids, and helped it to convince a skeptical industry that there was a market for computer-generated 3D animated features. It did so in part by combining its digital images with Disney-style aesthetics, a long-accepted standard for excellence.

During the late 1980s, Pixar and Disney worked together to create Computer Animation Production System (CAPS) software for 2D production. This included digital ink and paint (which eliminated the need to ink and paint by hand), compositing (blending elements), and rendering (putting images into motion, combining all directives). It was considered to be such an advance that it won a Scientific and Engineering Award from the Academy of Motion Picture Arts and Sciences. During the mid-1990s, Disney and Pixar furthered their relationship by signing a distribution deal that included *Toy Story*, *Finding Nemo* (2003), and other feature films. With every release a box-office winner, in 2006 Disney purchased Pixar—bringing John Lasseter back into its fold as a top executive. Meanwhile, the industry had expanded greatly, with CGI features appearing from numerous other studios as well.

Gaming

TRON was set in the context of a computer game, which is no surprise since they had become quite popular by the time that feature was made. The history of computer games can be

Disney's *TRON* (above) and *Toy Story* (right) created by the then-emerging Pixar Studios, were pivotal films in the development of the CGI feature industry. © Disney Enterprises, Inc.

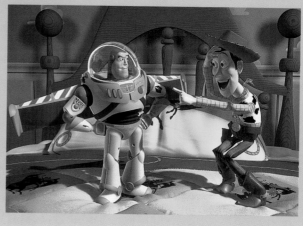

traced to the late 1940s, when Thomas T. Goldsmith Jr. and Estle Ray Mann created a game played on a CRT screen that involved a missile launched at targets. Other significant pioneers include A.S. Douglas, who invented a Tic-Tac-Toe game ("Noughts and Crosses"), also for a CRT, in 1952 in conjunction with his doctoral research on human–computer interactions. During the late 1950s, Willie Higinbotham created "Tennis for Two" using an oscilloscope at Brookhaven National Laboratory, a nuclear research laboratory in New York State. Just a few years later, in 1962, "Spacewar!" was developed at MIT as the first game made for a computer. However, it was still very much within the domain of research and development, and was primarily used by individuals at the Institute; few others could afford the computer needed to play it.

In terms of the general public, the true birth of gaming occurred during the early 1970s, with the release of the first arcade game, "Computer Space." It was created by Nolan Bushell, who also made "Pong," which came out in 1972, and founded Atari Computers, also in 1972.[15] An explosion in arcade-type game development followed during the next few years, at the same time home versions were emerging. Ralph Baer, an inventor with 150 United States and foreign patents in related fields, had disclosed his concept of playing video games on an ordinary television in September 1966. This resulted in the first commercial console set, the "Magnavox Odyssey" game, released in 1972.[16] Since then, gaming has developed into an international phenomenon that brings in untold amounts of money every year and greatly affects the development of animation technology, as budgets grow and demands on visual effects become ever greater.

Web Animation

The growth of the Internet has furthered opportunities for formerly marginalized animators, who can now produce work affordably and easily by themselves, and use the World Wide Web as a means of exhibition. Since the 1990s, when the Web started to become part of our everyday lives, it has provided a platform for animated imagery of all kinds.

In China, a number of artists have come to be called "Shanke," a term that essentially means "Flash animator."[17] Beginning in 1999, when Flash was introduced in China, the Shanke movement evolved rapidly. It has been closely tied to the FlashEmpire.com website, which in 2005 had a million registered users and links to more than ten thousand Flash animations. For these animators, like others across the world, the Web provides a forum for personal commentary that is often political and subversive.

The computer game pioneer Willie Higinbotham (above), created the "Tennis for Two" computer (top) in the 1950s. Courtesy of Brookhaven National Laboratory.

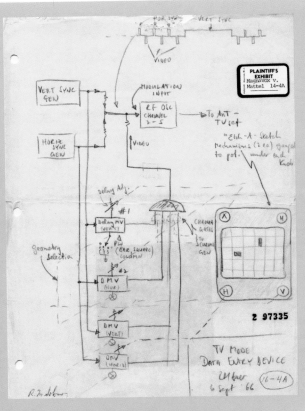

Ralph Baer's original schematic for the "Magnavox Odyssey" game (above). A photo from the game's release shows players using the set (left).

Case Study:
Juan Ospina

Colombian interactive media designer Juan Ospina works at Fabrica, a communication research center and creative laboratory near Treviso, Italy. Founded by the Benetton Group in 1994, the company employs artist-researchers from around the world who work in the realms of creative writing, film and video, industrial design, interactive media, music, photography, and visual communication. It carries out self-initiated research projects as well as commissioned works for private enterprise, nonprofit organizations, and cultural partners.

After joining Fabrica's interactive department in 2004 Ospina embarked on a series of projects, including Flipbook!, which is free, interactive software that allows Web users to make simple animated motion pictures online; it can be accessed at www.benettonplay.com/toys/flipbook. His work is consistent with the company's goal of providing hands-on training for young practitioners, with an emphasis on interdisciplinary work and recognition of cultural identity. It is also an excellent example of how animation can be used on the World Wide Web, and of the issues related to design and free speech that come with developing a new product for this environment.

Fabrica's participants have created many innovative works, including an interactive project that involved placing video and mail systems in a series of Benetton stores across the world, enabling interaction between strangers in faraway places. The online version of Flipbook! grew out of this project, initially appearing as a small offline installation.

Ospina explains that his concept for the work is rooted in aesthetic sensibilities found within the Fabrica environment. He says the company introduced him to the concept of relational art, "where the result is not a finished physical piece but the relation that emerges between the interaction of the piece and the viewer. It's an art piece that is never finished and that involves and encourages the viewer to give his/her input to complete the message or to propose new messages."[18] For the first (instore, offline) version of Flipbook! he borrowed from the structure and design of another Fabrica project, Draw, which was part of the "Dare" series showcased at the Museum of the Moving Image in New York in 2003. Ospina explains that users of Draw (a Shockwave application):

would come up to a touchscreen-enabled computer and using their fingers they could draw on the screen. Each user would start "drawing mode" by touching the screen, and then they could draw with their fingers for a short time before the computer went back to "playback" mode. The drawing would then be saved and played back in an enormous common animation sequence. The animation would be created by reproducing the way the drawing was made (the path that the hand followed to create the final frame), not by showing the sequence of different drawings by different people.

Juan Ospina at Fabrica (left). The online Flipbook! project began as an offline installation, using a single unit (above).

Draw was limited by its exhibition context; it had to be relatively simple to work in an art gallery space where visitors lingered for a short amount of time. The first version of Flipbook! borrowed from the structure and design of Draw, but Ospina built upon it to make animating a more complex frame by frame procedure. One of the main problems he faced was "how to make the interface intuitive enough for any user to learn and play in seconds, yet complex enough to allow the level of control required by frame by frame animation." Some of the specific questions he faced included:

– How should the program start "drawing" mode (with a button or just by touching the screen)?
– How long should the user be given to draw?
– How much time should pass before a frame was declared finished?
– Should onion skins (layers containing previous drawings) be shown, and, if so, how many?
– What color or colors of ink should be used?
– How thick should the line be?

Ospina worked on these problems conceptually, and then implemented his ideas, relying on Fabrica staff to provide feedback. Ultimately, he came up with a simple stand-alone Flash projector that works when someone draws a single frame on a touchscreen with their finger. He says, "The program records the drawing by keeping track of the x- and y-positions of the points that made up the lines. After some time of inactivity, the computer assumes the frame is finished, saves it, and returns to playback mode. Animation is created by showing the sequence of drawings made by user. The simplicity in interaction and fidelity to real flipbooks is kept by allowing only one type of line and only one color (black). The animations were played back at a low frame rate to allow people enough time to make out each drawing."

While he was creating this offline version of his project, Ospina became increasingly interested in exploring the World Wide Web as a platform for his work. He believes it is "the ideal platform for art, considering that it's accessible by many, information is available democratically and nearly instantaneously, and it's a cost-effective medium for distribution." The trade-off, he says, is that advanced artists can be discouraged by the relatively unsophisticated tools available within the Internet context—most users access it using low-end computers, a mouse, and simple creative tools—as well as by the technological limitations of the Web environment itself. He says, "I understand why this makes a lot of artists frustrated, but I see it as a challenge. Coming from a country where art galleries and money to fund them are small, I'm forced to make accessibility and democracy the absolute priority. Art must be public. Everyone must benefit."

The online version of Flipbook! resulted from not only Ospina's perspectives on art and the public good, but also the lessons he learned at Fabrica regarding relational art. He felt that an online, publicly accessible animation station would be the perfect vehicle for getting people involved in an art piece,

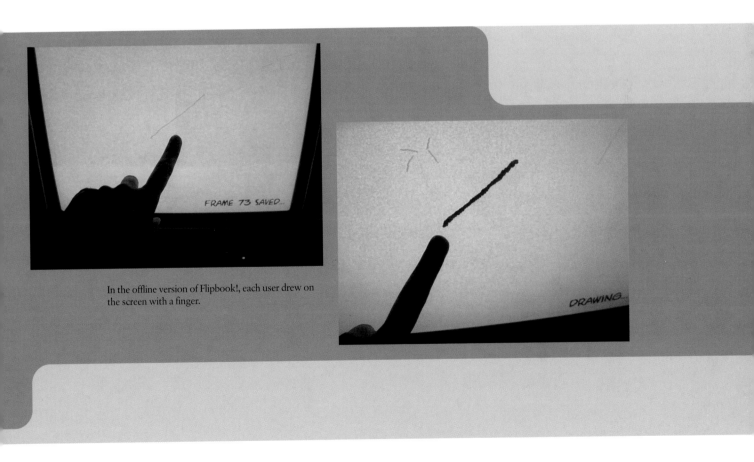

In the offline version of Flipbook!, each user drew on the screen with a finger.

and that the flipbook format would have a special attraction—for himself and everyone else who has ever scribbled a moving image on the pages of a notebook. He describes his project as "a digital-age alternative to the paper and pencil version with the added qualities of the communication age—the ability to share your work instantly."

After a relatively long research and development period at Fabrica, during which feedback was used to continually readjust the system, Flipbook! was launched online in February 2005. For the first few months, hits at the site were relatively few, but in June, after the software was featured in an episode of the American television series "Attack of the Show" on G4TV, contributions and traffic increased. Even greater visibility came about as the chain-reaction information flow of the Web resulted in links to blogs and message boards. At one point, the traffic swell shut down the server, causing Ospina to produce a leaner version, which could

handle the added volume. By 2006 the gallery had more than 160,000 animations, and was receiving between one and two thousand new ones a day.

Flipbook! was created using a combination of software applications, including Flash, which handles the drawing input part of the website. Ospina says, "The front-end Flash program records the animations as sets of points that describe the lines in the drawings. It is also used to play back this set of points as animations after they have been saved and retrieved." Unlike most Flash work, which is typically linear and self-contained, his version is able to communicate with other applications, and share, save, and remember previous interactions.

To make the animations play on the Web, Ospina worked with the "open source" software PHP (Hypertext Preprocessor) and MySQL (Structured Query Language). He used PHP both because of its open source

status, and because it was powerful enough to handle the job; it is relatively easy to incorporate into standard HTML documents, and thus it has widespread appeal. The central database was developed with MySQL, a popular language for adding, accessing, and processing data that works well with PHP.

Even after it had gone online, Flipbook! continued to be developed, responding not only to increased usage but also to Ospina's long-range goals. For example, a feature was added to allow the animations to be exported as PDF files, using the powerful open source FPDF (a PHP library). Ospina says, "This, in my vision, brings the concept full circle. The 'virtual' animations can be brought into the physical world and made into paper flipbooks, which were what inspired everything to begin with!"

The concept of free access works both ways for the project. It allows flipbooks to be freely produced, and it allows them to be

An image from Juan Ospina's *Colombian War Games.*

freely taken. Thus the issue of ownership is sidestepped in a way that encourages free expression.

However, Ospina has had to confront material that made him question his responsibility. He says, "Censorship and content moderation has been a difficult issue to handle. Since our goal is to allow everybody to contribute, we don't want to, and never will, censor or delete anybody's animation." However, he found out that others wish he would. He adds, "At first I never thought anyone would care if someone drew rough pictures of penises. The constant flow of emails complaining about this proved me wrong…. These complaints made me realize that people did indeed care." On the other hand, he was bothered by animation that showed racial and religious hatred. The

solution was to place the animations in two main categories: those with mature or explicit content and those that were "clean." Ospina says, "Flipbook! trusts authors to categorize their animations voluntarily." In addition, a "report" system allows the community itself to decide which animations are too controversial for the general audience. And a setting in the "preferences" option (turned off by default) allows people to decide whether or not they want to see controversial content.

To encourage users to make more and better animations, Ospina decided to include a rating system. However, after a couple of months it became apparent that a lot of users were voting many times, and also that the 1 to 10 rating was a bit complex. As a result, he developed an upgrade that included "a simplified voting interface and a tighter

security system to prevent cheating (or at least make it a lot harder). In the new system, people are only asked if they "like" the animation or not. This creates a positive and negative point record that is used to rank the animations."

Ospina continues to work on other projects that reflect his interest in creating art pieces that involve the users. For example, in *Spaik City*, which he developed for the clothing brand Killerloop, users can create graffiti in a fictional public space.[19] His *Colombian War Games* is personally involving in a more sinister way, as people "experience" crimes in the Colombian conflict.[20]

13

Spaik City, developed by Juan Ospina, allows users to create graffiti in a fictional public space.

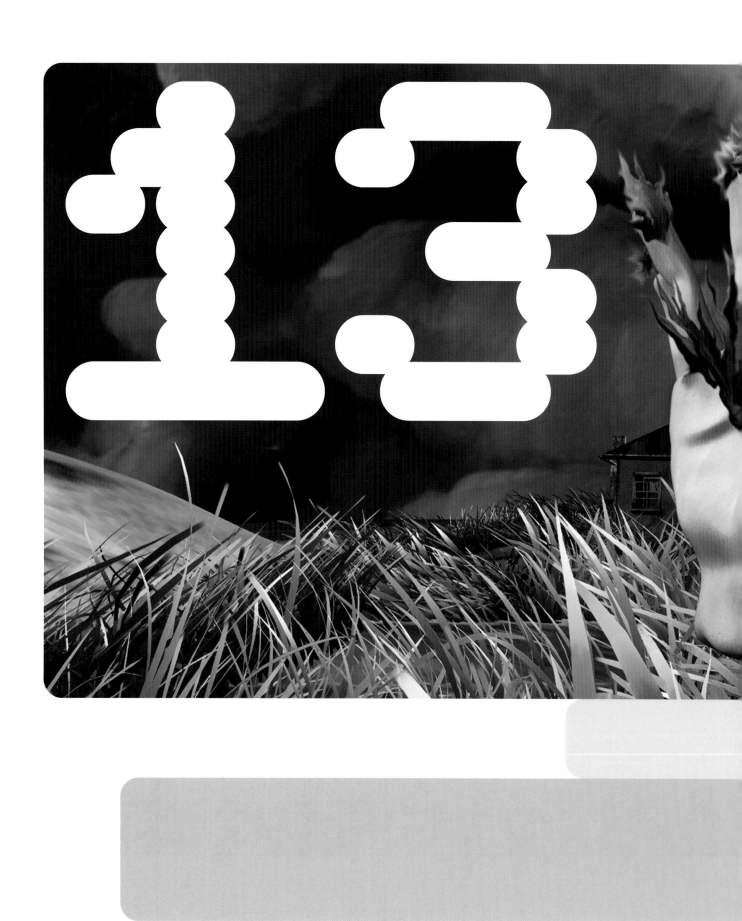

Digital Visions

The breadth of digital media is matched by the range of artwork that animators are creating with it. Some artists have embraced the computer and related technologies as a means of extending their interests in other art practices, while others have explored digital expression as a unique form.

Advantages of Digital Media

In the early twentieth century, shortly after the birth of the cinema, forward-looking painters embraced motion picture film as a way of exploring temporal elements of their work. In the early twenty-first century, digital media have attracted some artists, encouraging them to experiment with traditional techniques or enter new frontiers. For each of them, digital media offers different types of satisfaction.

Rachel Bevan Baker The Scottish animator Rachel Bevan Baker originally embraced digital technology because of the spontaneity it allowed her. As an independent artist, she valued the ability to control every aspect of the animation process, as she was freed from the constraints of a traditional studio setup. *Beaches* (2001) represents her transition into the use of digital media; it consists of eleven short works, ranging from forty-five seconds to four minutes in length, based on Bevan Baker's impressions of beaches around Scotland. She explains that the animation techniques she used were "a mixture—drawing on paper, drawing and redrawing on the same paper, drawing in sand, filming, and also animating on computer using Flash, which I hoped to use more in my work. *The Green Man of Knowledge* and *Beelines* [see page 191] were both shot on film—so the quality was great. But it's a very long, complex process. With Flash, I can see the results immediately—working fast like this means I can experiment more. I also like the different look—it's still drawing, but with a computer tablet."[1]

Bevan Baker felt her approach to *Beaches* was experimental in that she created "a lot of the animation 'on location,' as far away from studio as possible.... So some of the films were done in Flash, but some were done in layout pads, which I drew in onsite, starting on the back page first, then flipping page over page like a big flipbook. All the images were fleeting impressions of the beach activity in front of me."[2] She also worked on paper and acetate, animating with willow charcoal or oil bar, and using a small digital camera she set up at the outdoor location where she was situated. This allowed her to "respond immediately to surroundings," resulting in what she calls "impressionistic animation."[3]

Rachel Bevan Baker says *Beaches*, pictured here, was a transitional film because it bridged her traditional in-studio practices with digital and "on-location" work.

Ron Hui In 2003, Chinese animator Ron Hui used Maya to create *Ode to Summer*, a film that replicates the aesthetics of classical Chinese painting.[4] In the film it appears that the "camera" moves through space, beginning with a dragonfly floating around lilies, moving downward at an angle to observe a school of fish, lingering on a woman as she recites a poem, and finally pulling back to reveal a calligraphic poem.

Hui made the film at the Institute of Digital Media Technology, Ltd. (IDMT), in Shenzhen, China, where he was teaching Maya. Work on *Ode to Summer* commenced formally in November 2002, when the institute committed to the project, but for the previous year he had been experimenting with the software. He had studied Chinese and western painting, and while he created his tests he became interested in making a work in the style of the ink-painting master Qi Baishi. His goal was to avoid an obvious three-dimensional look; instead, he hoped to create the authentic appearance of Chinese monochrome painting.

The four-minute film was made in only three months, in addition to the pre-production that took place during the year of testing. It was decided that the story should be relatively simple, to hold it to a short length. Chen Yue, of the Institute's storyboard department, created a pencil-sketch storyboard, which assisted with the four-day process of layout. The rapid pace of production was made possible in large part because of the size of the crew provided by the Institute. Altogether, seventeen individuals made up the core production team. Animation was completed within three weeks; rendering was done at night, with unsatisfactory parts re-rendered the following day.

A central challenge was to re-create the look of the brushwork and borders in Chinese paintings. The crew experimented with different colors and techniques, but ultimately decided it was not necessary to be tightly restricted by the aesthetics of the traditional model; Hui's philosophy was to "keep a little, change a little, and abandon a little." One significant change is that the images are placed on a solid color fill rather than a "paper" background. Hui explains that when objects were moving, a paper effect looked strange. "We abandoned the thought of adding paper texture to the background and just added paper color instead."[5]

Kathy Smith Australian animator Kathy Smith began her artistic life far from the hub of media production; she grew up on a dairy farm in Australia, where she became attuned to the visual and aural patterns of nature, and landscapes in particular. She made a number of live-action Super 8mm films, beginning when she was a young child, and then trained as a painter.

Ron Hui directed *Ode to Summer* at IDMT, where a crew used Maya to create a film reflecting traditional Chinese aesthetics (below and right).

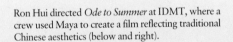

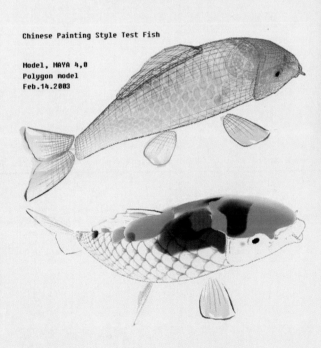

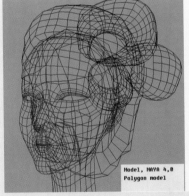

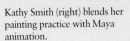
Kathy Smith (right) blends her painting practice with Maya animation.

Like Hui, Smith also uses Maya to explore the aesthetics of painting, though as an extension of her personal work.

Smith was exposed to 3D software in the mid-1990s, while she was in a residency at the Australian Network for Art and Technology, where she began to explore the possibilities of "transposing my 2D oil-painted imagery into a 3D environment."[6] Her film *Indefinable Moods* (2001) resulted from another residency—this time at the University of Southern California (USC), which led first to workshops and then to a permanent teaching position and her position as chair of the Department of Animation and Digital Art.

Indefinable Moods is based on twenty-three oil-painted panels she created on canvas-covered boards that ranged in size from about 8 x 12 inches (20 x 30 centimeters) to about 12 x 18 inches (30 x 45 centimeters). She says, "Each painting either dealt with a specific dream image, or was a construction of the unconscious images and thought processes that often come to mind when I paint." She placed her canvases side by side, and from these arrangements she began to sense what she calls "image movements." A narrative of sorts developed, and she sketched out motions, suggesting how the film would progress. The next step was to write notes that reflected her sense of the sound that would accompany each segment of the film. She worked with a composer, then mixed the sounds herself, purposefully throwing the "rhythms and timing out of beat to disorient the viewer and to reflect the imagery's constant collapse and reconstruction."[7]

Animation took three years, during which Smith learned more and more about Maya software. As she taught herself, she began instructing students, and helped USC shift toward digital technologies during the mid-1990s. However, she approached both her classroom lectures and the project more like a painter than a computer animator; *Indefinable Moods* was created as one entire scene, moving from start to finish. As a result, it is possible to see a progression in the software, from Maya 1.0 at the beginning of the work to Maya 3.5 at its end.

Smith feels that working with 3D software gave her the flexibility to "collapse, reconstruct, and journey through a landscape of symbolic narrative." She found inspiration in Renaissance and French Romantic painting:

Artists of these periods created magnificent oil paintings that alluded to the 3D world through the use of light, perspective, the study of the physical world of nature, and desire for movement (animation). The advent of digital technology has seen the "Renaissance" of animation internationally, and the information technology age greatly parallels what happened during the earlier Renaissance: the sense of discovery and perception of our world via new, exciting media and science.

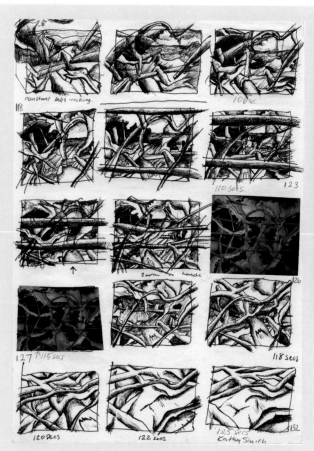

Kathy Smith visualized a series of "image movements" (left) to create an infrastructure for her film *Indefinable Moods* (above and right), which grew out of a series of her paintings.

Though Smith is immersed in digital technology in terms of both her production and teaching, she strongly believes "traditional animation techniques are not in decline. What you are seeing is a mixture of 2D and 3D elements combining organic media and digital technology. In fact, *Indefinable Moods* explores just that. Artists will always employ a variety of media to convey their ideas, and even—as software improves—to emulate painted or traditionally drawn worlds. Artists will still physically combine natural processes. Understanding traditional processes will always enhance whatever you do in the digital world."

Ying Tan Chinese visual music artist Ying Tan also is interested in the relationship between digital media and other art practices. She explores this relationship in work that depicts cosmic realms, the far reaches of the universe and our imaginations.

Tan has a special interest in the work of Jordan Belson, a seminal figure in abstract film known for his use of organic, mystical forms. After being introduced to his films at a visual music event, Tan worked closely with the artist. She made two short-film sequences, *Elements in Transformation #1* and *Elements in Transformation #2* (both 1998), to demonstrate to him that a computer could be used to create animation as organic and painterly as that made with more traditional

media. These films clearly reflect the influence of Belson's paintings and films. Like Belson's work, they feature swirling gases, planetary images, and ethereal lights. She made the films using SGI computers and Alias|Wavefront software provided by the computer science department of the University of Oregon, where she is a faculty member in the art department.

Tan makes extensive use of particle systems and texture mapping manipulation, and employs complex layering effects to produce fluid visual forms as in *Dawn* (1999) and *Like a Swarm of Angry Bees...* (2001), part of a body of work that is choreographed to music scores created by her collaborator, composer Jeffrey Stolet. While these animations are ethereal in nature, they also include more tangible images—for example, words on paper and fragments of an unknown fibrous material that tumble through space. Having worked in a high-end industrial studio before she began her teaching job, she has experienced production using state-of-the-art technology, and she sometimes misses the advantages of that work environment. However, she also values the lifestyle and other benefits offered by a career in teaching. In the final analysis, she feels that access to any given technology is less important than ideas—that software and platform matter less than the way they are applied and the concepts behind a production.

Ying Tan's film *Like a Swarm of Angry Bees...* (left) is choreographed to the score of her collaborator Jeffrey Stolet.

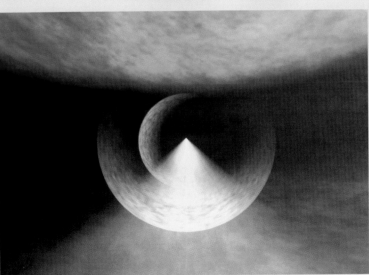

Ying Tan's *Elements in Transformation #2* (left) shows the influence of Jordan Belson's work, such as his 1967 film *Samadhi* (above).

Stephanie Maxwell Direct filmmaker and visual music artist Stephanie Maxwell (see pages 22 and 54) agrees with Tan when she downplays the overall significance of digital media in her work. She says, "Tools and techniques do not make the movie; there has got to be an idea or vision that needs to be expressed."

Early in her career, Maxwell established herself as a direct filmmaker, creating productions such as *Ga* (1982), an abstract work that suggests the relationship between predator and prey, and *Please Don't Stop* (1989), which interprets the experience of driving at night. In the late 1990s, after joining the faculty of the Rochester Institute of Technology (RIT), Maxwell began to experiment with digital techniques in *Outermost* (1998), *Nocturne* (1999), *Somewhere* (1999), *Fragments* (2000), *terra incognita* (2001), *Time Streams* (2003), *All that Remains* (2006), and other productions. However, despite her increased use of technology, handmade images remain at the heart of her work. She explains, "Digitalization allows the advantages of: A, editing and previewing the work quickly and in a very creative, spontaneous way at times; and B, 'effecting' or manipulating the images," though she keeps this practice to a minimum "to preserve the visual and energy aesthetics of the original direct-on-film effects (or other animation techniques that I may use in a work)."[8]

The development of music is integral to Maxwell's creative process and takes place simultaneously with her image-making. Her works are created using 35mm film, which she manipulates through painting, collage, and etching. Handmade imagery is placed under what she calls a "feed camera," a small device used to view and manipulate photo negatives (it looks somewhat like a microscope). It functions like a small optical printer unit, except that it does not record images. Instead, the lens transmits imagery to a Video LunchBox unit for frame-by-frame recording. A connected monitor allows Maxwell to see a magnified image of what is under the lens.

The feed camera allows her to manipulate the film in many ways. It has a small backlit panel to provide illumination and a lens that can zoom in very close ("to the size of a dime," she explains). It also has filters that enable Maxwell to adjust color and exposure, and change from positive to negative. There is enough room within the device for Maxwell to pick up the film and move it closer to the lens, twist or bend it, or otherwise manipulate it physically—like a piece of film that literally unfolds in *Time Streams*. She can also animate small objects that she wants to incorporate along with direct film materials; for example, in making *Time Streams* she captured images of a sponge being stretched in front of the lens and animated tiny black rubber bands placed on the backlit surface

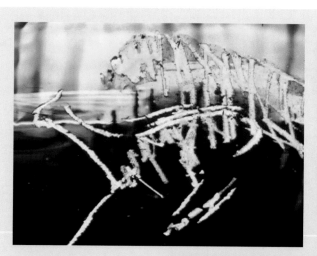 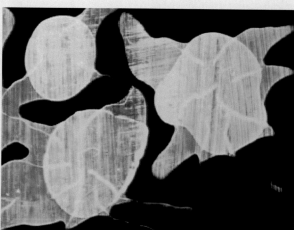

Images from *Ga* (above) and *Please Don't Stop* (above right) by Stephanie Maxwell.

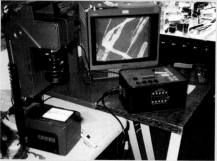

Stephanie Maxwell's studio (above left and right) includes her feed camera, a Lunchbox system, and a monitor, as well as a light table and a wide range of creative supplies.

of the feed camera. She also created black-and-white mattes by manipulating small pieces of black paper on the backlit surface, one frame at a time. These were later used for digitally compositing handmade imagery into their black-and-white fields.

After imagery is captured by a LunchBox, sequences are digitized (from the LunchBox Sync) or moved as files into an editing and/or compositing program for effects and editing. She explains, "I use Adobe After Effects for compositing and mild digital effects, like fades out and in, dissolves, and so forth. I use Avid, Final Cut Pro, or Adobe Premiere for laying down the soundtrack, editing, and perhaps some other simple effects that are applied to the visuals here and there or to give a final 'polish' to the fine cut of the work."

Maxwell is inspired by the French silent-era filmmaker Georges Méliès (see page 232) and the trickery of his films. Her primary filmic influence, though, has been Len Lye (see page 143), whose work launched her into direct film. While the visuals in her productions are abstract, she nonetheless begins with a sense of structure. She says, "The works grow out of ideas and concepts, and techniques are found that best realize the compositional, structural, and emotive elements in the work's design."

J. Walt Adamczyk In his "Spontaneous Fantasia" performances, American J. Walt Adamczyk creates visual music pieces, combining fantastic imagery created live with sound he has composed himself or existing music. An interactive designer, programmer, filmmaker, graphic artist, and composer, "J. Walt" has developed award-winning commercial production software that he has modified for use in these live performances.[9] He uses off-the-shelf hardware and writes his own software in C++ and Python, on top of OpenGL; it is constantly evolving as just about every piece requires a different interface or technique.

Each performance piece is created to accompany a particular composition. During the show, J. Walt creates gestural drawing and movements, improvising to some extent and working tighter or looser, and varying each time in the model of jazz performance. J. Walt's live images are mostly drawn with a Wacom graphics tablet and pen, though at one point he used a Wacom Cintiq loaner (which allows animators to work directly on a monitor). He also works with a joystick and 6-axis Spaceball to move his images through three-dimensional space. To shift colors, he uses the slider bars of an accompanying MIDI controller.

A piece of film unfolds under the camera in *Time Streams* (above) by Stephanie Maxwell.

J. Walt Adamczyk (above) creates live images for the visual music performances he calls "Spontaneous Fantasia" (left).

Case Study: Gokhan Okur

Turkish artist Gokhan Okur trained as an engineer, but in 1996 he started to draw comic strips for newspapers and publishers, and from 1999 to 2003 he illustrated three underground comic magazines: *Mengene*, *Les*, and *Girtlak*. At about the same time he began to work in animation; he shot his first short film in 1999 and completed an additional four over the next six years.Okur says he started to make animated works "for fun, but then it became a business for me. I am working independently, and I do not have a studio—it's just me and my computers." For high-volume editing and rendering, he also sometimes uses the facilities of Sabancı University, where he enrolled in a graduate program in visual communication design at in 2005.[10]

Okur's critically acclaimed short *Noci* (2005)[11] is a Flash 7 animation about symbols and their meanings; the title is "icon" in reverse. To create the piece, he began with three concepts: life, fire, and love. He visualized each one in various ways, using different symbols of his own design. For example, among other things, love was portrayed as platonic, confused, and fatal. The symbol for each visualization was created in black and placed against a white background. The concept words—life, fire, and love—also appear in black, with the specific visualization words (such as "fatal"), which are next to them, in red (creating the black and red combination "love fatal"). When all the visualization words and their symbols are on the screen (about fifty images), the symbols form a group and begin to interact. They slide across the screen forming new shapes, and also appear on different layers, in varying transparencies. As they move to create various forms, the film asks questions of its viewers; for example, "Life is samurai?" as the head of a warrior is seen. At the end of the animation, the mass of symbols creates the shape of a man's face thinking, a man's face smiling, the full figure of a man, and a cityscape. Throughout, the images are mainly black on a white background, with red used sparingly. The limited color palette and stark contrasts it creates emphasize the form of the work on the screen.

In animation, form always imparts information to viewers. It typically reflects how an entity feels or behaves—perhaps its "personality." In *Noci*, the emphasis on shape is particularly strong, as the film is about the way forms impart meaning. This made designing the images difficult. Okur writes, "Making symbols that represent 'life' is not an easy job. Life has many different meanings." He is interested in the fact that everyone interprets symbolic concepts in a different way, and says, "As we all communicate via symbols (more literally 'semiotics'), there always will be a misunderstanding—small or big—between humankind. I am not saying that the 'restroom' sign can be understood in another way, but that values, motivations, and meanings of ideas (concepts) may vary from person to person, culture to culture, time to time. Every person sees the world with his or her own values and ideas." As they shift around, the symbols impart the underlying message of the film: "It's how you see the world around you. The same symbols can tell different stories to different people."

The fifty or so images used in *Noci* were designed with pencil and paper over a period of two months, as Okur worked four to five hours a day. When they were complete, the symbols were transferred into a computer

love fatal

life is samurai ?

Gokhan Okur's Flash animation *Noci* uses a set of symbols to create images of varying complexity.

with a Canon Power Shot digital camera. The animation process took him about a week, working eight to ten hours a day. After he transferred the images to his Pentium 4 laptop, Okur set about vectorizing them, using Freehand 10 software. He explains, "I put a raw photo into a layer and on top of it I drew a vector version using the 'pen' tool."

The vector images were animated in Flash. Although Okur has been using it for a number of years—he started with Flash 4, which was released in the late 1990s—he does not consider himself to be a "Flash animator." The application suited this project because it accommodated the precise registration that was required. The symbols were moved primarily using its "tween" function, with relatively little key-framing to make each movement unique. The emphasis is on the interaction of symbols with each other, rather than the qualities of their motions. Okur created relatively complex movement using animations within other animations, which can be accomplished using Flash. Okur says the qualities of the software made *Noci* possible.

However, there were limitations in Flash that caused Okur to modify his original plans and affected the performance of the work. He says, "My original concept for *Noci* included much more complex animation than the final version, but Flash 7 was unable to show them properly. As a result, I had to reduce the complexity of animation and the number of different symbols on the stage. Suddenly I found myself counting tweened images that appear at the same instant. To help solve the problem, I distributed animations to the timeline, so I could have the optimum number of motions at the same time."

However, it was hard to move animation within the timeline in Flash, in contrast to other editing programs like Premiere, and Okur ended up dividing *Noci* into a number of scenes. When he used the "animations" function, he had to guess what the finished work would look like, as he couldn't see the movement until it had been exported. He says, "The basic problem with *Noci* was that Flash became slower with more tweening, but the overall file size grew as I created more key frame animation on the timeline. You have to think about the processor speed all the time."

The number of scenes in the film meant audio synchronization became problematic. Ultimately, it came down to priorities: smooth animation, or sound synchronized with the images? Okur explains, "In Flash 7, if you set the music as an 'event' it is separate from the video. In slow machines, *Noci* would be playing slower as animation but normal in terms of sound. Flash 7 does not allow you to set sound as 'sync' over several scenes; so, because I was working in separate scenes, I was unable to use sound in sync mode. Also, when you use sound in sync mode, the animation is tied into the sound, and in slower machines you lose the smoothness of animation because it is following the sound. To not lose the animation, in *Noci* I used music in event mode."

Okur's experiences making *Noci* demonstrate his contention that "the Flash animation process is about decision-making within your limits." Actually, the same observation could be made about the production process in general—the importance of understanding one's parameters and finding creative ways to work within them.

Case Study:
Bärbel Neubauer

Austrian Bärbel Neubauer (see page 141) is a visual music artist who lives and works in Munich, Germany.[12] Though she began her animation career as a direct filmmaker, she has steadily migrated toward the use of digital technology. In part this shift has been motivated by Neubauer's ability to compose, play, and record soundtracks using computer-based music media.

Since the beginning of her career in the 1980s, Neubauer has used a wide range of techniques working on 35mm, she stamped images to create *Algorithmen* (*Algorithms*, 1994), *Falter-Spot 7* (1994), *Roots* (1996), and *Absolut Neubauer* (1996). She scratched on film for *Mondlicht* (*Moonlight*, 1997), and made processed negative print for *Holiday* (1998), a work inspired by her visit to the Hiroshima International Animation Festival. In 1998, she also created *Sky*, a forty-second film for IMAX projection; Swell Productions commissioned it for exhibition in the United States, along with a selection of other animated productions.[13] Usually, Neubauer works in a straight-ahead mode, one image leading to the next, and takes three to four months to paint a four-minute animation.

Certainly, 1998 was a productive year for Neubauer. Aside from *Holiday* and *Sky*, she also released *Feuerhaus* (*Firehouse*), which was made by contact-printing onto 35mm positive print stock. In her darkroom, she placed plants and other natural elements on film that had a low light sensitivity, and then turned on a flashlight to make exposures in one of two ways. She either used it as a still spotlight to get a crisp outline of the object, or moved it up and down the length of the film, creating shadows and a sense of motion around the item. Colored filters were used on top of the flashlight and timing was intuitive. In a one-hour session, she could expose 30 to 50 feet (9 to 15 meters) of film. Neubauer was careful not to take too long as the small darkroom light would eventually leave a trace on the film.

When the footage was developed, there were no frame lines, so she could pull from the imagery any way she wanted. After she made creative decisions using a mock-up done on her computer, the original was optically printed to a negative, using a cut list of single frames she formulated while manipulating the imagery.[14]

Each of Neubauer's films explores the bond between sound and visuals. *Roots*, Neubauer explains, is a "metamorphosis of color and form which is painted, drawn, and stamped directly on blank film and corresponds to rhythm and music. The main symbols of the film are the sun and sun wheels."[15] Its images and sound were developed in parallel. She says, "When I started to make this film, I had some of the main images in my mind. I started by painting without having a concrete plan. I had composed some elements of the music on the computer so there was a rough structure. From there, both music and images were then developed in union."[16] Neubauer has been using a computer to compose sound for her direct films since she bought her first one, an Atari, in 1994.[17] For her, part of the appeal of using digital sound is the fact that the files become visual material that can be manipulated as curved lines, as sound waves—an experience that is quite different from composing in a traditional analog manner.

Eventually, Neubauer went further, and made even her images on a computer, rather than using direct techniques on film. The transition occurred in her twenty-five-minute *Flockenspiel* (*Play of Particles*, 2003), a four-part word she describes as "an associative journey from 2D to 3D through abstract digital images and music, soundscapes."[18] In the process of creating sound for the film, Neubauer used an Apple G4 800, a MIDI saxophone (which can be adjusted to play other sounds, such as those of a trumpet, steps, birds, and so forth), and a keyboard. For sound-related software, she used Metasynth (U&I Software), XX (U&I

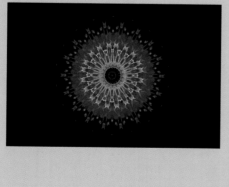

Bärbel Neubauer at work on her computer (left), creating images for *Morphs of Pegasus* (below).

"Storyboard" for "SKY"

70 mm
8 Perfs

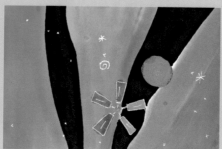

Bärbel Neubauer worked directly on film before she migrated toward digital media. Her film *Sky* (left) was animated directly on 70mm film; images from the film are sketched on her storyboard (above).

Software), and Logic Platinum (Emagic) with a variety of NI plug-ins: Spectral Delay (sound processor), KONTAKT (software sampler), BATTERY (drum sampler), and Pro 53 (software synthesizer). For her imagery, she employed Painter (Corel), VTrack (U&I software), Artmatic (U&I software), and Carrara Studio (Eovia).[19]

Neubauer likes working digitally because the media provide her with an intuitive, creative, and spontaneous way of working, while also allowing great control over every element in the film.[20] However, she is quick to point out that such technology can also be a liability, as it is possible to lose "track of your idea, creativity, and goal by having too much control, losing yourself in details, or flattening something that was better in its original version with 'mistakes.'"[21]

Despite her complete migration to digital media, Neubauer says *Flockenspiel*'s production process was similar to that of her previous films. She explains that "many steps of creation were the same as my direct-on-film work. The difference was that I could create not only images but parts of whole sequences in a short time, so that the rate at which I was creating was much closer to the

speed of my imagination than ever before." She adds, "But including all corrections and other requirements, the working time on the whole is the same as that of my analog films."[22] Some of *Flockenspiel*'s images were created with Painter software, which allowed her to paint on the computer in a way similar to how she worked on film in the past. While she was learning to use the software, she created a diary of images that later provided the foundation for the film.

Neubauer completed the sound used in the film during the summer of 2002, without having an animation project in mind. Ultimately, this music was used to define *Flockenspiel*'s themes, mood, and timing, which vary from part to part. For example, in part two, a sequence contains a percussion beat accompanied by kaleidoscopic flower-like snowflakes created in different colors and patterns. In part three, a sequence employs sampled human voices, altered to take on an ethereal "song-like" quality, which accompany images that are themselves celestial. Partly three-dimensional, partly flat and "screen-like," they suggest the experience of floating through space—or perhaps the inner structure of a snowflake. The imagery

constantly moves and shifts into new patterns.

Neubauer sees this film as fitting into:

> an organic transition from my analog ways of working to the various possibilities you have with digital tools, especially with the wonderful and powerful tools from U&I Software. It would not be possible to experiment spontaneously in an analog way with such complicated processes of many, many layers and algorithms that influence each other in different ways. As far as I can see it, my approach to image and sound are the same as ever, but the tools look different. It was a very happy time, developing my own language with the digital tools—that is, as always, an ongoing process.[23]

Neubauer continued this process in her next film, *Morphs of Pegasus* (2006), in which she employs soft-edged forms, such as clouds, nebulae, and moving light, that move through three-dimensional space.

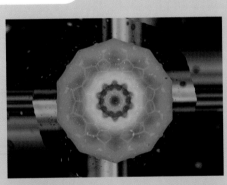

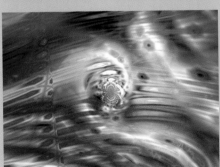

Images from *Flockenspiel* by Bärbel Neubauer.

Practical Considerations

Digital media can be great for a variety of reasons, as we see from the previous examples. However, they also bring their share of challenges. Artists using digital media face a number of practical considerations, including the rapidity of change, limitations of the media, and the fact that digital production methods are not always the best choice.

One of the biggest considerations artists face is the pace at which digital media evolve. The cost of necessary hardware and software updates every few years is significant. Applications can be complex in design and use, and their rapid evolution means that individuals working with them must constantly retrain in order to use new releases. An additional task is keeping track of archived elements from productions, to make sure they can still be accessed after a new system or updated software is installed. Good housekeeping in terms of file naming and hierarchical storage (use of file folders to organize related elements) and a devoted regimen of backing up files to save the work are essential aspects of the production process.

Stephen X. Arthur During the mid-1990s, Canadian artist Stephen X. Arthur (see pages 13, 38, and 68) came to realize how quickly computers were outdated. After completing *Touched Alive* in 1996, an animated production based on the paintings of Jack Shadbolt, he entered into an agreement with the National Film Board of Canada (NFB) to create a longer

work, *Transfigured* (1998), which incorporated much of the earlier film. At that time, fellow animator Leslie Bishko asked if he had plans to update his equipment.

Arthur replied that the change in personal computer systems over the past two years had been staggering:

> Now I discover that you can buy a complete system that will run more than ten times faster than mine, for less than half the cost. This rampant obsolescence happened in just the last year, even as I began my contract with the NFB to continue animating for another year with the system I have. The question of new equipment is an ongoing dilemma these days. You don't want to get addicted to progress, because you'll never have time to master your tools and be able to let the real, human, creative juices flow.[24]

Nonetheless, he conceded that it would be time for an upgrade after he finished his film.

Arthur first used digital technology in 1992, after seeing "a personal computer in a store that was displaying an actual moving image." At that time, he adds, high-resolution bitmap animation was "just becoming feasible on affordable computers." As an artist, Arthur leaned toward abstraction and kept images by Joan Miró, Desmond Morris, and Jack Shadbolt on his walls as inspiration for warm-up exercises. When he saw the moving computer images, he realized he

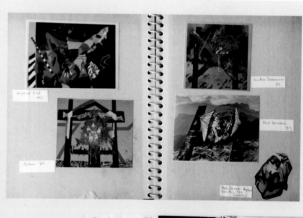

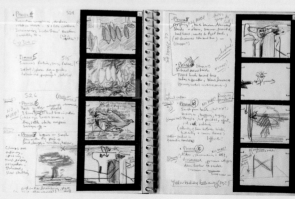

"could literally animate those actual pictures. They had a built-in theme and tone, and it would be an exciting challenge to try to express that through action." He used 2D bitmap animation, employing Autodesk Animator Pro and a shareware morphing program on 8-bit color images from Photo-CD. His work was all digital, employing scanned images of Shadbolt's acrylic-on-canvas paintings.

The new technology aided Arthur's work a great deal, because, he says, "As a lone filmmaker doing all levels of the production, computers have the obvious advantages of easy pencil testing and ink and paint, infinite cel levels, and limited forms of in-betweening.... The computer also allows me to create the complete soundtrack myself." However, at the time, home systems did not generally produce professional-looking copies for distribution purposes, so he had to find a creative solution. For *Touched Alive* he put the computer monitor beneath an Oxberry rostrum camera and shot from the screen; the colors on 35mm were warm and vibrant.

Arthur had previously designed his computer animation for "super-cheap, real-time output" to video, and was anxious to return to film. He also wanted to "create the Shadbolt animation in high resolution to offset the low color depth, so you don't see the pixels." Ultimately, his video output caused plenty of problems, in part because he did not anticipate the color requirements in various exhibition contexts—in particular, television. He says, at "the television premiere of my computer animation on local cable, it went berserk—strobing and superimposing random frames over the whole thing."

Karl Staven American animator Karl Staven was attracted to After Effects because it allowed him to place content on unlimited layers without losing quality at lower levels. Flexibility in timing was also a key feature. Using this software and elements created or cut out in Photoshop, Staven created the films *Composition in Blue and Green* (2000) and *Lafftrak* (2001). The former involves abstract figures moving through three-dimensional space in a homage to visual music artist Oskar Fischinger, while *Lafftrak* is a kind of collage film, featuring pictures of Staven's face as a boy, a teenager, and an adult.

It took five years for Staven to complete production of *Piano Dog* (2004), which employed Softimage for 3D sections and After Effects for 2D animation and compositing. The film tells the story of a group of animals, depicted in 2D, that venture into a surreal 3D "underworld" to rescue one of their friends. At the time he began the project, it was unusual to animate 2D characters in a 3D space.

He started by scanning in photos of artwork from a husband-and-wife team, Zbyszek and Tippi Koziol, who have a gallery in Key West, Florida. As a next step, "The images of the characters were cut apart in Photoshop and mapped onto flattened cubes in Softimage that were rebuilt into characters

Jack Shadbolt's paintings were the primary inspiration for Stephen X. Arthur's *Touched Alive* and *Transfigured*. Images shown are from the film and from Arthur's inspirational notebook (opposite) and production production storyboards (right).

with linked skeletons and IK chains. This was done before After Effects had either 3D space capabilities or the ability to parent/child objects" in order to link movements of hierarchically related parts of a figure.[25]

During the lengthy production period, Staven faced numerous problems. For instance, he had trouble with Softimage when it came to bending the mapped cubes that underlay his moving figures. He explains that the problem wasn't inherent in the software: It happened because of his design concept. He was "bending very simple cubes rather than subdividing them into more complex shapes with more vertices. By trying to keep the geometry simple when constructing my characters, I thwarted mapping movement mobility. If you bend a stiff piece of cardboard, you're going to get a sharp crease. If you bend a mesh screen, you'll get curvature of the surface."

Staven also had a problem rendering a long section of *Piano Dog* that included a forest made of large mushrooms. He explains that when he "attempted to render a frame, the computer couldn't handle all of the information. I had to go in and separate out the various rows of mushrooms, delete all but one row at a time, render out that row, and then reconstitute the forest in After Effects by compositing all of the individual rows." Eventually he just cut the scene. He also cut much of the rest of the film; at its original running time of twenty-six minutes, it did not do well at festivals. In its new version, it runs about nine and a half minutes, which fits into the typical "ten minutes and under" category found at competitions.

Thorsten Fleisch In *Gestalt* (2003), German animator Thorsten Fleisch works with fourth-dimensional fractals. With them he explores the "fourth dimension," the extension of space and time in a speculative realm that has fascinated artists, scientists, and others since the latter part of the nineteenth century.[26] With its ability to depict virtual worlds, digital media has aided in visualizing theoretical concepts of fourth-dimensional geometry.[27]

During his study of the fourth dimension, Fleisch found quaternion fractals, "bizarre shapes and forms that could be expressed by a single mathematical formula. Wondering how it would look if I changed some of the parameters over time, I experimented with animating them." To do so, he used Quat, a freeware (that is, "free") application written by Dirk Meyer that he found online. However, he had mixed feelings about the process: "I fiddled with every parameter that could be changed while gradually shifting one or more parameters to test if something promising would develop. This procedure posed a real challenge to my patience. Though I did only small resolution test renderings, they sometimes took half an eternity to finish." Rendering the sequences he liked at a higher resolution took almost a year. Another drawback was that the Quat-designed images were not compatible with professional 3D rendering software so the texture rendering looked "kind of raw."

Images from the films of Karl Staven, *Piano Dog* (above left) and *Lafftrak* (left).

In *Gestalt* (above), Thorsten Fleisch explores fourth-dimensional imagery.

Case Study: Lorelei Pepi

The process of creation often involves testing and retesting to achieve the desired outcomes, almost like the controlled research undertaken by scientists experimenting in a laboratory. Unfortunately, this experimental approach does not always lead to a completed project—sometimes results indicate that a new line of development should be pursued. Such was the case for Lorelei Pepi and her project *Ether*.[28] After a considerable amount of experimentation, she decided it should not be realized as animation using digital media because the results were unsatisfactory. However, her extensive tests, and investment of time and labor, were not wasted; rather they served as a valuable learning experience that taught her about her relationship with digital tools and the extent to which she could use them to satisfy her aesthetic goals in this project and others.

Pepi's animations are typically created using a blend of analog and digital media. She begins with "real world" images, but other aspects of her works are done digitally: animation, image manipulation, compositing, effects, editing, and sound design. In general, she is interested in the opposition of old and new, and strives to produce an "authentic" handmade look in her digital productions. For example, her film *Happy & Gay* (2006) employs 2D digital technology to create the vintage look of 1930s rubber-hose animation.

In her production testing notes, Pepi describes the *Ether* project as "a digital shadow-puppet animation movie." The puppet figures she made for the film were fashioned from frosted drafting mylar, clear plastic wrap, oil paint, charcoal, wire, and glue. Plastic wrap and mylar were also used to create textures. Pepi applied oil paint to the plastic wrap with her fingers, smearing and texturing the surface, then stuck mylar sheets to her window and taped the processed plastic wrap over them,

creating bumps and folds that were photographed with a digital still camera. She also made plastic wrap and wire sculptures, which she illuminated and photographed to create digital stills. The stills were imported into Photoshop, Illustrator, and Painter for image manipulation, and then brought into After Effects. She used ProTools for sound, the After Effects Production Bundle for animation of imported elements as well as compositing and visual effects, and Final Cut Pro for editing.

Pepi's experimentation in *Ether* was motivated by a range of previous experiences. One of the strongest influences was live theater—performance and set design, as well as the aesthetic and practical dimensions of lighting. She studied acting and theater production for years, and attended traditional and experimental puppetry shows. She says, "I particularly loved how one traveling group

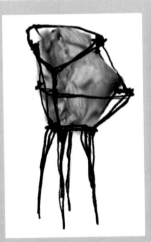

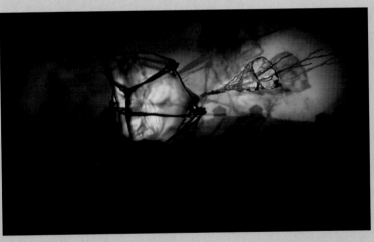

Lorelei Pepi created puppet figures (above left) that were digitally photographed for her film *Ether* (above).

Image (left) from *Happy & Gay* by Lorelei Pepi.

used flashlights to create a moving landscape of shadows on the screen. They moved the flashlights around behind the landscape silhouette, causing it to fracture into many levels of shadow and light, all the while moving the landscape as 'puppet.'"

Her awareness of lighting design extended to stop-motion and live-action production, and included the use of colored light. It also involved observing the environment around her. She spent time "watching how light sends shadows through trees and hand-cast windows and drops it in spaces around the house. The flittering quality of light, image, and gesture in these situations is tremendously beautiful and I could watch it all day. I took lots of low-resolution digital movies of these moments as reference and inspiration. These films became exotic miniature puppet shows in their own right."

She also studied traditions of puppet fabrication and the use of artist materials, such as paints, papers, skins, and plastics, searching for textural luminescence. She immersed herself in the study of traditional moviemaking techniques, and became knowledgable about

lens focal lengths, depth of field, f-stops, and related points. These technical concerns taught her how to create and manipulate levels of image in relation to a camera plane, and to create effects like lap-dissolves. In testing *Ether* she challenged herself to think about how to create a sense of three-dimensional space, using her technical knowledge.

Problem-solving and improvisation were key concepts in the tests. Pepi needed a creative attitude to come up with inventions that would help her achieve her goal: finding ways to imitate the "real," suggesting conventional animation techniques within a digital context. Part of the solution was to incorporate mistakes, "to keep it from being too processed. Mistakes in this instance are bumps, shifts, imperfect transitions, or movements; things that happen when real people work. I keyframe the movement, but add in bumpy moments to keep it alive. I think of things like, 'What if the puppeteer couldn't reach the whole way, and the puppet falls back from the screen a bit as she overreaches?' and I add that into the animation. It became all that more interesting to me as accident, visual

treat, and intimation of other forces at work in the narrative."

Pepi explains the main reason why she was motivated to use digital media to such a great extent for a project in which she was trying hard to imitate the real world. She says the digital approach,

released the work from some of the boundaries of reality, such as gravitational pull, and the material limits of form and flexibility. For instance, in the digital realm I could create a shadow puppet made to look like a water-filled jar with elements animating within the fluid, but that would not be possible and effective for me using real-world materials. With digital tools, I also have a much larger range of options in terms of image manipulation. I can coordinate the animation movements exactly as I want them and not have to redo entire sequences until correct, as I would if they were done in stop-motion in front of a camera.

Image from Lorelei Pepi's *Ether*.

Nevertheless, the final results were not entirely satisfying. Among the biggest problems was the complexity of the process, which overloaded the software and slowed down production. She says, "I managed to achieve some very beautiful and promising results, but the path of getting there was pretty arduous. It's a challenging thing to do in After Effects, and it really tests the limits of the program, because you're using very complex math processing. I found that after a few lights, 3D animated layers, animation in 2D, adding a few effects, and so on, it all started to drag so much that I wondered if it was worth it at all."

In the final analysis, Pepi was able to see that her choice of digital media was not a good fit for *Ether* for a number of reasons. She found it cumbersome working with the computer and says the project was so intensive for its CPU that it took "forever and a day" to update and redraw the images. She says, "I really can't think of any other way to do it using this software in particular. I lose my patience and the essence of spontaneity, and this deadens the experiment process for me. I lose interest after a while because I feel like I'm so subservient to the tools instead of it being a more interactive dialogue."

Digitalization Tips

Lorelei Pepi embraces a relatively scientific approach in her experimentation. What this really means is that she is highly organized and methodical—both virtues when it comes to the heavy investment of time and money required of the production process. Her advice to digital animators is:

— Test! Endlessly!

— Change one element at a time to isolate the results so you know what is affecting what.

— Keep a record of your tests so you know what you did.

— Save a new version every time you substantially change an approach. Keep these versions as documents so you can return to them as an information resource.

— Have as much RAM as you can get into the system, a fast co-processor, and an excellent video card.

— Use external drives for file archiving and general storage. Always back up your work. Back it up to two separate external drives if you can.

— And, importantly, begin with a reasonably informed idea about what goal you have, so your choices while utilizing the software will be "your own" as opposed to being randomly influenced by some software designer. It will also help you to get through the tasks of experimenting because you will be aware of the really important parameters.

Applications VII
Playing with Flash

Adobe Flash is relatively simple to learn, and yet it provides many advanced options for experienced users as well. This exercise will get you started.

Objective:

To provide a basic introduction to tweening forms and using layers, employing Adobe Flash.

You will need:

- Adobe Flash
- Computer and related hardware
- If desired, additional software or materials (possibly including a scanner) to create images

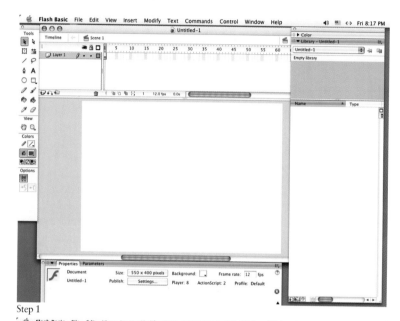

Step 1

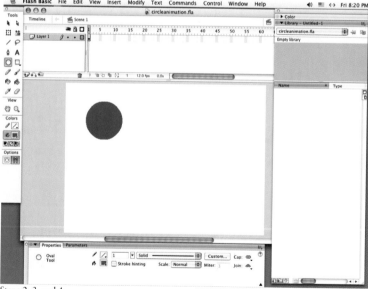

Steps 2, 3, and 4

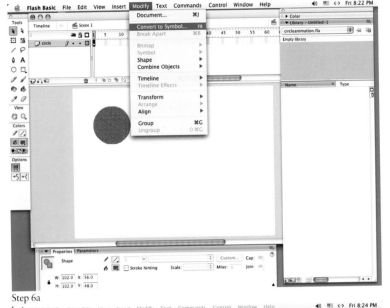

Step 6a

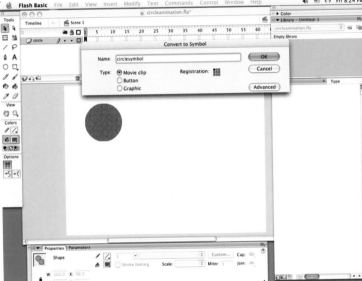

Step 6b

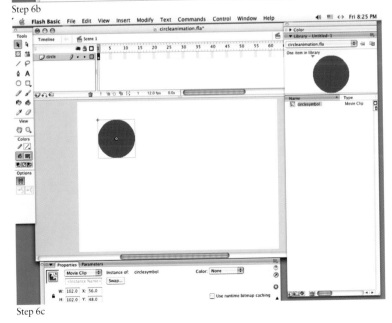

Step 6c

1

Open the Adobe Flash software. Using the drop-down File menu, select New. From the choices provided, open a Flash document. This will reveal a blank "stage" where you will place your images.

2

Acquire an image to place on the stage. There are various ways to do this. You can scan an image into the computer and use it; create an image using the digital tools in Adobe Illustrator or another drawing program; or make an image with Tools in Flash. For this exercise you need only a very simple shape, such as a circle.

3

Using the File drop-down menu, save the image using a descriptive title—in this case, "Circle Animation."

4

If it is not there already, place the image on the stage where you want it to be in the first frame. You are working on Layer 1. You will see its label and the Layer 1 timeline above the stage.

5

Click on the Layer 1 label to highlight it, and type in the name of the object that appears. In this example, it's "circle."

6

Before animating the image, you need to change it into a symbol. To do so, highlight the image with the "select" arrow from the toolbox, then use the Modify drop-down menu to select Convert to Symbol. Give the symbol a descriptive name (in this case, "circle symbol") and save it as a "movie clip." The image will appear in the Flash Library to the side of the screen.

Playing with Flash

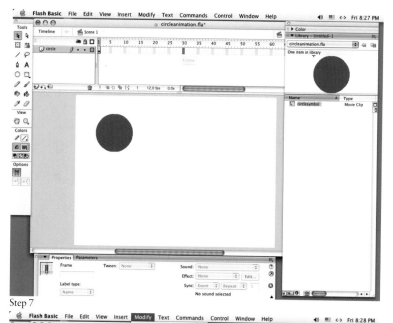
Step 7

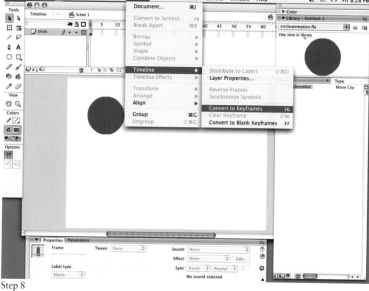
Step 8

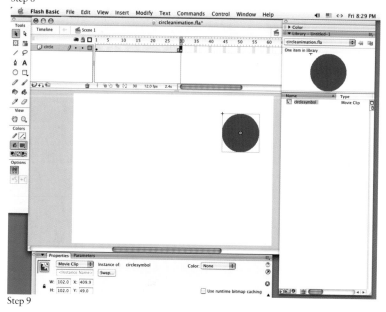
Step 9

7

Now set up the duration of the animated movement. You can use any length, but 30 frames is a good place to start. Using the select arrow, click on frame 30 within Layer 1. It will be highlighted.

8

The frame you selected (frame 30) must be converted into a "key frame." Using the Modify drop-down menu, go to Timeline and select Convert to Key frame.

9

Drag the symbol to where you want it to be on the stage at the end of its animated movement (at frame 30).

10

Now it is time for the in-betweening, which is done automatically through the software. To initiate the process, use the select arrow to click on the timeline of Layer 1 at any point between frames 1 and 30. In this example, frame 15 was selected.

11

Go to the Properties box at the bottom of the page, and under Tween select Motion. The in-betweening will occur. The image will move to a new place on the screen, depending on the frame you clicked on before you tweened. In this example, it will move to the spot designated for frame 15.

12

With the select arrow tool, click on the first frame of layer 1 to move the image back to its start position. To watch your animation, use the Command drop-down menu to select Play. If you want the action to repeat, first select Loop Playback from the Command menu.

13

This is only the first of many steps you can take. You can select a midpoint frame and also make it a key frame. By then dragging the symbol on this frame to a new position, you create a different tweening motion. You can also add additional motions to the end of frame 30 by adding key frames and moving the symbol.

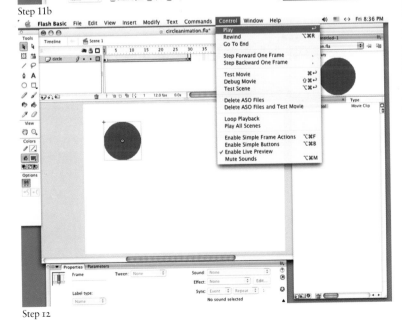

Steps 10 and 11a

Step 11b

Step 12

14

To add a second image, first place it on a new level. To create a new level, click on the Insert Layer icon below the timeline area on the screen. It looks like a piece of paper with a bent corner and a plus sign.

15

If you wish to experiment with metamorphosis, you can use different sizes of images (each one saved as a symbol) on the key frames. In the Property box, select tween Shape, rather than Motion.

16

You can also achieve effects through color and density, making objects change their appearance and fade from view.

Tips and Cautions:

— Try Flash for free by going to the Adobe website and registering for a thirty-day trial period.

— Save your work often.

— Lock individual layers when you are not working with them to avoid accidental movement—the lock is in the timeline area, near the name of the layer.

— There are many tutorials that will further your understanding of Flash, but don't let your imagination be limited by what they tell you to do! Look around the software and try everything, just to see the results you get.

Glossary

Academy leader The numbered countdown strip used at the start of films to help projectionists cue the beginning.

analogue A reproduction that has a physical correspondence to that which it depicts, such as a photographed image of a tree or a varying wavelength corresponding to a given set of sounds.

animatic A filmed storyboard, usually accompanied by some version of the dialogue track, and used to suggest the pacing of the action. Also known as a "leica reel."

animating on ones, twos, etc. Within the medium of film, the number of consecutive frames in which a single piece of artwork appears; at a film speed of 24 fps, animating on ones requires 24 separate images to be created, whereas animating on twos requires only 12, and animating on threes requires 8.

armature The structural support underlying a stop-motion figure, often made of wire or steel.

aspect ratio The shape of a projected image, expressed in a ratio of width to height, as in the "Academy ratio," which is four increments wide for every three increments high, usually expressed as 1.33:1; common widescreen aspect ratios are 1.85:1 and 2.35:1.

axes: x, y, z Directions of movement within space, as in left/right (x axis), up/down (y axis), and near/far (z axis).

bandwidth The amount of digital data that can travel over a network connection within a given amount of time, usually measured in kilobits per second (kbps) or greater units.

bi-packing Placing more than one piece of film together, so that both images can be projected onto a single screen or, more commonly, printed simultaneously onto a third piece of film. This process is often used in the process of compositing.

blue screen (*see* green screen)

cel animation Once the dominant method of industrial animation production, this 2D process involves the use of clear acetate cels that are inked on the front and painted on the back, and then filmed with a rostrum camera. Up to six cels could be layered on a background drawing.

CGI (computer generated imagery) Term commonly used in reference to animated images created using digital media.

color key The process of selecting colors for characters and backgrounds, and indicating them on a visual reference.

compositing Combining multiple images within a single frame; for example, inserting an animated character into a live-action environment. Once achieved through optical printing using mattes, bi-packing, and multiple passes of film images, compositing is now typically a digital process.

conventions Patterns of behavior or types of images that become normalized through repetition; for example, it is conventional for performers to break into song during a musical.

cycle A set of images that are used more than once in a row, such as the series of leg movements used to show a walk cycle or a background that keeps reappearing as a character runs across a setting.

digital A reproduction of an object that consists of mathematical data in the form of 0s and 1s, rather than any kind of physical correspondence; computer data is digital in form, whereas a photograph creates an analogue reproduction.

direct film Working directly on the surface of a filmstrip, without the need for a camera to record images; techniques typically include scratching onto black film, drawing onto clear film, or contact printing (creating a photogram) using unexposed film and a small light source to expose objects laid on top of it.

dope sheet (*see* exposure sheet)

DSL (digital subscriber line) A method of moving data over a phone line that allows for faster transfer of information than normal; generally it is described as "high band" because the bandwidth is increased, allowing for high-speed communication.

exposure sheet A visual record indicating how given images are to be recorded, including various layers, effects that take place during the process, or any other information that would be useful to show how a scene goes together. Also known as a "dope sheet."

extreme An image drawn by an animator to represent an important pose struck by a character; extremes may be linked together by a series of other drawings typically created by an assistant animator and possibly an in-betweener, though software now is often used to "tween" the work.

field size The relative size of an original piece of artwork or the amount of it that is to be captured by the camera, as indicated by a clear "field guide" that is laid over it; a 10-field image covers a larger portion of paper than a 2-field image.

file size Reference to the amount of memory space used to store a given image or animation; generally measured in kilobytes (K), megabytes (MB), or gigabytes (GB).

film stock A photographic material composed of a long strip of clear celluloid. It comes in various gauges, including Super 8mm, 16mm, 35mm, and 70mm. For many years, animated images were typically photographed sequentially onto negative film stock, which would then be used to create prints that were screened using a projector. (*see also* leader)

found footage Films of various sorts (commonly industrial or home movies) that have been found in some manner and repurposed in the context of another film.

frame A single still image, which is combined with a series of other images to create animated imagery; also the name given to the physical area of film stock housing the single image.

frame rate The speed at which images are combined in order to create animated movement; for example, sound film speed is 24 frames per second (fps), while NTSC video runs at 30 fps.

frosted cel An acetate cel that has been textured, so it has enough "tooth" to hold a wide range of media, including colored pencils and watercolors.

full animation Animation created using a high proportion of images for each second of the finished work, emphasis on action over dialogue, and few cycles; for example, the animation on ones created for Disney cel animated features.

gauge The size of a piece of film, as in 35mm gauge, or the thickness of wire used for stop-motion armatures (for example).

genre A category of narrative developed through repetition over time, and recognizable due to conventions in character types, themes, and plot actions. For example, westerns, musicals, and science fiction are all genres of popular culture media.

green screen A backdrop, typically green or blue in color, placed behind a performer or object, which is used for compositing a background into the shot; the desired image replaces all the areas that are green (or blue).

illegal colors Colors that do not reproduce properly within a given medium.

in-betweener An individual hired to create images linking the key or "extreme" poses created by an animator. Computers can be programmed to create in-betweens, but generally without the finesse of a human artist.

incremental movements Component parts of a continuous motion that are captured in sequence to create animation.

ink and paint Refers to the process of using acetate-adhering inks to outline figures on the front of cels, and then painting in colors using acrylic cel paints on the back of the cel. Once a department of animation studios populated primarily by female artists, ink and paint is now completed primarily through the use of 2D software programs.

installation Artwork that is installed in a particular space and designed to become part of that environment, allowing viewers to walk within and/or around it.

key frame Similar to an "extreme" in drawn animation, the term is typically used to describe important poses created within the context of digital production. These images are made by the artist and placed within the timeline, generally to mark the beginning and end of a particular motion.

layers Various levels on which artwork is drawn to facilitate movement of parts of an animated object. In cel animation, layers were limited to about six due to the density of the material, but in the digital realm, layers are virtual and therefore potentially can be unlimited in number.

layout An aspect of pre-production where the logistics of the animation are worked out through drawings: checking that the characters can move through their environment, establishing angles and shot sizes, and preparing other details needed to move into production.

leader Typically, a piece of black, clear, or white stock inserted within a reel of film, and most often attached to the beginning and end so it can be threaded through a projector. A leader is used as the basis for most direct film production (drawing, painting, and otherwise working directly on film).

leica reel (*see* animatic)

limited animation Animation created using a low proportion of images for each second of the finished work (animating on threes and higher). Emphasis is placed on dialogue to carry the story rather than action, and on abundant cycles. Made-for-television series tend to be created using limited animation, in part due to the fact it is

less expensive to create than the full animation typically found in feature-length productions.

line test (*see* pencil test)

lip sync The process of matching lip movements of an animated character to the dialogue it is speaking.

loop A single piece of film that is made continuous by attaching its start to its end. When threaded through a projector, the film loop runs over and over, without stopping.

maquette A three-dimensional, sculptural representation of a character used for planning purposes. It shows the figure in real space to help with perspective drawing and lighting.

matte Mattes are black images created as part of the process of compositing two strips of film onto a third piece. One matte is made to cover the area of each frame of one filmstrip that is to be replaced by images from the second filmstrip. A second matte represents the area of the original frame that is to be retained, and not overprinted by the second images. Thus the two mattes complement each other, covering opposite parts of the frame.

medium Any substance or technology used to create art or other forms of expression. The plural form of the word is "media."

metamorphosis Shifts in form over time.

model sheet A series of drawings of a character, representing it from different angles and in different emotional states, which help animators draw accurately, or stay "on model" over time.

modified base A technique of animation whereby a single image is modified repeatedly under the camera and filmed in incremental poses. It is in contrast to drawn methods in which many images are created individually and placed under a camera or on a scanner, to be captured one by one.

motion blur The blurring effect that occurs naturally in live-action cinematography of moving objects, and which is not apparent in the images of stop-motion figures shot in a series of still frames. Various techniques have been created to compensate for the lack of blur in order to create more realistic-looking animated movement.

motion capture A technique of animation employing a live performer who wears a body suit or other apparatus containing data markers. When the actor moves, the data is captured by a series of cameras and transmitted to a computer to become the basis for animated movement.

motion control camera A camera housed within an apparatus that can be programmed to move in a particular way. It is useful for stop-motion effects animation requiring multiple passes and for the development of complex camera movements through a set.

motion study Influential studies of human, animal, and other movements initiated during the nineteenth century as a means of understanding the dynamics of motion.

multiplane camera A camera set vertically over several panes of glass positioned at a distance from one another. This allows the manipulation of materials on them, such as oil paint, sand, or small objects, and creating the impression of deep space.

narrative Another word for "story," or the underlying structure linking a series of images; works that are not tightly structured around a story are sometimes described as "non-narrative."

NTSC (National Television System Committee) The standard for television and video signals used in the USA, Canada, and various other countries.

open source (OS) This term describes creative practices based on the concept of free sharing so others can build upon and further develop existing work. Open source software provides access to source code, which programmers are encouraged to modify and redistribute.

optical printer A device that includes both a projector and a camera, allowing the printing of images from one piece of film onto another.

optical sound A sound reproduction process involving a modulating line set into a portion of a filmstrip, which is read with light emitted from the projector.

optical toy An animation device, such as a flipbook, thaumatrope, or zoetrope, developed primarily to demonstrate scientific principles related to perception, but which has been absorbed into popular culture. Typically they are drawn or printed onto paper.

PAL (phase-alternating line) The television and video standard in much of Europe, and elsewhere.

PDA (personal digital assistant) A handheld digital organizer that functions as a varied communications device, possibly incorporating cell phone, fax, email, computing, and other functions.

pencil test A filmed test of animated movements, employing pencil drawings. Also known as a "line test."

performance animation The combination of live performance with projections of animated imagery.

personality animation This approach to animation utilizes components of movement (such as squash and stretch, anticipation, and follow through), along with distinctive voice and appearance, to create characters that are uniquely identifiable. For example, the personalities of the seven dwarfs in Disney's *Snow White* (1937) are all fully developed in these ways.

perspective A series of conventional, culturally specific art practices designed to create a sense of space. Linear methods involve drawing objects in relation to each other and using receding lines to suggest deep space, whereas atmospheric perspective relies on color and value to create atmospheric density between the viewer and the object being depicted.

phonemes The basic speech sounds. In combination, they form words underlying a language.

pixel Short for "picture element," it is the smallest component of a digitized image. Each tiny block contains color and brightness information. Collectively, the number of pixels defines the resolution (or sharpness) of an image.

pixilation An animation process employing live actors who are moved through incremental poses and captured frame by frame.

pose to pose animation A two-step process of creating a motion sequence, in which animators first draw only extreme poses, and then draw the images in between them. The second round of drawings may be completed by an assistant animator or in-betweener, whose work is constrained by the extreme poses of the original animator.

rendering The process of completing final animation art. In digital terms, it occurs through calculation of the various mathematical formulae determining the form, movement, angles, and other aspects of various objects. In other contexts, rendering can include tracing images from pencil sketches onto the final animation media (cels, drawing paper, and so on).

rostrum camera An animation camera suspended on a column above a movable platform, allowing the photography of individual frames of artwork.

rotoscoping Patented by Max Fleischer in 1917, this animation process involves filming live-action reference footage and projecting it frame by frame onto animation paper, so it can be traced and modified. The drawn images are then filmed, creating animated imagery that is highly realistic in its movement.

SECAM (Séquential Couleur à Mémoire) A video and broadcasting standard developed and used in France, much of Eastern Europe, and some other countries.

SLR (Single Lens Reflex) camera A so-called "still camera" that allows the photographer to see though the lens of his or her camera using viewfinder mechanisms.

stop-motion Animation techniques requiring frame by frame movement of objects; may include the use of clay, puppets, cutouts, and sand, among other things.

storyboard A visual representation of a project, drawn in a series of boxes that are typically accompanied by written dialogue. Storyboards can range from rough "thumbnails" to professional-looking "presenation boards."

straight ahead animation An approach to animation that involves creating images sequentially, beginning at frame one of a given sequence and progressing to the end. Some processes, such as puppet animation, require a straight-ahead technique.

surface gage A device used to mark the precise distance moved by a stop-motion puppet.

3D Refers to media having the three dimensions of width, height, and depth. Some computer-generated images are referred to as being "3D" because of how they look, though they are in fact created in the two-dimensional space of the flat computer monitor. Stop-motion sets are truly three-dimensional.

timeline The area within software that allows the user to see the various elements of his or her work (visuals, dialogue, score, and so on) lined up according to each frame, in a linear progression.

trace back An animation term for copying part or all of an earlier drawing. For example, if only an arm is moving, all of the rest of the character is traced back.

Further Reading   Notes

tweening The process of animating movement between key frames within a digital context. Software typically does tweening automatically, if desired.

2D Refers to media having the two dimensions of width and height, as in images drawn on paper. Any impression of depth must be created through optical illusion, using the rules of perspective.

universal access The concept of work being accessible to individuals with disabilities, including hearing and visual impairments.

variable speed cinematography Adjusting the rate at which the real-time movements of a living subject are captured—for example, slowing the frame rate of a motion picture camera, or accelerating it as a performer walks through a scene.

video assist A unit that works in conjunction with a camera to display frames of stop-motion animation so that an animator has a sense of how movements on a set are progressing.

visemes A visual (facial image) that corresponds to a particular sound, or phoneme, in a given language.

visual music Equivalents to music in visual form, using color, shape, and motion to suggest musical qualities in painting, animation, or other types of art.

walk cycle A series of body movements that are used over and over, creating a continuous walking sequence for a character.

Albers, Josef. *Interaction of Color*. New Haven: Yale University Press, 2006.

Amidi, Amid. *Cartoon Modern: Style and Design in Fifties Animation*. San Francisco: Chronicle, 2006.

Beiman, Nancy. *Prepare To Board! Creating Story and Characters for Animation Features and Shorts*. Boston: Elsevier Focal Press, 2007.

Bordwell, David, and Kristin Thompson. "Sound in the Cinema," in *Film Art: An Introduction*. New York: McGraw Hill, 1993.

Braun, Marta. *Picturing Time: The Work of Etienne-Jules Marey (1830–1904)*. Chicago: University of Chicago, 1992.

Coe, Brian. *Muybridge & the Chronophotographers*. London: Museum of the Moving Image, 1992.

"Flash Kit." Online at www.flashkit.com.

Furniss, Maureen. *Art in Motion: Animation Aesthetics*. Bloomington: Indiana University Press, 1998.

Goldmark, Daniel. *Tunes for 'Toons: Music and the Hollywood Cartoon*. Berkeley: University of California, 2005.

Griffin, Hedley. *The Animator's Guide to 2D Computer Animation*. Oxford: Focal Press, 2001.

Hashimoto, Alan. *Visual Design Fundamentals: A Digital Approach*. Boston: Charles River Media, 2007.

Hill, Helen. *Recipes for Disaster: A Handcrafted Film Cookbooklet*. New Orleans: Helen Hill, 2001.

Hooks, Ed. *Acting for Animators: A Complete Guide to Performance Animation*. Portsmouth, NH: Heinemann, 2003.

Jouvanceau, Pierre. *The Silhouette Film*. Translated by Clare Kitson. Genova: Le Mani, 2004.

Kunsthalle Düsseldorf. *Daumen kino: The Flip Book Show*. Cologne: Snoeck Verlagsgesellschaft, 2005.

Lemay, Brian. *Layout and Design Made Amazingly Simple*. Oakville, Ont.: Animated Cartoon Factory, 2006.

Lord, Peter, and Brian Sibley. *Creating 3-D Animation: The Aardman Book of Filmmaking*. New York: Harry N. Abrams, 2004.

Moore, Carol-Lynn. *Movement and Making Decisions: The Body-Mind Connection in the Workplace*. New York: Rosen Publishing, 2005.

Newlove, Jean. *Laban for All*. London: Nick Hern Books, 2003.

Peterson, Bryan. *Learning to See Creatively: Design, Color & Composition in Photography*. New York: Amphoto Books, 2003.

Raugust, Karen. *The Animation Business Handbook*. New York: St. Martin's Press, 2004.

Reiniger, Lotte. *Shadow Theatres and Shadow Films*. London: B.T. Batsford, 1970.

Robert-Breslin, Jan. *Making Media: Foundations of Sound and Image Production*. Amsterdam: Focal, 2003.

Russett, Robert, and Cecile Starr. *Experimental Animation: Origins of a New Art*. New York: Da Capo Press, 1988.

Schwartz, Lillian F., with Laurens R. Schwartz. *The Computer Artist's Handbook: Concepts, Techniques, and Applications*. New York: W.W. Norton, 1992.

Scott, Jeffrey. *How to Write for Animation*. Woodstock, NY: Overlook Press, 2002.

Stafford, Barbara Maria, and Frances Terpak. *Devices of Wonder: From the World in a Box to Images on a Screen*. Los Angeles: Getty Research Institute, 2002.

Wellins, Mike. *Storytelling through Animation*. Boston: Charles River Media, 2005.

White, Tony. *Animation from Pencils to Pixels*. Boston: Elsevier Focal Press, 2006.

Williams, Richard. *The Animator's Survival Kit: A Manual of Methods, Principles, and Formulas for Classical, Computer, Games, Stop Motion, and Internet Animators*. London: Faber, 2001.

Winder, Catherine, and Zahra Dowlatabadi. *Producing Animation*. Boston: Elsevier Focal Press, 2001.

Chapter One

1   Some creativity ideas from jpb.com. Online at www.jpb.com.

2   Beiman, Nancy. Email to the author, 3 August 2006. See also Beiman, Nancy. *Prepare To Board! Creating Story and Characters for Animation Features and Shorts*. Boston: Elsevier Focal Press, 2007.

3   Also see Barrier, Michael. *Hollywood Cartoons: American Animation in its Golden Age*. Oxford: Oxford University Press, 1999, 14–15.

4   In many countries, including Canada, the United Kingdom, and the United States, businesses and schools are required to make safety information available.

5   See Association of Moving Image Archivists. "Videotape Preservation Fact Sheets." Online at www.amianet.org/publication/resources/guidelines/videofacts/intro.html.

6   McCloud, Scott. *Understanding Comics*. Northampton, MA: Kitchen Sink, 1993, 51.

7   Engel, Jules. Untitled, in "The United Productions of America: Reminiscing Thirty Years Later," in *ASIFA-Canada*, ca. 1985, 15–17. Edited by William Moritz.

8   Bishko, Leslie. "The Use of Laban Movement Analysis for the Discussion of Computer Animation," October 1991. Unpublished essay, collection of the author.

9   Salm, Lorin. "Character Movement for Animators." Online at www.lorin.info/mvmtwrkshp-anim.html.

10 White, Tony. *The Animator's Workbook*. New York: Watson-Guptill, 1986, 46.

11 White. 136–37.

12 Hayashi, Hiroki. Interview with Geoffrey Tebbetts, in *Animerica* 7:8, 15, 33. Quoted in Drazen, Patrick. *Anime Explosion! The What? Why? & Wow! of Japanese Animation*. Berkeley, CA: Stonebridge, 2003, 22.

13 Drazen, 22.

14 Comet, Michael B. "LipSync—Making Character Speak," 1998. Online at www.comet-cartoons.com/3ddocs/lipsync/lipsync.html .

Chapter Two

1   Griffin, Sean. *Tinker Belles and Evil Queens: The Walt Disney Company from the Inside Out*. New York: New York University, 2000.

2   Carlsson, Sven E. "Introduction to Animation Sound." Online at www.filmsound.org/animation.

3   Descriptions of some of these elements are based on "Robert L. Mott's Nine Components of Sound." Online at www. filmsound.org/articles/ninecomponents/9components.htm.

4   Academy of Motion Picture Arts and Sciences. "Sound and Music: The Power to Enhance the Story." Online at www.oscars.org/teachersguide/sound/activity3.html.

5   Fels, Deborah. Telephone interview with the author, 24 August 2004.

6   Feisner, Edith Anderson. *Colour*. London: Laurence King, 2000, 3.

7   Feisner, 33–34, 37.

8   Arditi, Aries. "Effective Color Combinations," Lighthouse International. Online at www.lighthouse.org/color_contrast.htm. See also Ridpath, Chris, Jutta Treviranus, Patrice L. (Tamar) Weiss. "Testing The Readability Of Web Page Colors." Online at www.aprompt.ca/WebPageColors.html.

9   Feisner, 56–58.

10 Feisner, 38.

11 Baker, Jenny. Email from Megan Brain to the author, 13 January 2004.

Chapter Three

1   Winder, Catherine, and Zahra Dowlatabadi. *Producing Animation*. Boston: Elsevier Focal Press, 2001, 91. Winder and Dowlatabadi describe the role of an animation producer through all aspects of the production of feature films and television series, focusing on 2D and 3D computer-generated work.

See also Raugust, Karen. *The Animation Business Handbook*. New York: St. Martin's Press, 2004. This gives a detailed overview of producing concerns. This chapter draws upon these authors' works, but is necessarily more general in nature because it addresses a broader range of animation practices.

2 Winder and Dowlatabadi, 74.

3 Beiman, 2007.

4 Scott, Jeffrey. *How to Write for Animation*. Woodstock, NY: Overlook, 2002, 44.

5 Anonymous. "Story Mood Chart," in *Animation Journal* (Spring 1992), 88–91.

6 Peck, Nick. "Make Pictures Come to Life with Sound," Sound by Design. Online at www.digitalprosound.com/ 2001/03_mar/features/sound_design/sound_design1. htm. Much of the information in this section was gathered from Peck's article.

7 Tips for rehearsing with performers were developed in part with information from "Tales from Dutch Formosa." Radio Taiwan International. Online at www.cbs.org.tw/ english/TDF/art2-7.asp.

8 Beiman, Nancy. Email to the author, 6 August 2006.

9 Deitch, Gene. "How to Succeed in Animation," Animation World Network. Online at genedeitch.awn.com.

10 Beiman, Nancy. Email to the author, 6 August 2006.

11 Thompson, Frank. *Tim Burton's Nightmare Before Christmas*. New York: Hyperion, 1993, 93.

12 Anonymous. "Storyboarding the Simpsons Way." Online at www.animationmeat.com .

13 Winder and Dowlatabadi, 219.

14 Winder and Dowlatabadi, 105.

15 Winder and Dowlatabadi, 18.

16 Raugust, 47.

17 Creative Commons. Online at creativecommons.org.

18 This list is based in part on the supplies recommended at Anthony Scott, StopMotionAnimation.com. Online at StopMotionAnimation.com .

19 Winder and Dowlatabadi, 165–74.

20 Winder and Dowlatabadi, 167.

Chapter Four

1 For information on scene prioritization see Beiman, Nancy. "A-B-Sequence," in *Prepare To Board! Creating Story and Characters for Animation Features and Shorts*. Boston: Elsevier Focal Press, 2007.

2 Taylor, Richard. *The Encyclopedia of Animation Techniques*. Philadelphia: Running Press, 1996, 57.

3 Harris, Tom. "How Web Animation Works," How Stuff Works. Online at computer.howstuffworks.com /web-animation.htm.

4 Compiled from Frasier, Royal. "Conservation on the Web: Making GIFs Smaller," GIF Animation on the WWW. Online at members.aol.com/royalef/ conserva.htm; and Suzanne Stephens, "GIF Animation Tips," Web Page Design for Designers. Online at www.wpdfd.com/wpdanim2.htm.

5 For a good overview of Web applications, see Harris, Tom.

6 Lord, Peter, and Brian Sibley. *Creating 3-D Animation: The Aardman Book of Filmmaking*. New York: Harry N. Abrams, 1998, 68.

7 Lord and Sibley, 90.

8 Lord and Sibley, 127.

9 Lord, in Lord and Sibley, 144.

10 Lord, in Lord and Sibley, 141.

11 Winder, Catherine, and Zahra Dowlatabadi. "Producing Animation: The 3D CGI Production Process," in *Animation World Magazine* (4 January 2002). Online at mag.awn.com/index.php?article_no=1005.

12 Winder and Dowlatabadi.

13 For a map of video regions, see the "Global Standard Video Map," Ricardo's Geo-Orbit Quick-Look. Online at www.geo-orbit.org/sizepgs/ ntscp.html#anchor140633.

Chapter Five

1 King, Constance. *Metal Toys & Automata*. Secaucus, NJ: Chartwell, 1989, 14.

2 Jurkowski, Henryk. *A History of European Puppetry: From its Origins to the End of the 19th Century*. Coll. ed. Penny Francis. Lewiston, NY: Edwin Mellon Press, 1996, 223.

3 Jurkowski, 293.

4 Hillier, Mary. *Automata & Mechanical Toys*. London: Jupiter Books, 1976, 20, 28.

5 King, 33–34.

6 Hillier, 94.

7 Ballay, Ute. "Swiss Automata," in *Antiques & Collecting*, 98 (October 1993), 42–46; 44.

8 Foley, Dan. *Toys Through the Ages*. Philadelphia: Chilton Books, 1962, 53.

9 King, 20.

10 King, 19.

11 Tempest, Jack. "Princely Toys," in *Antiques & Collecting*, 100 (June 1995), 22–24. Hillier, 42. See also Kurokawa, Kisho. *Philosophy of Symbiosis*, chapter 11 summary. Online at www.kisho.co.jp/page.php?/308.

12 Mottram, Stephen. "Stephen Mottram on Puppetry." Unpublished essay, collection of the author.

13 Coe, Brian. *Muybridge & the Chronophotographers*. London: Museum of the Moving Image, 1992, 12.

14 Rossell, Deac. *Living Pictures: The Origins of the Movies*. New York: State University of New York, 1998, 31.

15 Coe, 13. Stanford was motivated by his desire to create better training methods for horse racing. See also Rossell, 31–32.

16 Musser, Charles. *The Emergence of Cinema: The American Screen to 1907*. Berkeley: University of California, 1994, 48.

17 Coe, 20.

18 Coe, 22.

19 Braun, Marta. *Picturing Time: The Work of Etienne-Jules Marey (1830–1904)*. Chicago: University of Chicago, 1992, 238–53.

20 Braun, 34–36. Various harnesses were developed even after Marey was able to create sequential photography. In 1887, for example, an apparatus was created to record oscillations of the vertebral column, shoulder, and hip. Braun, 143. In 1893, he created a device for measuring movements of the jaw, akin to facial capture. Braun, 158, 160.

21 Braun, 26–27.

22 Braun, 28.

23 Braun, 28.

24 Braun, 41.

25 Coe, 26. For a detailed discussion of the photographic gun, see Braun, 57–63.

26 Coe, 27.

27 Anonymous. "Pioneers of Early Cinema: 2." Braun, 187–90.

28 Rossell, 36.

29 Braun, 70.

30 The Phonoscope was patented on 3 March 1892. Coe, 29, 55–56. See also Touler, Emmanuelle. *Birth of the Motion Picture*. Translated by Susan Emanuel. New York: Harry N. Abrams, 1995, 28.

31 Braun, 176.

32 Stripping film had been developed by Eastman in the United States in 1884. Braun, 147. For a discussion of Marey's early motion picture film camera, see Braun, 150–70.

33 Braun, xix.

34 Damonte, Devon. "Rolling Man," Devonimation. Online at www.devonimation.com/rollingmanpage.html.

35 Griffin, George. "Cartoon, Anti-Cartoon," in *The American Animated Cartoon: A Critical Anthology*. Edited by Gerald Peary and Danny Peary. New York: E.P. Dutton, 1980, 261–68; 267.

36 In 1655, Huggens discovered a new way of grinding lenses that led to the development of a powerful telescope; he became the first person to see the rings of Saturn and at least one of its moons, plus details on the surface of Mars. Lamber, M. Lindsay. "In Praise of Christiaan Huygens," in *The Magic Lantern Society Newsletter* 53 (June 1998), 1–2; 2.

37 Musser, 17.

38 Musser, 32.

39 Magic Lantern Society website. Online at www.magiclantern.org.uk.

40 Rossell, 16–17.

41 The 3-foot- (1-meter-) plus panorama slide is in the collection of the Cinémathèque Française. See also Rossell, 15.

42 Musser, 43.

43 Rossell, 24.

44 Musser, 43.

45 Musser, 43.

46 Rossell, 107.

47 Newport, Raymond. "The Motion Picture Experiments of John Arthur Roebuck Rudge," in *The Optical Magic Lantern Journal* 8:2 (October 1997), 1–3.

48 Robinson describes the system as using racks, but the images were actually placed into circular disk forms. Robinson, "Rudge and Friese-Greene's Lantern Experiments."

49 Leskosky, Richard. "Two-state Animation: The Thaumatrope and its Spin-offs," in *Animation Journal* 2:1 (Fall 1993), 26–27.

50 Leskosky, 24.

51 Baker, Cozy. "Kaleidoscope Types." Online at www.brewstersociety.com/types.html.

52 Baker.

53 Beyer, Tim. "FAQ about Kaleidoscopes, or 'Ask the ScopeMaster!' by Tim Beyer," Kaleidoscopes of America. Online at www.kaleido.com/faqs.htm.

54 Chanan, Michael. *The Dream that Kicks: The Prehistory and Early Years of Cinema in Britain*. 1980. London, Routledge, 1996, 60–61.

55 Dobler's Austrian patent is dated 23 January 1847. Rossell. Email to the author, 16 December 2002.

56 Rossell. Email to the author, 16 December 2002.

57 Braun, 141.

58 See also "Praxinoscope/Praxinoscope Théatre." Bill Douglas Centre for the History of Cinema and Popular Culture, Exhibitions and Collections. Online at www.ex.ac.uk/bill.douglas/collection/optical/ ambridge.html.

59 Griffin, George, Victor Faccinto, Al Jarnow, Kathy Rose, and Anita Thacher. *Frames: A Selection of Drawings and Statements by Independent American Animators*. New York: Capital City Press, 1978.

60 Chimovitz, Melissa. "Declaration Of Independents: Independent Animation is Alive and Well in New York," in *Animation World Magazine* 3:2 (May 1998). Online at www. awn.com/mag/issue3.2/3.2pages/ 3.2chimovitznyc.html.

61 Griffin. From Philippon, Ann C. "An Interview With George Griffin," in *Animation World Magazine* 1:12 (March 1997). Online at www.awn.com/mag/ issue1.12/articles/philippon1.12.html.

62 Griffin. Email to the author, 5 July 2005.

63 Griffin. From Philippon.

64 Griffin. Email to the author, 7 July 2005. Griffin writes, "Metropolis Graphics began in 1971 as a partnership of four people (two documentary filmmakers, photographer and I) who knew each other at NYU (I was just hanging out there); those individuals were Gary Wright, Fred Aronow, and Rhetta Barron, my first wife. All three were involved in producing my first cartoon, *One Man's Laundry* (which Aronow wrote and co-directed). We called it Metropolis Photoplays as a kind of archaic hyperbole. By 1973, the other three had split off and by 1976, as I began publishing flipbooks in addition to film, I changed the name to Metropolis Graphics. Metropolis Graphics was finally incorporated (as a Limited Liability Company) in 1995."

65 Griffin. Emails to the author, 28 June 2005, 5 July 2005. Griffin explains, "I contracted with Noyes & Laybourne to produce segments for a children's series for HBO, and later directed and animated a spot for Vicks cough syrup."
66 Griffin. "Cartoon, Anti-Cartoon," 266.
67 Griffin. Email to the author, 23 September 2005.
68 Griffin. "Cartoon, Anti-Cartoon," 267.
69 Griffin. Email to the author, 23 September 2005.
70 Griffin. Email to the author, 23 September 2005.
71 Griffin. Email to the author, 23 September 2005.
72 Griffin. "Cartoon, Anti-Cartoon," 267.
73 Griffin. Email to the author, 23 September 2005.

Chapter Six

1 The Miniature Society of Florida. "What is." Online at www.miniature-art.com/whatis.html.
2 "History of Batik," Princess Mirah Design. Online at www.balifab.com/MAIN%20PGS/historybatik.html.
3 See, for example, "Man Ray (Emmanuel Rudnitzky), Rayograph, 1922." The Museum of Modern Art, 2002. Online at momawas.moma.org/collection/depts/photography/blowups/photo_005.html.
4 Hilton, Stuart. "Avoiding Animation." Lecture, City Lights Theater, Savannah, 2000. A tape of the lecture was provided courtesy of Jeremy Moorshead, Savannah College of Art and Design.
5 Lye, Len. "Why I Scratch, or How I got to Particles," in Figures of Motion: Len Lye/Selected Writings. Edited by Wystan Curnow and Roger Horrocks. Auckland: Auckland University Press, 1984, 95.
6 Jones, Henry. From Igliori, Paola. "Henry Jones," in American Magus: Harry Smith. Edited by Paula Igliori. New York: Inanout Press, 1996, 205–14; 213.
7 Smith, Harry. From Cohen, John. "A Rare Interview with Harry Smith," 1968, in American Magus: Harry Smith, 126–44; 130.
8 "Len Lye 18 ans plus tard (Len Lye 18 Years Later)," in ASIFA-Canada 11:3 (December 1983).
9 Lye. "Why I Scratch, or How I got to Particles," 95.
10 Lye. "Gene-Deep Myth," in Figures of Motion, 91.
11 McLaren, Norman. "The 'Lines' Films (1960–1962) (Vertical and Horizontal)," in Norman McLaren on the Creative Process. Edited by Donald McWilliams. Montreal: National Film Board of Canada, 1991, 74–78; 74. A variety of other materials were tried, but only the stainless-steel rules provided a rigid enough straight edge.
12 McLaren. "Mosaic (1965)," in Norman McLaren on the Creative Process, 79–80; 80.
13 McLaren, "Blinkity Blank (1955)," in Norman McLaren on the Creative Process, 88–90; 88.
14 McLaren, "Blinkity Blank (1955)," 89.
15 Woloshen, Steven. From Robinson, Chris. "Steven Woloshen's Fun with Science," in Ottawa 2002 International Animation Festival Reader. Ottawa: OIAF, 1992, n.p.
16 Woloshen. Email to the author, 7 August 2003.
17 Woloshen. "Mission Statement." Email to the author, 25 January 2003.
18 See also "Caroline Leaf," National Film Board of Canada. Online at www.nfb.ca/e/highlights/caroline_leaf.html.
19 Leaf. From Therrien, Denise. "Two Sisters,"in Perforations (April 1991). Reprinted in Pilling, Jayne. Women and Animation: A Compendium. London: British Film Institute, 1992, 47.
20 The proposal for The Albatross explains that "the animation techniques used to bring this alive are a development and extension of those used in Paul Bush's award-winning film His Comedy." Bush, Paul. "The Albatross," proposal. Courtesy of the artist.
21 Bush worked on a slightly larger surface to create Still Life with Small Cup, as images were blown up to 35mm/8 perforation film (sometimes known as VistaVision); another difference is that the film is monochromatic, so he did not have to use the same

range of techniques (to achieve varied colors) as in his other two direct films. Bush has created other direct projects. He made a direct film commercial influenced by "Blinkity Blank, Harry Smith, some of Len Lye and a bit of Paul Bush." He worked on the commercial with Bärbel Neubauer and Lucy Lee. It was produced by the London-based Picasso Pictures. He also developed a 4-minute film on 70/15 (IMAX) format for a London Cinema but "only got half the budget and the film was never made. Two test loops were scratched and projected at a number of shows including in London and LA. It looked pretty good and it was a shame to abandon the project." Bush. Email to the author, 3 February 2003. See also www.paulbushfilms.com.
22 Bush. Email to the author, 28 July 2003.
23 See also Street, Rita. "Rose Bond: An Animator's Profile," in Animation World Magazine 1:2. Online at www.awn.com/mag/issue1.2/articles1.2/streetbond1.2.html. For clips see www.rosebond.net.
24 Celtic Trilogy Intro (1997), Rose Bond Moving Pictures.
25 Bond, Rose. Email to the author, 5 August 2003.
26 Uman, Naomi. Email to the author, 24 July 2003.
27 Recoder, Luis. Email to the author, 24 July 2003. References to Recoder come from this email or one received 1 August 2003.
28 Recoder's films are available at recoderr@aol.com.
29 Tscherkassky, Peter. "How and Why? A Few Comments Concerning the Production Techniques Employed for the CinemaScope Trilogy." Online at www.tscherkassky.at. Quotations come from this source unless otherwise stated. Thanks to Eve Heller for her assistance in my writing on Tscherkassky.
30 See also Horwath, Alexandar. "Singing in the Rain. Supercinematography by Peter Tscherkassky," in Peter Tscherkassky (German/English). Edited by A. Horwath and M. Loebenstein. Vienna: Filmmuseum-Synema Publikationen, 2005.

Chapter Seven

1 For examples of Brakhage's work see www.fredcamper.com/Film/BrakhageS.html.
2 Camper, Fred. "About the Films," in By Brakhage: An Anthology. Criterion Collection DVD, 2003.
3 Brakhage, Stan. "Metaphors on Vision," in Film Culture 30 (Fall 1963).
4 Ascension is printed with a copyright date of 2001, but Brakhage's wife, Marilyn Brakhage, told Fred Camper the film was completed in 2002. Camper. Email to the author, 6 August 2003.
5 Camper. Email to the author, 2 August 2003.
6 Reeves, Jennifer. "Argument for the Immediate Sensuous: Notes on Stately Mansions Did Decree and Coupling," in Chicago Review 47-4/48-1 (Winter 2001/Spring 2002), 193–98.
7 Reeves, 194–95.
8 Reeves. "16mm Films by Jennifer Reeves" description sheet. Courtesy of the artist. Reeves explains that her film was named after a condition, the fear of blushing, known as "erythrophobia."
9 Fleisch, Thorsten. "Notes on Blutrausch—Bloodlust." Courtesy of the artist. See also www.fleischfilm.com.
10 Fleisch. Email to the author, 29 January 2003.
11 Fleisch. "Notes on Blutrausch—Bloodlust."
12 Fleisch. Email to the author, 3 February 2003.
13 Gibson, Sandra. Emails to the author, 7 May 2004, 11 August 2006.
14 Kuchar, Mike. Donna Cameron at Work. Video distributed by the Museum of Modern Art, Circulating Film and Video Library, New York.
15 Cameron, Donna. "Fine Paper Emulsion Painting as Film Object Image: Cinematic Paper Emulsion," 1989; revised 2002. Courtesy of the artist.
16 Cameron. Email to the author, 6 August 2003.
17 Cameron defines filtered pigment wash: "The pigment is pressed through sieves above the clear leader, together with minuscule paper pulp, and liquid (water

or oil) is simultaneously poured over it. This leaves an interesting impression of the moving liquid as it reaches the film through the sieve and particles of color and paper. The heavier particles stick in place, gravity claims the lighter, less viscous fluid and this leaves rivulet imprints as it makes its passage down, toward the earth." Email to the author, 7 August 2003.
18 Cameron. "Fine Paper Emulsion Painting as Film Object Image."
19 Cameron. "Narrative Resume." Courtesy of the artist.
20 Cameron, "Fine Paper Emulsion Painting as Film Object Image."
21 McLaren, Norman. "Technical Notes on the Card Method of Optical Animated Sound"; "Handmade Sound Track for Beginners." Produced at the National Film Board of Canada, 1969; revised 1984.
22 McLaren. "Handmade Sound Track for Beginners," 2.
23 van Cuijlenborg, Oerd. Emails to the author, 1 March 2003, 3 August 2003.
24 Reeves also counts Harry Smith as a significant influence. Reeves, Richard. Email to the author, 3 April 2003.
25 Reeves. Email to the author, 5 April 2003.
26 Reeves. Email to the author, 3 April 2003.
27 Reeves. "Information on Selected Animated Films Produced/Directed and Animated by Richard R. Reeves." Courtesy of the artist.
28 Reeves. "Line Sound Dream." Courtesy of the artist.
29 Reeves. Linear Dreams publicity sheet. Courtesy of the artist.
30 Pithers, Julie. "The Hometown Screening May 13–16, The Garry Theatre and The Quickdraw Animation Society," FFWD Weekly. Online at www.greatwest.ca/ffwd/Issues/1999/0513/cover.html.
31 Reeves. "Information on Selected Animated Films."
32 Pithers. "The Hometown Screening."
33 Povey, Thad. "The Scratch Film Junkies: Who We Are and What We Do," ca. 2003. Courtesy of the artist.
34 Povey. Email to the author, 14 August 2006. For participating members see www.thadpovey.com/sfj_index.html.
35 Povey. From Nelson, Peggy. "Message-in-a-bottle Filmmaking: An Interview with Thad Povey," in Otherzine (Spring 2001). Online at www.othercinema.com/otherzine/ozissue2/povey.html.
36 As a tribute, Jay Rosenblatt organized a collection of work, "Underground Zero," and invited Povey and other filmmakers to contribute to it. Povey. Email to the author, 7 July 2003.
37 Group members Colleen Silva and Danielle Booth contributed to Drink from the River.
38 Damonte, Devon. Email to the author, 26 July 2003. Quotations come from this source unless otherwise stated.
39 More specifically, "a quilting bee for eccentric filmmakers." Hardwater, Coco. "Direct Graphics Motion—The Films of Devon Damonte," MoCC/ Museu do chiado "Intermittent" exhibit. Courtesy of the artist. See also www. devonimation.com/Crackpot CraftersDescrip.html.
40 "A Barrel Full of Paul Klee." Online at www.devonimation.com/barrelkleepage.html. For information on Damonte's films, see Films by Devon Damonte. Online at www.devonimation.com.
41 Damonte. "Ironing on Film." Correspondence with the author, 22 February 2003.
42 Frederick, T.L. In Helen Hill. Recipes for Disaster: A Handcrafted Film Cookbooklet. New Orleans: Helen Hill, 2001, 69.
43 Carpenter, Maïa Cybelle. In Hill, Recipes for Disaster, 89.
44 Direct animators Marilyn Cherenko, Jose Luis Sistiaga, and Vincenzo Gioanola also participated in the project.
45 Segal, Steve. Email to the author, 8 August 2003.
46 Segal. Email to the author, 11 August 2003.
47 These contributions came from Heather Harkins, Lisa Morse, Richard Reeves, Christine Panushka, Devon Damonte, Rock Ross, Kevin D.A. Kurynik, Carol

Beecher, Jen Proctor, and Luke Jaeger. In Hill, *Recipes for Disaster*.
48 Moritz, William. Email to the author, 5 August 2003.

Chapter Eight

1   Pilling, Jayne. *2D and Beyond*. Crans-Près-Céligny, Switzerland: Rotovision, 2001, 28.
2   Pummell, Simon. Quoted in Pilling, 32.
3   Originally, Pummell wanted to depict the twelve stations of the Cross, but yielded to the suggestion of his producer, Keith Griffiths, that he begin with this first work. See also Pilling, 28–29.
4   Wang Shuibo. Email to the author, 26 April 2004.
5   Wang. Telephone interview with the author, 20 April 2004. References to Wang come from this interview unless otherwise stated.
6   Wang based the image of Mao on the famous one of America's Uncle Sam, as well as similar World War II images from both England and Russia.
7   *The Talking Eggs* was created for the W-GBH television series "Long Ago and Far Away."
8   Sporn, Michael. Email to the author, 19 March 2004. References to Sporn come from this email and a follow-up message sent in March 2004 unless otherwise stated.
9   Sporn. Voice-over commentary. *Whitewash* DVD.
10 A trace back is a term for copying part or all of an earlier drawing. If only an arm is moving all of the rest of the character is traced back.
11 Jürgens, Jo. "Frédéric Back: The Man Who Plants Hope," in *The Art of Animation* 1:1 (Spring 1994), 26.
12 "Creation of Milch: A Technical Overview," courtesy of Igor Kovalyov.
13 In 1997, Bevan Baker and partner Ken Anderson established Red Kite Productions, a studio in Scotland known for producing animation that uses a broad range of techniques.
14 Bevan Baker, Rachel. Email to the author, 19 April 2004.
15 Findlay, Moma. "Rachel Bevan Baker: Animator," Netribution Film Network, 2001. Online at www.netribution.co.uk/features/interviews/2001/rachel_bevan_baker/1.html.
16 Bevan Baker. Email to the author, 19 April 2004.
17 JJSP co-created "Captain Linger" with Cartoon Network writer Stuart Hill, and also produced the series with J.J. Sedelmaier directing. JJSP developed "Harvey Birdman—Attorney at Law" with creators Michael Ouweleen and Erik Ricter.
18 Sedelmaier, J.J. Telephone interview with the author, 13 April 2004. References to Sedelmaier come from this interview unless otherwise stated.
19 Sedelmaier. Email to the author, 29 June 2004.
20 Sedelmaier. Email to the author, 12 April 2004.
21 Smith Moorshead, Debra. Email to the author, 30 April 2004.
22 Plympton, Bill. Email to the author, 12 April 2004.
23 Segall, Mark. "Plympton's Metamorphoses," in *Animation World Magazine* 1:3. Online at www.awn.com/mag/ issue1.3/articles/segall.3.html.
24 Ehrlich, David. Email to the author, 21 March 2004. References to Ehrlich come from this email unless otherwise stated.
25 McIlleron, Anne. Email to the author, 8 June 2004.
26 Moins, Philippe. "William Kentridge: Quite the Opposite of Cartoons," in *Animation World Magazine* 3:7. Translated by William Mortiz. Online at www.awn.com/mag/issue3.7/3.7pages/3.7 moinskentridge.html.
27 Moins.
28 McIlleron. Email to the author, 8 June 2004.
29 Greg Kucera Gallery. "William Kentridge." Online at www.gregkucera.com/kentridge.htm.
30 Greg Kucera Gallery.
31 Iziko: South African National Gallery. "Guide to the Exhibition." Online at www.museums.org.za/sang/exhib/kentridge/projects/exhibition.

32 Dudok de Wit, Michael. Email to the author, 6 July 2004. References to Dudok de Wit, including quotations from him, come from this email and a series of other emails between 6 July and 12 July 2004.
33 They decided to use widescreen because they anticipated the conversion of British television sets to a widescreen format, but, according to Dudok de Wit, "the film has so far not been transmitted on British television."
34 *Chasse papillon* translates literally as "Hunt butterfly," and Vaucher writes that its "implicit meaning is 'The Butterfly Hunt.'" He decided on *The Song-Catcher* for the English title because he had been thinking of making a series of films in which music would be a character of sorts, and which would be called the "song catchers." Vaucher, Philippe. Email to the author, 6 March 2006.
35 Vaucher. Email to the author, 20 April 2004. References to Vaucher come from this email unless otherwise stated.
36 McLaren, Norman. "Technical Notes on La-Haut sure ces montagnes (1945) in the folksong series 'Chants Populaires,' No. 6 Black and White," 1945. Distributed by the National Film Board of Canada.

Chapter Nine

1   Bendazzi, Giannalberto. *Cartoons: One Hundred Years of Cinema Animation*. Bloomington: Indiana University Press, 1994, 403.
2   See also Kang, Helen. "Shui Mo Dong Hua: The History and Development of Brush Painting Animation," in *Animation Journal* 14 (2006).
3   Alkabetz, Gil. Email to the author, 26 April 2004. References to Alkabetz come from this email.
4   Dudok de Wit, Michael. "Notes," sent to the author 6 July 2004.
5   Hobbs explains that she "began with editions of artist's books and then started making them in the flipbook and Jacob's ladder model; animation was very much the logical next step for me. The films are made under the name Spellbound Animations." Hobbs, Elizabeth. Email to the author, 23 April 2004. See also www.spellboundanimations.co.uk.
6   Hobbs. Email to the author, 18 July 2006.
7   Gardner, Iain. Email to the author, 13 April 2004. References to Gardner come from this email and follow-up emails on 14 April and 23 April 2004 unless otherwise stated. The Glasgow Boys were young artists who challenged established traditions of art in Scotland during the late nineteenth century.
8   Gardner describes the technique: "Bi-packing is a process that allows for material from two or more sources to be printed onto a single piece of film in a seamless way. It involves the use of high-contrast film, developed as both positive and negative prints, which creates two opposing black mattes. The positive print of the high-contrast film is sandwiched next to the final unexposed film in the mechanism of the camera. The black mattes block out a portion of each frame during exposure. After the initial pass of the art is made, the film is rewound and another image is used under the camera, accompanied by the negative matte—which blocks out the opposite area of the frame. The final result is a full frame of image that has been captured in two (or more) separate passes, each time exposing a different part of the frame." Gardner. Email to the author, 6 April 2007.
9   *Akbar's Cheetah* can be viewed on the FilmFour website, at www.channel4.com/film/reviews/film.jsp?id=111108.
10 Gardner also used these inks in *Noah's List*, his first film at the Royal College of Art; he had received a free supply from the company. As a secondary choice, he depends on Dr. Ph. Martin's inks, which he feels are comparable in terms of texture and mixing quality.

11 Gardner notes that he had first seen china markers applied on cels by Richard Williams to give the Brigands, the characters in *The Thief and the Cobbler*, "a rough shimmer reflecting their vagabond existence."
12 Gros, Marie. "One-On-One With Alexander Petrov." Online at www.oldmansea.com/director/petrov.htm.
13 Carty, Alyson, and Chris Robinson. "The Old Man and The Sea: Hands Above The Rest?" in *Animation World Magazine* 4:12 (March 2000). Online at www.awn.com/mag/issue4.12/4.12pages/robinsonoldman.php3.
14 Chartrand, Martine. Telephone interview with the author, 16 April 2004.
15 Tilby, Wendy. Email to the author, 17 March, 2004. References to Tilby come from this email and others from 18 March and 27 March 2004 unless otherwise stated. See also Kenyon, Heather. "Animating Under the Camera," in *Animation World Magazine* 3:2. Online at www. awn.com/mag/issue3.2/3.2pages/3.2student.html.
16 At the time of writing, Tilby and Forbis's current project, *Wild Life*, combined "real" painted elements (mostly in gouache) with characters animated in Flash and then rendered using Photoshop.
17 Walley has donated his rig to the Royal College of Art, London.
18 Walley, Clive. Email to the author, 1 July 2004. References to Walley come from this email and others from 4 July, 8 July and 9 July 2004.

Chapter Ten

1   Annecy International Animation Festival, *Captured in Drifting Sand: Gisèle and Nag Ansorge*. La Roche-sur-Foron: Chevallier Imprimeurs, 1995, 35.
2   Annecy International Animation Festival, *Captured in Drifting Sand*, 26.
3   Leaf, Caroline. Quoted in Kenyon, Heather. "Animating Under the Camera," in *Animation World Magazine* 3:2 (May 1998). Online at www.awn.com/mag/issue3.2/3.2pages/3.2student.html.
4   Anonymous. "Buzz Box," The Kitchen. Online at www.thekitchen.org/MovieCatalog/Titles/BuzzBox.html.
5   David Daniels's commercial work can be seen at the website of Bent Image Lab, where he works: www.bentimagelab.com.
6   Gratz, Joan. "Artist Statement." Courtesy of the artist.
7   The Wan brothers (Laiming, Guchan, Chaochen, and Dihuan) used drawing to create the first animated short in China, *Uproar in an Art Studio* in 1926; and in 1941 two of them, Wan Laiming and Wan Guchan, completed the Shanghai Animation Studio's first feature-length animation, *Princess with an Iron Fan*.
8   Bird, Daniel. "Only the Images: A Profile of the Late Jan Lenica," in *Kinoeye* 1:6 (12 November 2001). Online at www.kinoeye.org/01/06/bird06.php.
9   Bendazzi, Giannalberto. *Cartoons: One Hundred Years of Cinema Animation*. Bloomington: Indiana University Press, 1994, 33.
10 Moritz, William. "Some Critical Perspectives on Lotte Reiniger," *Animation Journal* 5:1 (Fall 1996), 40–51.
11 Jouvanceau, Pierre. *The Silhouette Film*. Translated by Clare Kitson. Genova: Le Mani, 2004, 101.
12 Jouvanceau, 101.
13 Jouvanceau, 148.
14 Mouris, Frank. Email to the author, 28 July 2006. Quotations come from this email unless otherwise stated.
15 Kitson, Clare. *Yuri Norstein and Tale of Tales: An Animator's Journey*. Bloomington: Indiana University Press, 2005, 70.
16 Nomura, Tasutoshi. "How to Animate the Norstein Way," 1996. Translated by Leah Hertz.
17 Nomura. "How to Animate the Norstein Way."

18 Asano, Yuko. "How to Animate the Norstein Way," 1996. Translated by Leah Hertz.

19 Kitson, 64. Another significant contributor to *Tale of Tales* was cameraman Alexander Zhokovsky.

20 Kitson, 67.

21 Davies, Jon. "Action, Animation, Archival Abyss: *Fast Film* (Virgil Widrich, 2003)," in *Animation Journal* 14 (2006).

22 Unless otherwise stated, information on *Fast Film* is from www.widrichfilm.com/fastfilm/main_en.html.

23 Wehn, Karin. "The Renaissance of the Animated Short on the World Wide Web," in *Animation Journal* 13 (2005), 4–27.

24 Fleay, Lindsay. The Magic Portal. Online at www.rakrent.com/mp/mp.htm. References to Fleay come from this source unless otherwise stated.

25 Sibley, Brian, in Peter Lord and Brian Sibley. *Creating 3-D Animation: The Aardman Book of Filmmaking.* New York: Harry N. Abrams, 1998, 34.

26 "Plastazote could also be used for the core of the body, which needs to be hard enough to be drilled for fixing the puppet's limbs to it." Lord and Sibley, 96.

27 Elliot, Adam Benjamin. From Sellers, Simon. "Adam Elliot: Urban Eccentric," Sleepybrain. Online at www.sleepybrain.net/adam-elliot. References to Elliot come from this interview unless otherwise stated.

28 Elliot. Email to the author, 3 July 2006.

29 Wilson, Owen. "Adam Elliot," *Enough Rope with Andrew Denton*, online at www.abc.net.au/tenoughrope/transcripts/s1153948.htm.

30 Elliot. Email to the author, 2 October 2005.

31 Charles daCosta's comments are from a series of interviews conducted by the author via email, primarily during August, September, and October 1995.

32 See www.jacobsonchemicals.co.uk. The paints were not named, but were labeled "S.O."

Chapter Eleven

1 Sibley, Brian, in Peter Lord and Brian Sibley. *Creating 3-D Animation: The Aardman Book of Filmmaking.* New York: Harry N. Abrams, 1998, 34.

2 Kawamoto, Kihachiro. In Sibley, 34.

3 Tyrlová was the wife of Karel Dodal, creator of *Tajemst ví lucerny* (*The Lantern's Secret*, 1935), the first puppet film made in Czechoslovakia.

4 Bendazzi, 165.

5 "The Brothers Quay: Biography," Zeitgeist Films. Online at www.zeitgeistfilms.com/directors/tbrothers.

6 Anonymous. "The Legend of the Sky Kingdom." Press release sent to the author by Trish Mbanga, 23 April 2003.

7 Anonymous. "The Miracle Maker: Making the Film—Production." Online at www.themiraclemaker.com.

8 Rowe, Robin. "Bride Stripped Bare," in *The Editors Guild Magazine* 26:4 (July/August 2005). Online at www.editorsguild.com/newsletter/JulAug05/julaug05_bride.html.

9 Burton. Quoted in Rowe.

10 Rowe.

11 This solution was not unique. For example, Chiodo Brothers Productions, which has created stop-motion and puppet sequences for numerous television shows and features, had devised a similar system a few years earlier. Chiodo, Steven. Discussion with the author, 15 September 2005.

12 Barbagallo, Ron. "From Concept Art to Finished Puppets: An Interview with Graham G. Maiden, Head of the Puppet Department on Tim Burton's Corpse Bride." Online at www.animationartconservation.com/corpse_bride.html. References to Maiden are from this source, which is an extended version of Barbagallo's 21 July 2005 interview of the same name published in *Animation Magazine* (September 2005), 10.

13 Johnson, Mike. From "Mike Johnson and Allison Abbate" interview (San Diego ComicCon, July 2005), Comingsoon.net. Online at www.comingsoon.net/news/comicconnews.php?id=10412.

14 Johnson. Interview with Epstein, Daniel Robert. Ugo.com. Online at www.ugo.com/channels/filmtv/features/corpsebride/johnson.asp.

15 See also www.cartoonan.com/honey.htm.

16 Noonan, Gail. Email to the author, 5 September 2005.

17 de Nooijer, Menno. Email to the author, 20 October 2005. Unless otherwise stated references to Menno de Nooijer come from this and other email correspondence with the author from this period.

18 Anonymous. "One Hundred Years of Beauty," Denooijer. Online at www.denooijer.tv/06installations.html.

19 McLaren, Norman. "Further Notes on the Shooting of 'Neighbours,'" 1973. Unpublished, National Film Board of Canada. All McLaren's references to the production process of *Neighbours* production process are from this document.

20 Théberge, Jean. Email to the author, 12 July 2006.

Chapter Twelve

1 Ward, Paul. "Rotoshop in Context: Computer Rotoscoping and Animation Aesthetics," in *Animation Journal* 12 (2004), 32–52; 33.

2 Sabiston, Bob. Quoted in Anonymous. "Scanner Darkly Blurs Lines between Programming and Artistry," in *American Institute of Physics*, 14 July 2006. Online at www.newswise.com/p/articles/view/521943.

3 "Blender." Online at www.blender.org.

4 "Open Source." Online at www.opensource.org. References to the Open Source Initiative come from this source unless otherwise stated.

5 Carlson, Wayne. "A Critical History of Computer Graphics and Animation," 1. Online at accad.osu.edu/~waynec/history/lesson1.html. Information also was provided by Frank da Cruz of Information Technology at Columbia University; Frank da Cruz. Email to the author, 24 July 2006.

6 Carlson. "A Critical History of Computer Graphics and Animation," 3. Online at accad.osu.edu/~waynec/history/lesson3.html. While this source is not dated, it was part of a course website that contained a syllabus from 2005.

7 Kurcewicz, Gregory. "Lillian Schwartz: A Beautiful Virus in the Machine." Online at www.avantofestival.com/2003/en/film_lillians_2.html.

8 Schwartz, Lillian. Email to the author, 27 January 2006.

9 Cuba, Larry. Lecture at California Institute of the Arts, 24 March 2006.

10 Cuba. "3/78." Online at www.well.com/~cuba/Three78.html.

11 Cuba. Telephone conversation with the author, 27 March 2006.

12 Cuba. Email to the author, 27 March 2006. References to Cuba come from this email unless otherwise stated.

13 Cuba. "Two Space." Online at www.well.com/~cuba/TwoSpace.html.

14 Cuba. Email to the author, 3 April 2006.

15 Gemperlein, Joyce and Tenaya Scheinman. "An Interview with Nolan Bushnell," in *San Jose Mercury News* (19 January 1997). Online at www.thetech.org/revolutionaries/bushnell. Interestingly as a young man, Bushnell had hoped to work for Disney after graduating with a degree in Engineering, but the company did not hire him. He later went on to co-found the successful American chain of child-oriented "Chuck E. Cheese" restaurants, which used gaming arcades. Pong was released in a home version in 1975.

16 For a list of Ralph Baer's many patents see www.ralphbaer.com. Baer's accomplishments are documented at the Smithsonian's Lemelson Center for the Study of Invention & Innovation. Online at invention.smithsonian.org/resources/fa_baer_index.aspx.

17 Information on Chinese Flash animation comes from Wu Weihua and Steve Fore, "Flash Empire and Chinese Shanke: The Emergence of Chinese Digital Culture," *Animation* Journal, 13 (2005), 28–51.

18 Ospina, Juan. Email to the author, 3 January 2006. References to Ospina come from this email unless otherwise stated.

19 'Spaik City." Online at www.killerloop.com/spaik.

20 "Columbian War Games." Online at www.piterwilson.com/games.

Chapter Thirteen

1 For segments from *Beaches* see www.redkite-animation.com/flash/flashcollection.htm.

2 Baker, Rachel Bevan. Email to the author, 19 April 2004.

3 Bevan Baker. Email to the author.

4 References to Ron Hui in this chapter are taken from notes written by Hui for use at SIGGRAPH 2003. *Ode to Summer* is online at www.renderaid.com/launchMovie.aspx?cid=1020&sn=&rd=&pc=qt&s=l&w=480&m=1.5.

5 Hui, Ron. "Stills Gallery," Renderaid.com. Online at www.renderaid.com/StillsGalleryBrowse~uid~1060.aspx.

6 Quigley, Marian. "Kathy Smith," in *Women DO Animate: Interviews with 10 Australian Animators.* Mentone: Insight, 2005, 106–22. References to Smith come from this source unless otherwise stated:

7 Smith, Kathy. "Indefinable Moods." Online at www.kathymoods.org/im/aboutwork.html.

8 Maxwell, Stephanie. Emails to the author, 18 July 2003 and 4 August 2003; and telephone interview with the author, 3 August 2003. References to Maxwell come from these sources.

9 In 2006, Adamczyk won a Technical Academy Award for his development of the J-Viz pre-visualization system, which draws 3D scenes in real time and tracks the movement of a live-action camera. It is used for greenscreen shots, to roughly preview what a final composite will look like as it is being shot. An explanation of the pre-visualization system can be seen online at www.johnadamczyk.com/jviz. See also J. Walt's website at www.spontaneousfantasia.com/index.html. Quotations come from Adamczyk, J. Walt, email to the author, 12 August 2006.

10 Unless otherwise stated references to Gokhan Okur come from emails to the author, 29 November, 30 November, and 1 December 2005.

11 See www.kofti.com/sf/baaiit_eng.html.

12 See also "Bärbel Neubauer," Microcinema International Database. Online at www.microcinema.com/filmmakerResults.php?director_id=618.

13 "Bärbel Neubauer," ASIFA.NET. Online at asifa.net/+/neubauer.

14 Neubauer, Bärbel. Email to the author, 27 December 2002.

15 Neubauer. "Roots: An Experiment in Images and Music," in *Animation World Magazine* 3:6. Online at www.awn.com/mag/issue3.6/3.6pages/3.6neubauerroots.html.

16 Neubauer. "Roots."

17 Neubauer switched completely to digital in 2000. Email to the author, 24 July 2003.

18 Neubauer. Email to the author, 20 June 2003.

19 All sound-related plug-ins are from Native Instruments. Neubauer. Emails to the author, 24 July, 5 August 2003.

20 Neubauer. Email to the author, 24 July 2003.

21 Neubauer. Email to the author, 24 July 2003.

22 Neubauer. Email to the author, 5 August 2003.

23 Neubauer. Email to the author, 3 August 2003.

Picture Credits

24 Arthur, Stephen X. From Bishko, Leslie. "Power Tools: A Look at How Three Vancouver Film Animators have Explored Digital Imagery," in *ASIFA-Canada* (July 1997). Quoted material is taken from an excerpt published online at Arthur's website, mypage.direct.ca/w/writer/interview.html. References to Arthur come from this source or an email to the author, 22 January 2006.

25 Staven, Karl. Email to the author, 5 January 2006.

26 Fleisch, Thorsten. "Animating the 4th Dimension," in *Animation Journal* (2005), 86–97. References to Fleisch and the fourth dimension come from this source.

27 See www.fleischfilm.com.

28 Pepi, Lorelei. Email to the author, 9 October 2005; and unpublished notes on the production of *Ether*, sent to the author in October 2005. Quotations come from these sources.

Laurence King Publishing and the author wish to thank the institutions and individuals who have kindly provided photographic material. With the exception of those credits that appear with the image captions, all credit information is listed below. Numbers in bold refer to pages.

While every effort has been made to trace the present copyright holders, we apologize in advance for any unintentional omission or error, and will be pleased to insert the appropriate acknowledgment in any subsequent edition.

Chapter One
10–11: Courtesy Igor Kovalyov. **12**: Photo: Maureen Furniss. **13** (left): Courtesy Stephen Silver. **13** (right): Courtesy Stephen X. Arthur. **14**: Photo: Maureen Furniss. **15**: Images: Adam Fox. **16**: Société Radio-Canada. **17** (left): Photo used with permission of the National Film Board of Canada. © 1961 National Film Board of Canada. All rights reserved. **17** (right): © Michael Dudok de Wit. **18** (left): Courtesy Ke Jiang. **18** (right): Photo by Peter Schlaifer. Courtesy Frank Mouris. **19** (top left): Courtesy Clive Walley. **19** (bottom left): Courtesy Devon Damonte. **20** (left): Courtesy Rachel Bevan Baker. **21** (left): Courtesy Steve Segal. **21** (right): © Stephanie Maxwell. Courtesy Stephanie Maxwell. **23** (left): Image: Jessie Gregg. **23** (right): Image: Allyson Haller. **24**: Courtesy iotacenter. **25** (top): Image: Allyson Haller. **25** (bottom): Courtesy Bordo Dovnikovic. **26**: Courtesy Igor Kovalyov. **27** (right): Courtesy Maya Yonesho. **28** (left): Courtesy Netherlands Institute for Animation Film. ©Paul Driessen 1980. **28** (right): Courtesy Raimund Krumme. **29** (top): Courtesy Ralph Bakshi. Original production cel from *The Lord of the Rings*, part 1. Ralph Bakshi personal collection. **29** (bottom): Courtesy Denis Tupicoff. **32**: © Chiodo Bros. Productions Inc. / T.P. Cornpone. **34–35**: Courtesy Musa Brooker. **35** (top): Image: Allyson Haller.

Chapter Two
36–37: Image: Allyson Haller. **38** and **39** (left): Courtesy Stephen X. Arthur. National Film Board of Canada. All Rights Reserved. **40**: Courtesy Matt Hullum. **41** (top left): © 1995 National Film Board of Canada. All Rights Reserved. **41** (top right): Courtesy George Griffin. © George Griffin. **42–43**: Courtesy Susanne Horizon-Fränzel. **44**: Courtesy Lindsay Fleay. **45–46**: Images: Allyson Haller. **47**: Photos: Maureen Furniss. **48**: Images: Allyson Haller. **50**: Courtesy Toon Boom Animation. **54**: © Stephanie Maxwell and Michaela Eremiasova. **55**: Courtesy Bärbel Neubauer.

Applications I
57–59: Photos: Maureen Furniss.

Chapter Three
64–65: Courtesy Stephen X. Arthur. **66**: Photos: Maureen Furniss. **67**: Courtesy Ke Jiang. **68–69**: Courtesy Stephen X. Arthur. **71**: © 1957 National Film Board of Canada. All Rights Reserved. **72–75**: Images: Adam Fox. **76**: Images: Jessie Gregg. **77**: Courtesy Clive Walley. **78**: Courtesy Ke Jiang. **79** (left): Courtesy Virgil Widrich. **79** (right) and **80**: Courtesy Dave Borthwick. **81** (left): Photo: Nurit Israeli. Courtesy Gil Alkabetz. © Gil Alkabetz. **81** (right) and **82–83**: Photos: Maureen Furniss. **84** (left and center): Courtesy Igor Kovalyov. **84** (right: top and bottom): Images: Jessie Gregg. **85** (left): © Iain Gardner/S4C. **85** (top right): Courtesy Philippe Vaucher. **85** (bottom right): Courtesy Max Winston.

Chapter Four
86–87: Courtesy Ke Jiang. **88**: Reproduced with Permission by Cambridge Animation Systems Ltd. **90**: Courtesy Dae In Chung. **91** (top): Courtesy Bill Plympton. **91** (bottom) and **92**: Images: Adam Fox. **93** (top): Image: Jessie Gregg. **93** (bottom) and **94**: Images: Adam Fox. **95**

(left): Courtesy Will Vinton. **95** (right): Photo: Maureen Furniss. **96** (left and bottom right): Images: Jessie Gregg. **96** (top right): Photos: Maureen Furniss. **97** (left): © Chiodo Bros. Productions Inc. **97** (right): Photo: Maureen Furniss. **98** (top): Courtesy Virgil Widrich. **98** (bottom): Photo: Maureen Furniss. **99** (left): Courtesy Adam Elliot and Melanie Coombs. **99** (right): Photo: Maureen Furniss. **100** (left): © Aardman / Wallace & Gromit Ltd., 1993. **100** (right) and **101**: Courtesy Ke Jiang. **102**: Courtesy Charles daCosta. **103**: Courtesy Lindsay Fleay. **105**: Image: Jesse Gregg. **106–107**: Photos: Maureen Furniss.

Applications II
109–13: Images: Jessie Gregg.

Chapter Five
114–15: Courtesy Marty Hardin. **116**: V&A Images / Victoria and Albert Museum. **119**: Photos by Simon Annand. Courtesy Stephen Mottram. **120** (left: top and bottom): Collection German Technology Museum, Berlin. Photos: Maureen Furniss. **120** (right): Courtesy Devon Damonte. **121**: Courtesy Marty Hardin. **122–23**: Collection German Technology Museum, Berlin. Photos: Maureen Furniss. **124**: Courtesy Andy Voda. **125** and **126** (top left): Collection German Technology Museum, Berlin. Photos: Maureen Furniss. **126** (top right): Courtesy Andy Voda. **126** (bottom): Courtesy Steve Hollinger. **127** (left): Collection German Technology Museum, Berlin. Photo: Maureen Furniss. **127** (right: top and bottom): Courtesy Maya Yonesho. **128–29,130** (left), and **131**: Courtesy George Griffin. © George Griffin.

Applications III
132–37: Photos: Maureen Furniss

Chapter 6
138–39: Reproduced by Permission of the Len Lye Foundation. **140** (left): Courtesy Helen Hill. Photo: Becka Barker. **140** (right): Courtesy Rose Bond. **141**: Courtesy Bärbel Neubauer. **143**: Reproduced by Permission of the Len Lye Foundation. **144** (left): © 1955 National Film Board of Canada. All Rights Reserved. **144** (right): © 1965 National Film Board of Canada. All Rights Reserved. **145** (left and top right): Courtesy Steven Woloshen. **145** (bottom right): © 1990 Office national du film du Canada. Tous droits réservés. **146**: Courtesy Paul Bush. **147**: Courtesy Rose Bond. **148**: Courtesy Vincenzo Gioanola. **149**: Courtesy Naomi Uman. **150**: Courtesy Luis Recoder. © Luis Recoder. **150–53**: Courtesy Peter Tscherkassky.

Chapter 7
154–55: © 2006 by Donna Cameron. All rights reserved © Papercamfilms.™ **156** and **157** (bottom left): Estate of Stan Brakhage and www.fredcamper.com. **157** (top left and right: top and bottom) and **158**: Courtesy Jennifer Reeves. **159** (left: top and bottom and bottom right): Courtesy Thorsten Fleisch. **159** (top right): Courtesy Sandra Gibson. **160** (top): Courtesy Donna Cameron. **162**: Photo: Bill Olsen. © National Film Board of Canada. All Rights Reserved. **163**: © NIAF / Oerd van Cuijlenberg 2000. **164–65**: Courtesy Richard Reeves. **166–67**: Courtesy Thad Povey. Photos: Thad Povey. **168** and **169** (left): Courtesy Devon Damonte. **169** (center and right): Courtesy Helen Hill. **170**: Courtesy Steve Segal. **171**: Courtesy Eric Darnell.

Applications IV
172–175: Courtesy Devon Damonte. **176–79**: Courtesy Richard Reeves.

Chapter 8
180–81: Courtesy Michael Sporn. **182** and **183** (left): © KONINCK STUDIOS Ltd. **183** © 1998 National Film Board of Canada. All Rights Reserved. **184–87**: Courtesy Michael Sporn. **188**: Société Radio-Canada. **189**: Courtesy

END

END